Magazine Editing and Production

Magazine Editing and Production

Fourth Edition

J. William Click
Louisiana State University

Russell N. Baird
Ohio University

wcb

Wm. C. Brown Publishers
Dubuque, Iowa

Library of Congress Catalog Card Number: 85–73054

ISBN 0–697–00278–0

Printed in the United States of America
10 9 8 7 6 5 4 3 2

Contents

Preface

MAGAZINES disseminate more specialized information and commentary on a regular basis to diverse audiences than any other medium of mass communication. More magazines than television stations, radio stations, or newspapers are established each year. The expanding magazine field offers increasing career opportunities to recent college journalism graduates, many of whom begin as top assistants or even editors of professional association and company-sponsored magazines.

Although it usually takes longer to reach the top on large circulation consumer magazines, persons with some background in magazine editing and production frequently have the edge for entry positions on these publications and become productive staff members more quickly than those without this background.

Schools of journalism generally offer magazine instruction in two basic types of courses, one in magazine article writing and the other in magazine editing and production. The authors have planned this book to encompass the magazine editing process in all sizes of magazines, from the one-person staff of an association or public relations magazine to the complex, highly departmentalized consumer magazines. The general procedures are the same for both. Differences in frequency of publication, size, circulation, advertising linage, and budgets account for the degree of complexity and varied staff sizes.

Early chapters offer insight into the magazine and its role in American society in the last quarter of the twentieth century. Later chapters deal with editing strategy and functions, production, legal and ethical considerations, and distribution.

Teachers can use this book for courses in Magazine Editing and Production, Specialized Magazines, Industrial Journalism, Organizational Journalism, The Business Press, and similar courses. As more schools add a student magazine laboratory course to their curricula, it is important to have a single source of essential material to use in the preparatory course that usually precedes the laboratory course. This book is intended to fill that need, blending the necessary practical aspects with a sufficient amount of magazine history and background. It also should be useful to editors of small magazines who have not had formal course work in magazine editing and who may desire a ready source of information about editing techniques.

When the first edition of this book was prepared, the authors realized that the magazine industry's constant state of change would eventually require other editions. They did not anticipate, however, that the changes would be so many, so rapid, or so far-reaching in nature.

Most surprising has been the rapidity of change in the technology of production. The technical revolution that hit the newspaper industry in the early 1970s spread with lightning speed to the magazine industry as the decade drew to a close. In-house production facilities became commonplace almost overnight. *Folio* magazine reported in 1977 that already one-third of its survey respondents were doing all or part of their own typesetting, and almost two-thirds were doing their own paste-up or other mechanical work. Other respondents were in the process of bringing production activities in-house. Also at that time, all of the major newsmagazines and many other large publishing ventures had announced new production systems that incorporated electronic gear ranging from video terminals to satellites.

To incorporate these changes in the second edition, the production section was completely reorganized and substantially enlarged. An introductory chapter on traditional production processes was included as a reference point for an additional new chapter dealing with electronic and in-house systems. Additional material on layout and paste-up was included because of the increasing involvement of editorial staffs with these aspects of editing and production.

One of the largest additions to the third edition was a new chapter on The Editor and Typography, requested by many users whose curriculum provides little or no preliminary instruction in typography as a prerequisite for magazine editing. Others cited the need for a quick review of typographic principles as a supplement to earlier instruction on the subject.

Technological changes in printing production between the second and third editions required a totally new approach related to offset lithography rather than letterpress printing. The material on law and ethics was expanded slightly into two separate chapters.

For this fourth edition, primary emphasis has been on reorganization and the addition of considerable material dealing with the "how to" aspects of editing and production. These changes are the result of the experience of the authors in using this text, as well as suggestions from many instructors. The result, we hope, is a more effective teaching aid. The section on computer technology has been condensed and re-organized to be in better perspective. The material covering letterpress printing, once a major section, has virtually been eliminated.

The earlier chapters on the history and current status of the magazine industry by their nature require constant revision, and every effort has been made to bring them up-to-date.

Division of responsibility remains fundamentally the same as in the previous editions. Professor Baird took primary responsibility for Chapters 7 and 9 through 17, and Professor Click was primarily responsible for Chapters 1 through 6, 8, and Chapters 18 through 20.

For material provided for the first edition and retained in the later editions, we are grateful to John Goodwin, who drew the illustrations; Peter T. Miller, who photographed printing production processes; Robert E. Kenyon, executive vice president of the Magazine Publishers Association, Inc.; and Geraldine T. Keating, executive director of the International Association of Business Communicators.

Appreciation for providing materials and information is extended to American Business Press, Inc.; Audit Bureau of Circulations; Ruth Brown; Business Publications Audit of Circulation, Inc.; *Columbia Journalism Review;* Ralph R. Schulz of *Chemical Week;* John McCafferty of *DuPont Context;* Frank Bowers and Larry Werline of Fawcett Publications, Inc.; Herman Panyard, Athene Karis, and Forrest Still of The B. F. Goodrich Company; Bernard Gallagher of *The Gallagher Report; Ladies Home Journal;* John Good of the Lawhead Press, Inc.; McGraw-Hill Publications Company; Joseph A. Callanan of Marathon Oil Company; *Media Industry Newletter; Newsweek;* R. J. Malloy of Pacific Northwest Bell; Al G. Michaelian of Petersen Publishing Company; Edward H. Owen of *Printing Management; Reader's Digest; Redbook;* Byron T. Scott and Charles L. Scott of Ohio University; Max E. Shively; Time Incorporated; William B. Toran of Ohio State University; and Verified Audit Circulation Corporation.

For materials provided for the subsequent editions we are grateful to *Columbus Business Forum;* T. J. Donnelly and Audit Bureau of Circulations; *The Elks Magazine; Essence;* Downs Matthews and *Exxon USA;* Brenda Floyd of *Aide* Magazine; Peter G. Faur of Southwestern Bell; Herman Duerr and *Friends* Magazine; *Go* of Goodyear Tire and Rubber Company; *Graphic Arts Monthly;* Patricia Hagood of Oxbridge Communications; Reginald C. Hayes and Johnson Publishing Company; David G. Jensen and Ralph Schulz of McGraw-Hill Publications Company; James Jennings, who took the offset production pictures for the third edition; Ralph Kliesch of Ohio University; *The Lamp* of Exxon Corporation; *Louisiana Conservationist; Long Lines* of American Telephone and Telegraph Corporation; Marjorie McManus of *Folio;* Don Moser of *Smithsonian* Magazine; *NCR World* of NCR Corporation; *News/Lines* of Pennsylvania Bell Telephone Company; *Ohio Contractor;* Katheryn Powers and the Magazine Publishers Association; Carol Reuss of the University of North Carolina at Chapel Hill; James Richardson of *Modern Maturity;* John J. Tuohey and *U.S. News & World Report;* Robert Vereen, John P. Hammond, and Karen Stewart of *DIY Retailing;* and Lee Young of the University of Kansas.

J. William Click
Russell N. Baird

The Magazine Industry

THE birth of the first American magazine in February 1741 was a notable event. Colonists, most of whom were still struggling for survival in a strange, alien land, were amazed at the occurrence, and with good cause.

Any attempt to establish a magazine in the colonial environment would have been cause for astonishment; the fact that the birth produced twins, and that they were sired by two of Philadelphia's most sagacious publishers added to the wonderment.

Primary credit for the first American magazine goes to Benjamin Franklin, at the time a young but already successful printer and newspaper publisher. The enterprising Franklin was the first to conceive the idea of a monthly magazine, beginning his efforts in late 1740. The first issue of his *General Magazine and Historical Chronicle for all the British Plantations in America* bore the date January 1741 and was, after a tremendous struggle to get its 70-plus pages into print, finally offered for sale on February 16.

In a different printshop in Philadelphia, however, another of the town's respected publishers had heard of Franklin's intentions, and also had set about the task of bringing forth the first magazine. Andrew Bradford, Franklin's chief rival in the publishing business, hurriedly put together his *American Magazine, or A Monthly View of the Political State of the British Colonies,* and gave it the same birth date, January 1741. His product was offered for sale on February 13, three days before Franklin's.

Franklin managed to produce six issues before giving up the cause; Bradford produced only three. In retrospect, the experience of these publishing pioneers seems to have foretold what was to come in the history of American magazines. Although the lifetime for both their magazines was relatively short, it was only a short time before other magazines, sired by other publishers, found their proper niches and enjoyed long and prosperous lives.

From its inception, the magazine industry has been characterized by change, which continually produces a better and stronger industry. New magazines appear and existing magazines merge, are sold, or are discontinued, with the births overall outnumbering the deaths.

The magazine era of specialization accelerated in the 1980s. The early 1970s had seen the end of the general, mass circulation magazine as televison became the most widely accepted national mass advertising medium and an instantaneous purveyor of pictures and information, in addition to its role as entertainer.

The problem of the general magazine stemmed partly from a management practice originated in the 1890s and early 1900s. It was essentially in that period that the modern mass circulation magazine was born.

During that decade the United States hastened its move from an agricultural to an industrial economy. Improvements in transportation and mail service made it possible to distribute goods, including magazines, over wide geographical areas. The national distribution of products brought on brand names and the national advertising necessary to promote these brand names. At the time, the magazine was the ideal medium for national advertising, and the sale of space to advertisers boomed.

Competition among the magazines themselves created the situation in which the advertiser, not the magazine reader, carried most of the cost for a magazine. In order to get more circulation, which in turn generated the sale of advertising space, magazines offered readers bargain rates for subscriptions: club offers, premiums, long-term discounts, and other means. The discovery that advertising could be the "angel" that would pay the bills and provide for a profit was made at about the same time by the era's publishing giants. S. S. McClure of *McClure's Magazine,* John Brisben Walker of *Cosmopolitan,* Cyrus H. K. Curtis of the *Saturday Evening Post,* and Frank A. Munsey of *Munsey's Magazine* all joined in the move to soak the advertiser while letting the reader off cheaply. McClure entered the field in 1893 with a low 15-cent per copy price only to have Walker cut *Cosmopolitan's* 25-cent price in half. Then Munsey joined the battle by cutting his newsstand price from 25 to 10 cents. And so it went, until a tradition was built among American magazine readers that someone else would bear the brunt of the expense for bringing them quality magazines.

Signs of the need to change this became evident to some observers in the 1960s and to more in the 1970s. Magazines would build huge circulations and set advertising rates to cover the cost of the magazine and its profit, provided enough advertising pages were sold. Readers often got by very cheaply, and they wanted it that way.

This situation had been foretold in 1956 when the Crowell-Collier Publishing Company killed its last three magazines in less than six months. *American,* a general interest monthly with more than one million circulation, had lost more than half of its annual advertising revenue between 1946 and 1955, and it was discontinued with the August 1956 issue. That December the company's two remaining magazines, *Collier's* and *Woman's Home Companion,* each with circulation exceeding 4 million, were discontinued.

The weekly *Saturday Evening Post* struggled through the decade of the 1960s, and it came as no surprise when it ceased publication in 1969. As the 1970s began, it was clear that new magazines would have to rely on their readers for more of the funds needed to stay in business. Norman Cousins stated that need at the end of 1971 when he announced plans to start *World,* since merged into *Saturday Review.* Time Inc. introduced *Money* in 1972 at a higher than usual price.

Both *Saturday Evening Post* and the weekly *Life* tried to cut their circulation so they could sell more advertising at lower rates but neither succeeded. *Life* was discontinued with the issue of December 29, 1972, after having lost $30 million over four years. Many other magazines have succeeded in raising single copy and subscription prices substantially, but not while cutting circulation guarantees.

Magazines trying to maintain circulation guarantees and adequate advertising revenues continue low-priced introductory offers. In 1984 low-priced subscriptions were being offered by *Field & Stream, Outdoor Life, Home Mechanix, Esquire, Ms., Golf, Ladies' Home Journal, Road & Track, Savvy,* and *Cycle World,* among others. Over the decade of the 1970s, though, most magazines had increased the percentage of their total income that comes from readers. Income from circulation 1966–70 had been 30.7 percent of total income, according to a Magazine Publishers Association study. A similar study covering 1977–79 showed that figure had risen to 44.3 percent of total income.

The magazine field continually changes because it is relatively easy to start a magazine, and some entrepreneurs are convinced that their idea for reaching a sizable segment of the population with editorial matter and advertising is bound to succeed. Because it is easy to start a magazine, it is also easy to fail. A large amount of risk capital can be wiped out in a short time. Since it takes so long to get returns from all the newsstands for the first few issues, a publisher should have enough money for about six months' issues before he brings out the first one.

Once a magazine is established, it must be flexible enough to change with society. Thousands of names lie in the magazine graveyard, including the brilliant muckraking magazines of the early 1900s and H. L. Mencken's *American Mercury.* Not all died of ossification, but that is the cause of many fatalities. A magazine must be ready to change with the audience or industry it serves or face almost certain extinction. Change must be sufficient to keep pace, but not so great as to get away from the loyal reader.

The Media Mix

The typical American does not use one mass medium to the exclusion of all others, so discussions about the superiority of one medium are unproductive. Magazines rate high, along with television, radio, and newspapers, in overall use by contemporary American adults.

Not all heavy users of one medium are heavy users of all other media. One recent study found that 14 percent of American adults were heavy users of both magazines and television, 38 percent were heavy television and light magazine users, 30 percent were heavy magazine and light television users, and 18 percent were light users of both media. To reach the 30 percent who were heavy magazine and light television users, advertisers were advised to use magazine advertising. But magazine advertising also is needed to reinforce television advertising.

Media use varies significantly by education and income. One study found that 76 percent of the adults interviewed had bought magazines within the preceding year and 24 percent had not. In a group of "heavy magazine buyers," 84 percent earned more than $10,000 a year and 83 percent had completed high school while in the group of nonbuyers 67 percent earned less than $10,000 a year and 59 percent had not completed high school.[1]

Time spent with a medium is another factor to consider. Several surveys have reported that the average magazine issue is read an average of one and one-half hours per adult compared with 30 to 40 minutes per newspaper per reader per issue and a daily average of nearly three hours of television viewing per viewer. College educated viewers watch somewhat less.

The media are not directly competing against each other because each serves a different primary purpose and involves different kinds of effort from its users. Television and magazines are the two national media while newspapers and radio tend to be local or regional. Print offers advantages in material that is to be read and, perhaps, reread and saved. Television is advantageous for showing action and dramatizations. Radio prevails in reaching people who are doing other things, from bathing and shaving to driving to participating in leisure activities.

Consumers of any given medium are more likely to use additional media than are nonconsumers. So TV viewers are more likely to be magazine readers than nonviewers are, although there are differences in the extent to which one or the other uses each medium. During the period of rapid television growth, 1950–70, magazine circulation rose faster than the population and faster than newspaper circulation. A report by Daniel Starch & Staff, Inc., showed the readership of editorial content in magazines increased between 1959 and 1969.

Development of cable television and home information centers opens great opportunities for magazine publishers because the magazine format can be adapted easily to television. Just how soon cable magazines will be economically feasible and whether readers will find them as convenient as the print product remain to be seen. The majority of long-time print readers are likely to remain loyal to printed magazines while young consumers, more accepting of technological innovations and less accustomed to printed magazines, are more likely to accept the cable or home information center magazine.

Types of Magazines

The magazine can aim at a precise audience dispersed over a large geographical area, presenting illustrations and articles in a convenient format that can be read almost anywhere at any time. Although several magazines built tremendous circulations to reach "mass" audiences, others long ago defined their specific audiences and have been serving them for decades. These are special interest magazines, the majority of which are business publications. There are also thousands of magazines issued by companies for their employees, customers, stockholders, and other groups related to their communications and public relations programs.

There are numerous ways to classify magazines, but for our purposes it seems best to discuss a small number of basic groups. So we classify them as general consumer, special interest consumer, business, association, farm, and public relations.

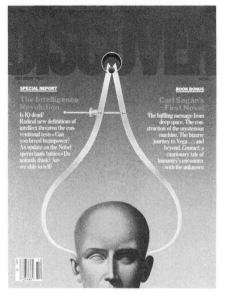

Figure 1-1 Successful market tests preceded the first regular issue of Time Incorporated's newsmagazine of science, *Discover,* in 1980. (Courtesy *Discover* copyright 1985 Time Inc.)

Figure 1-2 A business publication for the printing industry, *Graphic Arts Monthly and The Printing Industry* circulates on a controlled basis to qualified companies and departments. (Reprinted with special permission from the December 1984 issue of *Graphic Arts Monthly.*)

Consumer Magazines

Magazines sold at retail outlets are consumer magazines aimed at the general reading public. To many persons they represent the entire magazine industry, but they are no more than the visible tip of the iceberg. They are consumer magazines from the advertiser's viewpoint because their readers buy and consume products and services that are sold at retail and may be advertised in these magazines.

Basically, a consumer magazine can be purchased by anyone, through subscription or from retail newsstands. Many other types of magazines are not usually available to the general public.

Consumer magazines usually have the largest staffs and circulations, but there is wide variation, and many are put out by very small editorial staffs. Editorial positions on these books may be considered the most glamorous, but there is a limited number of such positions because consumer magazines are fewest in number.

Consumer Magazine and Agri-Media Rates and Data lists in its "Consumer Magazine" section more than 1,200 titles in 65 classifications, from airline inflight to youth, including groups, annual directory issues, and magazines that are published infrequently.

A few examples of the better known consumer magazines are *TV Guide, Reader's Digest, Better Homes and Gardens, Time, Newsweek,* and *Playboy.* Perhaps less familiar are *The Family Handyman, Travel/Holiday, Popular Hot Rodding,* and *Workbasket.* Nearly all consumer magazines today are classified as special interest books, which will be discussed in chapter 2. (In the trade, magazine editors and staff members refer to their magazines as *books.*)

Business Publications

Magazines that serve a particular business, industry, or profession are classified as business publications (and referred to by some as "trade journals"). Although the field changes continually, analysis of an issue of *Business Publication Rates and Data* showed nearly 2,600 listings of business publications that sell advertising and are published four or more times a year. Many of these are issued in newspaper format and stress news in their content. Some in magazine format also stress news in their content, thus blurring the distinction between magazines and newspapers.

Three types of publishing arrangements are used to issue magazines serving business. One is the independent, profit-seeking publishing enterprise that is not part of the field its publication serves. Theoretically, at least, such publishers can objectively view the field, pass judgment, and state their opinions as outside observers. A good example of this type is McGraw-Hill, a private publishing firm that issues publications serving businesses ranging from construction to electronics, engineering, and medicine. Other large business publishers include Fairchild, Penton/ IPC, Cahners, Harcourt Brace Jovanovich, Medical Economics, and Chilton.

A second type is the professional association that is part of the field served and that issues one or more periodicals as an association service to members. Because they are in the field served, these publications often boost their association or field without critical objectivity.

The third involves independent publishers who issue official journals of some associations, as, for example, Williams & Wilkins, who publish the *Journal of Immunology,* the official publication of the American Association of Immunologists.

Of 2,600 business publications listed in *Business Publication Rates and Data,* 1,500 are independently published, more than 600 are published by associations, and more than 400 are independently published for associations, notably in the medical specialties area. In round figures, these publications include 1,740 monthlies, 130 weeklies, and 20 dailies. The other 660 appear semi-monthly, biweekly, nine times a year, or at other intervals.

Continual change in the business publication field is shown by *Business Publication Rates and Data's* report that in 1980 it added an average of 31 new listings a month and removed an average of 10 a month.

Association Magazines

Far more than 600 association magazines are published. *Business Publication Rates and Data* lists only those that sell advertising, so untold hundreds of association periodicals are not listed. The 600 listed are primarily professional or business in nature. A number of association magazines, such as *The American Legion Magazine, The Kiwanis Magazine, The Rotarian,* and *Scouting,* are listed in *Consumer Magazine Rates and Data.*

Two of the best known and most financially stable association magazines are the *Journal of the American Medical Association* and *National Geographic.* Other examples of association periodicals include *The Quill* of the Society of Professional Journalists, Sigma Delta Chi, *Bioscience* of the American Institute of Biological Sciences, and *Texas Architect* of the Texas Society of Architects.

Among the hundreds not listed are *Journalism Quarterly, Journal of Communication Management,* and *The American Philatelist.*

Association magazines' staffs range from unpaid, volunteer part-time editors who do their editing on the kitchen table to large, well-paid staffs at such places as the Chicago headquarters of the American Medical Association. These magazines range from small issues with no advertising to thick ones in which ads occupy as much space as editorial content.

Farm Publications

Virtually the same as business publications are farm publications, edited and published for the agricultural industry. Many of these also are published by associations. They often are considered as a separate type and are listed in their own "Farm Publications" section of *Consumer Magazine and Agri-Media Rates and Data,* where 260 titles are listed in 11 classification groupings.

Farm publications typically deal with state or regional subject matter or with specialties, such as dairy and dairy breeds, field crops and soil management, or fruits, nuts, vegetables, and special products.

Examples of farm publications include *Farm Journal, Progressive Farmer, Successful Farming, Hoosier Farmer, Hoard's Dairyman, Soybean Digest, Wallaces Farmer, American Fruit Grower, The Peanut Farmer, Charolais Journal,* and *Wines & Vines.*

Public Relations Magazines

Magazines can effectively win and maintain friends for a business or nonprofit institution. No one really knows how many of these sponsored magazines there are because they do not sell advertising or qualify for second class postal rates. One estimate is 10,000. Many companies publish a number of magazines.

A public relations magazine is published by a sponsoring company or institution for circulation among one or more of its publics—employees, dealers, customers, stockholders, or other interest group—and carries little advertising, usually only for the sponsor.[2]

Most practitioners classify public relations magazines by their audiences as *internal, external,* or *combination internal-external* depending upon whether the readers are within the company, as employees; outside it, as customers; or a combination of both.

Some public relations magazines, notably the airlines' passenger (*inflight*) magazines, accept advertising. These are a combination of public relations piece for the airline and consumer magazine. Several are published by independent publishers for the magazines' sponsors. East/West Network of Los Angeles and New York publishes nine airline magazines, plus *Amtrak Express.* Halsey Publishing of North Miami publishes seven airline magazines. One of the earliest is *United,* established as *United Mainliner* in 1957 by United Airlines. *Consumer Magazine Rates and Data* lists 27 airline inflight and bus enroute magazines, most established since 1967. The largest include *American Way, Delta Sky, Eastern Review, Pan Am Clipper, TWA Ambassador,* and *United.*

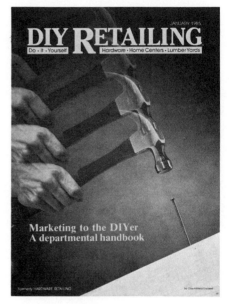

Figure 1–3 An association magazine that functions largely as a business publication is *DIY Retailing* published monthly by the National Retail Hardware Association. (Courtesy *DIY Retailing.*)

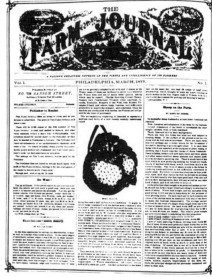

Figure 1–4 One of America's leading farm magazines, *Farm Journal,* dates from 1877. Publishing 14 issues a year, it led all farm publications with 1.1 million circulation in 1981. (Cover courtesy Prof. Lee Young, University of Kansas.)

Figure 1–5 The Marketing Division of Sentinel Communications Company, publishers of *The Orlando Sentinel* and several non-daily newspapers and shoppers, publishes *Sentinel Communications Quarterly* for Central Florida and the newspaper industry. It is a quarterly public relations magazine. (Courtesy of Sentinel Communications Company.)

One-Shot Magazines

Publishers capitalize on a hot topic, phenomenon, or idea by issuing a single magazine about it. Examples range from magazines on the Apollo moon shot, to television shows such as Star Trek and Dallas, to remembrance books about Elvis Presley, Bing Crosby, and John Lennon immediately following their deaths.

Often published by a special projects division of the publishing company, one-shots may reappear from time to time, and eventually become a regular magazine. One-shots on crafts, needlework, home repairs, and the like have developed into regularly issued periodicals.

The one-shot is risky. Considering the lead time required, it is difficult to sell much advertising, and success depends greatly upon timing. If you publish while interest in the topic is at its zenith and you beat your competitors to the newsstand, you may do very well. But if you are late, you may find it a costly venture. One advantage publishers of well-established magazines have in these undertakings is that it is easier for them to get rack or newsstand space by using the name of the established magazine. For example, "A Woman's Day Super Special" is frequently used on one-shots by CBS Publications, publishers of *Woman's Day*. And the special can protect the regular magazine's rack space by using it after the regular magazine has sold out its most recent issue.

Magnitude of the Industry

Mere figures cannot convey the magnitude of an industry so diverse as the magazine industry. Raw numbers of magazines, combined circulations, dollars of income, advertising volume, and the like may be both impressive and misleading. Also, the magazine industry is more than magazines. Some editors insist that magazines are incidental in their companies' overall operations, which may include book clubs, book publishing divisions, direct mail merchandising, and sales of the magazines' mailing lists as the big money makers. And hundreds of associations and businesses that issue sponsored magazines don't consider themselves part of the magazine industry.

Establishing exact dimensions of the magazine field is nearly impossible. Although we can accept estimates of about 1,200 consumer magazines and about 2,600 business periodicals, including some association magazines, we never really know how many there are because no one has an accurate count of the number of public relations and association magazines.

The *IMS Ayer Directory of Periodicals* limits its listings to business, consumer, technical, professional, trade, and farm publications issued four or more times a year. It specifically excludes publications of "primary or secondary schools, or houses of worship" and "internal publications." The 1984 edition listed 10,809 periodicals. Frequencies were 182 daily, 21 triweekly, 73 semiweekly, 1,376 weekly, 390 biweekly, 268 semimonthly, 4,096 monthly, 1,348 bimonthly, 1,711 quarterly, and 1,344 at variant intervals.

The Standard Periodical Directory attempts to be more inclusive, to the point of listing publications that appear at least once every two years. Its 1985–86 edition listed 62,400 United States and Canadian periodicals, including 13,258 magazines, 3,916 "house organs," and 8,631 journals. This edition added 10,000 new titles and deleted approximately 3,000 periodicals that had ceased publication or could no longer be located. Newsletters, college yearbooks, public relations magazines, and advertising shopping guides are included in *The Standard Periodical Directory*, which does not contain tables listing frequency of publication.

A 1980 Audit Bureau of Circulations study showed that magazines, farm publications, and business publications had total average circulations of nearly 477 million copies per issue. Magazines averaged 454,000, farm publications 74,000, and business publications 29,000 circulation per issue.

Circulations range from small and unreported figures to millions. In June 1984 *Hypertension* had a circulation of 3,732, *Pittsburgh Business Times* 6,711, and

American Demographics 7,896. At the same time, ABC listed 64 magazines with more than one million circulation, not including comic books and magazine groups. The largest included *Reader's Digest, TV Guide, National Geographic, Better Homes and Gardens, Family Circle,* and *Woman's Day.*

Time led all magazines in advertising revenue in 1984 with more than $335 million, according to *The Gallagher Report.* Giant consumer magazines expectedly led in advertising revenue (table 1–2), but major business publications ranked well (table 1–3). *Computerworld,* with more than $50 million in advertising revenue, would have ranked 25th if compared with consumer magazines, behind *Redbook* and ahead of *Sunset* in the 1984 *Gallagher Report* listing.

TABLE 1–1
Magazines Exceeding Two Million Circulation (Audited by ABC)

Rank	Magazine	Circulation (million)
1	Reader's Digest	18.0
2	TV Guide	17.3
3	National Geographic	10.2
4	Modern Maturity	9.8
5	NRTA/AARP News Bulletins	9.6
6	Better Homes and Gardens	8.0
7	Family Circle	7.0
8	Woman's Day	6.8
9	McCall's	6.2
10	Good Housekeeping	5.2
11	Ladies' Home Journal	5.1
12	National Enquirer	4.7
13	Time	4.6
14	Guideposts	4.2
15	Playboy	4.2
16	Redbook	3.9
17	Star	3.6
18	Penthouse	3.2
19	Newsweek	3.0
20	Prevention	3.0
21	Cosmopolitan	2.9
22	Sports Illustrated	2.6
23	People Weekly	2.6
24	American Legion	2.5
25	Southern Living	2.2
26	Glamour	2.2
27	U.S. News & World Report	2.1
28	Smithsonian	2.0
29	Field & Stream	2.0

Source: *ABC Fas-Fax,* June 30, 1984.

TABLE 1–2
Top 15 Consumer Magazines in Advertising Revenue

1984 Position	1983 Position	Magazine	Advertising Revenue 1984	1983	Percent Increase or Decrease
1	1	Time	$335,589,383	$299,341,979	+12.1
2	2	TV Guide	304,264,688	269,430,110	+12.9
3	3	Newsweek	247,094,704	218,722,832	+13.0
4	5	People	232,888,231	175,308,068	+32.8
5	4	Sports Illustrated	230,766,138	183,055,377	+26.1
6	6	Business Week	184,782,417	156,208,266	+18.3
7	7	Good Housekeeping	133,313,233	127,096,131	+ 4.9
8	8	Family Circle	130,691,623	118,767,567	+10.0
9	9	Better Homes and Gardens	126,134,446	109,010,213	+15.7
10	11	Reader's Digest	111,854,487	101,634,629	+10.1
11	12	Fortune	111,678,974	97,006,134	+15.1
12	10	Woman's Day	110,366,689	105,644,690	+ 4.5
13	14	Forbes	109,728,789	84,459,135	+29.9
14	13	U.S. News & World Report	101,480,471	93,759,710	+ 8.2
15	15	Cosmopolitan	95,144,052	81,136,017	+17.3

Source: Copyright © *The Gallagher Report,* Second Supplement to January 28, 1985. Reprinted by permission.

The number of pages of advertising published places magazines in a different perspective because this measure allows for the variation in circulation and advertising rates. The top 15 magazines in ad page volume in 1984, according to voluntary reports to *The Gallagher Report,* are listed in table 1–4. Business publications dominate the list, illustrating that there is a large volume of advertising aimed at potential customers in a specific industry or profession through their specialized publications.

TABLE 1–3
Top 15 Business Publications in Advertising Revenue

1984 Position	1983 Position	Publication	Advertising Revenue 1984	1983	Percent Increase or Decrease
1	1	*Computerworld*	$50,160,048	$42,850,900	+17.1
2	2	*Restaurants & Institutions*	30,578,500	22,613,500	+35.2
3	3	*Electronic Design*	27,740,000	22,091,000	+25.6
4	7	*EDN*	25,575,000	19,391,000	+31.9
5	5	*Aviation Week & Space Technology*	24,459,000	19,973,000[b]	+22.5
6	4	*Medical Economics*	22,620,000	21,591,000	+ 4.6
7	6	*Institutional Investor*	22,400,000	19,700,000	+13.7
8	8	*Design News*	21,867,755[a]	15,877,456[a]	+37.7
9	9	*Datamation*	18,982,000	15,004,000	+26.5
10	10	*Journal of the American Medical Association*	15,779,394	14,206,847	+11.1
11	16	*Electronic Engineering Times*	15,500,000	11,100,000	+39.6
12	20	*Electronic Buyer's News*	15,400,000	10,300,000	+49.5
13	21	*Nation's Restaurant News*	14,681,000	10,300,000	+42.5
14	26	*Computer Systems News*	14,300,000	9,700,000	+47.4
15	15	*Restaurant Business*	13,350,000[a]	14,000,000	− 4.6

[a]Includes annual, special editions.
[b]Includes Paris Air Show issue.

Source: Copyright © *The Gallagher Report,* Second Supplement to January 14, 1985.
Reprinted by permission.

TABLE 1–4
Top 15 Magazines in Advertising Pages Published

1984 Rank	1983 Rank	Magazine (Issues per year)	Advertising Pages 1984	1983	Percent Increase or Decrease	Circulation
1	2	*Travel Agent* (104)	7,706	7,676	+ 0.4	33,628
2	3	*Computerworld* (52)	6,350	6,011	+ 5.6	125,067
3	1	*Electronic Design* (26)	6,340	7,881	−19.6	114,062
4	4	*EDN* (26)	6,111	5,004	+22.1	120,979
5	6	*Business Week* (52)	4,972	4,641	+ 7.1	775,223
6	9	*Design News* (24)	4,969[a]	4,064[a]	+21.8	155,844
7	5	*Medical Economics* (26)	4,752	4,701	+ 1.1	169,965
8	20	*Electronic Buyer's News* (52)	4,459[b]	3,170[b]	+40.7	50,378
9	10	*Restaurants & Institutions* (26)	4,364	3,550	+22.9	126,771
10	14	*People Weekly* (51)	4,063	3,446	+17.9	2,695,431
11	7	*Byte* (12)	3,919	4,330	− 9.5	409,387
12	8	*Oil & Gas Journal* (52)	3,885	4,147	− 6.3	62,467
13	15	*Forbes* (26)	3,834	3,401	+12.7	726,736
14	12	*TV Guide* (52)	3,800	3,632	+ 4.6	17,345,473
15	18	*Aviation Week & Space Technology* (52)	3,678	3,202[c]	+14.9	140,010

[a]Includes annual, special editions.
[b]Oversize page. Equivalent 7″ × 10″ units = 7,447 and 5,294.
[c]Includes Paris Air Show issue.

Source: *The Gallagher Report,* Second Supplement to January 14, 1985, and Second Supplement to January 28, 1985; *ABC Fas-Fax,* June 30, 1984; *Consumer Magazine and Agri-Media Rates and Data,* August 27, 1984; and *Business Publication Rates and Data,* December 24, 1984.

The *Folio 400* each year reports estimates of subscription revenue, single copy revenue, advertising revenue, and total revenue and lists average circulation per issue. Table 1–5 lists the top 15 magazines in total revenue from the *Folio 400*.

Media Conglomerates

Much strength in the magazine industry comes from multiple publishing and diversification of enterprises that spread risks among more operating divisions and permit support of a money-losing magazine, at least for a period, with profits or surplus from other magazines or divisions. McGraw-Hill Publications Company, the largest business publisher in terms of gross income, is part of a corporation that also operates McGraw-Hill Book Company, McGraw-Hill Information Systems Company, Standard and Poor's Corporation, McGraw-Hill Broadcasting Company, Data Resources, Inc., and McGraw-Hill International Book Company. Besides corporate strength from such diversity, multiple publications using the same news service (McGraw-Hill World News), and sharing the overhead, can obtain news that they could not afford as single publications.

Several corporations have branched into other media, notably television or cable or community antenna television (CATV), and some have become conglomerates selling insurance, mailing lists, and games, and operating book clubs, record clubs, direct mail merchandising, radio stations, and newspapers. In some cases the magazines are kept in business to provide active mailing lists for the mail order enterprise.

CBS Inc. is an example of a corporation that entered publishing to diversify its interests. Its publishing group includes Holt, Rinehart and Winston and other educational publishing operations, 21 major special interest consumer magazines, the Popular Magazines unit that publishes 21 special interest magazines distributed only on newsstands, and Popular Library paperback books.

The largest division of CBS, of course, is its broadcast group. Other groups are the records group and the Columbia group, which includes Columbia House, retail stores, musical instruments, and the toys division.

The American Broadcasting Companies, Inc. (ABC) more than doubled its gross income from publishing by acquiring *Los Angeles,* Chilton Company, Hitchcock Publishing Company, and McCall's needlework and crafts publications over the years 1977–1979. Yet publishing accounted for only 9 percent of the corporation's gross revenue in 1979. ABC was publishing six consumer magazines, seven farm publications, and 31 business publications in 1984.

TABLE 1–5
Top 15 Magazines in Total Revenue from *The Folio 400* **(Estimates for Calendar year 1983)**

Rank			Est.1983 Total Revenue ($000)	Total Revenue Growth %	Est. 1983 Ad Revenue ($000)	Est. 1983 Sub. Revenue ($000)	Est. 1983 Newstd. Revenue ($000)	Est. 1983 Ad Pages	Est. 1983 Average Circ.	Est. 1983 Average Subscript. Circ.	Est. 1983 Average Newstand Circ.
1983	1982	Magazine Name									
1	1	TV Guide	695,524	5.0	269,422	186,086	240,017	3,644	17,170,799	8,113,564	9,057,235
2	2	Time	487,639	14.7	298,612	166,586	22,441	2,699	4,667,469	4,413,927	253,542
3	5	People Weekly	325,722	13.1	175,515	39,521	110,686	3,449	2,741,029	1,004,784	1,736,245
4	3	Newsweek	319,139	10.5	218,723	84,212	16,204	2,958	3,030,780	2,826,961	203,819
5	4	Reader's Digest	295,498	2.5	101,649	177,069	16,779	1,033	18,118,068	17,101,135	1,016,933
6	6	Sports Illustrated	283,860	15.3	188,222	86,289	9,349	2,761	2,476,147	2,375,354	100,793
7	8	Family Circle	208,834	9.7	118,830	1,595	88,409	1,788	7,251,531	127,504	7,124,027
8	10	Good Housekeeping	207,304	12.4	127,243	42,721	37,339	2,097	5,406,959	3,431,335	1,975,624
9	14	Woman's Day	188,664	16.4	105,865	598	82,201	1,607	6,987,317	50,491	6,936,827
10	7	National Enquirer	187,048	− 1.8	28,300	9,427	149,321	1,404	4,890,644	472,864	4,417,780
11	15	Business Week	185,685	14.9	156,499	25,833	3,353	4,644	852,821	820,269	32,552
12	11	National Geographic	184,760	11.5	27,379	157,381	0	264	10,492,039	10,492,039	0
13	9	Playboy	177,710	− 5.8	60,562	46,817	70,331	1,047	4,229,824	2,326,939	1,902,886
14	12	Better Homes and Gardens	177,659	7.3	109,038	58,339	10,282	1,376	8,032,373	7,461,148	571,225
15	16	Parade	168,564	7.2	168,564	0	0	742	23,168,789	0	0

Source: *The Folio:400/1984* © Folio Publishing Corporation. Reprinted by permission.

Professional Organizations

Concerned with issues and problems facing magazines as an industry, a handful of professional organizations binds together publishers, editors, writers, and art directors. The most prominent of these, and whose emblem is printed in many member magazines, is the Magazine Publishers Association (MPA), established in 1919. Membership includes association, religious, business, scholarly, metropolitan, and professional magazines as well as consumer magazines. MPA sponsors and publishes industry-wide research about magazines and their roles as communication and advertising media, and it attacks industry problems such as proposed postal rate increases.

Affiliated with the Magazine Publishers Association is the American Society of Magazine Editors (ASME), founded in 1963 by Edward Weeks, editor of *The Atlantic,* Dan Mich, editor of *Look,* and Ted Patrick, editor of *Holiday.* They aimed for ASME to give magazine editors a leadership position among magazine executives and to serve as a forum for discussions on professional problems, as a voice to express their concerns and viewpoints, and as a means for developing public relations programs of long-range benefit to magazine journalism. Chief editors and their senior associates of consumer magazines, business papers, and farm publications are members.

Professional programs for editors include seminars and round tables on current operating problems and luncheons on topics of general interest to editors. Public relations programs are the National Magazine Awards and a magazine internship program that brings students to New York each summer to fill junior staff positions on several magazines.

The National Magazine Awards are presented annually to honor editorial excellence and to encourage editorial vigor and innovation. They were established in 1966 at the invitation of ASME with a grant from MPA and are administered by the Graduate School of Journalism at Columbia University. In 1970 the award was expanded to five categories, and it has been modified until it had 10 award categories in 1981.

The Association of Business Publishers traces its beginning to 1906 and the Federation of Trade Press Associations, later called Associated Business Publications. The group established standards of practice for the industry in 1913. Membership was limited to publishers whose circulations were audited by the Audit Bureau of Circulations.

The growth of publications using controlled (free) circulation to persons who met certain qualifications within the industry led a group of these publishers to found the National Business Papers Association in 1940. The name was changed to National Business Publications in 1948, and the organization accepted members with both paid and free circulations.

In January 1965 the two organizations merged to form American Business Press, Inc., with headquarters in New York City. The merger was a natural outgrowth of business conditions, with many publishers issuing both paid and controlled circulation magazines and some belonging to both organizations. ABP requires a publication to be audited by an independent, nonprofit, tripartite auditing organization, to be independently owned and tax-paying, and to adhere to ABP's Code of Publishing Practice (see chapter 19), which places the interest of the reader first, in order to be eligible for membership. Publishers of about 390 titles are members of ABP. The name was changed to the Association of Business Publishers, Inc., in 1985.

Since 1954 ABP annually has presented to individual editors the Jesse H. Neal Editorial Achievement Awards in five editorial categories in each of three business publication classifications to reward editorial excellence in audited, independent business publications.

ABP permits journalism school graduates who are interested in the business press to use its job placement service.

Association magazines formed their organization in the mid-1960s, the Society of National Association Publications, with headquarters in Washington, D.C. By

1978 its membership included nearly 200 national trade, professional, and business associations that publish 265 national magazines, and it was beginning an internship program for university journalism students.

Editors of public relations magazines may join the International Association of Business Communicators, which had its beginnings in the 1930s as the American Association of Industrial Editors and in the 1940s as the International Council of Industrial Editors. The two groups merged to form IABC in 1970.

IABC sponsors an annual Gold Quill Awards competition that includes categories in internal magazines, external magazines, magapapers, design, and photojournalism. It also conducts an annual convention, presents educational seminars, has an "accredited business communicator" program, and issues *Communication World*. Its headquarters are in San Francisco.

Two other organizations with involvement in the magazine industry are the American Society of Business Press Editors, with headquarters in Evanston, Illinois, and the Agricultural Publisher's Association, with headquarters in Chicago.

Future for Magazines

Man's need for knowledge, entertainment, and ideas assures the magazine industry of survival, probably in a greater variety of formats and forms than now exist. The possibility of an electronic magazine has been held out for years, but the exact form it may take has not been determined. A subscriber may receive his magazine by facsimile through cable television. That would require expensive paper and considerable time. He may have a cathode ray tube he can hold in his lap and read, after either ordering the pages he wants to read from computer storage or inserting a video cassette into his home communications center. Either system would pass more of the cost on to the consumer.

Some magazines may come as audio or video cassettes. But the future of print seems assured. Even with the additional channels of a cable operation, the cost of transmission would be too great for many of the association and public relations magazines and probably for many special interest magazines of less than 100,000 circulation. *Ladies' Home Journal* may be stored in a computer so one can call up just what is wanted, or one may subscribe to and pay for only certain sections of it. But economics probably will encourage *Railroad Model Craftsman,* with its 89,000 circulation, to continue as a printed magazine.

Postal rate increases coupled with increased printing and paper costs may increase the feasibility of the electronic magazine as well as make it imperative to pass along substantial cost increases to magazine subscribers and advertisers. Some magazines will be able to adjust to higher postal rates, but others will find that almost impossible. In an attempt to cut delivery costs, magazines have been experimenting with alternate delivery methods since 1972. Independent delivery services appear to be the most feasible means. The situation provides ample reason for new magazines to set subscription rates high enough to lure only those readers sincerely interested in the editorial product. It is much more difficult to raise subscription rates successfully after readers have become accustomed to a certain price range.

In whichever form, electronic or print, magazines will need editors who can process information, entertainment, and ideas into effective communication packages and distribute them efficiently to consumers. In spite of the economic challenges, the future for the magazine is bright, perhaps brighter than at any previous time this century. The magazine field is strong overall and offers writing, editing, photographic, design, and production opportunities to intelligent, skilled, creative persons who have a never-ending curiosity and a desire to do things better.

Entry is usually not via the big books headquartered in New York City. The largest number of jobs is on public relations, business, and association magazines, which have smaller staffs and perhaps less turnover. The prospective editor may have to search out his own vacancy to fill, but with so many thousand magazines like these, jobs usually are available. The new employee often appreciates working on these books more because he is given wider latitude for expressing himself, a greater variety of tasks, and greater responsibility in seeing that the book meets its production schedule. Many new journalism graduates become one-person editorial staffs within a few weeks after graduation, having the thrill of planning the book, editing copy, designing layouts, ordering illustrations, and seeing the entire book through to completion wholly to themselves.

Conclusion

Although there have been notable changes in individual magazines, the magazine industry as a whole is stable, and more new magazines are being established than discontinued. Americans are reading an average of eight issues a month, although they spend less time with magazines than with television or newspapers. The vast majority of magazines are business or public relations publications, but the largest individual circulations are claimed by consumer magazines. Variety in content, circulation methods, and income sources makes generalization about the magazine industry extremely difficult.

In the United States, magazines have evolved from a form of popular entertainment and nationalizing influence in the 1800s and early 1900s to a specialized form of mass communication emphasizing the information function, especially with the development of television in the 1950s and 1960s. Magazines, from the muckraking 1910s through the newsmagazine 1930s, always have provided information, but informative ones grew more rapidly and fiction became less emphasized in the 1950s and 1960s. Magazines now meet specialized information needs that cannot be met adequately by the mass medium of televison or the local medium of newspapers.

Notes

1. *How & Why People Buy Magazines* (Port Washington, N.Y.: Publishers Clearing House, 1977), pp. 29 and 31.
2. These magazines are sometimes referred to as *house organs, industrial magazines, company magazines,* and *organizational magazines.*

Special Interest Magazines

2

FROM fly fishing to flying, flower gardening to model railroading, gun lore to philately, there's a magazine for almost any interest you may have. A family's magazine reading may cover the spectrum from a home and garden magazine that takes no stands on controversial issues through children's magazines, women's magazines, business magazines, a fraternal magazine, a travel magazine, and a hobby or craft magazine, to a fiercely controversial journal of opinion.

Readers may look upon these as individual entities rather than as a group of magazines, but collectively they represent the backbone of the magazine industry.

Special interest magazines have long been on the American scene. *Harper's Bazaar* dates from 1867, *McCall's* from 1870, *Sports Afield* from 1887, *National Geographic* from 1888, *Vogue* from 1892, *Travel/Holiday* from 1901, and *Flying Models* from 1927. But the rapid expansion of population, markets, and family income since World War II has aided their great increase in numbers.

Women's and Home Service Magazines

Long the strongest portion of the American magazine publishing industry, women's and home service magazines continue to have large circulations and large amounts of advertising. Similar in many respects in their focus, the home service magazines appeal more broadly to the family than do the women's magazines, which slant toward women, including their interests outside the home.

Six of the 11 largest circulation magazines are women's and home service books: *Better Homes and Gardens, Woman's Day, Family Circle, McCall's, Ladies' Home Journal,* and *Good Housekeeping.* Each has more than 5 million circulation.

Ladies' Home Journal was the foundation of the Curtis empire. Prior to its founding, Cyrus H. K. Curtis had indifferent successes with a few publications operated on small budgets. He was editing the women's department of the *Tribune and Farmer,* a four-year-old weekly in which he was a partner, in 1883, when Mrs. Curtis took over editing it after telling him his material sounded funny to a woman. The department grew to a page, then an eight-page supplement, then in December 1883 it became the *Ladies' Home Journal.*

Following a difference of opinion, Curtis gave his partner the *Tribune and Farmer,* which soon failed, and kept *Ladies' Home Journal.* When Mrs. Curtis retired as editor in 1889, the *Journal* led all women's magazines with 440,000 circulation. Her successor, Edward Bok, was a 26-year-old Dutch-born bachelor who also became a great editor, guiding the *Journal* for 21 years. He told his readers about venereal disease and civic planning, started a lovelorn column he personally wrote, and had a doctor answer questions about the care of children. Under Bok, the *Journal* was one of the first magazines to reach one million circulation.

Bruce and Beatrice Gould followed Bok and presided over what some term the silver age of that magazine, although it began to lose money before they retired in 1962.

Both *Cosmopolitan* and *Good Housekeeping* are Hearst magazines. *Cosmopolitan* has long been known for selling most of its copies via newsstands (95.7 percent) at a relatively high cover price. Those who choose to subscribe must pay not

Figure 2–1 John Mack Carter began his magazine journalism career at age 21 as an assistant editor of *Better Homes and Gardens.* Two years later he was managing editor of *Household.* Before becoming editor of *Good Housekeeping,* he was also executive editor of *Together,* editor of *American Home,* executive editor of *McCall's,* editor of *McCall's,* and editor of *Ladies' Home Journal.* (Photo courtesy of John Mack Carter.)

only the full cover price of all 12 issues, but also the added cost of mailing. *Good Housekeeping,* edited in recent years by John Mack Carter, sells nearly two-thirds of its circulation by subscription.

Most women's fashion, beauty, and grooming magazines are in the 500,000 to 1 million circulation bracket, except for *Glamour* at more than 1.9 million. Condé Nast publishes *Glamour, Mademoiselle,* and *Vogue.* Hearst issues *Harper's Bazaar.* Fairchild publishes *W.*

The beginning of the 1980s saw several new women's magazines burst upon the scene, including *Savvy, Self* from Condé Nast, McCall's *Working Mother, Woman* from Harris Publishing, and *Woman's Week,* a weekly available only on newsstands. Some of these will succeed, but some are bound to disappear.

Essence, Lady's Circle, Ms., New Woman, Parents, Playgirl, Redbook, Shape, True Story, Weight Watchers, Women's Sports and Fitness, Workbasket, and *Working Woman* are among the other magazines for women. Several dressmaking and needlework books are issued, usually two or three times a year, by several publishers, as are special interest books on decorating, hairstyles, cooking and baking, and Christmas ideas.

Usually called shelter books in the trade, the home service magazines cover a wide range of topics: food, appliances, decorating, gardening, health, autos, family entertainment, travel, home maintenance, and consumer buying. Circulation leader in the field is a relative newcomer, *Better Homes and Gardens,* established in 1922 by E. T. Meredith of Des Moines. From the beginning his magazine aimed at men as well as women readers and stressed service to the point of insisting that each article help the reader do something.

Both *House Beautiful* and *House & Garden* preceded Meredith's magazine (1896 and 1901 respectively), but both have always been class-oriented and each near 1 million circulation, compared with about 8 million for *Better Homes and Gardens.*

L. W. Lane, an advertising staff member of *Better Homes and Gardens,* bought *Sunset* in 1928 to make it a homeowners' magazine for the West Coast. It had been started by the Southern Pacific Railroad in 1898 to promote rail travel on its Sunset Limited and to extol the virtues of the West. Its employees bought it in 1914 and made it into a regional literary magazine. *Sunset,* the Magazine of Western Living, now exceeds 1.4 million circulation and charges extra for subscriptions outside its nine-state service area.

Southern Living, begun by *The Progressive Farmer* of Birmingham in 1966, achieved 875,000 circulation within five years. Circulation was 2.2 million in 1984.

Leisure Time and Avocational Magazines

A trip to any well-stocked newsstand reveals a variety of leisure time and avocational magazines that have developed as the work week has grown shorter and income and leisure time have increased. *Consumer Magazine Rates and Data* has more than a score of classifications for these magazines, ranging alphabetically from art and antiques, automotive, camping, and crafts and hobbies to romance, sports, travel, and TV and radio. It lists more than 30 automotive magazines, 14 started in the 1970s and 9 in the 1980s, and 17 motorcycle magazines.

Four coin publications circulate an average of 89,500 copies per issue reaching a total circulation of 358,000 per issue. *Lapidary Journal* circulates 43,000 copies per issue, *Tropical Fish Hobbyist* 42,000, and *Flying Models* 27,000. These circulations are small in comparison with the circulation giants, but the coin collector, rockhound, and other hobbyists are intensely interested in their publications, making those publications the most efficient means for reaching potential customers.

Numerous travel magazines are published, usually bimonthly or monthly, from automobile club publications to *Travel & Leisure* and *Travel/Holiday.* Magazines for owners of recreational vehicles have become increasingly popular in recent years.

One of the notable post-war successes is Robert Petersen of Los Angeles. Laid off a $35 a week movie publicity job, he and his partner Robert Lindsay started

Hot Rod in 1948 on $400 cash and credit with a printer. They hung around race tracks to sell copies, and within a year the magazine was making money. Petersen's other magazines include *Car Craft, Circle Track, Dirt Rider, 4 Wheel & Off Road, Guns & Ammo, Hunting, Motorcyclist, Motor Trend, Petersen's Photographic, Pickups & Mini-Trucks, Sea and Pacific Skipper, Skin Diver,* and *'Teen.*

Two duck hunters waiting in a blind got the idea of *Field & Stream* and established it in 1895. Now owned by CBS Publications, it is edited for outdoor sportsmen and their families, giving them advice on hunting, fishing, camping, boating, archery, conservation, sportsmen's dogs, and travel. *Sports Afield* was started in 1887, and Colorado sportsman John A. McGuire originated *Outdoor Life* in 1898.

Aiming at the gun enthusiast is *Shooting Times,* published by PJS [Peoria Journal Star] Publications. In the same vein are *Guns & Ammo, Guns, Gun World,* and *Handloader,* all issued by magazine publishing companies. *American Rifleman* is the official publication of the National Rifle Association. *Skeet Shooting Review* serves members of the National Skeet Shooting Association, and the Amateur Trapshooting Association has *Trap & Field* published for its members by the Indianapolis organization that publishes today's *Saturday Evening Post.*

Outdoor magazines focusing on specific regions include *Western Outdoor News, Western Outdoors, Southern Outdoors, Salt Water Sportsman,* and *Midwest Outdoors.* A number of state publications serve outdoor interests, too, including *Lousiana Game & Fish, Michigan Out-Of-Doors,* and *Texas Fisherman.*

Artnews, long a small-circulation magazine in a specialized field, broadened its appeal and posted a 38.4 percent circulation gain between June 1976 and June 1977. Billboard's *American Artist* maintained a large circulation edge. Another art magazine is *Art in America.* Each has a slightly different readership appeal.

Romance magazines persist even after 60 years of radio and television soap operas, though in the seventies they declined as there were fewer romance magazines, fewer groups of romance magazines, and smaller circulations for the magazines that continued publishing.

Circulations of many of these look-alike magazines with sound-alike names are small, and advertising in them usually is sold on a group or combination basis. Advertising in the Macfadden Women's Group can be bought as a package of seven monthly magazines reaching 2.3 million circulation. This group includes *True Story,* established in 1919, *True Confessions, True Romance, True Love, True Experience, Secrets,* and *Modern Romances.*

Several attempts at publishing senior citizens magazines have failed because the potential readers wanted to read about and identify with younger people, and advertisers were interested in reaching a younger market. The handful of successful magazines in this field has been aimed largely at the relatively small group of professionally organized senior citizens. Whitney Communications publishes *50 plus* monthly for 312,000 subscribers, but the others are issued by such organizations as the American Association of Retired Persons (which publishes both the *AARP News Bulletin* and *Modern Maturity*), the National Association of Retired Federal Employees (*Retirement Life*), and the National Retired Teachers Association (*NRTA Journal*).

Metropolitan and Regional Magazines

After having been largely bland chamber of commerce puff publications for so many years, metropolitan magazines became more independent and vigorous in the late 1960s. Some of the credit belongs to *San Diego* magazine, which was begun by an independent publisher in 1948 and became the liberal voice in a conservative city served only by equally conservative Copley newspapers after the Democratic paper ceased publication in 1952.

Philadelphia made a name for itself by helping to update the city's airport and blowing the whistle on questionable real estate maneuvers under the guise of urban renewal. A one-time chamber of commerce newsletter, it had become independent and included full-color in its handsome format. In 1970 *Philadelphia* won the National Magazine Award for specialized journalism. It since has won additional National Magazine Awards and has won an award for the best religious article in a secular magazine.

Although an official chamber of commerce magazine at the time, *Atlanta* made news with its frank discussion of the city's higher than national average suicide rate, and discussed segregation, poverty, and political issues in addition to covering the arts, local authors, and sports and hunting in the area.

When *American Machinist* won the National Magazine Award in 1969 (a single award at that time), a metropolitan book, *The Washingtonian,* was one of three magazines to receive "special recognition."

No fewer than 126 metropolitian, regional, and state magazines are listed by Standard Rate and Data Service. *Honolulu,* a monthly, dates from 1888 and reaches more than 35,000 paid circulation. *Philadelphia* goes back to 1908. But of those listing founding dates, one-half were established in the 1970s and one-fourth in the 1980s. This portion of the magazine industry experienced dramatic growth in the last half of the 1970s and first half of the 1980s. As in any rapidly growing field, a number of the new starts were unable to continue to publish.

About 20 states have state-aided travel or outdoor magazines. Although obviously promoting their states, they strongly appeal to their readers, and several are known for their excellent photography and color reproduction. The leader is *Arizona Highways,* a monthly started in 1925 as a black-and-white bulletin of technical engineering information. It later developed into a state travel magazine world renowned for its color photos and reproduction. Closest in circulation and editorial quality is *Vermont Life,* a relative newcomer begun in 1946. Originally filled mostly with black-and-white layouts of historical articles, the quarterly magazine now has 24 full-color pages in each sixty-four-page issue. Most of the others are well under 50,000 circulation.

To make up losses incurred in publishing the magazines, *Arizona Highways* and *Vermont Life* both sell related products: calendars, engagement books, copies of pictures, and bound volumes of magazines. Most similar magazines require some subsidy.

Editorial questions facing some of these magazines include how to balance tourist promotion with conservation and wildlife content. Some states have separate magazines for those areas of content, but the editor of *Outdoor Indiana* said he was facing the decision of whether to throw the magazine entirely to tourist promotion or continue mixing in wildlife, conservation, and travel. *Vermont Life,* established

Figure 2–2 The Louisiana Department of Wildlife and Fisheries publishes *Louisiana Conservationist,* a bimonthly state magazine of nearly 200,000 circulation. This Christmas issue featured an unusual wraparound cover. (Courtesy *Louisiana Conservationist.*)

to attract new residents to that state, now faces the problem that attracting more new residents may no longer be desirable. Yet 85 percent of the magazine's subscriptions and 70 percent of its newsstand sales are outside the state. *Oklahoma Today* tries to point out the things "that are right and good about Oklahoma," while *Outdoor Oklahoma* is more of a wildlife publication.

Several independently published magazines are regional in nature. *Yankee* is a 6 × 9 inch magazine jammed with advertising and several articles on New England each month. Its publishers in Dublin, New Hampshire, say it is "published for New Englanders everywhere." Its mid-1984 circulation was 950,000.

Sunset has 95 percent of its circulation in the Pacific and Mountain states; *Southern Living* does equally well with its readers in the South.

Related to all these are the American Automobile Association and Canadian Automobile Association magazines, which also are essentially regional in nature as well as concerned with travel.

Opinion Magazines

A handful of magazines that deal with public affairs in a broad sense, usually from a well-defined point of view, have been influential by raising social issues in their pages before the issues become generally popular. These opinion magazines typically have circulations of 20,000 to 100,000 and need subsidizing to remain in operation. Although they are similar in these characteristics, they do not agree on their views.

Oldest of these is *The Nation,* established in 1865 by E. L. Godkin, who had immigrated from Ireland in 1856 to write about conditions in the South. He was critical of much of what he saw in America, and his magazine condemned Tammany Hall, the Populists, and the railroad barons, but it also attacked trade unionism and the eight-hour work day. In 1918, after Oswald Garrison Villard had become editor, one issue was held up five days by the Post Office as unmailable until President Wilson intervened.[1]

In his analysis of *Magazines in the Twentieth Century,* Theodore Peterson writes about *The Nation:*

It denounced Mussolini at a time when he still had apologists in the United States. It foresaw the threat of Hitler long before the invasion of Poland. . . .

The *Nation* promoted a number of causes after Carey McWilliams became editor in 1955: making racial equality an immediate reality, setting life imprisonment as the maximum punishment for any crime, achieving equal voting strength in state government for citizens in city and country, conserving natural resources, treating drug addiction as a medical rather than criminal problem. But its prime cause seems to have been disarmament and rule by international law, and it gave considerable space to the peace movement and to the dangers of nuclear war. It continued to give attention to foreign affairs, and it maintained its concern for civil liberties.[2]

The Nation is published weekly. Another liberal magazine is the *New Republic,* started in 1914 and issued weekly. The conservative *National Review* of William F. Buckley, Jr., is the most recent entry, 1955.

Three religion-related magazines can be counted in this group: *Christian Century,* a Protestant weekly begun in 1900; *Commonweal,* a Catholic lay magazine begun in 1924; and *Commentary,* a Jewish monthly originated in 1945.

John Schacht observed that the print medium is ideal for discussion of complex issues of human society, and that these magazines are influential as a result of continued repetition of basic themes. "In major issues the journals' views have preceded, not coincided with or followed, government action and changes in public opinion," he said.[3]

These magazines usually keep a major issue in their readers' minds over a period of years, not just when the issue is hot in the other magazines and media. Their approach is usually philosophical, ethical, and analytical, and calculated to bring about positive action.

Schacht's analysis shows that almost one-fifth of all magazine material in the United States on the social security issue between 1932 and 1935 appeared in the opinion magazines, but this dropped to less than one-tenth as the mass magazines began running more but different material on the subject. About one-third of the articles on censorship, free speech, and freedom of the press listed in the *Reader's Guide* are to be found in the opinion journals, he said.

One publisher of an opinion magazine says the magazines in this group don't have to be popular, so they can either say things the big magazines won't say or say them earlier. If there are no fireworks after the opinion magazine runs the piece, a big book may pick up the issue and do a better or a broader story. Another publisher claims that the leader or activist turns to his journal for the argument about the issue.

Little Magazines

Magazines that publish artistic work that, for commercial reasons, is not acceptable to large circulation magazines are called little magazines or little literary magazines. They come and go rapidly. On the average, one that makes it through the first year likely will not last longer than five. One writer for such magazines has suggested that the little magazine can do its work in two or three years and need not survive longer.

Little magazines lose money, so their owners have to keep them small and often modest in physical quality. They claim originality, intellectual honesty, and literary influence, and they protest the smugness and security they believe accompanies commercial success. Little magazines are more for their writers than for their readers. However, a study in 1946 concluded that little magazines had discovered about 80 percent of the important novelists, poets, and critics who began to write after 1912, and that they introduced and remained the basic magazines to publish 95 percent of the poets of this period.[4]

The first modern-type little magazine in the United States was the short-lived *Dial,* edited by Emerson, Thoreau, and Margaret Fuller (1840–44). There have been at least three *Dial*s since. *Poetry,* founded by Harriet Monroe in 1912, has survived. So have the *Partisan Review* (1934), now published at Rutgers, and *Hudson Review* (1948). Most that have survived are subsidized by colleges or universities.

The *Sewanee Review* dates from 1892 and is published by the University of the South, Sewanee, Tennessee. The *Midland* of Iowa City lasted twelve years and inspired *The Prairie Schooner* (1927) and *The Frontier,* later combined and published as *The Prairie Schooner* at the University of Nebraska. The distinguished *Kenyon Review,* established in 1939, fell victim to budget cutting at Kenyon College in 1970. After it was re-established in 1979, it achieved more than twice its previous circulation record in less than two years.

Quarterly Review of Literature is published by Princeton. *Kansas Magazine* was succeeded by *Kansas Quarterly* in 1968. The *South Atlantic Quarterly,* headquartered at Duke University, has published literature and history since 1902. *Southern Review* is published at Louisiana State University.

Major universities believe that a journal of humanities is a worthwhile venture, by either keeping an established magazine going or beginning a new one. Some of these combine public affairs, politics, humanities, and the arts with literary content, as does *Southern Humanities Review* (Auburn University), which goes into criticism and poetry. Most are quarterlies, but some are published less often.

A knowledgeable magazine publisher intending to make money would not start an opinion magazine or a little magazine, nor would a journalism graduate plan a career editing such a publication. Neither type is conventional magazine journalism, and both types of magazines will find unique persons to be their editors.

Adless Magazines

Thousands of public relations and association magazines carry no advertising, but only an infinitesimal minority of consumer magazines rely solely on subscription and single-copy income to remain in business. A few are worth noting, as are a few that have changed and begun to accept advertising.

Consumer Reports was established in 1936 to report monthly on the independent testing of consumer products by Consumers Union. The magazine does not accept advertising. It forbids use of its test findings and recommendations for commercial purposes and has won several suits against companies that have violated that prohibition. *Consumer Bulletin,* established in 1927, is similar in intent. It is published monthly by Consumers' Research, Inc.

Editor Harvey Kurtzman and Publisher William Gaines fathered *Mad* from a hardback book into a satire magazine in comic book format in 1955. *Mad* accepted some advertising for a time, but it seemed incongruous with the overall tone and format and eventually faded away. It was estimated in 1970 that *Mad* was selling 2 million copies an issue.

American Heritage began in 1949 as a spare time project of Earle W. Newton, publisher of *Vermont Life*. He issued the quarterly magazine with the help of one paid employee and with backing from the American Association of State and Local History. The magazine was sold in 1954.

While making good profits from an estimated 300,000 circulation in 1958, *American Heritage* brought out *Horizon* as a magazine of the arts. The company started *Americana,* a handsome bimonthly on topics "with roots in the American past that people are participating in today," in 1973. In 1984 all three were publishing advertising and were under separate ownership. Bimonthly *Americana* had a circulation of 340,000, bimonthly *American Heritage* 135,000, and *Horizon,* 10 times a year, 58,000.

Changing Times deals with family finances or personal economics. Willard M. Kiplinger, who had made a name with his *Kiplinger Washington Letter,* started work on his magazine in 1946. He discarded both the first and second issues at press time because he thought they were not good enough. He finally went to press with the January 1947 issue, a 7×9 inch pamphlet with perforated pages, so articles could be easily passed along to friends. Page size later was enlarged and, because of cost, perforations were eliminated. The magazine sold poorly on the newsstand but achieved circulation success—one million by April 1961—from promotion on radio and television. The magazine began accepting advertisements in 1980 and by mid-1984 had a circulation of 1.4 million.

Public Relations Magazines

Millions of American families regularly receive magazines from their auto dealers, employers, or corporations in which they own stock. This area of magazine journalism perhaps started in 1840 when the *Lowell Offering* was begun as an outlet for the literary expression of the Lowell Cotton Mills' women workers in Lowell, Massachusetts. Other early company-sponsored magazines were *The Mechanic* of the H. B. Smith Machine Company of Smithville, New Jersey in 1847, and the two oldest magazines extant, one started as *The Travelers Record* of the Travelers Insurance Company in 1865, and the other *The Locomotive* of the Hartford Steam Boiler Inspection and Insurance Company in 1867.

These magazines were issued for general circulation. *The Travelers Record* circulated 50,000 copies of its first issue to hotels, clubs, barber shops, and other gathering places. At that time *The Saturday Evening Post, Harper's Weekly,* and other leading magazines had fewer than 75,000 circulation. The great growth of general interst periodicals in the 1890s led the Travelers Insurance Company to change its magazine to *The Agents Record* and reduce circulation by limiting it to its agents. It was combined with *The Agents Bulletin* in 1918, and the name was changed to *Protection.*

The first known periodical specifically for employees was *The Triphammer,* begun in 1885 by the Massey Manufacturing Company, later to be Massey-Ferguson. *Factory News* of the National Cash Register Company was established in 1890 as a twelve-page monthly. It was succeeded in 1967 by a smart, black-and-white, 32-page bimonthly, *NCR World.*

Many terms have been applied to periodicals of corporations and businesses. The early term *house organ* has undesirable connotations to many in the field, having been applied at a time when those publications often were blatantly one-sided and unreliable. The term still is in widespread use, both by detractors and impartial observers.

When practitioners in this field organized their professional groups in the late 1930s and 1940s, the terms *industrial journalism* and *industrial publications* emerged. The term *industrial magazine,* however, often is confused with business publications that are not sponsored by a single company, and in their 1961 book Baird and Turnbull settled on *company publication* as an appropriate descriptive term. Some editors prefer the term *organizational magazine.*

Because these publications nearly always are issued to advance the aims of the company, and their objectives are compatible with corporate policy, we have adopted the term *public relations magazines* as appropriately descriptive. These magazines are aimed at specific publics of the company in an attempt to achieve certain objectives. They may be issued by the public relations department, corporate relations, corporate communications, or even the personnel department, but their objectives are public relations in nature.

Types of Public Relations Magazines

Public relations magazines come in varied sizes and frequencies, with assorted purposes. Large companies, like Ford Motor Company, have an entire publications division. Very small companies may have an editor in charge of the company magazine, the employee newspaper, and special brochures or other publications.

There are at least six major types of public relations magazines.

1. *Employee magazines* grew up telling employees about each other and their achievements, company policy and procedure, cutting waste, and how personal health and safety benefit both the worker and the company. As companies become larger, they often assign many of these functions to employee newspapers that can be locally edited within a plant or regional service area. The magazine then becomes more a voice of corporate policy and goals, augmented by general interest content and features that humanize portions of the company.

A telephone company magazine shows installers in a new mammoth office building or directory assistance operators at work. Billing and other personnel get attention, too, to show the person behind the job. An oil company magazine dramatizes work on an off-shore drilling rig and discusses the depletion allowance. But a major story in each issue is likely to be how the company is facing a current challenge, accepting its social responsibility, or trying to maximize profits, wages, and employee benefits in the face of spiraling operating costs. Content concerns broad topics and issues that affect both employees and the company.

It's sometimes hard to tell an employee magazine from another type, like a stockholder magazine, merely by looking at it. The attention to broad issues and general interest content makes them look alike. More emphasis on employees, employee policy, or employee promotions and service anniversaries generally characterizes the employee magazine.

Seventy Six of the Unocal Corporation, *Long Lines* of the Long Lines Division of American Telephone and Telegraph Company, and *Enterprise* of Southwestern Bell Corporation are examples of employee magazines.

The typical employee magazine recognizes employee activities and achievements, lists service anniversaries, and regularly features company news. A few include a column or a question-and-answer column by the company president.

2. *Customer magazines* are among the best edited, most interesting magazines in the country. *Friends* of Chevrolet is graphically exciting, excellently designed, and skillfully edited to assure readers an interesting magazine each month. *Ford Times* and its small format—because Henry Ford wanted a magazine he could put in his pocket—are legend. Going to approximately 1.6 million customers each month, the magazine is paid for partially by local dealers. Among other things, this helps to keep the mailing list current.

A magazine for customers, besides providing entertainment, reminds customers of the desirability of owning that company's product, gives ideas for use of the product and information about care and upkeep of the product, and introduces new models of the product to readers.

Friends is done for Chevrolet by Ceco Publishing Company in suburban Detroit. *TWA Ambassador* and *Delta Sky* are published for their sponsors, Trans World Airlines and Delta Air Lines, by Halsey Publishing in North Miami. East/West Network in Los Angeles and New York also publishes several inflight magazines, including *Eastern Review* and *United*

3. *Stockholder or corporate magazines* are aimed at investors, who are interested in earnings and dividends, operating costs, research and new products, legislation that affects the company, and the company's international operations. Besides, many of these magazines include material of more general interest to avoid overplaying the company's hand in the magazine. Many corporations send the corporate magazine to employees in addition to the newspaper or other format publications specifically intended for employees.

The Lamp of Exxon Corporation, *The Texaco Star,* and *Marathon World* of Marathon Oil Company are three examples, each a handsome quarterly replete with four-color illustrations and bright writing.

4. *Sales magazines* tell about products and how to sell them, aiming to help company salesmen operate more efficiently.

5. *Dealer magazines* maintain a constant flow of information about company products. Because the dealer often sells other brands of the same product, these magazines attempt to build brand loyalty, pass along successful merchandising ideas, and make an effort to increase cooperation between the merchandiser and manufacturer by explaining and interpreting company policies. *GO,* The Goodyear Tire Dealer Magazine, usually features one or two tire dealers, reports on unusual uses of Goodyear tires, and includes some company news in each issue.

6. *Technical service magazines* are found especially in those fields in which technical data are important in making the best possible use and applications of the sponsor's products. One objective is to contribute to the prestige of the sponsor and its products; others include giving technical data for use of products. *Materials Technology* is issued by the Engineered Materials Group of General Electric Company. General Motors issues an engineering journal, and RCA an electronics magazine.

Figure 2-3 A large circulation customer magazine. *Friends* has been going to Chevrolet owners for more than 35 years. (Courtesy *Friends Magazine.*)

Figure 2-4 Basically a customer magazine, *The Furrow* is published worldwide by Deere & Company and its subsidiaries in 12 languages for qualified farmers. (Courtesy The Furrow.)

Figure 2-5 *Merchandiser* is a bimonthly magazine for Maytag dealers and salespersons. (Courtesy *Merchandiser.*)

In the corporate setting, editors often find it mandatory to have material cleared within the company prior to publication. In one survey, 20 percent of the respondents had to go through five or more clearances for some major stories, although nearly 40 percent said they could publish after one or two clearances. Large companies required more clearances than smaller ones. Using 5,000 employees as the point between the two, the survey found that 69 percent of the large companies and 51 percent of the small companies required three or more clearances.

Editors within corporations also have to be careful about the use of the company's trademarks and, in employee magazines, about labor law and National Labor Relations Board decisions. In both cases they work with company counsel and have copy cleared before publication.

Business Magazines

Philadelphia Price Current is reported to have been the first U.S. business publication—established in 1783. It provided wholesale commodity prices and marine information to merchants and shippers. Other early ones were *New York Prices Current,* 1795; *Butchers' and Packers' Gazette,* 1808; *General Shipping and Commercial List,* 1815; *American Journal of Pharmacy,* 1825; and the *American Railroad Journal,* 1832. Growth of these paralleled growth of industry in general, and by 1900 there were about 300 business publications.

Factors that led to national markets for national brands also led to the need to reach wholesalers and retailers with information about their own business fields, and to keep them in touch with other industries. Businessmen who are involved in building appliances or automobiles need to read about the steel industry; and those who make auto accessories read about the auto, steel, rubber, and plastics industries,

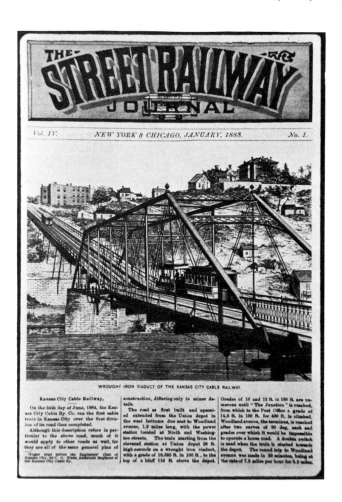

Figure 2–6 The first great success of James H. McGraw, founder of McGraw-Hill, was the *Street Railway Journal,* published for managers of horsecar lines. This is the January 1888 issue. (Courtesy McGraw-Hill.)

engineering, and finance. Many publications operate to disseminate the information about the products of their industries to other industries that use those products.

The range of business magazines, of course, spans the breadth of American industry. *Business Publication Rates and Data* has 173 classifications of publications, from Advertising and Marketing through Brewing, Brick, and Science, Research and Development to Wire and Wire Products, and Woodworking. The number of classifications changes, too, as new industries become established and need business publications.

A few of the larger magazines in the business field include *Computerworld, Datamation, Oil & Gas Journal, Machine Design, Electronic Design, Chemical Engineering, Chemical Week, Aviation Week & Space Technology, Medical Economics, Purchasing, Iron Age,* and *Industry Week.*

Figure 2–7 Three new business magazines started by McGraw-Hill in the 1970s are *Modern Plastics International,* 1971, *The Physician and Sportsmedicine,* 1973, and *Data Communications,* 1974. (Courtesy McGraw-Hill Publications Company.)

Figure 2–8 A business publication aimed at advertisers and ad agencies, *Magazine Age* started with this January 1980 issue. (Courtesy *Magazine Age.*)

Figure 2-9 Executives in the magazine industry are served by *Folio: The Magazine for Magazine Management.* The monthly started as a controlled circulation bimonthly and evolved into paid circulation and monthly frequency. (Courtesy *Folio: The Magazine for Magazine Management.*)

Growth in the number of magazines has resulted from three factors: new industries or businesses emerging to serve new technologies or markets; specialization within an industry that results in the splitting off of one or more new specialties, and regionalization of magazines to serve areas like the West or South.

There is almost no end to what could be written about special interest magazines. As long as there are enough readers interested in a particular topic and enough advertisers interested in those readers, a special interest magazine on that topic is feasible—and likely to be attempted.

Notes

1. Theodore Peterson, *Magazines in the Twentieth Century,* 2d ed. (Urbana, Ill.: University of Illinois Press, 1964), pp. 417–20.
2. Ibid., pp. 420–21.
3. John H. Schacht, *The Journals of Opinion and Reportage: An Assessment* (New York, Magazine Publishers Association, 1966), p. 38.
4. Frederick J. Hoffman, Charles Allen, and Carolyn F. Ulrich, *The Little Magazine: A History and Bibliography* (Princeton, N.J.: Princeton University Press, 1946), p. 8.

Success and Failure

3

MAGAZINES succeed or fail for many reasons. They succeed primarily if they represent the right idea at the right time, offering information or editorial service that appeals to a sufficient number of potential readers who in turn appeal to a sufficient number of advertisers. Any successful magazine can expect competition that will try to perform the same service and win away advertising dollars from it.

Magazines fail because of the lack of an editorial reason for existence, the lack of an advertising basis for existence, or the lack of knowledge of the magazine field in general and of the specific competition. Edmund Wilson also asserted that a magazine is much like a living organism, growing mature, then eventually growing old, declining, and dying.[1] Magazine success stories far outnumber the failures. Here, briefly, are some.

Of Lasting Interest

As a college student, DeWitt Wallace read extensively in current publications and noted that some articles were of more than passing interest and value. He began a card file on high points of the best articles, a technique that led to *The Reader's Digest* 12 years later.

After college he became a promotion writer for the Webb Publishing Company in St. Paul. The company published, among other things, *The Farmer,* and Wallace noted the excellence of scores of pamphlets, mostly unknown to farmers, issued by the U.S. Department of Agriculture and state agricultural experiment stations, that came to the publication's editorial desk. He prepared a 120-page booklet listing these publications and left his job with Webb after getting credit from the company for his new venture. Titled *Getting the Most Out of Farming,* it was issued in 1916 from the Webb press, and Wallace sold it to banks, who could imprint their names on the cover and distribute it to their farming customers. Touring Minnesota, North Dakota, Montana, and parts of Washington and Oregon, he sold 100,000 copies of the booklet before returning to St. Paul.

He next began to digest articles from advertising and merchandising trade journals, testing the idea by offering the digest service to department stores in country towns. He abandoned this venture in the experimental stage. Then one summer night, in a Montana bunkhouse, while thinking of the agricultural and business digests, he suddenly realized that the digest concept could be applied also to general magazines. Before he could develop his idea, war broke out and Wallace volunteered.

Wallace was hit by shrapnel in France in October 1918 and, while spending several months in the hospital, experimented with his magazine idea, clipping dozens of articles and digesting them, reducing some by as much as 75 percent without substantially altering the writer's style or meaning.

Discharged in April 1919, Wallace returned to St. Paul and spent six months collecting material. When he decided his idea was ready, he had several hundred copies of a sample issue printed and dated January 1920. The title page identified the contents as "31 articles each month from the leading magazines, each article of enduring value and interest, in condensed and permanent form." He mailed copies to leading magazine publishers and potential backers. None were interested, and Wallace was bitterly discouraged.

He took jobs in real estate and grocery wholesaling, then in 1921 got a job with the new International Publicity Department of the Westinghouse Electric and Manufacturing Company in Pittsburgh. The depression of 1921 affected the company, and after six months, Wallace was laid off. He began to write promotion circulars for his proposed magazine, sending them to teachers and nurses. He also spoke to women's clubs and professional groups.

That October in Pleasantville, New York, he married Lila Bell Acheson. From a Greenwich Village basement they started *The Reader's Digest* with a borrowed $1,300 and $5,000 brought in as provisional subscriptions from promotional mailings. Volume 1, Number 1, dated February 1922, was an unillustrated pocket-sized, and inexpensive-looking periodical, done in a serious vein. The legend on the cover was the same as that on the sample issue, except that "compact" replaced "permanent." Five thousand copies were printed.[2]

Reader's Digest was originally planned for women, but the Wallaces soon added men to their audience. Their three criteria for selecting articles were applicability—the reader should feel that the subject concerned him; lasting interest—an article should be worth reading a year later; and constructiveness.[3]

James Playsted Wood summarizes the *Digest's* contents:

The Reader's Digest has presented digested material with unfailing mass appeal. Stories of human kindness, of successful community experiments, of new inventions and devices, popularized medical articles, biographical sketches of entertaining characters, and anecdotes of simple human goodness triumphing over inimical forces are its stock in trade.

Articles on the art of living, on health, and medical topics are *Digest* staples. Issue after issue has described, sometimes almost rhapsodically, new and quick cures for new and old diseases. Homey success stories, stories showing how ambition, thrift, and kindness pay high rewards, sometimes material as well as spiritual, but always spiritual, usually to lovable little people in small towns or in the country, are unfailing in the *Digest*.[4]

The *Digest* was solely a text magazine for 17 years, then the first black-and-white line drawings were introduced in November 1939. A change in presses allowed four-color line illustrations to be used in 1948, but photographs were not used

Figure 3–1 (Above) DeWitt and Lila Acheson Wallace, co-founders of *The Reader's Digest*. (Courtesy of *Reader's Digest*.)

Figure 3–2 (Right) Cover of the first issue of *The Reader's Digest*. (Courtesy *Reader's Digest*.)

THE READER'S DIGEST

THIRTY-ONE ARTICLES EACH MONTH FROM LEADING MAGAZINES ⟶ EACH ARTICLE OF ENDURING VALUE AND INTEREST, IN CONDENSED AND COMPACT FORM

FEBRUARY 1922

until the *Digest* admitted advertising in April 1955 and began to use glossy paper for the advertising and part of the editorial content.

The *Digest* succeeded as an all-editorial magazine, rapidly gaining circulation, until 1954 when it faced a $1 million deficit. Although production and distribution costs had risen greatly, the magazine was still selling at its 1922 price, 25 cents a copy or four dollars a year. A research survey found that 81 percent of the readers preferred having advertising introduced into the book rather than having to pay a higher price per copy, and the *Digest* announced late in 1954 that it would accept 32 pages of advertising per issue beginning with the April 1955 issue. Requests for space poured in. Within two weeks it had received orders for 1,107 pages, more than three times as much as could be published the entire first year. Before the *Digest* published any advertising, it had orders for $11 million worth. The April 1955 issue contained 216 pages instead of the usual 168, and by April 1956 advertising was permitted to occupy 20 percent of the pages in an issue. By 1967 that figure had risen to 47 percent.[5]

The magazine had begun originating some material and established regular departments in 1933. Some *Digest* originals were prepared in expanded form and placed for first publication in other magazines, then reprinted in digest form. About 42 percent of the articles appearing between 1939 and 1943 were straight reprints and the other 58 percent were originals, some appearing for the first time in *Digest* pages, some prepared cooperatively with other magazines. By 1971 original material constituted about 60 percent of the *Digest's* editorial content.[6]

The condensed book was introduced in 1934, and the Reader's Digest Condensed Book Club published its first edition in 1950 for 183,000 charter subscribers. Anthologies were issued beginning in 1941, and three special books were issued. Then the *Digest* entered the book publishing field directly with the acquisition of Funk & Wagnalls, Inc., and its affiliate, Wilfred Funk, Inc., in 1965. (The *Digest* had first issued records in 1959.)[7]

The Reader's Digest Association tested *Families,* its first magazine launch since 1922, in September 1980 with an issue that contained 67 pages of advertising, all sold at full rate. Even before that issue went on sale, Digest executives planned a second issue for the following spring, and monthly publication the following fall. The test covered 28 markets.[8] National publication was scheduled for the May 1981 issue and the monthly issues starting that October with a circulation guarantee of 500,000.[9] The magazine did not catch on, though, and was suspended after two issues.

The Weekly Newsmagazine

The reader may get the idea that the way to succeed in magazine publishing is to begin with no magazine experience and clip the material he publishes. These characteristics of the beginning of *Reader's Digest* are shared by the beginning of *Time.*

Briton Hadden and Henry R. Luce were both 24 years old when they founded Time Inc., in 1922. During his childhood, Hadden had issued a newspaper, the *Daily Glonk,* for his schoolmates. Following graduation from Yale, he got a job on the New York *World* after having told Herbert Bayard Swope, its editor, who had tried to get rid of him, "Mr. Swope, you're interfering with my destiny." His destiny was to start a publication on his own, and the job on the *World* was to provide the experience.[10]

Hadden and Luce managed the undergraduate newspaper at Yale and conceived the idea of a publication that would present news in a more orderly fashion than the day's newspapers and cover world events more adequately than the day's magazines. Their magazine would organize the week's news into departments, give the news in narrative form, and describe the people who made the news. As Wood describes it, "*Time* would select the facts, tell what the facts meant, and state or strongly suggest what the reader should think or feel about them. The new magazine was to be 'curt, clear, complete,' so written and arranged that each issue would be an orderly and coherent account of the preceding week's news."[11]

Figure 3–3 *Time's* first cover. (Courtesy *Time,* Inc.)

Figure 3–4 (Left) Cover of the first issue of *Fortune*. (Courtesy *Fortune Magazine*.)

Figure 3–5 (Right) *Life's* first cover featured Margaret Bourke-White's photo of a dam at Fort Peck, Montana. (Courtesy *Life Magazine*.)

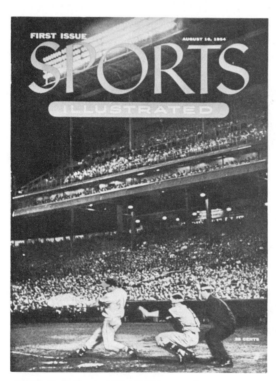

Figure 3–6 Cover of the first issue of *Sports Illustrated*, August 16, 1954. It took nine years and $20 million before this magazine showed a profit. (Illustration courtesy *Sports Illustrated*.)

Figure 3–7 Henry R. Luce. (Photographed by Alfred Eisenstaedt, courtesy *Life Magazine*.)

The idea was nurtured during their service together at an officers' training camp during World War I and later while working on Frank Munsey's Baltimore *News*. Early in 1922 they quit their jobs to begin raising money for their magazine, which they called *Facts*. With the help of friends and acquaintances, they raised $86,000, renamed the magazine *Time*, brought out a specimen issue dated December 30, 1922, and published the first issue March 3, 1923 (fig. 2–2).

Raw news was clipped from the daily newspapers, especially *The New York Times*. Hadden and Luce took turns editing and at times writing 50 to 70 percent of the magazine. The staff was small, requiring only one taxi for the ride to the printer.

Time lost $39,454 by the end of 1923, and in September 1925 the operation was moved to Cleveland for economy's sake. It lost $23,829 in 1925 but had a circulation of 107,000 and advertising income of $100,000. In August 1927 Luce and Hadden returned to New York, where there was a supply of young intellectuals they could hire for comparatively small salaries and where they could get the *New York Times* ten hours earlier. The first year a profit was shown had been 1926—$8,546.[12]

Hadden thought the news of advertising needed to be summarized as *Time* summarized general news, and in April 1927 the company began *Tide*, an advertising trade magazine. After Hadden's death in 1929, executives were more concerned with the company's new magazine, *Fortune*, and late in 1930 *Tide* was sold to Raymond Rubicam of Young & Rubicam advertising agency. Rubicam sold it in 1948, and after four other ownership changes, *Tide* ceased publication in 1959.

Fortune also was a spin-off of *Time*, whose business section was too small to carry all the material produced by the staff. Henry Luce suggested starting a magazine of restricted circulation to utilize *Time's* leftover business material, and also suggested the name. The company established a department in 1928 to work out plans for the new magazine. By late 1929 it had produced a dummy, and the first issue of *Fortune* (February 1930) appeared shortly after the stock market crash (fig. 2–3).[13]

Time Inc. acquired the 40-year-old *Architectural Forum* in 1932, changed the name in 1950 to *The Magazine of Building*, then divided it into two magazines, *Architectural Forum* and *House & Home*, in 1952. McGraw-Hill became publisher of *House & Home* and, in the late 1970s, changed its name to *Housing*. *Architectural Forum* suspended publication after becoming a Whitney Communications publication.

In 1936 the name *Life* was brought from the former humor magazine and attached to the company's new picture magazine started that same year. *Life's* early success could have killed it. Advertising rates had been set on an estimated 250,000 circulation, but its first press run of 466,000 sold out (fig. 2–4), and for months the more copies it sold the more money it lost. Because of the high cost of coated paper required for good picture reproduction, the loss, instead of being small as anticipated, hit $50,000 weekly, totaling $6 million before *Life* began to pay back on its investment.[14]

A "think" magazine was developed in 1947, but it was never published. However, after a year of experimenting with a recreation magazine, the company narrowed the scope to sports and brought out *Sports Illustrated* in August 1954 (fig. 2–5). It had 250,000 subscribers from mail promotion before it had a name, and after six months' publication its circulation was 575,000.

Time Inc. had three magazines listed under the "News-Weeklies" classification of *Consumer Magazine Rates and Data* in 1984: *Time* at 4.6 million circulation, *Sports Illustrated* at 2.6 million, and *People Weekly* at 2.6 million. *Newsweek's* circulation was 3.0 million and *U.S. News & World Report's* was 2.1 million.

Money, begun in October 1972, still had not been a smashing success with its 883,000 circulation by June 1981, but the unexpected bonanza had been *People*, launched with the issue of March 4, 1974, and in the black within 18 months. *People* has little in common with the other Time Inc. magazines because it is a newsstand magazine sold primarily in supermarkets, is read by more women than men, does not spend heavily on name writers or news bureaus, and has no editorial color.[15]

Figure 3–8 The first national weekly magazine launched in 20 years, *People* exceeded expectations for its success by showing a profit within 18 months. (Courtesy *People*.)

Figure 3–9 As a monthly with an editorial concept different from its predecessor weekly publication, *Life* debuted with the October 1978 issue. By 1984 circulation was 1.5 million with 42 percent being sold as single copies. (Courtesy LIFE copyright 1978 Time Inc. Reprinted with permission.)

The first national weekly launched since *Sports Illustrated* 20 years earlier, *People* also was the first magazine Time launched using market research. Two prices and two degrees of promotion were tested in 11 cities in August 1973. A follow-up issue was never published but was printed for testing in October "with a decidedly improved design." The board of directors approved the start October 18.[16] *Time* reported that 85 percent of the test issue copies were sold, spurring the decision to begin regular publication, and that the decision not to promote mail subscriptions was prompted largely by increased second-class postage rates.[17] At mid-1984 *People* was selling 62 percent of its circulation on newsstands.

Although *Well* and *View* had been under development to follow *Money* onto newsstands, *People* was the one that introduced and succeeded beyond expectations. Time continued its magazine development and, in late 1977, had a demonstration copy of *Woman* prepared for reader reaction, based on two years of study.[18]

Woman was planned to be a pocketbook-sized weekly sold mainly through supermarkets and appealing more to the type of women who read *Ms.* and *Working Woman* than those who read *Woman's Day* and *Family Circle*.[19] The 92-page prototype issue was the only one to be produced.

Fortune, a monthly of 627,000 circulation, increased to 26 issues a year in January 1978. As a biweekly its circulation continued to climb and was at 709,000 in 1984.

Life was re-established as a monthly magazine in October 1978, and was circulating 1.5 million copies per issue in 1984.

Time entered the highly competitive field of science magazines with *Discover* in October 1980. The first issue carried 62 pages of advertising and reader demand exceeded expectations to the point that the rate base was increased by 50 percent to 600,000 effective April 1981,[20] and grew to 990,000 by mid-1984.

Perhaps the greatest launch in magazine history was announced by Time Inc. for 1983. *TV-Cable Week,* with a commitment of $100 million over five years to establish the magazine, was to begin in seven markets in April and expand to 20 or 30 cable systems by the end of the year. A separate edition would be published for each cable system that signed an agreement with the magazine.

Conceptually the magazine dated to 1971 and *View*. It was backed by more than 20 months of corporate planning. More than 50 10-year business plans were evaluated. The worst one had *TV-Cable Week* losing $1 billion in the first year. *Select* and *View* were considered as names but dropped in favor of *TV-Cable Week*.

The 1971 idea of an entertainment magazine about television, film, and theater was considered to be too costly. A 1978 proposal for a guide only for cable was dropped. But in 1981 a task force took on the project and investigated a partnership with the cable industry and selling the magazine through cable operators to their subscribers. A production specialist spent nine months developing a system to sort millions of cable listings and transmit them electronically to regional printing plants. Focus groups offered critiques of existing cable guides in more than two dozen cities.

As the planning continued, competitors signed cable systems in some cities. A Buffalo, New York, system began promoting *TV Guide,* for example.[21] *TV-Cable Week* got out of the gate in April as planned. It moved into its eighteenth market in San Diego in September. And it ceased publication with the September 25 issue.

Time Inc. developed into a mass communication conglomerate from a single magazine. In 1963 the magazines accounted for about three-fourths of the company's revenue, but by 1976 that proportion was nearer 40 percent and Time Inc. reported $67 million profit on $1 billion revenues, its first billion-dollar year.[22]

Magazines accounted for 22 percent of the corporation's operating profit in 1980.[23] Besides magazines, Time's operations include Time-Life Books, the Book-of-the-Month Club, Inc., a cable television operating company, Home Box Office, and a television station.

John Johnson and *Ebony*

John H. Johnson's magazine publishing success story is both different and typical. He became a successful minority publisher at a time when that was nearly impossible, yet his methods have broad application.

In Chicago, Johnson was editor of the school newspaper, president of the senior class, and president of the student council. Because of his leadership, he was invited to attend an assembly of outstanding high school students from throughout Chicago, where the president of Supreme Life Insurance Company of America was the speaker. Afterward, Johnson went to talk with him and told him he wanted to go to college but needed a job. The president suggested he stop by in September.

Starting as an office boy with Supreme Life, Johnson later was assigned to clip articles about black people for the president, who did much of the work in publishing the company's *Supreme Liberty Guardian.* Soon Johnson was promoted to assistant to the editor.[24]

As he clipped newspapers and magazines and gave his company's president a digest of what was happening each week in the black community, he would ask friends if they had read this article or that one. Usually they hadn't. So he thought there might be a market for a *Negro Digest.* He approached friends to go into business with him and people with money to invest, but no one was interested. He eventually convinced his mother to let him borrow $500 on her furniture. He discussed his idea with the president of Supreme Life and was offered the company's mailing list of 20,000 names.

Johnson used the borrowed $500 for a mailing to determine how many people would be interested in a black magazine, asking them to send him $2. About 3,000 replied, and he used that $6,000 as a base to persuade the printer to extend him credit. By working nights, he and his wife prepared copy for the first issue of 5,000 copies, which appeared in November 1942 and sold out within a week. Within a year, circulation reached 50,000 a month.[25]

Johnson's associate Ben Burns, after putting in a day's work with the *Chicago Defender,* would edit the magazine at his home.[26] Circulation plateaued at 50,000, until Eleanor Roosevelt wrote the first piece in a series by white people, "If I Were A Negro." Her statements were picked up by the press, and following the wide publicity, circulation shot from 50,000 to more than 150,000 within thirty days.[27]

As World War II came to an end, Johnson thought the returning servicemen would be looking for light, interesting reading material, and he had a pictorial magazine in mind which became the formula for *Ebony.*[28] Burns put that one out with freelance contributions until the first staff was recruited in 1946. *Ebony,* more than any other magazine, demonstrated to advertisers the importance of black consumers.[29]

Johnson points out that *Ebony* has been successful because it changed with the times and has a commitment to its readers. When the magazine started, success was equated with material things—a Cadillac or a mink coat. As the magazine

Figure 3–10 John H. Johnson, founder, president, and publisher of Johnson Publishing Company in Chicago. (Courtesy Johnson Publishing Company.)

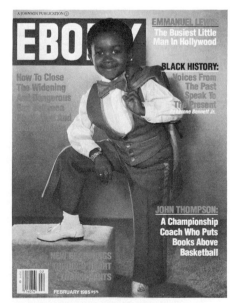

Figure 3–11 Although not the first Johnson magazine, *Ebony* became the flagship publication of the company after being launched in 1945. (Courtesy *Ebony.*)

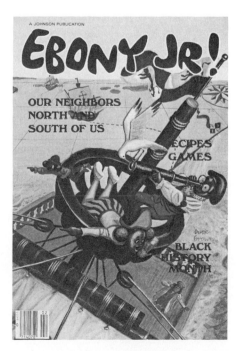

Figure 3–12 *Jet* and *Ebony Jr!* make Johnson Publishing a diversified and multiple-magazine publishing company. (Courtesy *Jet,* and *Ebony Jr!*)

developed and matured, it found that success is accomplishing whatever one sets out to do.[30] *Ebony* plays a positive role, telling people what they can do. Any black person doing a successful job in a unique situation is an *Ebony* story, Johnson says.[31] Ebony has helped black people become proud of their heritage and proud of themselves, and it gives them information and inspiration they cannot find anywhere else.[32]

In 1950, Johnson started *Tan,* which was similar to *True Story* or *True Romance.* After the October 1971 issue, the name was changed to *Black Stars* and the magazine concentrated on the black entertainment world—blacks who have been successful in films, records, night clubs, and the like. *Black Stars* was discontinued in 1981.

Jet was begun in 1951, and was one of the few pocket-sized news magazines that survived into the 1960s. It was designed to give a brief weekly summary of what is happening in the black community, and was a success from the beginning.

Negro Digest was phased out in 1951 because it was felt to be performing a function similar to *Jet.* Old readers kept asking for it back, so it was revived in 1961. Its name was changed to *Black World* in 1971, then the magazine was discontinued in 1976.

There was a 12-year span between the founding of *Jet* and that of *Ebony Jr!,* which is directed at the 6- to 12-year age group with emphasis on reading mastery at early ages. This magazine carries only house advertising for *Ebony Jr!* and its book division.

Johnson Publishing Company started its book division in 1961 and entered radio broadcasting in 1973, buying WGRT and changing the call letters to WJPC. The company moved into its own newly constructed, 11-story corporate headquarters on Chicago's South Michigan Avenue in 1971. Johnson received the Henry Johnson Fisher Award as the publisher of the year from the Magazine Publishers Association in 1972.

Movement to Special Interest Magazines

The departure of *Look* in 1971, followed by that of *Life* in 1972, signalled the virtual end of the general interest mass magazine. Other magazines had larger circulations, but they were special interest men's, women's, TV, or shelter magazines.

Special interest magazines had been forging ahead, serving rapidly expanding markets and audiences, as those in the general interest category declined. The efficiency of carrying advertising within a specialized area to persons obviously interested in that activity appeals to advertisers catering to such an area and makes these magazines ideal media for their ads at lower overall cost and with minimal waste circulation.

Essence

Essence grew out of a black capitalism meeting called by a Wall Street brokerage firm in 1968. A 24-year-old New Jersey Bell ad salesman suggested the idea for the magazine, and the adviser steered him to a printing expert, a financial planner, and an insurance salesman. They got volunteer assistance from Time-Life, *Newsweek, Psychology Today, New York,* CBS, Young & Rublicam, J. K. Lasser Tax Institute, Cowles Communications, McCann-Erickson, and Lorillard Corp. and took the name Hollingsworth Group, using some stationery Cecil Hollingsworth, the printing expert, had left over from a graphics consulting firm he once started.

Their original proposed budget of $5 million was cut to $1.5 million, and they eventually sold the idea to First National City, Chase Manhattan, and Morgan Guaranty banks. They got Gordon Parks, noted black photographer and writer, to be editorial director and assembled a full-time staff of 26, including four whites. Eighteen months after that first meeting, the stylish monthly for black women appeared with a May issue in April 1970, and a circulation base of 150,000.[33] Its sworn circulation by the end of 1971 was 162,000 but by mid-1972 it was not yet breaking even.[34]

Media Industry Newsletter reported the March 1973 issue as the first break-even issue, with 42 pages of advertising. Investment had grown from the original

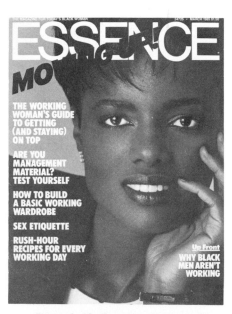

Figure 3–13 *Essence* was started to give the black woman a magazine that portrayed her role as it should be viewed in society. (Reprinted courtesy *Essence Magazine.* Copyright by Essence Communications, Inc., 1985.)

$120,000 to $2 million, and in its first three years *Essence* had switched from a fashion magazine to a women's service magazine and had grown to 200,000 circulation. The staff, which had been increased to 39, had again been cut to 27.[35]

The magazine idea had come from an historical perspective of how black women had been viewed in American society and what was happening in 1968 in terms of how black women were being used and viewed in older magazines. No one was talking to the black woman about her aspirations, needs, and desires, or was portraying her in the role as she should have been viewed in society as a beautiful and intelligent human being, according to Publisher Edward Lewis.

The magazine's working title had been *Sapphire,* to connote the precious jewel qualities rather than the Amos 'n Andy image of the black woman that had to be overcome. But the negative associations were so great among women interviewed that the title was changed to *Essence.*[36] *Essence* was originally intended to be strictly a fashion and beauty book, but it soon became apparent that that would not be enough for the *Essence* reader. Its content was broadened to include consumer reports, child care, food, health, fiction, fashion and beauty, and some politics and religion. Special one-theme issues were begun in 1972 on topics such as college and education, careers, travel, and home sewing.[37]

Essence advertising policy requires ads showing people to include a black woman and insists that ads in no way demean black women.[38]

The editor-in-chief who saw the book achieve its first break-even issue and septuple its advertising income, as well as having served the longest tenure as editor, is Marcia Ann Gillespie. She came to *Essence* as managing editor in November 1970 from Time-Life Books and became editor-in-chief in May 1971 at age 26. She saw circulation grow to 550,000 and advertising income grow from $557,000 in 1971 to $3.76 million in 1976.[39] *Essence* was targeted to hit 750,000 circulation by 1979-80.[40]

Gillespie came to *Essence* because she "had wanted to combat the negative imagery which for centuries had been foisted on blacks." She also said, "I didn't want little black girls growing up as I had thinking only white women were beautiful. I wanted them, through *Essence,* to see and to feel what black women really are—incredibly vital people who have been boxed in intellectually, creatively, and emotionally."[41]

Gillespie left *Essence* after the tenth anniversary issue of May 1980. Circulation stood at 600,000 and over the next year increased to 650,000 as first Daryl R. Alexander and then Susan L. Taylor succeeded her as editor-in-chief. Circulation stood at 700,000 in 1984.

Figure 3–14 Marcia Ann Gillespie became editor-in-chief of *Essence* at age 26 and led it into profitable operation. (Photo courtesy *Essence Magazine.*)

More New Magazines

Smithsonian, by the Smithsonian Institution National Associates, started with the April 1970 issue, reached 186,000 by the end of 1970, and 277,500 by the end of 1971.

Smithsonian's success continued as its audited circulation reached 1.5 million in June 1977 and 2 million in June 1984.

Intellectual Digest was founded by Martin Gross in September 1970 as a pocket-size magazine. Communications/Research/Machines Inc. took it over in 1971 and made it the basic 8½ × 11 inch magazine size, gave it more eye-catching graphics, and supplemented the digest material with original pieces, mostly photo essays and interviews that made up 15 percent or more of each issue. *Time* credited editor Martin Goldman with having made the concept work in only one year, doubling circulation and approaching a break-even operation.[42] When CRM and Boise Cascade got out of the magazine business, *ID* was sold to Ziff-Davis and later ceased publication.

American Express launched *Travel & Leisure* as a controlled circulation magazine for its credit card holders with the February-March 1971 issue. Published bimonthly, it sold 210 pages of advertising in its first five issues, guaranteeing advertisers 3 million circulation. Caskie Stinnett, former editor of *Holiday,* took over as editor with the third issue.

Travel & Leisure experienced some of the problems of success that had burdened *Life* and *Psychology Today* when circulation growth fast outran advertising rates and the number of American Express card holders reached 5 million in autumn 1973. When that happened, it was decided to split the group into two equal circulation lists of 2.5 million each and publish 12 issues a year, each group receiving alternate issues, beginning in January 1974.[43]

The process was extended to make the magazine a fully paid monthly over a 17-month period. Three mailings were used, and by July 1975 the magazine had 500,000 paid subscribers against a projected goal of 460,000. Subscribers exceeded 700,000 by the end of October and had reached 800,000 by June 1976. The eventual goal was 1 million, with the ideal range for *Travel & Leisure* having been plotted at 800,000 to 1.2 million.[44] Circulation averaged 944,000 the first half of 1981 and 957,000 in 1984.

New Woman was established in 1971 with a circulation base of 200,000. An additional 100,000, not figured as part of the advertising base, was to be circulated to beauty salons, department store buyers, and other women's groups. Margaret Harold, president of Allied Publications in Fort Lauderdale, Florida, said she was committing five years' support to the magazine.[45] *New Woman's* sworn circulation was 242,000 by the end of 1971, including 40,000 nonpaid, but publication was suspended in June 1972. The magazine later resumed publication as a bimonthly, largely reprinting material from other publications, and built an ABC circulation of 670,442 for the June 1977 reporting period, an increase of 102.3 percent over the preceding year.

Success continued for *New Woman,* as its circulation reached 1.3 million, two-thirds sold on newsstands, in 1981, and it announced a move to monthly frequency with the March 1982 issue.[46] It was bought by Rupert Murdoch's magazine group and in 1984 its circulation averaged 1 million.

In August 1971 General Mills licensed a new company to publish a bimonthly magazine tied in with the Betty Crocker name. At that time the magazine had no name, but later became *Sphere/The Betty Crocker* Magazine with its first issue scheduled for January 1972.[47]

The magazine developed into a handsome, colorful magazine emphasizing food, achieved circulation success, and increased its frequency to 10 issues a year. The Betty Crocker reference was dropped in 1975, and in 1978 it started a name change by using the name *Sphere's Cuisine* and in 1979 completed the change to *Cuisine.* CBS Publications bought the magazine and built its circulation to 755,000 by 1984. The December 1984 issue was the last, however, as CBS sold the subscriber list to *Gourmet,* which had a circulation of 654,000 at the time. *Media Industry Newsletter* observed that there was no advertising base in that field to support the magazines.

Ms., a feminist magazine, debuted in *New York* magazine's 1971 year-end issue. Clay Felker, editor and publisher of *New York,* offered to run excerpts from the first issue of *Ms.* a month before regular distribution and agreed to pay the production costs for 300,000 copies of the first issue in return for half the profits on newsstand sales and all the advertising revenue.[48]

The first issue, published in January, was dated Spring '72, sold out and helped draw in 125,000 subscribers for Volume 1, Number 1 dated July 1972. Nevertheless, *Ms.* had only 16 pages for paid advertising in its first regular issue of 138 pages.

The original publisher left the staff in March 1972, and Patricia Carbine moved from editor of *McCall's* to editor-in-chief and publisher of *Ms.* She had been executive editor of *Look* before moving to *McCall's* 18 months earlier. *Ms.,* of course, also had Gloria Steinem.

Ms. was controlled by its staff, and even though Warner Communications invested $1 million of the estimated $1.5 million needed to begin publication, it became only a minority stockholder.

Time proclaimed the magazine a success in its December 25, 1972, edition, noting that December circulation had reached 395,000.

Ms. continued modest growth in the late seventies. Circulation went from 454,000 in 1976 to 500,000 in 1977, where it remained relatively stable at 504,000 in 1981, dropping to 463,000 in 1984.

Ms. had reorganized as a not-for-profit corporation named the Ms. Foundation for Education and Communication, Inc. Another consumer magazine published by a not-for-profit corporation is *Mother Jones,* published by The Foundation for National Progress.

In the industry the longest-anticipated new magazine of 1972 was *Money,* which Time Inc. had been working on for more than three years. *Money* and a health magazine, *Well,* had tested very well in surveys and sample promotions.

Earlier, Time Inc. had had Louis Harris and Associates conduct an attitude survey on six possible magazines that could be bound into *Life* or issued separately. Paul Wilkes mentioned in *New York* magazine January 12, 1970, that the circulation possibilities were *Movie,* 1.5 million; *Your Health,* 1.2 million; *Your Money,* 900,000; *For Children,* 800,000; *Travel,* 735,000; and *Food,* 667,000. The latter two were considered unacceptable risks, but *Life's* new leaders decided to test the possible food magazine further because it was well-conceived and well-edited.[49]

The industry heard in spring 1972 that Time would bring out *Money* in October, and probably follow with *Well,* the latest name for the health magazine, by mid-winter. Two other magazines were still in the works: *Camera Month,* a photography magazine, and *View,* a magazine of "the moving image."

The decision not to go ahead with the health magazine appeared to be confirmed in the mid-seventies, when the American Medical Association sold its consumer health magazine, *Today's Health,* which was eventually combined with *Family Health. Family Health* had started as a monthly in 1969 and had achieved 994,000 paid subscriptions by the end of 1971, but by December 1976 its A.B.C. circulation was 919,000 (with *Today's Health* merged into it), and by June 1981 had dipped to 854,000. Also in 1981 the name was changed to *Health* and it was publishing 10 issues a year. Circulation had risen to 974,000 by 1984 and it was publishing monthly.

The Early Eighties

As the eighties began with double-digit inflation affecting consumers' pocketbooks and corporations' budgets, established magazines were about holding their own in circulation and advertising, with some posting gains and some posting losses. New magazines, however, were bursting on the scene. A new genre of women's magazines was developing, science books were hot, and personal computing and home video were spawning new magazines.

Women's Magazines

Narrowcasting through cable television became more widespread in the 1980s and the same trend increased in the magazine industry through new books aimed at narrower, more specific interests. While the giant circulation women's books lost some of their circulation and advertising, more specialized books were started to aim at such interests as physical and emotional well-being and concerns of women executives.

Condé Nast's *Self,* launched in January 1979 as a monthly focusing on self-improvement and the realization of individual potential, claimed to be the most successful new women's magazine—in both circulation and advertising—in more than 35 years. It achieved 900,000 circulation[50] and attracted 521 pages of advertising in less than one year. The magazine was a $20 million venture developed by a full staff for a year before the premiere issue.[51] *Self* published 1,157 pages of advertising in 1984, ranking 51st among consumer magazines, and had a circulation of 1 million.

More than 57,000 letters and responses from *McCall's* readers convinced the publishers of the editorial need for *McCall's Working Mother,* a bimonthly started with the May 1979 issue. The first six issues averaged 58 ad pages and circulation of the February-March 1980 issue was guaranteed at 275,000. At the time the magazine was being developed there were said to be more than fifteen million working mothers with children under 18 in the country.[52]

Savvy, the magazine for executive women, went on newsstands November 27, 1979, to sell for six weeks at $1.75 and with a circulation guarantee of 125,000. The 100-page premiere issue had a press run of 145,000.[53]

Editor Judith Daniels had slowly developed the idea over several years, starting when she was managing editor of *New York.* "Something important was happening in the world of business and professional women I knew," she said. "I knew two things for certain: *Work,* above all else, was shaping their lives. And there was an increasing self-confidence, an increasing self-awareness that professional women had something unique to share."[54]

She moved to the *Village Voice* as managing editor in 1974 and the following summer made a list of 150 story ideas to demonstrate that the concept had both breadth and depth. She also worked on possible titles. "At first I thought it might be called *Executive Woman* or *Professional Woman.* Then I went through the A's: *Aspire, Achieve, Ascend*—but they all sounded like federally funded programs for the disadvantaged. But the name *Savvy* had flexibility and a little pizzazz. I wanted to convey a sense of sophistication and smarts. It was slangy without being pejorative. It had an energy to it, and it captured exactly the right state of mind."[55]

Daniels became managing editor of *New West* in July 1976, wanting to convince some of the right people on the West Coast that the time was right for *Savvy.* Two months later she quit that job to work full-time on a real preview issue of *Savvy* because she wanted more than a dummy.

In 1977 *New York* and *New West* ran a 44-page insert of *Savvy,* which drew 13,000 subscribers. The preview was done with the *New York* staff, so Daniels still had to assemble a staff for *Savvy,* as well as raise the start-up money. She first negotiated with an investment banking firm, but nothing materialized. A team of lawyers and accountants worked from May to December 1977 to design a limited partnership plan with attractive tax shelters for potential investors. Those plans fell through. Daniels turned to several publishing companies; still no luck.

In the fall of 1978 she started working with Alan Bennett, who had converted the small, local *New York Photographer* into an immediately successful national *American Photographer* in late 1977. Editor Daniels and publisher Bennett finally raised $75,000 needed to do a direct mail test by going hat-in-hand to their friends, who staked them in $5,000 and $10,000 units. At the end of 1978 they used 40 mailing lists to send out 250,000 pieces of direct mail to test different prices and editorial packages. The response was a healthy 4 percent, and the test results helped them find the $1.4 million needed to start from 28 sources.[56]

The bulk of the $1.4 million was put into circulation mailings that generate revenue and renewals, which continue to generate revenue, rather than into salaries and production costs. Three mailings totaling 7 million pieces were made in July and September 1979 and January 1980, all with good returns.

Savvy aims at the top 5 percent of America's 43 million working women, the ones with real clout and earning power. A subscriber survey found that *Savvy* readership is 100 percent female, 87 percent college educated, 48 percent married, 92 percent employed full-time, 83 percent in professional/managerial positions, and has a median age of 35 and a median household income of $31,900.[57]

Big Beautiful Woman went into national distribution with its second issue, June-July 1979. After five issues the bimonthly's circulation guarantee was 190,000 and monthly publication was being considered.[58] Harris Publications introduced *Woman* in October 1980 as a bimonthly dealing with women's feelings and emotions and including continuing features on health, exercise, food, money matters, and medical advice.[59]

Also in October 1980 the North American subsidiary of Heinrich Bauer Verlag, publisher of eight women's magazines in West Germany, tested *Woman's World* after spending two-and-one-half years on research, analysis, and development. The weekly carried no advertising and was sold only by single copy at 75 cents. Distribution started in Chicago and the northeast quadrant of the United States in January 1981 with 700,000 copies. It was to expand to the West Coast by June and a goal of 2 million copies in the United States and Canada by fall was announced. The publisher, Heinrich Bauer North America, Inc., was involved in all phases of magazine production and was acting as its own publisher, printer, distributor, and wholesaler. Whether advertising would be sold depended upon circulation success, the vice president of sales said.[60]

Science Magazines

Increasing interest in science fact and fiction led to the establishment of *Omni* in 1977 by Robert Guccione, publisher of *Penthouse* and *Forum*. The success of *Omni* foretold the flurry of 1979 and 1980 when four science magazines were developed and launched.

Science 80 was started by the American Association for the Advancement of Science in November 1979 as a bimonthly to promote an understanding of the latest scientific developments among the general public. It increased its frequency to 10 times a year on its first anniversary. Started as a subscription-only book, it started newsstand sales near the end of its first year. The sponsoring association already had a magazine, *Science,* aimed at the scientific community.

Next, the magazine of the future, was the first consumer magazine in the Litton Publishing Group, started bimonthly with the March-April 1980 issue. It announced a rate base of 400,000 for September 1981, when it was scheduled to go monthly,[61] but in 1981 Litton was acquired by International Thomson, who sought a buyer for the magazine. When none was found, *Next* was discontinued with the August issue.

A Hearst magazine established in 1936, *Science Digest,* was remade into a standard-size magazine with the premiere issue in the new size dated November-December 1980. The bimonthly converted to monthly with the March 1981 issue. The cover price had been increased to $2 from the previous 75 cents, and the rate base was more than doubled from 150,000 to 400,000.[62] Circulation in 1984 stood at 575,000.

Discover was started in September 1980 by Time Inc. with a typical Time promotion to 10 million persons and a circulation guarantee of 400,000. It planned to treat science as a continually changing news story and to have short lag times of 3½ to 2 weeks between articles going to press and hitting the newsstands in order to be timely and to make it, as its subtitle said, the newsmagazine of science.[63] As mentioned previously, its circulation was 990,000 in 1984.

Scientific American, the oldest science magazine (dating from 1845), continued to lead the newcomers in advertising pages and revenue, though it trailed in circulation at 665,000 in 1984.

Bernard Goldhirsh acquired the defunct *High Technology* in October 1980 and announced he would convert it from a business publication on electronic research and development to a consumer magazine to fill the gap between the straight science magazines and the how-to books.[64] Bimonthly *High Technology* appeared with the September-October 1981 issue. By that time Goldhirsh had announced another bimonthly start, *Technology Illustrated,* to be launched with an October-November cover date. The latter has since been suspended and *High Technology* is published monthly with a circulation of 307,000.

Computing Books

Personal computing magazines were the biggest growth area in the industry in the early 1980s. McGraw-Hill's *Byte* dated from 1975 and was third in advertising pages and 32nd in advertising revenue among consumer magazines in 1984. *Byte* had a companion, *onComputing,* starting in 1979 as a quarterly. The name was changed to *Popular Computing,* and the frequency increased to monthly in 1981. *Creative Computing* had been established in 1974, Hayden Publishing's *Personal Computing* in 1976, and *80 Micro* in 1980.

New books were started for owners of specific brands of personal computers and even for specific models. By 1984 *Consumer Magazine and Agri-Media Rates and Data* listed 46 computer magazines published ten or more times a year. Thirty-four had been established in the 1980s, 14 in 1983 alone. Circulations ranged from 5,000 for *PCM—The Magazine for Professional Computing Management* to 536,000 for *Personal Computing. Computers & Electronics,* a 1981 conversion of Ziff-Davis' *Science & Electronics,* was a close second at 523,000. Most, though, had circulations of 70,000 to 250,000.

Computer magazine editors who participated in a 1984 Louisiana State University survey predicted that most of the computer magazines eventually would fail. The December 1984 *Folio* reported that 23 computer magazines had been started in the first nine months of 1984 and 29 had discontinued publication. Ten of the shutdowns had published their first issue in 1984. *Folio* listed more than 100 computer magazines. As in any burgeoning field, many of the new entrants cannot succeed and stability takes time to be established.

Video Books

Magazines for the home video market also were introduced in the 1980s. *Video* started as a quarterly in 1977, and became a monthly in 1980. *Video Review* started in 1980 and later absorbed *Home Video,* which had been begun in 1979. *Videoplay,* a bimonthly started in 1978, was discontinued in 1984. By the end of 1984 the field did not appear to be expanding, although *Video Now* had been announced as a new entry. Each magazine had a circulation between 250,000 and 300,000.

Factors of Failure

Magazine failures can be attributed to three principal reasons, according to Herbert Mayes, former editor of *Good Housekeeping* and *McCall's:*

First, overoptimism concerning potential market—the kind and number of readers who will be interested and the companies that buy advertising space; second, undercapitalization—the amount of money needed to achieve a viable circulation, plus the cost of staff and paper and printing and distribution; thirdly, the failure to recognize new competition soon enough and that readers and advertisers can change quickly and drastically.[65]

Harlan Logan, former publisher's consultant and former editor of *Scribner's,* once examined a long list of magazines that failed and noted the following weaknesses always were present:

1. Lack of editorial reason for existence.
2. Lack of clearly defined editorial pattern.
3. Lack of advertising reason or existence.
4. Lack of realistic budget projections.
5. Lack of realistic schedule of time required to gain either readers or advertising acceptance.
6. Lack of knowledge of the magazine field in general and of the specific competition.
7. Lack of accurate information about the personnel which is hired to produce the new magazine.
8. Lack of an objective and independent (nonstaff) audit of the potentialities of the new magazine and of the publishing program that has been set up.[66]

Logan pointed out that the more frequent the publication the greater the investment required. A weekly may need, for example, about 4 1/3 times as much risk capital as a monthly.

Success of New Magazines

Change and dynamism are key words in the magazine business. As constant readers and industry observers mourn the demise of old standbys, new magazines spring up. To predict long-term success for any magazine would be unwise. Deficits nearly always run larger and longer than anticipated, and some magazine ideas simply are not capable of sustaining long-term success.

A statistical study of 1,432 consumer magazines over the 25 years ending 1977 showed a median life of 13.4 years and a mean life of 23.2 years. Magazines with large circulations and low costs to reader had longer lives. A mass special interest magazine had more than a 70 percent chance of surviving its first 10 years. A small special interest magazine had more than a 50 percent chance of failing in the first five to nine years, according to Anne P. Bowers, who did the study. A general interest magazine had a 60 percent chance of failing to reach the 10-year mark. Of the magazines that lasted at least 10 years, a small special interest magazine had only a 26 percent chance of reaching the 25-year mark, she reported.[67]

The long-term experience of history and the short-term developments of the last decade or two bear out the conclusion that more new magazines succeed than fail, and the magazine industry continues to be a vital, growing part of the mass communication system.

Notes

1. Edmund Wilson, "The Literary Worker's Polonius," in *The Shores of Light* (New York: Farrar, Straus and Giroux, 1952), p. 593.
2. James Playsted Wood, *Of Lasting Interest: The Story of The Reader's Digest,* rev. ed. (Garden City, N.Y.: Doubleday & Co., 1967), pp. 8–14, 16, 21–24, and 26.
3. Theordore Peterson, *Magazines in the Twentieth Century,* 2d ed. (Urbana: University of Illinois Press, 1964), p. 228.
4. James Playsted Wood, *Magazines in the United States,* 3d ed. (New York: Ronald Press, 1971), pp. 241–42.
5. Wood, *Of Lasting Interest,* pp. 148 and 223–28.
6. Wood, *Magazines in the United States,* pp. 242–43.
7. Wood, *Of Lasting Interest,* pp. 174–75, 186–87, 189, and 192.
8. *Media Industry Newsletter,* Sept. 10, 1980, p. 1.
9. *Media Industry Newsletter,* November 19, 1980, p. 3.
10. Peterson, *Magazines,* p. 235.
11. Wood, *Magazines in the United States,* p. 207.
12. W. A. Swanberg, *Luce and His Empire* (New York: Charles Scribner's Sons, 1972), pp. 59, 62–63, and 66, and Peterson, pp. 236–37.
13. Peterson, pp. 237–38.
14. Swanberg, p. 144.
15. John Mack Carter, "The pros said it couldn't be done, but *People's* making it," *Folio,* February 1976, p. 58.
16. Carter, p. 58.
17. *Time,* March 4, 1974, p. 42.
18. *Media Industry Newsletter,* June 13, 1977, p. 1, and August 8, 1977, p. 1.
19. Ibid.
20. *Time Incorporated 1980 Annual Report.*
21. *USA Today,* Feb. 10, 1983, pp. 1D and 2D.
22. Peterson, p. 243, and *Time Incorporated 1976 Annual Report.*
23. *Time Incorporated 1980 Annual Report.*
24. "Lessons of Leadership: John H. Johnson of Ebony," *Nation's Business,* April 1974, p. 48.
25. Ibid., p. 46.
26. Peterson, p. 66.
27. *Nation's Business,* April 1974, p. 49.
28. Ibid., p. 48.
29. Peterson, p. 66.
30. *Nation's Business,* April 1974, p. 50.
31. " 'Failure is a word I don't accept,' an interview with John H. Johnson," *Harvard Business Review,* March-April 1976, p. 85.
32. *Nation's Business,* April 1974, p. 49.
33. *Time,* May 4, 1970, pp. 79–80.
34. *Newsweek,* July 17, 1972, p. 71.
35. *Media Industry Newsletter,* February 23, 1973, p. 3.
36. Speech by Publisher Edward Lewis to the ASME Editorial Luncheon, September 14, 1976.
37. Marjorie McManus, "The Essence Magazine Success Story," *Folio,* December 1976, pp. 28–29.
38. Ibid., p. 28, and Lewis.
39. McManus, p. 28.
40. Lewis.

41. McManus, p. 28. © Copyright 1976 *Folio: The Magazine for Magazine Management.* Reprinted by permission.
42. *Time,* September 25, 1972, pp. 99–100.
43. John S. Conners, "Paying for Your *Travel & Leisure, Folio,* June 1976, pp. 50 and 52.
44. Ibid.
45. *Advertising Age,* November 30, 1970, p. 12.
46. *Media Industry Newsletter,* August 13, 1981, p. 8.
47. *Advertising Age,* August 9, 1971, p. 2.
48. "Ms.: Gloria Steinem's Big Gamble," *Dodge Adventurer,* March/April 1973, p. 6.
49. Wilkes, p. 32.
50. *Media Industry Newsletter,* January 9, 1980, p. 6.
51. John Love, "Birth of a Notion," *TWA Ambassador,* October 1980, p. 47.
52. *Media Industry Newsletter,* February 28, 1978, p. 3, and December 26, 1979, p. 9.
53. *Media Industry Newsletter,* January 9, 1980, p. 6.
54. Love, p. 49. Reprinted from *TWA Ambassador Magazine* with permission of the author and publisher. Copyrighted 1980 by Trans World Airlines, Inc.
55. Ibid.
56. Ibid., p. 50.
57. Ibid., pp. 49 and 52.
58. *Media Industry Newsletter,* December 26, 1979, p. 2.
59. *Folio,* April 1981, p. 43.
60. *Folio,* February 1981, p. 31, and *Media Industry Newsletter,* January 21, 1981, p. 3.
61. *Media Industry Newsletter,* January 9, 1980, p. 5; June 4, 1980, p. 4; and October 22, 1980, p. 8.
62. *Media Industry Newsletter,* June 4, 1980, p. 1.
63. *Media Industry Newsletter,* April 23, 1980, p. 1, and June 4, 1980, p. 6.
64. *Media Industry Newsletter,* October 22, 1980, p. 8.
65. Herbert R. Mayes, *The Magazine Maze* (Garden City, N.Y.: Doubleday & Company, 1980), p. 88.
66. Harlan Logan, "Tomorrow's New Magazines," *Magazine Industry,* Summer 1949, p. 19, cited by Theodore Peterson, *Magazines in the Twentieth Century,* 2d ed. (Urbana, Ill.: University of Illinois Press), 1964, p. 81.
67. *Media Industry Newsletter,* July 31, 1978, p. 4.

4

Editorial Concepts

A PLAN to serve women with information and features that will help them at home, in self-improvement, and in their careers provides a basic concept for a magazine. A concept is a mental image that may be abstract and general, or concrete and specific. Usually an editorial concept begins as general and largely abstract and is refined and developed toward the specific and concrete. As this process takes place, the editorial concept is developed into an *editorial formula* from policy decisions that have been made about the kinds of content the magazine will publish, the kinds of readers it will cater to, and the kinds of advertisers it will attempt to attract.

Magazine Formulas

There is no universal definition of an editorial formula. Basically, it is the mixture of editorial material that makes up a magazine, the content that establishes the magazine's personality. Formula is the continuing or long-range editorial concept of the magazine expressed as specific kinds of content or topics. It can be broken into at least three major components:

Departments. The most obvious component of a magazine's formula is its departments that continue from issue to issue. Readers are familiar with the departments in their favorite magazines, and that is one reason to departmentalize content. In *Better Homes and Gardens* these include food, gardening, health, decorating, travel, parenting, education, building, money, and cars. Articles in *Skiing* are grouped under where to ski, how to ski better, what to buy, special, and exclusive. The continuing columns and features are listed as departments.

Southern Living's departments include the current month's features, travel and recreation, garden and landscape, homes and building, foods and entertaining, and directories.

Columns, bylined or on specific topics, also function as departments. *Ladies' Home Journal* offers "Can This Marriage Be Saved?" and "The Working Woman" as features of this type. *Family Circle* has "Readers' Idea Exchange," "Beauty & Fashion Hotline," and "Here's News in Medicine" among its regular departmentalized features.

Articles Within Departments. Some departments are large enough to contain several articles, and some of these specific articles may be repeated in every issue. A continuing feature from issue to issue in *Better Homes and Gardens,* for example, is "Prize Tested Recipes" in the food department. "Travel South" is a fixture in the travel and recreation department of *Southern Living.*

General Types of Content. In place of or in addition to departments and continuing articles within departments, magazines have more general types of content as part of their formulas. Fiction is an example. The fiction may not appeal to the same type of reader each issue and may be on vastly different subjects from issue to issue, but fiction itself is a continuing element of the formula. Another magazine may have a travel piece each issue. One time it may appeal to readers interested in inexpensively roughing it along the Atlantic seashore, another time it may tell about luxurious accommodations in Aruba. Although the appeals are different, travel is a component of the formula. Poetry, cartoons, jokes, news, editorials, and photo essays are forms of content that can be included under this heading.

Formula itself is an austere or sterile term. It is obvious that a magazine's character or personality results from creative editing by an imaginative editor and editorial team. Beyond the subject matter discussed in the magazine are the angles, writing style, illustrations, graphic display—many, many nuances that cannot be reduced to formula.

In a sense, the editorial concept or objective is a basic plan agreed to by the publisher and editorial staff about what the magazine is to be. The formula itself deals with editorial content, both in terms of subject matter and mode of presentation necessary to carry out the concept.

The key to success is to first attract people to buy the magazine, and then to keep their interest with content that is in tune with the reader's thinking issue after issue. The magazine must be reader-oriented, and appeal to enough readers to keep circulation up and advertisers interested. On a sponsored or controlled circulation magazine the trick is to get the publication read by the intended audience.

Some editors insist they never edit to a formula. They may be right, but any magazine edited with a degree of consistency has a formula, though it may be implicit in the editor's thinking rather than in the form of a written statement. Most of these editors certainly know where their magazines are headed and try to steer them on a clear course. Norman Cousins is one of these. In an editorial for *Saturday Review,* he wrote, "The one thing I learned about editing over the years is that you have to edit and publish out of your own tastes, enthusiasms, and concerns, and not out of notions or guesswork about what other people might like to read."[1]

As he was launching *World,* Cousins said:

There are two ways to produce a magazine. You can get a marketing organization to tell you what people want and then edit to meet their needs. Or you can edit to please yourself, as I do, and hope that enough people share your enthusiasm and concerns to make the magazine a success.[2]

Actually Cousins had several continuing departments, features, and monthly supplements in his magazine—what could be called a formula. But he was one of those editors whose ideas and tastes fit in with those of his readers well enough that he didn't have to consciously tell himself what his readers were interested in. He also traveled extensively, and kept in personal contact with national and international leaders and major issues.

This suggests the ideal editor, one who is so close to his readers and their enthusiasms and tastes—in fact usually a step ahead—that his interests dovetail with theirs well enough to maintain their loyalty while attracting new readers. Most great editors have had that characteristic: George Horace Lorimer of the *Saturday Evening Post,* Edward Bok of *Ladies' Home Journal,* and DeWitt Wallace of *Reader's Digest.* For a few such geniuses, an editor's decision to edit a magazine to please himself may work, but for most editors, guidance by a formula is essential.

The "Publisher's Editorial Profile" of each magazine listed in Standard Rate and Data Service publications describes the magazine for advertisers and potential advertisers. The statements tend to be general and in some magazine classifications, such as women's magazines, almost indistinguishable. Nonetheless, they are useful in giving a capsule description of the editorial formula or, in a few instances, the editorial concept.

TV Guide's entry starts with editorial concept, and concludes with editorial formula:

TV Guide reports, probes and analyzes various aspects of network, cable and pay television. Its national editorial section contains in-depth reports on the television medium, and a wide array of updates, backgrounders, special profiles and features, many of which deal with the medium's relationships with news, sports, science, finance, politics, government, literature, the arts and social issues. The local section provides network, local and pay/cable programming information for each local edition area.

The Publisher's Editorial Profile of *InfoWorld* goes more into formula:

InfoWorld is edited for microcomputer users. The magazine is divided into five sections covering applications (Using Micros), computer-to-computer communication (Communicating), programs (Software), computers and peripherals (Hardware), and the companies and people that make and sell microcomputers (The Industry). *InfoWorld* features news and important opinions in the front of the magazine each week and sets the standard for product reviews in the microcomputer industry.

Redbook's entry deals with the target audience and then goes into a general description of formula:

Redbook Magazine is edited for young women today, who are juggling the demands and rewards of husband, child and jobs. Articles are geared towards helping her make "first-time" decisions in her complicated life ranging from personal relationships, home, money management, children and childcare to beauty, fashion, fiction, food and nutrition.

Southern Living's entry closely parallels the departmentalized content of its monthly issues:

Southern Living is edited for, and concerns, the tastes and interests of contemporary Southerners. The magazine regularly traces developments in the areas of travel and recreation, homes and building, gardening and landscaping, and food and entertaining.

Determining the formula requires consideration of several major factors, according to Roland Wolseley, which include:

1. Purpose of the magazine.
2. Market for the magazine.
3. Standard of living of the potential readers.
4. Educational and cultural level of the potential readers.
5. Competitors in the field and *their formulas*.
6. Tested formulas—whether existing formulas have worked.
7. Climate of opinion of the public generally, and how it might react to the proposed magazine.
8. The financial horizon or limits set on the formula by the financial condition of the magazine's owners.

His last point suggests that the owners should be able to sustain the intended formula over a long period of time until the magazine becomes established, or the magazine may drastically change when portions of the formula are eliminated or modified for economic reasons. Such changes might involve dropping extensive four-color printing, eliminating articles by top-name writers, going to less expensive paper stock, or sacrificing other content that is too costly.

Editorial Objectives

Editorial objectives are more abstract in concept than formulas. An objective is a desired goal or end that the magazine wants to achieve. It may be tangible or measurable. An objective could be to get a specific bill passed in Congress. The magazine editorially supports passage until the bill is passed or defeated. If it is passed, the magazine has achieved an objective.

Public Relations Magazine Objectives

Especially in a corporation's public relations program, objectives for employee, customer, and dealer magazines may be stated so all involved are re-reminded where the magazines are headed. In each instance, the readers' interests and the corporation's interests must be considered in developing reasonable objectives.

On an employee magazine, the editor is in the middle. For example, the employee wants good wages that continually increase, while the company wants punctuality and a good level of productivity. If the editor wants to make the employee aware of the company's expectation, he must do so in terms of the employee's expectations and from the employee's point of view to be effective.

Employee magazines may pursue objectives such as the cutting of waste in supplies or raw materials by pointing out how economy can help increase profits or productivity and perhaps lead to higher wages. Or they may try to alleviate employee anxiety about installment credit purchases, home mortgages, insurance coverage and premiums, alcoholism, or other issues that relate to absenteeism, productivity, or safety. If a company keeps statistics, results eventually may be inferred, but the magazine should not claim credit for just any improvement in the problem area in question unless it has some way of substantiating its claim.

After examining both the employee's and the company's expectations, a listing of objectives may be developed. Common objectives for *employee magazines* include:

1. Informing employees of company news and policies.
2. Explaining and interpreting company policies in terms of employees and their interests.
3. Developing employees' pride in their jobs and their company.
4. Developing loyalty to the company.
5. Helping to improve the company's efficiency and cut down on waste materials and time.

Purposes and objectives can be worked out for other company magazines. *Sales magazines* usually have as their purpose helping salespeople operate more efficiently to maintain or increase the level of their sales. To do this they include articles about new products, new applications for existing ones, and how salespeople have made big sales; company promotional activities, such as advertising campaigns and point-of-purchase displays; company regulations and policies regarding merchandising, returns, guarantees, sales contests, and discounts; competitors' activities and sales pitches; success stories of company salespeople; and techniques of selling. They often contain a large amount of light and humorous material, in keeping with the tradition that conversation is a salesperson's stock in trade, and for the purpose of winning readership.

Dealer magazines are generally expected to build brand loyalty, therefore, they tell about the company's products, describe successful merchandising ideas, and endeavor to increase cooperation between the merchandiser and the manufacturer by explaining and interpreting company policies.

Customer magazines attempt to contribute to the prestige and good will of the company and, in the long run, to build sales. The formula usually centers on entertainment plus ideas for use of the product and expert information on maintenance of the product, especially in the automotive field.

Some of the most exciting magazines, graphically, are *stockholder* or *corporate magazines*. These are the top-of-the-line company magazines aimed at shareholders who usually are not active in the management of the company, but are interested in it. They are especially interested in earnings and dividends and the general position of the company within its field. A trend in this field is toward discussing large, important issues—what the company is doing in relation to ecology; what its world marketing position and strategy are—and away from topics dealing with employees and fringe benefits. A stockholder magazine generally has two major functions: (1) to inform readers about the company specifically and about the industry it is a part of, and (2) to win or hold the readers' approval of management's activities and policies. Several stockholder magazines have broadened their scope of coverage so they can be issued to customers and the general public as well. These usually contain more general features not related directly to the company.

In planning how to meet the magazine's objectives, the editor of a public relations magazine must keep in mind that the publication must earn and retain the acceptance and respect of readers as well as skillfully present the management viewpoint.

Editorial Plans to Meet Objectives

The formula and objectives imply long-range plans, which involve imaginatively determining what kinds of pieces in the formula to run in each of the next several issues. Depending upon the type and frequency of magazine, editors work several issues and several months ahead. *Better Homes and Gardens* provides its promotion department with editorial plans 11 months ahead of an issue's publication date. The Hallmark *Cards* magazine published around Easter, for example, has content about

Figure 4–1 *GO, The Goodyear Tire Dealer Magazine*, advises tire dealers each month of products and successful sales and strategies. (Courtesy Goodyear Tire & Rubber Company.)

Christmas cards so merchants can plan ahead for the oncoming Christmas season. The editor may have been getting the issue ready the preceding Christmas. June bride issues have to be planned around Christmas, and some of the biggest issues of bridal magazines hit the newsstands in January, meaning the writers and editors were working on them around September.

The astute editor plans ahead to have the right article at the right time—not just a timely article that fits the department or formula, but the article that will appeal to the mood of the public at the time it is published.

The editor is planning several issues ahead as well as closing the current one at any given time. He or she has to keep in mind how long it will take to get assigned articles from staff writers and free lancers. A public opinion survey may take two or three months to plan and conduct before someone can even begin to write the article. Translating objectives into specific articles that will meet them is a major challenge of editing. The topic, the angle to interest readers, the length, and illustrations all affect the ultimate decisions. To successfully meet this major editing challenge, records of article ideas and assignments made for each issue are imperative to keep track of how things progress toward deadline.

Balancing Content

Part of editing is balancing content both within one issue and over a long period of time, say a year's issues, in fulfilling the formula and objectives.

Readers like variety and quickly sense monotony in topics or content. The formula itself suggests balance of content. Some magazines even break their formulas into percentages, such as *Management World,* which states, "In a year, editorial content covers: general management trends and practices (30%); human resources management topics (20%); information systems management—equipment and procedures (25%); new products, services, publications (25%)."

Hospitals aims for 27 percent on administration and professional practice, 18 percent on finances and economics, 17 percent on news, 9 percent on purchasing and product information, 8 percent on planning and construction, 7 percent on technology, 6 percent on support services, and 8 percent on other topics.

A public relations magazine for employees may have a general formula and balance, such as 40 percent company news and features, 20 to 40 percent general (noncompany) features, 5 to 20 percent employee news, and 5 to 15 percent employee participation and opinion.

How content is balanced varies from editor to editor. Some do it all in their heads and come out beautifully. Others go as far as to store in computers the amount of each type of article so they can get printouts showing percentages for each issue and the year-to-date. In between, some keep lists or charts of the kinds of content in the formula, the article types, titles, and amounts for each issue, and cumulative figures for the year. Whatever system is used, the editor must make a conscious effort to balance content.

Balance involves (1) variety, (2) breadth of coverage, (3) consistency, and (4) purpose. Few readers can take a steady diet of heavy articles or light articles; a mixture must be provided to maintain interest and to let the reader pace himself through the issue.

Variety in types of content is essential, too, such as balancing human interest articles against serious articles, text against illustration, long pieces against short ones, sprightly or inspirational material against bland or routine subjects, or company news against general features. Good editors cover a broad range of topics of interest to readers, from recurring themes and routine material to new ideas and developments. Editors continually generate new ideas to go along with their blend of standard or traditional fare, such as the January and February income tax tips and the March and April gardening tips.

A final reminder on an issue's content from Herbert Mayes, former editor of *McCall's:* "Vital to a magazine are the regular columns intended to capture readers' issue-to-issue attention. . . . They are the bread and butter on the editorial menu." And, he advised, "Never consider a magazine schedule ready to go unless it is at least as good as the last one, and when possible introduce an unexpected feature."[3]

Regional Editions

More than 70 national magazines offer regional or demographic editions to capitalize on regional advertising revenue. This way a business in a large metropolitan or sizable geographic area can reach prime prospects at reasonable rates while avoiding wasted circulation of its ad in copies of the magazine distributed in other parts of the country.

The number of regional editions a magazine publishes depends on its circulation and the location of that circulation. Demographic editions can be offered if the magazine has enough subscribers in a given occupation or income group.

At *Time* magazine in 1976, for example, regional and demographic ads accounted for about 20 percent of total ad pages and about one-third of the magazine's revenue, excluding international editions. In 1984 *Time's* national circulation of 4.6 million was divided into 11 regional editions, such as the Eastern edition of 1.5 million circulation. *Time* also offered 50 primary spot market editions on alternating weeks. Its demographic editions included *Time* Business edition for 1.6 million business executives; *Time* Student/Educator edition (550,000), *Time* Top Management edition (610,000), and *Time* Top Zips of 1.25 million subscribers in 2,000 highest income Zipcode areas located in 200 areas of dominant influence (ADIs) in 43 states and Washington, D.C. State editions were available for all 50 states. That's 98 editions of *Time* in the United States.

In regional editions alone, *U.S. News & World Report* listed 15, *National Geographic* and *Playboy* 6 each, and *Ski* and *Skiing* 3 each.

Although advertisements in some of these editions, particularly for small circulation areas, are sold in only full-page units, many are not. The result is that many of these editions need editorial matter to fill the space left after regional or demographic ads have been dummied. How the editorial operation fits in with regional editions varies among magazines.

In a study limited to magazines with six or more regional or split-run editions, Carol Reuss found that about one-third of the magazines have no editorial involvement at all in regional editions, about one-third maintain a bank of material that the makeup or production editor can use to fill the remaining space in regional editions, and about one-third generate at least some material for specific regions or demographic groups.[4]

Only two magazines in the study, *Farm Journal* and *Outdoor Life,* regularly run special sections of editorial content in regional or demographic editions. *Farm Journal* has been issuing geographic editions since 1952, when it began with three. These were later increased. Then Dairy Extra, Beef Extra, and Hog Extra editions (8- to 48-page inserts bound into copies of the magazine going to subscribers who are livestock growers) were added. Advertisers requested even more editions, until there were 29 in 1973, according to editor, Lane Palmer.

Outdoor Life published six regional inserts, each an 8-page section on yellow stock, for its six regional editions. The articles varied from short news items to multiple-page articles, with all copy oriented to the outdoor activities and life of the region involved.

Typical of the operations that maintain a stockpile of material was *Woman's Day.* The vice president-executive editor described it:

Because of the extreme time-squeeze on the production of the regional editions, all editorial material for them is prepared off-schedule. Text is in galley, engravings are made and layouts are done without reference to any specific issue. The material is laid out in the standard spaces we know we will be going to fill—one-column, half-page, two-column units, etc. At closing the advertising makeup department prepares laydowns of the regionals. These show the positioning of ads and the space available to editorial. The editorial makeup people then indicate what editorial material they wish to position in this space. Advertising has no say as to content.[5]

Since much of this material is not regional in nature but only regional in use, it can be used in several or all editions before being discarded. *Better Homes and*

Gardens, which has nine regions that are further broken into 141 editions, uses staff-produced and free-lance articles. After ads are dummied, the makeup editor fills the unoccupied space with editorial matter. The group administrative editor said:

Every attempt is made to use the regional editorial in every regional edition before it is discarded. It may be reworked several times in the process as the space units often vary from one regional edition to the next. This puts a real burden on the makeup editor to be sure that the material is used to the fullest extent and yet never appears in the same regional edition twice.

Magazines that reported creating special copy for regional or demographic editions included *McCall's, Successful Farming,* and *Nation's Business. McCall's* has an editor and full-time associate in charge of editorial content for the 10 regional and demographic editions.

Knowing the Reader

Effective editing involves meeting objectives, balancing content, and, ultimately, appealing to the reader. Each editor learns to know his own readers, but communication research tells us something about readers in general that can help us be more effective editors.

1. People tend to read, look at, and listen to material they already are interested in. People who are interested in a subject, even if they don't know much about that subject, welcome information about it. But those who have no interest are a poor target for such information. This may appear to be obvious, but many information campaigns have failed because those in charge overlooked their readers' interests.

2. People tend to read and listen to material that they agree with and to avoid that with which they do not agree. If people are confronted with material they disagree with, they tend to interpret—or misinterpret—that material to make it conform to what they already believe. People see the world through a filter of attitude patterns, and they try to keep those patterns intact by screening out material which would disrupt them.

3. People tend to check their opinions with authorities. Through personal influence, these opinion leaders can be important in causing people to make up or change their minds. These authority points seem to be scattered throughout the entire population and not concentrated in any single social class. People find these opinion leaders at their own level, although they may have different authorities for advice on different subjects.

   This is not a simple proposition of media to opinion leader to follower. Opinion leaders are heavy users of mass media, but they also get opinions from other opinion leaders. It is an intricate network of personal influence and media.

4. People tend to check their opinions and attitudes against those of the groups to which they belong. Attitudes with anchors in the group are hard to change. When the media's content comes up against these attitudes, little headway is made in changing opinions, values, or behavior.

Mass communication can be very effective if the standards of the group are weak or do not exist at all. During World War II, Allied propaganda made little impression on the Wehrmacht while morale was high. But when parts of the German army began to fall apart, so did the group standards that had buoyed up the individual soldier. And then propaganda telling the soldier how he could survive did a good job of promoting surrender.

Another finding that keeps cropping up in research is that if a reader is really interested in a subject, he will plod through the most wearying of prose and layout to read about it. The content and the reader's interest in it are the crucial aspects.

Magazine Influence

Some magazine editors believe they have great impact on large numbers of their readers. Other editors feel a close "personal" relationship with their readers, even if they have not met them. Many editors take almost any feedback from readers as evidence of great success, and a few even wonder if their readers are paying attention to what they are publishing.

What is the influence of a magazine and its editor?

All mass media probably have their greatest influence over a long time span; a single magazine issue or television broadcast seldom has a noticeable effect. One article may trigger a newspaper editorial, a rash of letters to legislators, a Congressional speech or bill, or an article or series in other publications. But this is the exception rather than the rule, and magazine influence usually is more subtle and less noticeable.

Because of what research has found, Theodore Peterson suggests there is no good way to separate magazines from the culture in which they are a force and by which they are conditioned—no way to separate the effects of magazines from those of other forms of communication. He concludes, though, that the nature of the magazine suits it for introducing new ideas to a democratic society, for providing a forum for discussion, for sustaining campaigns over long periods, and for working toward cumulative effect rather than single impact. Like other print media, the magazine's appeal is more to the intellect than to the senses and emotions of its audience. "In short, the magazine by nature well met the requirements for a medium of instruction and interpretation for the leisurely, critical reader" in the first two-thirds of the twentieth century, he said.[6]

Peterson mentions several accomplishments of magazines in the twentieth century. Magazines have (1) helped foster social and political reforms, (2) interpreted issues and events, and put them in national perspective, (3) fostered a sense of national community, (4) provided millions of Americans with low-cost entertainment, (5) been an inexpensive instructor in daily living, and (6) been an educator in man's cultural heritage through their historical articles, biographical articles, and attention to art. The variety of magazines was noteworthy, arising from selectivity of audience. As Peterson wrote, "the typical magazine was not edited for just 'everybody'; it was edited for a following with some mutual activity or outlook. Because they sought out little publics within the population at large, magazines in the aggregate represented a wide range of tastes and opinions."[7]

A magazine is very much like a living organism and should not be overinstitutionalized in the editor's thinking. Magazine history suggests that an editorial concept can grow and mature after "birth," but that as society changes, so must the concept and formula.

Notes

1. "Final Report to the Readers," *Saturday Review,* November 27, 1971, p. 32.
2. Newspaper Enterprise Association interview, *Columbus* [Ohio] *Citizen-Journal,* April 11, 1972, p. 12.
3. Herbert R. Mayes, *The Magazine Maze* (Garden City, N.Y., Doubleday & Company, 1980), pp. 97, 119–20.
4. Carol Reuss, "Editorial Involvement in Regional/Split Run Editions," paper presented at the Association for Education in Journalism Convention, 1973; updated 1976.
5. Ibid., 1976 addendum.
6. Theodore Peterson, *Magazines in the Twentieth Century,* 2d ed. (Urbana, Ill.: University of Illinois Press, 1964), p. 442.
7. Ibid., pp. 450–51.

5

Editorial Administration

ASPIRING editors often think almost exclusively in terms of working with words, photographs, and graphic materials to create an appealing editorial product, but no matter how small the magazine, *administration* is also an important part of magazine editing. Magazines are businesses as well as literary creations, and they require the help of adequate capital, sound organization, and efficient administration to achieve success.

Types of Ownership

Magazines operate under a variety of ownerships. Three common structures are the multiple-magazine publishing company, the media conglomerate or diversified corporation, and the single-magazine publishing company. The multiple publisher issues several magazines and may operate each as a subsidiary, division, or profit center, or may operate groups of magazines that way. If a single magazine or group loses money, corporation funds can be used to maintain operation until the magazine makes money again or is suspended.

The media conglomerate operates in several media fields, such as magazine publishing, cable television, television, radio, and possibly newspaper publishing. It also may have book clubs and direct mail sales operations. There is no big difference between it and a multiple publisher except that, as we describe them, the conglomerate is more widely diversified and magazine publishing may be actually only a small part of the operation.

One example is CBS Inc., whose Publishing Group includes consumer magazines, business magazines, educational publishing, and international publishing. CBS publishes about 20 magazines, including *American Photographer, Audio, Field & Stream, Home Mechanix, Tennis USA,* and *Woman's Day.* Broadcasting and recordings continue to account for most of the corporation's revenue.

Perhaps the best-known single-magazine publishing company is The Reader's Digest Association. Although it has entered into some auxiliary enterprises and its magazine has international editions, it is essentially a one-magazine publisher. Other single-magazine publishing companies of note include The New Yorker Magazine, Inc., Scientific American, Inc., and Newsweek, Inc., a subsidiary of The Washington Post Company.

Publisher

In virtually all magazine organizations, the publisher is the top executive, with final authority over all departments, both editorial and business.

The publisher, as owner or the owner's representative, is the ultimate policy maker for the magazine. In a multiple publishing house or conglomerate, he or she may be publisher of a group of magazines. Directing both editorial and business operations, the publisher usually is more inclined toward the business side because he or she has probably come up through the business ranks. The editor, then, must spend much time making the editorial staff's objectives, intentions, and positions known to the publisher and proposing policy that will benefit the total magazine in the long term.

The editor, too, realizes that without adequate income and profits, the magazine is not likely to continue publication, and is primarily concerned for editorial excellence in the context of successful business. The necessity for business success on the single-magazine publishing operation is obvious. The magazine either makes a profit or finds an angel to subsidize it—or it goes out of business.

Within the magazine organization (see fig. 5–1), the editor is likely to be one of three persons who report to the publisher, perhaps through an assistant publisher. The other two are the advertising director and the circulation director. Editors try to remain apart from the advertising and circulation operations, but they assist with promotion and appreciate the interrelationship among editorial, advertising, and circulation that must be part of a successful magazine.

Editor

Titles of top editors vary—editor-in-chief, executive editor, editor. For simplicity and clarity, *editor* is used here. The top editor on most magazines of any size is an administrator who seldom puts pencil to copy or writes a piece unless he or she remains in seclusion at home or stays late at the office to get it done.

Most of the editor's time is spent in four major activities: (1) staff relations and communication, (2) editorial supervision, (3) planning, and (4) public relations. The editor, whose name is at the top of the masthead, is usually obsessed with shaping the magazine to his or her editorial plans and tastes and with keeping errors out of the book. He or she delegates as much work as possible, especially the routine, but dozens of undelegated concerns come to the editor daily and occupy much time.

Realizing that one person cannot put out a magazine alone, an editor spends a lot of time with the staff individually and in small groups to explain actions, ideas, plans, and aspirations for the book. Personal contact and communication with the staff are essential for the staff's work and the book's content to be cohesive. This time spent in a combination of editorial supervision and staff relations may appear to be inconsequential to the casual observer, but it is essential to keeping a magazine on-target and on production schedule.

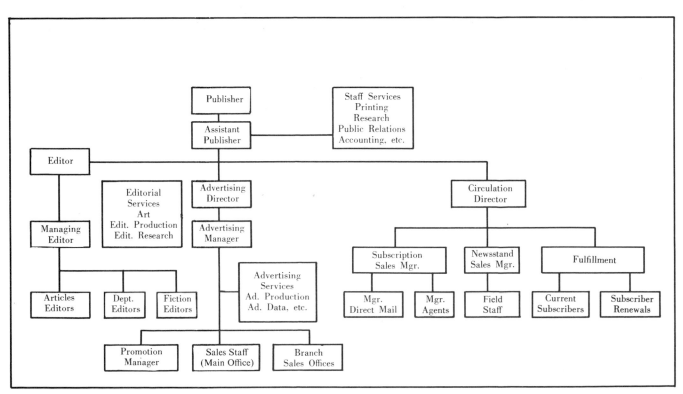

Figure 5–1 Magazine organization chart.

Walking through the office chatting with staffers, suggesting changes or pointing to new directions, spotting errors or incorrect emphasis, may look like socializing or meddling. But done with businesslike informality, it contributes to efficiency and effectiveness. The editor must determine the best way to use his or her unique attributes—personality and editorial judgment—to motivate and supervise the staff, giving it sufficient freedom to be creative, while at the same time firmly maintaining editorial standards.

The editor must be thinking ahead several issues while supervising completion of the current one. One thinks in terms of seasons (groups of three or four issues) or points of emphasis in the specialized field—trade shows, conventions, new model introduction. The editor may be concerned with appropriate content to get a consumer magazine through the usual summer slump in consumer magazine interest, and other content to capitalize on renewed interest in the book that fall. He or she may be planning a depth report or analytical feature that can make an impact for the book when it covers the annual trade show or the annual introduction of new models in its field. An editor thinks in general terms six months to a year ahead (on a monthly), while jelling the next three or four issues in his or her mind. Typically, the April issue this year will suggest ideas for next April's issue, and some plans toward it may begin immediately.

Editors keep the advertising department advised of editorial plans, especially if doing so may mean selling a few more ads in a particular issue. Although no respected editor would promise a favorable article about a company or its product, it is legitimate and good business for the advertising sales personnel to know the subjects and themes of upcoming issues to help them sell space.

Planning often will result in an *editorial calendar* that can be used by the advertising department to sell ads related to the major emphases or features in each issue. Business publications, especially, plan their coverage around trade shows and individual areas of expertise within the industries they cover. McGraw-Hill's *Housing* listed an editorial calendar that included the following items:

Issue	Editorial Emphasis/Special Features
January	NAHB Show: New Products Preview/Housing Demand Index
February	Merchandising Tactics: Good ways to turn lookers into buyers/Cost Index
March	Factory-Built Housing: Is it the answer to affordability?/Non-Residential
April	Remodeling: Problems and opportunities in updating older homes/Housing Demand Index
May	Custom Homebuilding: How to appeal to the high-end market/Cost Index
Mid-May	Kitchens and Baths/Special Showcase
June	The California Influence: Translating California design ideas to other regions/The Public Builder: Annual Report
July	Landscaping: How to enhance the value of a site/Housing Demand Index
August	Buyer's Guide/Desktop Reference Cost Index
September	Energy Update: The latest in energy-saving design and products/AIA/*Housing* Homes for Better Living Awards
October	Non-Residential Opportunities and Pitfalls: What homebuilders should know about commercial and industrial development/Housing Demand Index
Mid-October	Kitchens and Baths/Special Showcase
November	Recycling Old Buildings: Solving the special problems of adaptive reuse/Cost Index
December	Coping with High Density: Planning and design ideas for livable, high-density for-sale housing/Home-Shopper Survey[1]

Promotional angles also will be conceived and communicated to the promotion manager. And if newsstand sales are a significant part of total circulation, promotion may want tie-in material, such as point-of-purchase placards, cover stickers, newspaper ads, television spots, or other devices to boost circulation.

Editors tend to be strong-willed individuals who see the broad picture, working at fitting the pieces together, promoting their magazines, and seeking favorable relations with readers, constituent groups, and advertisers. They normally won't withdraw from the excitement of keeping everything moving, although they may need to keep in mind what they can do best and what other staffers do best. They know the magazine cannot exist without the editorial department, but they may have an internal sense of humility when reminding themselves that only about 10 percent of a magazine's income is spent on its editorial operation. The remainder goes to production, promotion, sales, and profit. Although continually fighting for a larger budget, the successful editor recognizes the importance of controlling expenses and carefully manages the budget.

An important function within any organization is internal communication, and this supports the case for a small, efficient staff. The most effective communication usually is the give-and-take of interpersonal communication or face-to-face conversation. Informal discussions about plans, articles, and editorial treatments are likely to be more productive than communications forced into a rigid structure. Some memos are inevitable (vacation policy, sick leave, fringe benefits), but personally checking with staff members to see that you are understood and that you understand their frustrations and emotional problems, as well as ideas, is imperative. If they get too far, emotional problems of even one staff member can materially affect production of your book, and throw it behind schedule.

The editor and publisher participate in basic decisions, Herbert Mayes, former editor of *McCall's,* observed. They determine circulation objectives, what advertisements will be accepted or rejected, the quality of paper to be used, the printer, and, with the circulation director, the size of each issue's print order. They join in determining the magazine's immediate and long-range goals.[2]

Public relations activities take a big chunk of an active editor's time. Public speaking opportunities are seized upon to advance ideas and promote the magazine's strength in its field. Publishers' groups, professional groups, civic groups, and groups of influential readers all will want to hear a vigorous or thoughtful editor at times. And the editor will want the opportunity to speak and to get feedback, new ideas, and different angles from the members of these groups. The editor must get out and see what's going on in the field, as well as in the magazine office.

Although trying not to get tied down to the day-to-day operation, editors insure a smooth work flow and efficient use of time and talent in the office. They may occasionally solve problems or establish new systems to increase efficiency, but they avoid routine mechanical functions.

Managing Editor

While the editor is involved in long-range planning, scheduling, and administration, the managing editor is concerned with the day-to-day and moment-to-moment chores of closing the current issue, taking care of the nitty gritty of fitting all the pieces of a single issue into place and getting everything completed on time. One difference between an editor and a managing editor may be that the editor is looking further ahead and getting ready for the next three to six issues, while the managing editor is of necessity focusing on the current one.

For many journalists, the real action is in the managing editor's position. That's where decisions about whether to keep or discard a picture, how to phrase a title or blurb, or how to display an article, are ultimately made. The managing editor works closely with writers, editors, art directors, and photographers to get the specifics right for the current issue.

Art Director

A well-staffed magazine is likely to have a full-time art director, who designs the magazine, selects type faces for title treatment or headlines, and plans display of pictures and of nonphotographic illustrations. He or she may or may not execute art work for the magazine.

Art direction has been emphasized for years, since few editors are qualified to look simultaneously at the verbal and visual, and carry off a successful article display. This may be one reason why the art director often is the No. 2 person on the masthead, between editor and managing editor. In any case, the art director works closely with both of them to make the content as visually appealing as possible.

Quarterly and smaller magazines are more likely to have an outside art director from a design studio or advertising agency do their issues.

News-oriented magazines often have less need for art direction, having established a formula or format that prescribes headline size and face, photo display, and departmental design, much like a newspaper's headline schedule and makeup plan. In this sense, *Time* and *Newsweek* are designed more like newspapers than magazines.

If the art director can also turn out finished art, so much the better, because art usually is ordered after the manuscript is in hand, and by that time the printing deadline is rapidly approaching. It's good to have a variety of art sources, but a good working relationship with one or two artists who understand your magazine, and who work rapidly, can yield excellent art almost by any deadline. Important maps may be produced in minutes; covers in a matter of hours. Artists who can do line drawings, make acetate overlays, and turn out charts, graphs, and maps are relatively abundant throughout the country, and their services are relatively inexpensive.

Free-lance artists are readily available in most cities, as are writers and photographers. In places like New York and Chicago, they are listed in the telephone directory, and in other cities they can be found in ad agencies, creative printing and design studios, and sometimes in industrial design shops from which they may moonlight for publications.

Smaller and less frequently published magazines that cannot support a full-time art director often find that their printer offers an excellent art service at reasonable fees.

In a magazine it is as important to maintain art quality as it is to maintain writing and photography quality. If some art you buy is not up to a publishable standard, do not hesitate to discard it. Far better to pay for unpublished art than to ruin the quality of the magazine. Instead of thinking that you have paid for the art and, therefore, should use it, think in terms of paying for overall magazine quality that may occasionally include the cost of discarded material that was carefully purchased.

Even when the art director is the No. 2 person behind the editor, it is important to remember that a magazine editorial staff can have only one boss, one person in charge. Herbert Mayes advises and warns:

Art directors need to be pampered, praised, loved, especially in public. Now and then an art director could begin to feel he should be left to his own devices, his work not subject to the editor's veto. Permitted to get away with it, he becomes a burden. If I have said it before, it's worth saying again: There can be only one boss. It can't be the art director.[3]

Staff

Staff size is a function of the amount of work to be done and the level of efficiency desired. Editors often find that a small staff of six to twelve can work very efficiently without bumping into each other, duplicating effort, or having a clique on the fringe trying to be creative and becoming frustrated when their material is not used.

It has been stressed that magazines are highly individual enterprises and that the structure for one often will not work for another. What seems to be typical may not be exactly that for a large number of books. But generalizations are inevitable and give guidance to persons viewing the magazine scene or planning to work in it.

An entirely staff-written magazine is not typical of the industry. At the same time, free-lance writers find it relatively rough going if they don't also have a full-time job or, at least, a contract to do so many pieces a year for a magazine. Some material will be staff generated—departments, continuing features, news sections, reader service features. Other will be commissioned out to columnists or regular writers who seldom come to the office.

Proper staffing is important to success. A magazine staff is not a machine or an organization chart into which editors and writers can be plugged like parts off a stockroom shelf. People who can work together, given sufficient freedom and a healthy amount of tension, can put together a lively magazine. An editor doesn't have to be like Harold Ross of *The New Yorker* was in order to have a quality magazine, but he or she does have to realize the tenuous balance between vigorous leadership (including decision-making ability) and staff freedom. The successful magazine is not a democracy, but a product shaped, molded, and led by its editor.

In the office, a small monthly magazine may find it efficient to have six to 12 key staff members, including:

1. Editor or Executive Editor
2. Art Director
3. Managing Editor
4. Editorial Secretary
5. Articles Editor or Senior Editor
6. Copy Editor
7. Production Manager

Additional staff may include writers of staff-generated material, another copy editor or two, and a senior editor or two in addition to an articles editor. The staffing, titles, and structure must be designed for the individual magazine, not borrowed from someone's organization table or a textbook.

Major differences in staff size stem from frequency of publication (a weekly needs a larger staff than a monthly, a monthly a larger one than a quarterly) and the type of content (a news or home service magazine requires more staff writers than a think or opinion magazine that can commission much of its content).

The economics of magazine publishing prohibit employing unproductive staff members and encourage heavy use of commissioned articles that can be obtained at lower cost than staff-written material. Many of these articles will be commissioned on the basis of queries received from free-lance writers, while others will be commissioned to writers who have a good track record and long association with a magazine. Some writers appear so frequently that readers tend to believe they are on the magazine's staff.

Larger magazines with heftier budgets contract with free-lance writers for a specified number of assignments each year. Under these arrangements the contract writer covers the assignment and is paid whether his article is published or not.

Those magazines that generate more content in-house may expand the number of persons in the basic positions that have been described, but they will also staff departments of the magazine.

Among those with larger staffs, *Mademoiselle* lists 64 editorial staff members on its masthead, *Better Homes and Gardens* lists 63, and *Woman's Day* has 67 editorial employees on its masthead, not counting 10 contributing editors, departmentalized like this:

1. Editor
2. Executive Editor
3. Art Director
4. Managing Editor
5. Special Projects (4)
6. Articles (2)
7. Books and Fiction (2)
8. Beauty (2)
9. Decorating (2)

10. Equipment (2)
11. Fashion and Patterns (3)
12. Food (4)
13. Needlework and Crafts (2)
14. Photographic Studio (3)
15. Reader Service

16. Workshop
17. Art (7)
18. Editor-Writers (2)
19. General Editorial (26) (2 Assistants to the Editor, 1 Copy Editor, 2 Designer-Editors, 6 General, 4 How-To, 6 Production, 3 Reader Mail, 1 Research, 1 Shopper's Showcase)

One monthly that is largely staff-written lists 46 editorial staffers. Another monthly with a smaller editorial well and more commissioned pieces lists 30. A magazine that uses book excerpts and outside contributions has 13 editorial staffers. Staff size relates to budget, work load, and other factors.

The one-person editorial staff performs the same functions as the large staffs, but on a smaller scale. The one-person staff has the added challenge of having to achieve sufficient self-discipline to get all the work done on time, from planning and scheduling through copy editing, title writing, layout, production, and reading galley and page proofs.

Even one-person situations vary widely, from unpaid volunteer editors of association magazines that rely on members for manuscripts and photos to the well-financed corporation magazines whose editors can buy manuscripts, superb photos, and art direction by a studio. When budget permits adding a staff member, the first addition may be an art director-artist if the editor prefers to continue writing and editing copy or a writer-editor if the editor has expertise in graphics and layout. In some instances a photographer would be added, but it takes a huge amount of photo assignments to keep one photographer occupied full-time.

As a magazine gains financial strength, there is a temptation to add staff just because the money is available. But some editors recognize that they are likely to sacrifice efficiency for size and keep as small a staff as can get the work done.

Encouraging Editorial Productivity

Editorial administration involves getting as much high quality editorial work as is possible out of each editorial employee, including yourself. Varied approaches and procedures may be effective for different people. Howard S. Rauch of Gralla Publications has offered advice in the areas of hiring productivity, staff productivity, and personal productivity.

Hiring Productivity

Spend less time in the screening process while selecting the best job candidate to increase hiring productivity. State a specific salary range in your ad to eliminate a lot of applicants who are far beyond the range. People who want more than the highest-stated salary will still apply. Cover that in the phone call arranging for the interview, making clear how negotiable you can be.

Toss aside any resume not accompanied by a cover letter, and any resume accompanied by a form letter with only a box number or the company name. This may eliminate up to 25 percent of the applicants, all who have not attempted to write a creative cover letter.

Classify all remaining resumes as A, B, or C. The A resumes most closely relate to the job needs. Interview and test the A candidates. Administer a one-hour exam on grammar, basic editing skills, headline writing, and news sense. (At Gralla, about 85 percent of the applicants fail.) Make no exceptions to testing. Advanced, experienced candidates should not be permitted to rely only on their clippings to prove their ability.

Conduct extensive interviews with all remaining candidates. Considerations in evaluating the candidate include: punctuality for the interview, the introductory greeting, appearance, job history (including longevity), speaking and interviewing ability, enthusiasm for the job, travel experience, organization in approaching a new job, specific related skills and experience, ability to relate experience to your magazine's needs, professional samples, and productivity history—ability to produce volume quickly.

Staff Productivity

Start with orientation and training. If you make a new assistant editor as knowledgeable as possible as quickly as possible, you will spend less time supervising that person. Both you and your employee become more productive as a result. One approach is to start with a 90-minute orientation on your magazine's policies the first day on the job, followed by an hour-a-day for two weeks to review facets of your field, editing techniques, your magazine's writing style, and other information the employee needs to function efficiently. Much of this training can be done by creating workshops on specific topics that can be repeated for other new employees later.

Recognition can increase productivity. List new editors on the masthead and give them business cards right away. Give them a good assignment and reward them with a byline as quickly as possible. For the ardent journalist, nothing tops seeing his byline in print.

Develop realistic standards of performance. Analyze routine work—how long it takes to write regular departments, paste up pages, read proof. Establish quantitative standards for how many new product items an assistant editor can write in three days or how many pages an associate editor can dummy in two days. If the standards are not achieved within 90 days, a conference with the employee is needed.

Specific quantitative standards are preferable to vague guidance, such as "the article is too long" or "you haven't done enough work" or "this is dull." Use the Fog Index as one measure of writing. Give specific assignments, and be specific in critiques of those assignments.

Quantitative standards help you determine the size of staff you need. Using a 20-day work month, make realistic estimates of how long it will take to make the assignments, write the material, edit the material, write the headlines or titles, design the pages, prepare illustrations, proofread the type, and, if necessary, paste up the pages. Assign these tasks to individuals in your analysis. One person may have five days of routine writing, three days of editing, two days of writing headlines, and two days of proofreading. This 12-day routine work month leaves eight days for other assignments, such as attending a three-day convention and writing two articles about it, or doing a major story that requires interviewing a dozen good sources.

With an analysis like this for each staff position, you can plan a reasonable and productive work schedule for every staff member, including yourself. Knowing how long it should take to write a single-source feature, or to edit the columns for one issue, helps everyone gauge productivity. If a staff member complains of having too much work, ask him or her to keep a record of how long it takes to do every task during a typical month, usually in days or half-days, and bring the results for discussion. A staff member may come up with 25 days of work for a 20-day month. Or the staff member may come up with only 15 days of work for the month and decide the job is not overwhelming after all.

Analysis of the amount of editorial content produced by all staff members can assist management. Calculate how much published material, in pages or column inches, was contributed by each staff member. Compare the results and analyze them. At Gralla, for example, staffers were expected to produce 200 to 250 column inches a month. One staffer who produced only 70 inches a month was found to be submitting inferior work that could not be published. Another had only 30 inches a month published, but that was because his editor was giving him poor assignments that could not result in publishable pieces. In one case the employee needed to be replaced, and in the other the editor needed to make better assignments.

Personal Productivity

Magazines vary, and so do editors' jobs, but a check list Rauch proposed can be helpful to most editors. The editor:

1. Writes at least one important feature for every issue (of a monthly).
2. Has a timely and well thought out regular editorial column.
3. Spends at least three working days each month in the field meeting readers.
4. Often seeks new contacts among readers, as opposed to relying on old friends all the time for story material.
5. Takes personal interest in developing the skills of inexperienced staff members.
6. Has created written, flexible job descriptions for all staff members.
7. Provides errant staff members, when necessary, with written job objectives to be achieved within a specific time period.
8. Supports the editorial chain of command, if one has been established.
9. Introduces at least a half-dozen new, exciting, timely features every year.
10. Secures speaking engagements on at least three or four industry programs every year.
11. Spends company money as if it were his or her own, and administers corporate policies as if they are personal policies.
12. Reviews competing magazines consistently for strengths, as well as weaknesses.
13. Reads his or her own magazine carefully upon publication to become aware of all the mistakes the editor or someone else should have caught.
14. Meets all publication deadlines, setting an example for the rest of the staff.
15. Refuses to accept second-best performances from staff and self.
16. Refuses to accept alibis such as "not enough time" and "had to fill space" for running second-rate material in the magazine.
17. Willingly does routine, nitty-gritty work in emergencies or when the workload is unusually heavy.
18. Keeps personal business to a minimum while on office time.[4]

Handling Manuscripts

The greatest amount of staff time and attention typically is expended on manuscripts, especially if the magazine accepts free-lance work. It is essential to establish and maintain a precise routine for handling manuscripts if chaos is not to overtake the operation.

The editorial secretary usually will have a full-time job keeping track of manuscripts and queries. When a manuscript or query is received, the editorial secretary should immediately send a printed post card acknowledging receipt and make a record with the author's name, basic information about the query or manuscript, date received, and person to whom routed.

Generally junior editors will review over-the-transom manuscripts and queries and will have authority to reject the ones that obviously do not fit the magazine's formula. Because these should be handled within a matter of days, a writer who does not receive a rejection within two or three weeks should be buoyed with hope that he is at least receiving serious consideration.

Ideas and manuscripts of promise should then be routed to top editors, with the editorial secretary making proper notation on the author's record. If the editorial secretary has not received action on an idea or manuscript within an established number of days, say 10, he or she should insist that the junior editors reach a decision so the rejection can be sent or the idea forwarded to senior editors.

The critical facet of a smooth-flowing operation is the fact that one person knows at all times where every query and manuscript is, and has a record of rejections and acceptances sent out, including dates, deadlines, and prices offered. This may seem trivial or obvious, but it is neither—the load can be overwhelming. Before it discontinued accepting free-lance material, *Today's Health* was receiving 40 manuscripts a day. Other monthlies report 12,000 to 24,000 a year.

Files are kept by authors' names so the individual author's track record can be readily available (number of submissions, acceptances, rejections), and not by title, because titles often are not submitted with articles and submitted titles usually are changed.

If the manuscript or query goes to a senior editor, articles editor, or editorial committee, as in the case of scholarly and professional magazines, a decision still must be made within a reasonable amount of time and conveyed to the editorial secretary, who then issues the appropriate letter to the author.

A series of form letters to authors is advisable to keep the work flowing and to minimize dictation time. Several types of letters may be kept at hand to deal with different types of situations. Four basic examples are:

1. Frank rejection—a letter that simply states that the article or idea submitted is not suitable for publication in the particular magazine.
2. Rejection with a warm paragraph—a rejection letter that indicates appreciation for having been able to see the manuscript or for the quality of its writing, perhaps with mild encouragement to the author for future submissions.
3. Conditional acceptance—letter that says the magazine would like to see the article the author queried us about, but only if the author will submit it on speculation. This gives the author the chance to follow through on his or her article idea, but does not guarantee acceptance when completed.
4. Acceptance plus personal note—accepts the idea and includes a paragraph dictated by the editor including the desired slant or angle, due date, price to be paid, and anything else that is relevant to the assignment. If an article was submitted, the letter accepts it and specifies how much will be paid. Payment may accompany the letter or go out from the business office after publication of the piece.

Evaluation of queries and manuscripts more often than not is informally but carefully done. One junior editor may want to check with one or several others, both on especially good manuscripts and on borderline cases. An editor who likes a manuscript will want to share it with anyone who happens by. The same is true at the senior editor level, where the top editor may take a manuscript home overnight to see if it's as good as a glance or another editor told him or her.

Editorial boards make decisions on some magazines, but boards listed on mastheads more often are window dressing to impress readers that some well-known writers contribute to the magazine. Professional association and scholarly magazines are more likely to have a formal mechanism for reviewing and voting on manuscripts than on consumer, business, or public relations magazines. On most magazines, the editors have a clear idea of what they want and exert leadership to see that they get it.

While a manuscript is being considered, everything about it—correspondence with the author, notes by other editors—goes along with it in a folder so that any editor reading it will have the full details available at all times. It saves the time otherwise required for going back to get files when letters or notes are wanted for reference.

Editors sometimes contact writers by telephone, especially if they have been published in the magazine before. After a telephone call the editor must dictate a memo to the file to note specifics, such as due date, amount of payment offered, any expenses authorized, and suggestions to the writer for treatment of the subject.

Some magazines pay on acceptance, though many do not. Some buy well ahead of issue dates, and others work close to the next deadline. An adequate stockpile must be maintained so the magazine will not run short of copy, but not so large an amount that it becomes outdated and useless.

After publication, the magazine keeps a manuscript and all the material related to it—galley proofs, page proofs, relevant notes—for six months to a year in case objections, questions, or lawsuits arise.

Throughout all phases of contact, writers should be treated as cordially and politely as possible. Editors realize that these writers are an important part of their livelihood—without free-lance and commissioned articles, most magazines would not be able to continue publishing.

Photography

As in the case of manuscripts, it is cheaper to use a free-lance photographer than to pay a photographer's salary and maintain a darkroom. Another reason outside photographers are used is based on the fear by some editors that an in-house photographer will see things the editor's way too easily, and they prefer someone who will think of different angles and be more creative while on their own. Telephone directories in most cities list photographers who can do good work, and photographers seek out magazines and offer to shoot assignments. Fellow editors can recommend free-lance photographers also.

Besides outside photographers, editors can call on picture services, both those that maintain files of pictures, any of which can be used quite inexpensively (as Wide World), and those that have on call a network of free-lance photographers who can shoot assignments of excellent quality (as Black Star or Magnum).

In-house photographers usually are prohibitively expensive for a monthly. Exceptions are obvious. *National Geographic* uses staff photographers in addition to free-lance work of known quality. A multiple publisher like McGraw-Hill or Chilton can amortize the cost of photography over several books and not saddle one with high overhead. But the typical magazine will find greater flexibility and availability in working with outside photographers who can work important assignments into their schedules relatively easily.

While providing the photographer with area for creativity, the editor must be thorough in making the assignment. Essential information the photographer must know includes (1) the subject matter, (2) specific people, activities, or scenes, (3) suggested emphasis or mood of the photos, (4) number of photos expected to be used, (5) deadline, and (6) amount of payment. A photography work order form (as fig. 5–2) often is used to formalize the details and keep track of them in written form.

When buying photos, the editor usually purchases only the rights for one-time publication in the magazine. The editor has complete rights to photography done by staff photographers, of course, and can sell rights to those prints if they are marketable.

Photos can be used for public relations purposes in association, public relations, and other small magazines. After publishing a feature on officers, employees, local officials, or anyone else who might have some real interest in the publicity, an editor routinely sends a set of the prints to the person or persons photographed, or otherwise involved, as a goodwill gesture. Some go as far as to have vinyl plastic folders

PHOTOGRAPHY WORK ORDER

Description of picture wanted: ________

Size: ☐ 8 × 10 ☐ 5 × 7 ☐
Format: ☐ Horizontal ☐ Vertical ☐ Square

Need contact proof by: ________
Need finished print by: ________

Picture to be shot at: ________
Location: ________
Name of person to contact: ________

Authorized by: ________

FOR PHOTOGRAPHER'S USE ONLY:

Picture shot: ________ Negative developed: ________
Contact proof made: ________ Print made: ________
Identification of persons in picture: ________

F-7015

Figure 5–2 Photography work order.

made with gold lettering: "Congratulations, you were recently featured in *Veeble-fetzer World*." Inside are copies of the magazine or clippings plus the photo or set of photos. Of course the folders must be made up and dispatched shortly after publication to make the maximum impact with the persons featured.

Production

Magazine production has traditionally been done outside the office, but the introduction of relatively inexpensive typesetting equipment and computers has brought that phase of production in-house in many magazines. A production manager oversees a smooth flow of work from editorial and ad staff to the printer to assure that production schedules will be met. Magazine presses usually are booked solid, and missing a deadline can both cost extra money and create a significant delay in printing and delivery.

The book has to close on time if it is to be printed and mailed on time. Editors are keenly aware of budgets and sometimes seem unreasonable in their demands to meet the schedule.

If composition is set in-house, the production manager supervises the employees who operate the typesetting machines and works with the artist who makes the *mechanicals* (paste-ups of pages ready to be photographed for printing) to insure that printing deadlines are met.

A production manager also may be involved in the mailing of the magazine, and the filing of the circulation audit statements—particularly on a smaller magazine.

Budget

No editor wants to be a slave to a budget, but none can ignore it. Wide variations in magazine sizes, overhead, salaries, type of content, income, and printing preclude the possibility of making firm statements about budgets. Most magazines do not own their own presses. They create an editorial product, try to get it printed and distributed at a reasonable price, and try to remain in business by making a profit. Operating one's own printing plant greatly decreases flexibility and ties up capital that cannot be afforded for that purpose. Several publishers operate subsidiary printing plants, but these usually must sell printing outside the company to generate sufficient work and income.

As with other aspects of magazine publishing, there is no typical budget. Insight into magazine finances is offered, though, by an analysis of 101 magazines, all members of the Magazine Publishers Association, for the years 1977–79. In these inflationary years, expenses increased and operating profit decreased each year. Table 5–1 presents the data for 1979.

Although a direct comparison with a similar study of 74 magazines over the years 1966–70 is not wholly valid, one can see a slight increase in operating profit, from 7.3 percent in the earlier study to a three-year average of 10.1 percent; an increase in subscription revenues from 22.9 percent to 30.2 percent that more than offset the slight increase in subscription selling, promotion, and fulfillment costs from 13.5 percent to 14.7 percent; and a decrease in editorial costs from 10.0 percent to 7.9 percent. All figures are percentages of total magazine revenues.

Budgeting

A budget is a plan for a business for a stated period, usually one year, and covers all income, expense, and profit items. A profit and loss budget, a balance sheet budget, and a cash flow budget are essential to the financial department. In addition, there are special budgets, such as advertising pages, subscription sales, and single-copy sales, and often payroll budgets and capital budgets.[5]

The process of budgeting, besides developing a plan for operations, gets people to think about their activities, examines alternatives, involves key people in decisions with each other, evaluates performance against the plan, guides control of the operation, and informs people of the total plan and their role in it.

Table 5–1
Magazine Revenue and Expenses, 1979 (Amounts expressed as a percentage of total magazine revenues)

Revenue	Percentage
Net advertising revenue (after all discounts and commissions)	55.20
Gross subscription revenue	30.15
Gross single copy revenue	14.65
Total magazine revenues	100.00
Expenses	
Advertising	
Selling costs	5.09
Research and promotion costs	2.91
Total advertising expenses	8.00
Circulation	
Commissions to subscription agencies	4.82
Other subscription promotion costs	7.47
Commissions on single-copy sales	4.12
Other single-copy promotion costs	1.72
Fulfillment costs	2.37
Total circulation expenses	20.50
Editorial costs	7.90
Manufacturing and Production	
Paper costs	17.68
Printing and bindery costs	17.55
Total manufacturing and production expenses	35.23
Distribution expenses	9.41
Other operational expenses	
First class postage costs	1.32
Third class postage costs	1.40
Other postage and operating costs	1.06
Total other operational expenses	3.78
Administrative costs	5.94
Total magazine costs	90.76
Operating profit	9.24

Source: Magazine Publishers Association Price Waterhouse Financial Survey for 1979; *Folio,* January 1981, p. 26.

Budget periods should coincide with accounting periods so that comparisons with actual figures easily can be made. This is by issue in the magazine business, except for weeklies where it becomes too time consuming to be worthwhile.

The most effective budgeting process involves everyone who has responsibility budgeting for his or her own area, and the overall budget results from coordinating and putting all these individual budgets together. A bureau chief in Miami budgets for his bureau. The director of the photo studio or photo editor budgets for the studio or photo department, and so on. Ultimately the editor puts all the editorial budgets together for the editorial budget that is submitted to top management.[6]

This budgeting approach is effective because people are more likely to comply with a budget they helped formulate, it involves broader thinking and planning throughout the company, more people become involved and feel that they are part of the team, and by going into individual units and subunits—the lowest positions on the organization chart—more detailed knowledge of the function and its costs go into the budget.[7]

The process usually begins several months before the end of the company's fiscal year when the financial department issues background material to help plan the upcoming budget. These data vary but can include the current budget, actual figures to date and projections for the remainder of the year, anticipated inflation factors and price changes, economic conditions, status of the field covered, and the company's general approach to the upcoming year.

Department heads prepare their budgets and discuss them with the next person up the line. Sometimes other persons are consulted, and the department head reworks the budget. The process continues with study of major and minor alternatives until the overall budget is adopted.

As the year progresses, it is important to compare the actual figures distributed by the financial department against the budget to determine whether significant differences between budgeted and actual figures warrant action. If expenses are outrunning income or budget, controls or cuts may be necessary. If income is exceeding expectations, additional expenditures may be necessary to produce the additional editorial material and print the additional pages needed to go with the additional advertising pages being sold.

Major changes may necessitate rebudgeting. Some companies rebudget as a matter of practice every three to six months. When rebudgeting, it is advisable to keep the original budget and compare it as well as the new one with actual figures. Careful budgeting is time consuming and should be done as needed but not so often that it overburdens the staff.[8]

An Actual Budget

Here is a late-1970s budget for a trade association magazine listed in *Business Publication Rates and Data* that has a seven-person staff and a circulation of 42,000. The editor describes budgeting as fairly easy because the magazine is stable in circulation and number of pages; 10 issues each year average 50 to 55 pages of editorial and the convention and post-convention issues average 65 pages.

His first step in budgeting is to determine unit costs for composition, printing, postage, and paper either by month or by page. These mechanical costs account for about half the magazine's total expenses and are directly related to the number of pages printed. Unit costs are obtained by dividing total expense by number of pages printed or number of issues published.

Unit costs for the year used as the basis for budgeting were

Composition	
Typesetter rental and supplies	$ 395 a month
Purchasing typesetting	40 a month
Negatives	395 a month
Separations, four-color	200 a month
Miscellaneous composition, supplies	55 a month
Total Composition	$1,085 a month
Printing	$87.75 a page
Postage	
Controlled circulation	31.20 a page
First Class	200.00 a month
Paper and Mailing Services	
Paper	75.00 a page
Freight, wrappers, mailing labels	745.00 a month

The next step was to estimate the number of pages that would be printed in the succeeding year. In the current year there had been 500 advertising pages and 720 editorial. Using salesmen's reports and industry projections, the budget was based on 12 issues containing 515 advertising pages and 735 editorial, or 1,250 total. He also had to allow for a 7 percent postal rate increase the second half of the following year, paper price increases in January and July, and the fact that the magazine's printing contract would expire at the end of June and costs probably would increase.

Given these facts and assumptions, the budget came out looking like this:

Composition	
$1,085 a month plus 6% less savings of $1,151.20 on changes in production procedure	$ 12,650
Printing	
550 pages first 6 months at $88	48,400
700 pages second 6 months at $93	
(6% increase rounded down)	65,100
Postage	
550 pages at $31.20 first 6 months	17,160
700 pages at $33.40 second 6 months (7% increase)	23,380
First Class at $200 a month	2,400
Total Postage	42,940

Paper and Mailing Services

Paper, 550 pages at $82.50 (10% increase in January)	45,375
Paper, 700 pages at $86.50 (5% increase in June)	60,550
Freight, wrappers, mailing (5.4% increase rounded down)	9,420
Mailing labels, 6 months (prior to anticipated conversion to in-house computer services)	5,000
Total Paper and Mailing	120,345
Total Production Budget	$289,435

The next budgeting step was to estimate editorial costs. The magazine would need an average of 25 pages a year of freelance written material at a rate of $60 a page. Three regular monthly columnists also would be paid at agreed rates of pay. The editorial budget, then, looked like this:

12 columns at $165 each	$1,980
12 columns at $145 each	1,740
12 columns at $40 each	480
25 freelance pages at $60 each	1,500
Miscellaneous editorial charges	300
Total Editorial Budget	$6,000

Art costs were similarly figured. Front covers had averaged $423, about $160 had been spent on film and developing, and $40 on one cartoon a month. So the new budget looked like this:

12 covers at $450	$5,400
Miscellaneous art, $50 a month	600
Cartoons at $40 a month	480
Special project art	1,020
Film and developing at $25 a month	300
Art materials and equipment	400
Special convention photography by professionals	800
Total Art Budget	$9,000

Expenses for advertising sales promotion were budgeted to include 10 issues of a soft-sell newsletter to key advertising, marketing, and sales executives, rate cards and editorial schedules, annual market guide to the field served, special issue promotions, media kit data sheets, Business Publications Audit and Media Comparability Council data forms, materials for five regional marketing seminars, ads in SRDS and *Industrial Marketing,* surveys of competitive advertising, reader inquiry fulfillment, readership study, reader attitude study, marketing and purchasing studies, and convention expense for booth, hospitality suites, and displays. From all this expense was deducted the estimated income from renting the circulation list, and net expense for advertising sales promotion, which came to $34,000 or 4 percent of estimated gross advertising revenues.

Miscellaneous Administrative Expense includes the magazine's share of expenses of services provided by the association, such as the secretary-treasurer, accounting department, mailroom, copying machines, some outgoing mail and all return postage, office supplies, and fixed asset expenditures. All these came to $33,700.

Much higher Circulation costs than usual were budgeted to cover expenses of a switchover from outside verification service to an in-house computer operation. The circulation budget broke down like this:

Verification mailings to current recipients to qualify for BPA audit	$7,000
BPA auditing charges	1,500
Computer service bureau	8,800
Dun & Bradstreet prospect list	5,400
Total Circulation Budget	$22,700

A Miscellaneous Dues item covers membership in various organizations, staff attendance at professional seminars, and magazine subscriptions. Budget: $2,000.

TABLE 5–2
Budget for Monthly Trade Association Magazine
42,000 Circulation Averaging 104 Pages a Month

Printing, Engraving, Postage & Mailing	$290,000
Editorial & Art	15,000
Sales Promotion	34,000
Miscellaneous Administrative Expenditure	33,700
Circulation Audit	22,700
Dues, Suscriptions & Miscellaneous	2,000
Staff Salaries	153,700
Staff Travel & Expense	26,500
Telephone & Telegraph	8,000
Rent	15,500
Total Expense	$601,100
Advertising Revenue	$609,140
Net Profit	$ 8,040

Staff salaries and benefits totaled $153,700 for seven full-time employees: editor and publisher, managing editor, business manager, editorial production assistant, circulation clerk, secretary, and advertising salesman.

Staff Travel and Expense, based on averages of past expenses for travel and expenses of the editor and publisher, managing editor, and one advertising salesman, totaled $26,500.

Telephone and Telegraph was estimated at $8,000.

Rent of space provided by the association was $15,500.

Advertising Sales is a complex item to budget. The average gross income per page had been $1,575, and a 5 percent rate increase would take effect the following January. Gross income was estimated at $1,650 per page, and if the 515 pages were sold, they would produce income of $849,750. From this are deducted agency commissions (15%) and cash discounts (2%) totalling $141,910 and sales commissions to advertising salesmen, both salaried and publisher's representatives, of $94,500. For bad debts from advertising agencies, one-half of 1 percent ($4,200) was set aside. This left an estimated income of $609,140 against a budget of $601,100, leaving a potential profit of $8,040, or less than 1 percent of gross sales.

The overall objectives, the editor said, are to publish 12 good issues at no cost to members, and make a modest profit for the association.

A City Magazine Example

Working up a budget involves summarizing records, then making projections and supporting them with a written statement about plans reflected in the budget. Information about previous years can be disseminated to department managers in the same form as their budget worksheets. In this example, figure 5–3 gives information for the editorial department of a 30,000 circulation monthly city magazine. Figure 5–4 shows the budget developed by the editor. The copy editor had received a salary increase during the year and was budgeted for a relatively smaller increase than other editors the following year. The year's totals do not always equal 12 times the January figure because items vary from issue to issue.

This magazine had revenue of $1,250,000 a year, but was barely breaking even. A new owner believed proper budgeting and control could produce a reasonable profit, and his assumptions as budgeting began included a 5 percent increase in advertising rates, a 5 percent increase in advertising pages, an increase of 500 subscriptions, no changes in single copy sales or circulation prices, a few new expenditures, and a profit of $50,000.[9]

Budgets submitted by department heads showed $100,000 increase in revenue, but a $128,000 increase in expenses. The new owner then reviewed each activity and dollar figure with the department head who submitted it. No salary increases were altered, but some editorial plans, including converting two pages of two-color

Figure 5-3.

EDITORIAL DEPARTMENT INFORMATION
CURRENT YEAR

	January	February	March	etc.	Total
Pages					
Cover & contents	3				36
Listings	8				84
Reviews	5				63
Editorial	1				11
Contest	2				24
Columns	5				63
Short Stuff	3				42
Letters	2				23
Features	31				386
	60				732
B & W	42				494
2-Color	10				133
4-Color	8				105
	60				732
Expenses					
Salaries					
Editor	$ 2,000				$ 24,000
Managing Editor	1,500				18,000
Art Director	1,450				17,400
Senior Editor	1,250				15,000
Local Editor	750				9,000
Copy Editor	750				10,000
Editorial Assistant	600				7,200
Part-Time	500				6,200
	8,600				106,800
Columnists	600				7,200
Art and photo	550				7,000
Engravings	650				8,000
Manuscripts	2,000				29,000
Travel, entertainment	150				2,000
Editorial research					
Other	200				2,600
	$ 12,750				$162,600
Cost per edit page	$213				$222
% of total revenue	10.8%				13.0%

James B. Kobak, "Magazine budgeting: a case study," *Folio,* August 1976, p. 82. © Copyright 1976 *Folio: The Magazine for Magazine Management.* Reprinted by permission.

Figure 5–3 Editorial Department Information. James B. Kobak, "Magazine budgeting: a case study," *Folio,* August 1976, page 82. Copyright 1976 *Folio: The Magazine for Magazine Management.* Reprinted by permission.

a month to four-color at a cost of $200 a month, were postponed. Budget revisions called for a 7 percent advertising rate increase, a $1 increase in subscription price, a reduction to 50-pound paper stock from 55-pound, and addition of editorial and advertising research at a cost of $10,000 at the insistence of the new owner. These changes brought anticipated profit to $38,000, and the owner went back to each department to share some costs to reach the $50,000 profit figure.

In this first year of new ownership, a single budget was adopted, but the owner decided that the following year high, low, and most-likely budgets would be developed and there would be another advertising rate increase.

In the budgeting process, a schedule making the number of editorial pages directly dependent upon the number of advertising pages at a ratio of about 60 percent advertising to 40 percent editorial was established, with a minimum of 55 editorial pages per issue and a maximum of 75.

As the year progressed, monthly expenditures that exceeded the budget were reviewed with each department head to arrive at a mutual decision about where the needed cutbacks would be made.

Figure 5-4.

EDITORIAL DEPARTMENT BUDGET WORKSHEET
SUCCEEDING YEAR

	January	February	March	etc.	Total
Pages					
Cover and contents	3				36
Listings	10				96
Reviews	5				60
Editorial	1				12
Contest	2				24
Columns	5				60
Short stuff	4				48
Letters	2				24
Features	32				384
	64				744
B & W	46				506
2-Color	8				120
4-Color	10				118
	64				744
Expenses					
Salaries					
Editor					$ 25,700
Managing editor					19,000
Art director					18,500
Senior editor					16,000
Local editor					9,000
Copy editor					10,300
Editorial assistant					7,400
Part-time					6,000
	9,325				111,900
Columnists	625				7,500
Art and photo	580				7,300
Engravings	840				10,500
Manuscripts	2,500				40,000
Travel & entertainment	170				2,200
Editorial research					
Other	250				3,000
	$ 14,290				$182,400
Cost per edit page	$223				$245
% total revenue	?				?

James B. Kobak, "Magazine budgeting: a case study," *Folio,* August 1976, p. 84. © Copyright 1976 *Folio: The Magazine for Magazine Management.* Reprinted by permission.

Figure 5-4 Editorial Department Budget Worksheet. James B. Kobak, "Magazine budgeting: a case study," *Folio,* August 1976, page 84. Copyright 1976 *Folio: The Magazine for Magazine Management.* Reprinted by permission.

Other information essential to keeping income and expenses in line throughout the year was reported to management on the Circulation Sales Report (fig. 5–5), the Production Report (fig. 5–6), and the Advertising Space Report (fig. 5–7).

Magazines experiencing rapid growth or decline in circulation or advertising pages need to rebudget frequently or develop alternative budgets that can be invoked when needed.

Figure 5-5.

CIRCULATION SALES REPORT

This Month				Year to Date		
Last Year	Budget	This Year		This Year	Budget	Last Year
			New subscriptions			
			Direct mail			
			Advertising			
			Insert cards			
			Others			
			Renewal subscriptions			
			Other income			
			Reprints			
			List sales			
			Other			

James B. Kobak, "Magazine budgeting: a case study," *Folio,* August 1976, p. 85.

Figure 5–5 Circulation Sales Report. James B. Kobak, "Magazine budgeting: a case study," *Folio,* August 1976, page 85. Copyright 1976 *Folio: The Magazine for Magazine Management.* Reprinted by permission.

Figure 5-6.

PRODUCTION REPORT

This Month				Year to Date		
Last Year	Budget	This Year		This Year	Budget	Last Year
			Pages—Advertising B/W			
			Advertising 2-Color			
			Advertising 4-Color			
			Editorial B/W			
			Editorial 2-Color			
			Editorial 4-Color			
			Color usage			
			-2-color			
			-4-color			
			Print order			

Due on the 17th of the month of publication.
Estimated dollar figures to be added later.

James B. Kobak, "Magazine budgeting: a case study," *Folio,* August 1976, p. 85.

Figure 5–6 Production Report. James B. Kobak, "Magazine budgeting: a case study," *Folio,* August 1976, page 85. Copyright 1976 *Folio: The Magazine for Magazine Management.* Reprinted by permission.

Figure 5-7.

ADVERTISING SPACE REPORT

This Month				Year to Date		
Last Year	Budget	This Year		This Year	Budget	Last Year
			Pages—Display			
			Classified			
			Shopping Mart			
			Restaurant			
			Make Good			
			Filler			
			Black & White			
			2-color			
			4-color			

Due on the 12th of the month of publication.
Dollar billing figures to be added later.

James B. Kobak, "Magazine budgeting: a case study," *Folio,* August 1976, p. 85. © Copyright 1976 *Folio: The Magazine for Magazine Management.* Reprinted by permission.

Figure 5–7 Advertising Space Report. James B. Kobak, "Magazine budgeting: a case study," *Folio,* August 1976, page 85. Copyright 1976 *Folio: The Magazine for Magazine Management.* Reprinted by permission.

Notes

1. *Business Publication Rates and Data,* July 24, 1981, p. 259.
2. Herbert R. Mayes. *The Magazine Maze* (Garden City, N.Y.: Doubleday & Company, Inc., 1980), p. 234.
3. Ibid., p. 99.
4. Howard S. Rauch, "Measuring editorial performance," *Folio,* November 1984, pp. 123–28.
5. James B. Kobak, "Budgeting for fun & profit," *Folio,* June 1976, p. 46.
6. Ibid.
7. Ibid., pp. 46–47.
8. Ibid., p. 48.
9. For the complete discussion, see James B. Kobak, "Magazine budgeting: A case study," *Folio,* August 1976, pp. 81–85.

Creative Editing

EDITING is a highly individual process. An editor's intellect and personality have great effect on the other staff members and the magazine, so generalizations about magazine editing have their exceptions because of the individualism and variety in the magazine field.

Editing is supervision of the whole range of editorial functions from planning content to preparation for the press run. Long-range plans are made, article ideas considered, articles assigned, manuscripts scheduled into specific issues, illustrations planned and ordered. Articles are edited, titles written, layouts planned and approved. Copy is sent to the typesetter, proofs are read and corrected, dummy is pasted up, page proofs are checked. Finally, the issue goes to press.

Specific activities of an editor at any given time depend upon the frequency of the magazine, the size of the staff, and his or her mode of operation. A top editor may seldom touch a pencil to a piece of copy. He or she may be an executive who assigns articles, selects manuscripts, and gives direction to the rest of the staff. It is these executive activities that give a magazine its special character, that make it different from all others in the field. Because they are so varied and often intangible, these activities are difficult to catalog, define, or measure. Yet some magazines succeed in maintaining reader appeal over long periods of time because of the creative talents of their editors, while others fail because their editors lack those talents. These special talents first show themselves in general planning.

Planning Is Crucial

Planning, the crucial step, is where the editor's expertise really shows. If the editor can plan the right editorial content for the readers, assign the right writers to the right topics or personalities, and get the right illustrations for each issue, the magazine can succeed. Looking ahead to future issues is important to the well-being of any magazine. An editor must have a clear idea of what is coming up and shape current issues to that concept.

To get ideas, evaluation, and occasional articles, any successful editor must have a large number of personal contacts. He or she must use good editorial judgment to keep them in balance, realizing that the people closest to an editor are not necessarily representative of people in general or of the magazine's readers. A wide range of contacts can open the way to significant manuscripts by important persons as well as insightful and entertaining pieces by competent free-lance writers. An all-staff-written magazine can benefit from occasional outside articles and photo features.

The small magazine often relies more heavily on over-the-transom pieces. Religious and association magazines particularly need material offered by free lancers, plus articles requested from members and authorities.

Planning may be largely a one-person operation, a cooperative conference with an editorial board or staff, or a combination of the two. Except in some association and professional journals, most editors insist on decision-making power, thereby avoiding editing by committee.

Staying a Step Ahead of the Reader

Editorial imagination or creativity is something that is learned rather than taught. It grows from the individual editor's background, interests, abilities, and contacts with the staff and other persons. How an editor thinks of devoting an entire issue of a magazine to a book like *Hiroshima* by John Hershey, as *The New Yorker* did, or to a week's American combat fatalities in Vietnam or a Hemingway novella, as *Life* did, is not easily pinpointed. Some editors' creative ideas work—and some don't.

Why one editor invites a respected psychologist to become a regular contributor to the magazine, perhaps just hours or days before another editor tries the same, is not easy to say. Sometimes it can be chalked up to inspiration, other times to serendipitous insight, digging, suggestions from colleagues, or a casual remark overheard at lunch. Too much time spent evaluating an idea may mean missing the opportunity; not enough may invite a blunder. It's not pure luck, although some of that helps.

The great success of George Horace Lorimer as editor (1899–1936) of the *Saturday Evening Post* has been attributed to his ability to appeal to the businessman and his family, perhaps projecting him an income level or two beyond his status and showing him a life he might achieve if he persisted and gained economic success. Lorimer aimed at a middle class readership and never strayed far from its tastes, although he did publish short stories by F. Scott Fitzgerald and William Faulkner. His magazine was a conservative, stabilizing influence, not an agent for social change.

Edward Bok, editor of *Ladies' Home Journal* (1889–1920) advised women how to rear babies and campaigned against French fashions. He moved the women's magazine from its preoccupation with moralizing and sentimentality to a service publication that appealed to women's interests and practical problems. He had architects prepare plans for houses and sold blueprints by the thousands. He campaigned against venereal disease in 1906. His campaign to clean up American communities stirred action from backyards to municipal projects. He succeeded in having a large billboard at Niagara Falls removed, and his mere threat to publish prevented erection of a huge sign at the Grand Canyon. His crusades of national importance usually succeeded, but those of purely feminine concern failed.

DeWitt Wallace had an idea he couldn't give to a publisher. So he and his bride made it work themselves. Henry Luce originated a magazine concept that has been modified over its 50 years, but *Time* remains pre-eminent in its field in circulation and advertising income.

Truly creative, imaginative editors are not plentiful, even in a country with thousands of magazines. The magazine with a predictable formula from issue to issue remains in the majority. Some magazines are so departmentalized and institutionalized that the reader can almost tell in advance which kind of tulip will be

Figure 6-1 Creative editing of visual and verbal components has won two National Magazine Awards for reporting excellence, one for visual excellence, and one for general excellence for *Audubon*, the magazine of the National Audubon Society. (Courtesy *Audubon*.)

mentioned in the gardening article next month. This in no way lessens the service rendered by that type of magazine. It may, however, challenge editors to put more effort into developing fresh treatments of service articles that readers are counting on. After all, April 15 is income tax deadline every year, and taxpayers need advice on how to complete the gauntlet with a minimum of pain. Solid, straightforward information simply presented often is the answer.

National Magazine Award winners exemplify creative editing. *Audubon* won successive awards for reporting excellence—in 1976 for an account of the consequences of an ill-conceived irrigation project in South Dakota, and in 1977 for a "readable, succinct, but comprehensive" report on PBB, a toxic chemical accidentaly dumped into cattle feed in Michigan. *Philadelphia* won the 1977 public service award for an emotionally powerful article, "Forgotten Children," on the loneliness and despair in a state institution for the retarded. The specialized journalism award in 1977 was presented to *Architectural Record* for spurring international competition to find architectural solutions to slums.

To organize and conduct the international design competition for a settlement to house an impoverished community in a developing country, *Architectural Record* established the nonprofit International Architectural Foundation and announced the competition in its April 1974 issue. Consultation and support were received from the United Nations Environment program, the Union Internationale des Architects, and the Philippine Government. The foundation received 2,531 registrations from architect entrants in 68 countries and 476 submissions to be judged by a distinguished international jury. The winning designs were presented in the May 1976 "Human Settlements" issue.

The citation for the 1975 specialized journalism award to *Medical Economics* said the award was for "a striking and courageous attack upon the inadequacy of the medical profession's commitment to self-discipline. It documents past outrages and points out the implications, for the profession as well as the nation's health, of a continuing closed world." *Modern Medicine* won the service to the individual award in 1976 for its treatment of basic questions facing physicians and medical researchers in "Ethics, Genetics and the Future of Man."

Business Week received the 1976 public service award for its survey of the changing role of women in top management, and *Redbook* won the 1975 fiction and belles-lettres award for William Kotzwinkle's remarkable novella, "Swimming in the Secret Sea," which "brilliantly demonstrates the author's mastery of narrative

Figure 6–2 *Architectural Record* received the National Magazine Award in specialized journalism for its support of international competition to find architectural solutions to slums. (Courtesy *Architectural Record*.)

Figure 6–3 The cover story in this issue of *Business Week,* a survey of the changing role of women in top management, received the 1976 National Magazine Award for public service. (Courtesy *Business Week*.)

Figure 6–4 The cover story on productivity in this issue helped *Business Week* win the National Magazine Award for general excellence in 1973. (Courtesy Business Week.)

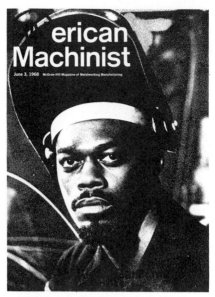

Figure 6–5 *American Machinist*, a McGraw-Hill magazine, won the National Magazine Award the last year it was a single award, primarily for this issue devoted to hardcore unemployment. (Courtesy *American Machinist*.)

Figure 6–6 An outstanding regional magazine, *Texas Monthly* won the National Magazine Award for public service with this issue's cover story of teacher education and certification. *Texas Monthly* also has won the National Magazine Award for reporting and for specialized journalism. (Reprinted with permission from the September 1979 issue of Texas Monthly Photo by Andy Uracin. Copyright 1979 by *Texas Monthly*.)

and his ability to handle potent and painful material delicately and yet with telling effect. It also demonstrates *Redbook's* courage in publishing fine fiction on subjects not usually encountered in popular magazines; in this case, a breech delivery, death and burial of a young couple's first son . . . grim, heartbreaking, real."

A detailed two-part series, "Supertankers," that brought to public consciousness the dangers to man and to the environment posed by huge ships that transport the world's oil won the reporting excellence award for *The New Yorker* in 1975. That year *Esquire* won the service to the individual award for a series of "three delightful and informative essays by Richard Selzer on such apparently unpromising if ubiquitous objects as livers, kidney stones and surgeon's knives. Selzer, a doctor, is also a scholar and a literary stylist. *Esquire* magazine deserves high praise for uncovering this unique talent and setting it to work in an area usually inaccessible or uninteresting to the ordinary reader," the citation stated.

Mother Jones won the 1980 reporting award for "The Corporate Crime of the Century," which the judges described as "a meticulously researched and cleanly written expose of large-scale dumping in third-world countries, often with United Stated Government aid, of hazardous products declared illegal within the United States." That year *Saturday Review* received the award for service to the individual for an article on children and cancer, called by the judges "a compassionate and compelling report of great potential service to families facing the tragedy of a child afflicted with the disease."

An article dealing with the inadequacies of teacher training and certification in Texas won the 1980 public service award for *Texas Monthly*. The judges said the subject had "broader implications for the future of our entire public education process."

A free-lance article about a boy who was tortured to death by his mother and stepfather won the 1981 public service award for *Reader's Digest*. "The Murder of Robbie Wayne, age Six" by Mary Jane Chambers "dramatically brought to millions of readers the too-often hidden problems of child abuse," the judges said. Mrs. Chambers had become interested in the trial of the mother and stepfather when it took place in Oklahoma in 1979.

A magazine must give readers a lot of what they want, but it must go beyond and give them what they want before they know they want it. Some of this material may have low readership, but a cumulative effort eventually will result in some gains. Talented editors are in touch with their areas of concern or subject matter well enough to be ahead of the reader. They sense when to add a new department or treat a new topic.

Forecasting Trends

Success comes to the editor who can see a trend developing and plan the magazine's approach to it, timing it to break just when the readers are most receptive to it. Trends usually develop slowly, even in today's fast-paced society, and so quietly that they often are missed until too late. Wide contacts with people "where the action is" is one key to forecasting trends.

Robert Cirino roasted the media for missing important social issues.[1] His analysis of selected magazines, newspapers, and television newscasts over an eight-year period showed they had overlooked coverage of population and birth control, world hunger, hunger in the United States, illiteracy, the brain drain, prison brutality, venereal disease, chemical-biological warfare, abortion, and the military-industrial complex. Instead he found an inordinate amount of coverage of athletics, entertainers, space exploration, business corporations, Vietnam, and religion. By the time his book was published, some of the media were covering several of these topics, but his point was well taken. The media, including magazines, had an opportunity to address significant issues of society and had instead remained preoccupied with traditional coverage rooted in the past. All the concerns he listed eventually were thoroughly covered, but there will be new social problems that the media should face. Many magazines, of course, choose not to cover social issues and, knowing that information about athletes and entertainers sells well, feature that material.

Fads fly by, and readers tire after several successive articles on some subjects, but the magazine editor must remain alert to leads and follow up those with promise.

Editorial leadership, though, can quickly resolve itself into a fad and lose its impact, and the magazine its distinctiveness. The fad often is the method of treatment of a topic by magazines, rather than the topic itself. For example, women's liberation, as a movement, started slowly. By the time readers and editors got interested in it, every magazine had to have a women's lib piece, usually with Gloria Steinem on the cover. The fad was the spate of articles on women's lib and the use of Gloria Steinem to exemplify it, not the movement itself.

Sometimes the difference between following a fad and continuing a legitimate service is difficult to discern. There are always many articles on a new occupant in the White House, but magazines carried it to ridiculous extremes with the Kennedys. Movement leaders like Gloria Steinem get space in numerous magazines, and popular movie and TV stars get coverage when they are hot and maybe through rediscovery a year or two after. At various times Christie Brinkley, Princess Diana, Farrah Fawcett, Cheryl Tiegs, Brooke Shields, Elizabeth Taylor, and Raquel Welch have appeared on numerous covers in a short span of time. Perhaps it is editors who tire of the frequency of these people on covers more so than the public, but editors who want covers to sell their magazines will stick with the most popular people on them.

Working Ahead to Have the Right Article at the Right Time

Striving to be the leader in a field, as if not difficult enough for the creative editor, is complicated by the need to work well ahead of publication dates. A consumer monthly may outline its ideas a year in advance and make assignments as the ideas jell. By three or four months in advance, most articles need to be in good shape, ready for copyreading and art direction. Now and then a piece may be polished and inserted on deadline, but an entire issue cannot be produced that way.

Completing some articles on schedule is comparatively easy in fields like fashion, where the showings to buyers take place months in advance of retailing the merchandise. The whole process is scheduled so the fashion magazines can show what's new and whet appetites for the apparel soon to be in the stores. Many business publications, whether for housewares or durable goods, are in a position to follow similar courses. The tough decisions can be what the big social problem will be in six months, which best-seller will appeal to parents of teen-age children, what actor will make a good story, what should be published on the domestic economy. Every editor seems to have about as many tough decisions as easy ones in keeping the book vibrant, muscular, and on the leading edge of reader interests.

Good editors have a knack for coming up with the apt topic and a twist in its treatment to make it different. They are idea people and they come in contact with numerous interesting people who also have ideas. They read voraciously and think about what they read. A person who doesn't have more ideas than he or she can develop and publish isn't likely to be a successful editor.

Besides planning ahead on seasonal and topical articles, editors buy an inventory of pieces that can be used as the months roll along. The inventory shouldn't be so large that some of it is likely to become out of date, but there should be a cushion of material so that the editors are not forced to rush headlong into their next issues at the last moment with a bare minimum of usable material. Thorough acquaintance with the subject matter, the field, and the magazine's readers make planning ahead easier. Planning is work and takes conscious effort.

Working with Outside Sources

Staff writers, photographers, illustrators, and correspondents are sources for the bulk of material in today's magazines. Outside sources account for a substantial amount, especially in the idea and opinion books.

Editors approach top-name talent for specific pieces. Occasionally a bidding war among magazines takes place, but that's not commonplace. The relationship may begin when free-lance pieces arrive at the office and the editor likes them so much he or she buys almost anything the writer can turn out. Eventually the writer's material may not be as well written or as relevant to the audience, but the editor feels a certain appreciation for past service and loyalty toward the writer. Such was the case with Clarence Budington Kelland, who over 40 years sold numerous pieces of fiction to *Saturday Evening Post*. After Ben Hibbs departed the editorship, three novels by Kelland, for which Hibbs had paid $50,000 each, reposed in a box in an office closet. Hibbs also had paid $100,000 for a biography of General Douglas MacArthur that the *Post* never published.[2]

After the assassination of President John F. Kennedy, memoirs by close associates brought high prices. Ted Sorenson was expected to have the most valuable ones, and *Look* got them for $150,000. *Saturday Evening Post* approached Arthur Schlesinger Jr. with a $50,000 offer for his, which drew a laugh because he already had an offer of more than $100,000 from *Life*. The *Post* dropped out of the bidding, but later engineered a small coup when it bought and published the story of Kennedy's long-time personal secretary. As Otto Friedrich tells it,

We received a copy of a tearful little memoir by Kennedy's devoted secretary, Mrs. Evelyn Lincoln. It had already been turned down by all the other big magazines, but that was because the other magazines had failed to perceive its maudlin virtues. What none of them had realized was that Mrs. Lincoln had observed Kennedy a lot longer and a lot more closely than most of his entourage, and although she might have nothing more to say than that she picked up Kennedy's socks after his nap on the White House sofa, that was all the average reader needed. Very few people really cared about the political revelations in these memoirs—who can remember the details of any of them?—for what everyone wanted was simply a retelling of the legend, a sense of reunion with the fallen prince, and thus a momentary feeling that he was not really dead. So for $15,000 we bought Mrs. Lincoln's little book, and, with a handsome cover portrait of Kennedy by Karsh, we outsold both *Life* and *Look*.[3]

It was the third straight sell-out issue of *The Post,* and with a piece that had been turned down by *McCall's, Ladies' Home Journal, Life,* and *Look.*

Revision and Rejection. Relations with outside authors and photographers usually are less spectacular. Free-lance offerings arrive with regularity in most magazine offices, and those free lancers want and deserve prompt responses. A writer has invested valuable time digging into a subject and putting it in writing. Presumably the writer is familiar enough with your magazine that he or she thinks the piece is the type you usually publish or should publish. What a typical serious writer wants most is your honest answer as soon as possible.

If you reject the piece, reject it promptly so it can be submitted elsewhere. If you think the writer has promise, but needs editorial advice before starting a piece, suggest that he or she query you in the future before writing.

A piece that is good but needs revision should be returned with the specific suggestions for revision. Holding a manuscript for a week or a month or more won't improve it and won't likely make your decision any easier. If others on your staff must be consulted, do that, but keep the paper moving. Don't let an advisory or associate editor halt the process by leaving it in his or her *in* basket. The American Society of Journalists and Authors Code of Ethics and Fair Practices formerly stated that a writer was entitled to an answer about a magazine's intentions with regard to purchase, revision, or rejection of a manuscript within 21 days of its submission. That has been deleted in a revision of the code, but it is a good guideline for an editor to follow.

The code specifies:

A writer is not paid by money alone. Part of the writer's compensation is the intangible value of timely publication. Consequently, if after six months the publisher has not scheduled an article for publication, or within twelve months has not published an article, the manuscript and all rights therein should revert to the author without penalty or cost to the author.

A magazine's policy dictates how and when it pays. Professional writers obviously prefer to be paid upon acceptance, and they're more likely to try to do a good piece for that type of book in the future. The American Society of Journalists and Authors has a terse bit in its code on this:

The writer is entitled to payment for an accepted article within ten days of delivery. No article payment should ever be subject to publication.

Many editors do pay only upon publication, and although it never should happen, a writer occasionally has a piece accepted for payment upon publication only to have that editor be succeeded by another who ships back the manuscript.

Imitation as a Road to Success

The leader in the field may remain the leader, but there usually is opportunity for imitators to achieve commercial success. Confession magazines present a good example of imitation. *True Story* appeared in 1919, and was an obvious success by 1926. Magazine success cannot be hidden, so other publishers brought out similar magazines. Bernarr Macfadden, originator of *True Story,* himself started imitations of that magazine.

Imitation was the major factor in several other types, including the factual detective, fan, pulp, and men's magazines. *Playboy* was an imitation of *Esquire,* or what *Esquire* had been. Numerous imitations spring up over the years to capitalize on *Playboy's* success. Like other magazines, *Playboy's* readers grew older and *Penthouse* stepped in as a contemporary imitation of what *Playboy* had been. Rather than change its successful formula, *Playboy* countered with *Oui,* which it has since sold.

Reader's Digest was imitated by a number of digest magazines in the late 1920s, but most dropped by the wayside. Specialized topics were served by the digests that stayed around, like *Science Digest* (1936), *Catholic Digest* (1936), *Children's Digest,* and *Baseball Digest* (1942).

Time (1923) was well established when two other major national magazines, *Newsweek*—founded by the first foreign news editor of *Time*—and *U.S. News* appeared in 1933. *Business Week* (1929), which resembled *Time* in its coverage of business news, was a conversion of McGraw-Hill's *Magazine of Business.*

Any successful editorial idea suggests possibilities for other magazines, often most successful when applied in a special interest area or toward a different audience. No box score of imitative successes and failures is available, but failures seem to have outnumbered the successes. Imitation in editorial formula, as well as article topics and treatments, will be tempting to editors and publishers for a long time to come.

Editors of popular magazines will continue to get leads on significant topics from magazines of opinion, professional and scholarly conventions, and news reports. The border between imitation and creativity or leadership isn't always clearly distinguishable.

Seasonal Content Recurs

At first you may wonder what it might be like to write something "new" for *Casket and Sunnyside,* a magazine for funeral directors. But most magazines in a special interest field have the same situation. Readers have a basic interest in the field or they wouldn't ask for the magazine, but how does an editor get them into this issue's articles and keep them on the hook?

Lane Palmer, when editor of *Farm Journal,* discussed this at length with an agricultural journalism class at the University of Wisconsin and later in a bulletin issued by the Department of Agricultural Journalism. Farmers obviously are interested in farming, but how much will they read if it's something they already know?

Three basic questions guide the editors of *Farm Journal* and relate to editors of other magazines: 1) What's on farmers' minds this month? (The surest way to get a reader's attention is to promise him help with a problem that's on his mind at the moment.) 2) What is there new to say about it? (You have to promise him something he doesn't already know.) 3) What does it mean to the farmer in Lincoln County? (It may be interesting as an example, but what does it mean, what can it do for the typical reader elsewhere?) Newspapermen edit for the milkman in Omaha or the little old lady in Dubuque. *Farm Journal* editors edit for the farmer in Lincoln County, where editor Ralph Wennblom grew up in South Dakota. If it would appeal to Wennblom's farmer brother back in Lincoln County, it would have possibilities as a *Farm Journal* article.[4]

Significance, or meaning, is what Palmer calls the "so-what" of an article. An article full of examples, but no so-whats isn't helpful to readers; they want the so-whats, not just the examples. But Palmer adds:

There is as great or a greater danger in writing with too much "so what" and too few examples. I suspect that this is the problem with many of the lectures in classrooms. It's what we mean when we say that a prof lectures almost entirely in theory. It's what students mean when they say they want teaching with more relevance—they want theory related in some form familiar to their every-day experience.[5]

Suppose the article has some solid information and some reader interest, but it just doesn't grip you enough as an editor to make you believe your readers will stay with it. Palmer's four-word description of the ideal *Farm Journal* story applies to most magazines:

NEW, YOU, NOW, and HOW. We want to write the NEW ideas which YOU, the average farmer, can use NOW and here's HOW. We seldom find a story strong on all four counts. If it is really a NEW idea, it is probably not ready for use NOW. Farms vary so much by enterprise and size that we probably can't tell farmers HOW to use the idea in a single article.[6]

News and continuing concerns are part of every field. Magazine editors know, too, that a big portion of their readers continually change. So the same topic can be brought back occasionally if it does not become bothersome to the loyal reader.

Gardening magazines have about the same subjects season after season—issue after issue, but different or unusual gardens can be found to show as examples; varied plantings of the same basic plants can be designed; issues can be themed around trees, then shrubs, then flowers, and content emphasis and approach can be varied in other ways. A home service or personal finance magazine may run a series of articles every winter on how to do your income tax. If the tax laws don't change the tax forms do, and people forget about details of deductions, dividends, and the like from one year to the next.

The *new* may lead into repetition of continuing details that need to be repeated—as what is deductible from income tax and under what conditions. *How* and *now* always have strong appeal when the topic is relevant to the reader. Late summer and early fall magazines occasionally carry a title like, "What You Can Do Now To Cut Your Income Tax Next April." And magazines write lots of articles in the second person, talking with the reader as *you* instead of in the impersonal third person used by newspapers.

Later chapters discuss editing manuscripts, and details of that need not be covered here. But after all the techniques, style, grammar, and other details are mastered, Palmer adds:

Superior or great writing calls for something that you don't find in the rule books. The best an editor can do is to recognize it when he sees it and prints it. The nearest I can come to describing it is to say that the sort of informational writing I've been talking about speaks mainly *to the mind*—to the readers's *reasoning powers*. Great writing does this, too, but it speaks as well *to the heart*—to the reader's *emotions*.[7]

Visual Versus Verbal

Any photographer can tell you a picture is worth 10,000 words, but most editors come up through the writing and editing ranks and think verbally more than visually. The photojournalist recognizes the importance of words as correctives for distortion, and for two-dimensional representation of a three-dimensional scene. He or she knows that words are needed to identify, explain, and complete the story begun by the picture.

There's no need for an either-or argument. Both pictures and words are needed, and the best editor is the one who most expertly considers how words and illustration, including graphics, can go together to present content effectively to the reader. Wilson Hicks, first picture editor of *Life,* once gave a speech titled "One Word is Worth 10,000 Pictures."

An editor may not be his or her own art director or photo editor, but it's obvious he or she must think as they do, as well as about manuscripts. Going back for pictures after a manuscript is completed may not be the most effective or most efficient way to do it.

Ideally, the planning of illustration should begin with the planning of the story. Before you sit down at the typewriter—in fact before you start interviewing—you should ask yourself: "What will be the most effective way of telling this story? Can I tell it mostly with photographs? With drawings? With charts? The word-oriented writer particularly should force himself to go through this thought process. Otherwise, he'll find himself going back to his sources for pictures after the writing is done. He will always be illustrating his manuscript rather than telling the story in the most effective form.[8]

National Geographic, though, prefers to have the completed manuscript in hand before shooting the pictures. Editing cannot be reduced to a formula or step-by-step process applicable to all magazines; an editor's creativity must always provide the dash of seasoning that is never measurable precisely, but always vital.

Notes

1. Robert Cirino. *Don't Blame the People* (Los Angeles: Diversity Press, 1971).
2. Otto Friedrich, *Decline and Fall* (New York: Harper & Row, 1970), pp. 12, 102–3.
3. Ibid., p. 207.
4. Lane M. Palmer, *Publishing Magazines to Meet Reader Needs and Interests* (Madison: Department of Agricultural Journalism, University of Wisconsin, 1971), pp. 43 and 45.
5. Ibid., p. 50.
6. Ibid., p. 45.
7. Ibid., p. 52.
8. Ibid., p. 66.

7

Editing for Content

IN the previous chapter, the point was made that editorial decisions based on thorough planning often make the difference between quality magazines and run-of-the-mill magazines. In extreme cases, the creative decision-making of top editors can actually determine the ultimate success or failure of their publications.

But month after month, or week after week, editorial activities are carried out that bring these creative decisions to fruition or let them slip into oblivion. These activities are also important aspects of editing because they result in specific *verbal-visual* packages for readers. Here the editor takes up where the writer leaves off, and the key to success is represented by the combination of those two words: verbal and visual.

Unlike the writer, the editor cannot think in terms of words alone. In processing the manuscript, the editor must visualize it in a final form. The graphic treatment given to the title, the space allocation, the spot used for it, the page layouts, the typographic treatment assigned to the text, and the illustrations to supplement the words all are interrelated and cannot be separated. Putting the article in perspective with the rest of the content in a magazine further complicates the work of the editor as he or she processes manuscripts.

In this chapter we shall be considering the three steps in article editing that relate to content: (1) evaluation; (2) polishing; and (3) verification. The fact that these aspects of editing will be separately discussed does not mean that they, in fact, can be accomplished separately. The separation occurs here only to give order to our discussion; it must not be permitted to obscure the fact that the physical, visual product presented to the reader forms the basis for acceptance or rejection of the product.

Evaluation of Manuscripts

Selection of content tests editors' mettle more than any other single task. As they apply their knowledge of reader interests to the evaluation of manuscripts, editors must also be applying their professional and technical skills. These skills are needed for their visualization of the final product that might emerge from the raw material they are evaluating. In manuscript evaluation, the concept of visualization is all important. Weaknesses in the raw material can be corrected, and a good editor should be able to see through them. Prose can be sharpened. A weak title can be strengthened. Confusing, complicated data can be clarified with graphs, charts, or other visual aids. Organizational faults can be eliminated if the writer is guided carefully through meaningful revision.

As they use visualization as an aid to evaluation, editors must constantly remind themselves that they are serving as their readers' gatekeepers, determining what information will flow to the reader and what will get no farther than the editor's desk. Whether they open or close the gate should depend on the interest and needs of readers, not their own biases or interests.

To be their responsible gatekeepers, editors must know their readers intimately. They must know their interests, their strengths, and their weaknesses. An editor is both a follower and a leader; having to know and follow the interests of readers while providing the guidance and leadership they need. Magazine editors have always known that they must follow the interests of their readers if they are to succeed, and they have felt reasonably certain of their ability to measure reader interest. Their own experience plus that of the editors who have gone before provides an empirical set of rules for measuring reader interest. These guidelines can be reinforced with quantitative results of readership surveys.

There is no doubt that readership studies are a valuable tool for an editor in evaluating manuscripts. Good magazine editing demands periodic measurement of readership of all elements within a magazine. But readership studies, even at their best, can be truly reliable only for guiding an editor in following readers' interests; they reveal what the reader was sufficiently interested in to read in a previous issue. Their value in pointing out new directions—in providing a base for leadership by a magazine—is limited.

Editorial leadership is important for all contemporary magazines, and for the large number of specialized business publications and other similar magazines, this aspect of editing is exceptionally important. But how is an editor to know what his or her readers *need* to know now, especially if readers have no strong feelings about the material? Or, how can an editor know what his or her readers will need to know in a few months or a year so he or she can present the needed material in advance? These are the demands of editorial leadership, and they are difficult to meet.

Editors, however, do have some advantages over their readers when it comes to determining present and future needs. They have the ability to attend conferences and brainstorming sessions with leaders in the field covered by their magazine. They have the opportunity to gather and analyze information on a much broader and more detailed basis than an individual can. And they probably have working for them a staff of field editors, department heads, and other specialists who can provide a breadth and depth of knowledge that no reader could be expected to have.

So it is possible for editors to provide leadership by pooling their knowledge with that of their staff and applying it to manuscript evaluation. This leadership must be exerted at an early stage of manuscript evaluation—the stage when the subject, as contrasted with the manuscript as a literary package, is being evaluated. And it is most important when consequence (as contrasted with interest) of a subject is being considered. Does the subject now have or will it in the near future have some bearing on the well-being of a large number of readers? If so, it has consequence. Readers often have little or no initial interest in material that may eventually prove to be of considerable consequence to them. Editorial leadership is being exerted when subjects are covered that may not have shown up too well on readership reports, but are of real importance to readers nevertheless.

Once the consequence of a subject has been determined, potential verbal-visual treatments must be considered. Editor Lane Palmer of the *Farm Journal* once gave an excellent example of this aspect of evaluation.[1] The subject under consideration was zoning, which Palmer said "was as important to farmers as they were indifferent to it." The *Farm Journal* had run earlier articles on the subject and was "rewarded with a deafening silence." This time, Palmer said, "We decided to go all out with illustration. We settled on three of the worst things that can happen to a community as a result of having no zoning: a car junkyard, a roadhouse, and a highway cluttered with a jungle of roadside signs. With the help of three picture agencies, we ran down the best, or perhaps I should say the worst, photos of the three we could find. Then we tied the three together with a huge ink blot and carried it under the title 'Want One of these Blotting Your Farm?' We were rewarded with reprint requests from all over the country, which taught me this lesson: If the subject really matters to your readers, you, the editor, are the only reason why it will not be read."

In this example, the *Farm Journal* combined the knowledge of what its readers needed with the ability to visualize and follow through with an approach that caught reader interest, thus providing true editorial leadership. Editor Palmer, like other editors who have made their magazines leaders in their fields, has given a lot of thought to bases for manuscript evaluation. He says:

The editor debating whether to use readership studies or his own judgment is in exactly the same position as a president or governor wondering whether to follow the polls or to attempt to lead them. In a democracy, the majority of voters (customers, readers) rules, and the politician or editor who ignores that fact does so at the peril of his own career. Yet at the same time the public wants to be led, wants to be taught, to be challenged.

So indeed the editor walks a tight-rope between readership and leadership. Knowing what subjects will interest your readers—deciding what to print and what to leave out—is, by all odds, the greatest challenge in editing. . . . How you say something and how it looks to the readers are important, but the most important thing of all is what you choose to write about.[2]

Magazines of different types face somewhat different manuscript evaluation problems. A highly technical periodical, for example, may require the use of an advisory board during the selection process. Because no editor and no staff of such a periodical could be expected to be sufficiently knowledgeable in all aspects of the magazine's coverage, manuscripts may be circulated to outside experts for assistance in evaluation. Academic magazines often use a similar system.

Regardless of the evaluation system used, and regardless of the source of the manuscript (free-lance or staff writer) the decision often cannot be a simple "yes" or "no." In fact, it probably is most common for the decision to be a "no" or a tentative "yes," because it is typical for magazine manuscripts to go through some revision before being published.

Polishing and Shaping Up Manuscripts

Assuming that its subject gains approval, the manuscript is considered as a verbal-visual offering that must come up to certain literary and graphic standards. Bringing it to an acceptable level may require only minor change or extensive revision, token graphic treatment or a full-blown visual dressing up.

Polishing and shaping up requires careful attention to an article's approach, direction, organization, completeness, literary style, and mechanics of style.

An article's approach to a subject is a primary determinant of readership. Some changing and sharpening of the approach is perhaps the most common improvement an editor can produce as he or she works with a manuscript. Sometimes called the "slant" or the "angle," the approach should be signalled by the title and carried forth quickly and vigorously in the article's beginning. If the purpose of the article is to provide assistance to the reader, the reader's potential benefits from that assistance should be alluded to immediately. If, on the other hand, the article's reason for existence is entertainment, its opening should set the stage for what is to follow.

For editors of specialized vocational and technical magazines, working for a new approach to basic subjects is a constant problem. Some subjects must recur because they are basic to the industry being served, but the approach must be varied—new and different each time if readership is to be expected. Cooperation between writer and editor is needed if the best approach is to be found. In one instance, *Farm Journal* Editor Lane Palmer worked with one of his new editors through four beginnings of an article on farm record-keeping before he was satisfied with the approach.[3] Two of the beginnings were roughed out by Palmer, the other two by the original writer. The final version was worth the effort, however, because it gave action and life to an oft-repeated subject.

Some revision is often required, too, because an author loses sight of the direction his or her article should take. Once the beginning sets the approach, a well-structured article will follow a straight course to its conclusion. Side trips, though they may be interesting, cannot be permitted to let an article lose its direction. Although it is a more common fault among beginning writers, straying from the central subject occurs in the product of seasoned professionals also. The temptation to toss in a bit of interesting but extraneous information is just too tempting, especially if that bit of information was acquired only after some hard digging. It is the job of the editor, however, to "blue pencil" the article back on course.

Flaws of subject organization can be kept to a minimum through effective outlining, but restructuring at the editing stage often is necessary. Serious organizational faults usually require further work from the author, but skillful editing can do wonders with minor rearrangement of facts, the addition of transitional devices, and similar structural aids.

The lack of some bits of pertinent or sometimes vital information is another common shortcoming that must be corrected before publication of a manuscript. Depth of coverage is highly essential for any magazine article, and shallow treatments must be subjected to further work. Incomplete manuscripts must be bounced back to the author with sufficient comment to guide him or her in gathering the missing material and incorporating it into the piece.

So far our discussion of the role of the editor in processing manuscripts has dealt with substantive matters: evaluating the subject in terms of reader needs and interest; checking the approach, direction, and depth of an article; and correcting flaws in organization. Editors must also be concerned with literary quality as they process manuscripts.

Magazines represent the broadest possible range of literary effort, from concise news presentation to the most creative and best of prose. The breadth of the subject makes a thorough discussion of literary style impossible here; such a discussion would take volumes. In the last few years, however, there have been certain basic trends and points of emphasis in writing for all magazines that we can give attention to. These have included the demand for clarity and effective communication, as reflected in the work of many with readability research; the emphasis on humanizing even the most complex subjects in order to hold reader interest; and the emphasis on anecdotes, description, and narration in fact-article writing.

Beginning with the readability research of Rudolf Flesh in the 1940s, the work of several individuals in attempting to measure the effectiveness of writing has had a strong effect on magazines. Clarity of presentation is sought by virtually every magazine, and any method for measuring and improving writing on that score would naturally be welcomed. To exactly what degree the specific techniques of various systems are accepted and applied varies widely, but the effect of principles enunciated by these "readability experts" has been almost universal.

The Chilton Company, a Philadelphia-based publisher of specialized business magazines, employed Robert Gunning (*The Technique of Clear Writing* [New York: McGraw-Hill, 1968]) as a consultant for several years and applied his measurement system to its magazines. Three issues a year of each Chilton magazine were tested and the results shown on a graph that told the individual editors exactly where their scores placed their product in relation to a minimum standard. Gunning's system records a "fog index," the score based on average number of words per sentence and the number of "hard" words (three syllables or more). With a score of 13 as acceptable, Chilton officials were pleased to note a drop in score from their industrial publications from 14.4 to 12.9 in eight years. Merchandising magazines produced by Chilton also improved from 13.2 to 11.7. The company management was convinced that the improved scores reflected true improvement in their editorial offerings.

Not all magazine publishers use readability measurement in the same fashion. Nor do they all use the same systems or the same consultants. But, in general, the accepted conclusion has been that there are certain measurable aspects of writing that indicate the effectiveness of the writing sample in getting its message to readers. For those with an interest, some detailed study of readability systems will be helpful, but many editors concern themselves only with some general principles stemming from all the systems together. These include the following basic guidelines:

1. Short sentences are more effective than longer ones.
2. Shorter words are better than longer ones.
3. Common words are better than the uncommon.
4. Human interest, as measured by such things as personal references, adds to readability.

Although these guidelines tend to oversimplify the formulas of readability measurement, and the formulas themselves are imprecise yardsticks, there is merit in their use. In the unscientific world of written communication, even an imperfect base for judgment is welcome.

The first three readability guidelines are rather easy to apply. By reducing a words-per-sentence average from 50 to 18 or 20, an editor can be reasonably sure that he or she has improved the chances of reaching the receivers with the meaning of the message. If the editor can cut the syllables-per-word average from two to nearer to Flesch's suggested 1.5, he or she can also be relatively confident that reader comprehension will be better. And if the ratio of common words to total words improves, it is a tangible bit of evidence indicating improved readability.

The fourth guideline, however, is perhaps most important and most in need of attention. Readability research here is substantiating a long-standing empirical judgment of editors and writers: the interest the reader has in the subject has a direct bearing on his or her ability to read and understand written material. Given the subject, the editing job then is to maximize the reader's interest in it.

Humanizing for Maximum Interest

The dominant conclusion about getting and holding reader interest from which editors approach their work is that subjects need to be humanized whenever possible. To tell a story in terms of human beings instead of statistics—to show consequence in terms of one person or one family rather than to a mass—is to get a jump on readability by maximizing interest.

For example, a writer may submit an article on a subject that is of consequence and interest to a magazine's readers. In this case, let's assume the article is for a business publication serving retail office supply outlets and the title is "Ten Ways To Improve Stapler Sales." You know the article is based on interviews with several merchants who have been successful in greatly increasing their sale of staplers. The article as written is concise and highly readable from the three rhetorical aspects of readability measurement; sentences are short and words are short and common. The advice the article offers seems sound, and there is a built-in interest because the subject offers assistance to readers. The effort to inject more human interest into the article might, however, call for some revision. The approach might be changed to fit a new title: "Six Dealers Tell: HOW WE BOOSTED OUR STAPLER SALES." Instead of straightforward preaching to readers, the article would relate, in the words of the successful dealers, their own success stories. Additional readership would be expected because of the introduction of people and their experiences. Editorial hunches and readability measurement agree: people do like to read about people.

Anecdotes, Examples, and Description

The trend toward humanizing subjects when possible has been paralleled closely by an increased awareness of the need for adding color to writing. Competition for reader time has forced more effort in this direction. Also, the new generations brought up with a perpetual flow of entertainment coming from their television sets are forcing magazines to make even vital information take on some flavor of entertainment, if the magazines want them as readers. The result has been more and more emphasis on rhetorical devices traditionally rooted in fiction writing.

The anecdotal approach has become so pervasive that observers have complained about some articles being big Dagwood sandwiches with layer on layer of anecdotes, making it almost impossible to find the factual meat in between.

Be that as it may, skillful editors guide their writers into an approach that uses anecdotes, examples, and description to add color, action, life, and interest to articles of any subject. A good case in point is an article in *Medical Opinion,* a magazine written to a large extent by medical personnel. The article reached out for readers with the title: "Dream On, Bureaucracy, Dream On," and led into the text with the subtitle: "After you scrub with pHisoHex and relax with a cold Fresca, imagine that you're sitting in the FDA [Food and Drug Administration] and overhearing the discoveries of insulin, penicillin, and digitalis plead their cases for safety." Dr. Frank B. Nordstrom, the author, then began with an anecdote:

The ringing of the telephone dragged me away from Howard Cosell and the Monday night football game.

"This is the emergency room, Doctor. Mrs. Mortis has just brought her son in with a scalp laceration."

"Excellent. It's almost half time. I'll be down in a few minutes and sew him up."

Mrs. Crossman, our efficient ER nurse, had the area shaved and all the instruments laid out by the time I arrived. Donning gloves, I had started to clean the wound when Mrs. Mortis interrupted.

"You're not going to put that oily white poison on little Rigor's skin, are you?"

"Why, Mrs. Mortis, that isn't oily white poison. That's pHisoHex, an excellent germicide. It's more effective than. . . ."

"Apparently you don't keep up, Doctor," she replied in a voice edged with steel. "No son of mine will ever be smeared with the likes of that by the likes of you. Come Rigor, let's find a more competent physician."

Stunned, I drove home to the glowing TV tube, but not even the corn-pone brandishments of Dandy Don could erase the image of that bizarre scene.

The doctor continued his article with some dialogue that led into another anecdote, this one relating to the Food and Drug Administration's banning of a cyclamate soft drink. He then used a dream device with dialogue between a fictional FDA authority and the discoverers of insulin, penicillin, and digitalis leading to the banning of their discoveries because of side effects. The result was a fast moving satirical piece that made its point effectively and would produce a high score on any interest-measuring system besides.

Not all articles can get this type of treatment, and not all writers are able to carry it off, especially in highly technical fields. But when the opportunity does present itself, most editors welcome the anecdotal approach, especially if such opportunities are not commonplace.

The Mechanics of Style

Editors are expected to be experts in the mechanics of language. As they process manuscripts, one of their chores is to bring a meticulous correctness to the language being used. Although magazine audiences vary as to their sophistication and knowledge of language, it behooves every editor to strive for this correctness, because all audiences contain some self-styled grammarians who bitterly object to sloppy usage.

The primary problem for the editor, of course, stems from the fact that language does change and there is no absolute agreement on some points in the first place. But despite this truism, good editors will arm themselves with the best dictionary they can find plus a good manual of style and follow them as closely as they can and with consistency. By so doing they can be reasonably assured that their usage will pass muster with even the most discriminating readers. For editing changes made in the name of better usage, the final test must be, however, clarity of meaning.

Of special importance for any publication is uniformity in the mechanics of style. Clarity stems, to a great extent, from uniformity. For example, if comma usage is consistent throughout, variations in opinion on the use of commas at least do not interfere with intended meaning. Uniformity in capitalization, use of figures, and other variable aspects of mechanics (insofar as is possible) also contributes to an impression of careful editing and reliability.

Careful editing is essential to creation of a good editorial product. But care must be taken to prevent editing from interfering with an author's style. Authors often deliberately set aside some fine points of grammatical construction in order to achieve a special style dimension for their prose. This is their right, and editors should tolerate these variances, provided only that meaning is clear and the style peculiarity is, in fact, an effective device. Throughout all his work in processing manuscripts, the editor must be sensitive to the rights of his authors. Any change constituting meaningful revision should be referred back to the author for execution.

Creating Titles That Sell

Pound for pound, line for line, and word for word, titles that are both eye-catching and informative are the most effective sales tool an editor has for selling the content of a magazine. With only a few choice words, a title has more power to determine whether an article will be read than any other single element with which an editor has to work.

Along with photographs, titles are a primary tool for getting the reader's attention. Then, working with subtitles, they carry the basic responsibility for luring an audience into reading the articles they describe.

Therefore, regardless of what else might be said about titles, we must start with an appreciation of their goals: to capture readers, grab their interest, and persuade them to read an article.

Probably the best source for aid in writing and presenting effective titles is the work of the best professionals who, weekly or monthly, create and publish titles that pass their tests in the marketplace.

Also, there are textbooks for magazine article writing that contain much useful information about creating effective titles because writers, too, are involved in their preparation. In some instances, writers phrase very effective titles that can be used as they are, or with only slight modification. Sometimes even a free lancer, who has studied the market well, hits the bullseye with a title.

But in the vast majority of instances, the final published titles show the fine hand of the editor. In developing titles, whether modifying an author's efforts or starting anew, editors work with better perspective because they have a complete verbal-visual package in mind. They don't restrict themselves to phrasing alone, or type display alone, or placement alone. They are also aware of their illustrations and the assistance that can come from a subtitle. They work as if all these elements are members of a team, each to be used for maximum effect in achieving readership. And all along the way they know they must work within certain space limits and that brevity and conciseness are mandated.

In many ways, titles are an editor's severest test of word skill and judgment; he or she must pick the exact few words that will most accurately describe their subject and, at the same time, appeal to the greatest possible number of readers. Titles can also represent the editor's toughest test of creativity as he or she tries to make them unique, or at least different enough to be appealing.

Writing Effective Titles

Title writing is creative because there are no limits to their form. Anything goes as far as literary devices are concerned. Form follows function, however, if titles are to be truly effective. Consequently, we shall first look at titles from the standpoint of content.

In content, titles usually fall into one of these two groupings: *descriptive* or *suspenseful,* those that tell and those that tease. A descriptive title is written primarily to give information about its article; it is assumed that interest will be aroused because the article's subject and approach are interesting. A suspenseful title is written to tease, to arouse curiosity by withholding some basic information for the article itself to reveal. Most editors, confident in their content, place greater reliance on descriptive titles.

Descriptive Titles

The preference for descriptive titles stems from a conviction that most readers look to a title for a quick answer to one basic question: "What is this article about?" Some editors are even convinced that readers are sometimes alienated when attempts to be cute or to build suspense delay the answer to this question beyond the title.

Descriptive titles can be dull and unimaginative, but they need not be. As we shall see, they can vary widely in form; the fact that they are intended to be straightforward answers to basic questions does not limit creativity in approach.

This demand for creativity of approach varies somewhat with the potential lack or latency of interest of readers. It also increases with the competition for reader attention from other media or other activities. The reader who has a built-in interest in a subject and picks up a specialized interest magazine looking for information can be enticed to read on without any special gimmicks. If the title tells readers in specific, accurate terms what the article is about, they'll probably read it. Even in these instances, however, it is not wise to accept an audience as "captive" and proceed to bore it with unimaginative titles; all audiences are subjected to competition for their time from other media or activities.

Nonetheless, what is perhaps the most common descriptive title is a simple label consisting of only a noun, or a noun with a modifier or two. Although there is nothing spectacular in its rhetorical form, this basic type is widely used in magazines of all descriptions, as these examples indicate:

Farm and Ranch Vacations (*Family Circle*)
Skier's Picnic (*Ford Times*)
Newark's Street People Teachers (*American Education*)
The Miraculous New Eye Exams (*Woman's Day*)
The Tempting Siren Called Speed (*Reader's Digest*)
Those Fantastic Planes of World War I (*Boys' Life*)

The following examples, although they are somewhat different because they begin with a verb form, are substantially the same from the standpoint of content:

Learning To Like New Zealand (*Holiday*)
Scouting in Denmark (*Boys' Life*)
Decorating with Quilts (*House and Garden*)
Stalking Wild Foods on a Desert Isle (*National Geographic*)

The titles in both these lists simply represent, in each instance, the attempt on the part of an editor to give a simple, direct answer to the reader's natural question: "What's this article about?" The same objective is present in these examples:

Machiavelli: The Man and the Reputation (*Reader's Digest*)
Health Care Politics: How the Game Is Played (*Medical Opinion*)
Communications Update: Intercoms (*Modern Office Procedures*)
Richie: My Son, My Enemy (*Reader's Digest*)
A Dry Basement: The Myth That Becomes a Reality (*Good Housekeeping*)

In the above five instances the editors are shifting the word order of each so that the central subjects can be given primary display, with the modifiers being pushed into a secondary position. A variation of this form incorporates a question following the subject designation.

Employee Loyalty: Where Is It? (*Journal of Organizational Communication*)
Web Offset Air Pollution: Just How Serious Is It Today? (*Inland Printer and American Lithographer*)
U.S. Military: Servant or Master? (*Reader's Digest*)
Being a Working Wife: How Well Does It Work? (*Reader's Digest*)
Paris High Society: Is It in Decline? (*Newsweek*)
The Three-Year B.A.: Boon or Bust? (*AAUP Bulletin*)

Although the question portion of this title form may, in some instances, constitute an effort to arouse a reader's curiosity, it usually is designed to help the title be more specific. One of the basic tests of a good descriptive title is the degree of specificity it has. Any title that would fit, without alteration, more than one article, is probably in need of revision. It almost certainly is too general in scope. Articles take specific approaches to subjects, and titles should reveal that approach. Consider, for example, an article on hogs for a farm magazine. It might be titled with just that one word. But that obviously is too general because readers have been exposed to scores of hog articles before. The title might be made more specific if it is given one modifier and becomes "Hog Care," but actually it still would not be sufficiently tailored to the writer's approach to the subject. Even "Tips on Hog Care" is still too general, as well as trite. In one such article for the *Farm Journal* the author's approach was to show that farmers suffer losses on hogs that get bruised on their way to market. More specifically, his piece related examples of specific dollar losses resulting from bruised carcasses. The title as it appeared was "It Costs $5 to Kick a Hog," a statement that was specifically tied to the article's approach, or slant. It brought a high readership score for the article.

One way to show the approach of many articles is to start a title with *how, what,* or *why.* This title form is especially common among specialized magazines because the readers of these magazines are often looking to them for information about the hows, whys, and whats of their profession or avocation. But their use is not restricted to any single magazine type, as these examples show:

How To Hang Anything on a Wall (*Family Circle*)
How To Care for Gift Plants (*Good Housekeeping*)
How To Make Schools Fit for Children (*Better Homes and Gardens*)
How To Talk to a Baby (*Reader's Digest*)
What It Takes To Keep a Big Rig Planting (*Successful Farming*)
What Revenue Sharing Means to Education (*American Education*)
Why the Vietnam War Drags On (*U.S. News & World Report*)
Why Father Zicarelli Is Now in Poughkeepsie (*New Yorker*)

In several of the examples already presented the title writer obviously tried to inject some extra spice and variety by employing special word tricks. Such rhetorical techniques for titles are unlimited. In fact, when it comes to form, the classifications of titles seemingly have no limit. Every gimmick a word artist can conceive is a potential title device, provided only that some caution and good sense are used. Gimmickry that stands out as gimmickry can be worse than a straightforward approach. But the unique, the offbeat, the clever twist that gives a title something special is a source of pride for the editor and a joy to readers.

Some Special Title Gimmicks

Rhyme, alliteration, puns, figures of speech, coined words, deliberate repetition, and literary allusion are some of the devices that can be enlisted in the effort to get special appeal for titles. Here are a few examples from contemporary magazines:

Take a Gander at These Geese (*Better Living*)
The Guest Is Best at Saratoga (*Sports Illustrated*)
The Pill in Perspective (*Reader's Digest*)
The New Liberated Lingerie (*Woman's Day*)
Boy on a Barge (*Boys' Life*)
Age of Shovelry (*Reader's Digest*)
Rip-roarin' Rural Sport (*Country Living*)
Blazering Along the Gunflint Trail (*Chevy Camper*)
Bungalows for Bluebirds (*Ford Times*)

Quotations also serve as a handy title device. Personal accounts naturally lend themselves to quotation titles which may, in their form or content, fit other categories. The mimicking brought on by a rash of such titles as "I Was a Spy for the FBI" has not deterred editors from using them, including the rhyming and alliteration that has subjected them to mimickry. Entertainment magazines (movies, radio-tv) make most use of quotation titles, but so do some general and other special interest periodicals, as the following examples indicate:

"The Summer I Wrapped Cabbage Heads" (*Reader's Digest*)
"How I Played Third Base" (*Boys' Life*)
"I Thought We'd Take the Din out of Dinner" (*Reader's Digest*)
"Bill Cosby Reveals: 'Why I Am Becoming a Teacher' " (*Family Circle*)
"What I Learned from Three Cultures" (*Redbook*)

Involving the Reader

The reader can be brought into the title through the use of direct address; hopefully, readers will be enticed into the article because the title is directed to them. As can be seen in some question titles any literary form can be involved in direct address ("Do You Know How to Play With Your Child?" and "How To Impress Your Coach"). Here are other examples:

If You Want Help on Your Income Tax Return (*Reader's Digest*)
So You Think You Own Your Own Land! (*Farm Journal*)
You, Too, Can Find Connubial Chaos (*Reader's Digest*)
Take Your Pick of the World's Jazziest Hamburgers (*Family Circle*)
How To Drive Your Children Sane (*Reader's Digest*)

Asking a Question

A common alternative to the basic label telling what an article is about is the question title. If an editor knows his or her readers well enough to select a subject that solves a common problem or answers a question on their minds—and then asks that same question or poses that problem in the title—he or she has a natural winner. The question form seems to rank second in popularity only to the basic label, perhaps because in many ways it is simply a disguise. Analyze these two question titles:

Do You Know How To Play with Your Child? (*Woman's Day*)
Raise Hogs in the Dark? (*Farm Journal*)

Both could have been presented as positive statements: "How To Play with Your Child," and "Raising Hogs in the Dark." Both would then have been typical descriptive titles. By putting them in the form of a question the editor attempts to make them a little more thought-provoking and intriguing. But they nevertheless answer the basic question: "What is the article about?"

Suspense Titles

On the whole, however, the primary goal of the question form is to arouse interest and create suspense to carry the reader into the article. Note that these deliberately withheld information:

What Chance for a United States of Europe? (*Reader's Digest*)
Are Kids Psyching You Out? (*Learning*)
Does More Time in School Make a Difference? (*Saturday Review*)
Should You Own Property Together? (*Better Homes and Gardens*)
Is the U.S. Going Broke? (*Reader's Digest*)

Readers have to go at least to a subtitle before they know the answer to these questions; it is hoped that their interest has been piqued sufficiently to get them to read beyond that.

Another form used to create suspense is the provocative statement, one that is so startling, so contrary to a reader's knowledge or assumptions, or so general that it teases him to read on. With these titles the goal is to arouse questions in the readers' minds that can be answered by the article. Each of the titles below raises such questions:

Dr. Land's "Impossible Dream" (*Popular Science*)
2,400 Miles by Hand Power (*Sports Illustrated*)
Convoy to Nowhere (*Aramco World*)
Fables, Foibles, and Fools (*Ohio Bell Voice*)
A Moment Can Last Forever (*Reader's Digest*)
Love, Marriage—And Crime (*Reader's Digest*)

All of the literary gimmicks can be employed in suspenseful titles, too. Alliteration, puns, and the like are not restricted to any particular category. As a matter of fact, our attempts to categorize titles does not mean that rigid classifications really exist; even a quick look at the examples presented will reveal instances in which titles fit several categories. Nor do we mean to imply that editors do or should approach titles with categories in mind. Ever-present should be the image of the reader and the goals that a title should achieve. If a title appeals to readers sufficiently to "flag them down" and encourage them to read further, it is a good title.

So far, our discussion has been limited primarily to the main title. It is obvious that in many cases, especially those that deliberately tease the reader by withholding information from the main title, subtitles will be needed. Although subtitles have a value as a visual transition from large type to small type, their more important function is to increase the reader interest that the title has spawned. They are vital bridges between title and text.

In order to cause reader interest to grow, subtitles are usually written to provide detail that wouldn't fit into the main section. Their goal can be related to the sales role of titles; any sale requires a clincher, something the customer can't resist, something to "close" the sale. The effective title sparks the interest, while the subtitle closes the sale.

Subtitles may follow the approach started by the main title, or they may shift the direction. For example, if the top title is a label, the subtitle may simply be an attempt to add some interesting facts; it carries forward the assumption that, if the article is accurately described in the title, readers will come to it. Or the label title may be followed by a question or some other device to suspend reader interest by creating curiosity. With suspended interest titles the same options are open—follow with a subtitle that is in the same vein, or shift to one that is descriptive. All the literary techniques, from allusion to puns, are also appropriate for subtitles.

Let's look at some of the titles already cited as examples to see how various editors employed subtitles. Following its title based on an allusion to the well-known advertising line, "When You're No. 2, You Try Harder," *Sports Illustrated* added specific facts and word tricks:

WHEN YOU'RE NO. 2, YOU DIET

When Jurgensen was hurt, Billy Killmer became the No. 1 Redskin quarterback. However, don't count Sonny out, he's counting calories

And in another article, *Sports Illustrated* followed with facts that came in question form:

2,400 MILES BY HAND POWER

Or how else would you get a surfboard from Boston to Miami?

Following a catchy title, *Woman's Day* used a subtitle beginning with a question and ending with more specific facts:

THE NEW LIBERATED LINGERIE

What's going on? Nothing much!
That's what's great about the
new underthings. They're airy,
light, stretchy, comfortable. Just
like a second skin, only better

The preceding examples all show subtitles as independent units following a main title. Even this aspect of usage is subject to variation. Some titles are really dependent, either reading into the title or out of it and not standing independently. Or, as the following example from *Popular Science* illustrates, it can combine both techniques.

Come for a ride on
BILL LEAR'S NEW STEAM BUS
A light steam turbine drives this converted bus.
Will it perform reliably?
Free of emissions?
And how does it compare with the diesel?

Here, also from *Popular Science,* is a short subtitle leading into the longer main title:

Now They're Building
AIRPORTS THAT TAKE THE HASSLE
OUT OF CATCHING YOUR PLANE

Fortune led into a moderately long title with a subtitle of about 30 words:

"Beneath the ritual histrionics of the presidential campaign, deeply divisive forces are tearing at the U.S. political system. The Republicans will have trouble of their own, but a far graver threat is

THE TIME BOMB INSIDE
THE DEMOCRATIC PARTY

The editors of *Women's Day* gave excellent graphic treatment to a main title (Pick Me Ups Under $10) that led into a routinely displayed subtitle:

> Add a little magic to a familiar
> sunny-day wardrobe—new snap,
> new shine—to lift the spirits
> without lightening the
> purse too much

The Blurb Background as a Subtitle

A few words about the author or circumstances surrounding the preparation of an article are often used in much the same fashion as a subtitle. Called "blurbs," these word groups are displayed just as subtitles are, and often perform the same function. The stamp of authority can be put on an article through use of a blurb that establishes the qualifications of the author; audience interest can be stimulated by promotional material contained in the blurb.

When in Doubt, Use Subtitles

The examples of subtitles given here are only a small sample of the potential variations; as with titles, there is really no limitation on their manner of presentation. These examples do show, however, the importance and need of subtitles. As a general rule, titles need the extra, more specific information that comes from a subtitle before they really tell a reader what he or she wants to know before deciding to read an article. When in doubt, it is wise to assume that the reader needs a subtitle as the second part of a one-two combination.

So What Are Subheads?

Subtitles are sometimes called *subheads,* but actually the terms are not synonymous. Subheads are units of type display usually used between paragraphs as headings for the portion of the article immediately following. They have traditionally been used as a means for some typographical relief in a large mass of body type. They can be used in a wide variety of forms, however, and they can also serve a more useful function.

Rather than being used merely for visual relief, with little or no attention being given to their content, subheads can be useful "rechargers" of reader interest. If they are to be effective, care should be exercised in their writing so they do encourage a reader to continue. Without meaningful content, subheads are often no better as visual aids than white space which, when judiciously used, can break up type masses and provide optical reference points just as well as type.

Figure 7–1 Subheads, if given special treatment, can relieve monotony and create interest. (Courtesy *Journal of Organizational Communications, American Education, Tempo.*)

Common forms for subheads include single boldface lines that are centered or placed either flush to the left or flush to the right. Capitalization and special boldness given to the first few words of a paragraph can also create the effect of a subhead. These are traditional newspaper forms, and they find their best usage in the magazine field among "newsy" magazines.

Other magazines, some of them not concerned with news material, have developed forms that give more responsibility to subheads. Meaningfully written and given special size, important position and/or special graphic treatment, these subheads are, in reality, titles for the portions of articles they precede. Figure 7–1 shows how some editors have employed subheads effectively.

Headlines in Magazines

Headlines, like the traditional subheads, are a product of the newspaper. As the name implies, headlines are standardized lines of type used to head a story and are placed at the top of their story. In selling news to readers, they are probably unbeatable. They have been perfected in newspaper offices with that goal in mind, and there is no reason why they should not serve the same functions in magazines.

Their use has served *Time, Newsweek,* and *U.S. News & World Report* well because of the content and general style of these newsmagazines. There are also many specialized newsmagazines, such as *Editor & Publisher, Chemical Week,* and scores of others, that also rely on newspaper-style headlines. Timeliness and a news orientation are usually the characteristics that point magazines toward headlines rather than individually designed titles.

The attributes of a good magazine headline are the same as those of a newspaper headline.[4] They usually contain one to three lines of display type, all of the same size and style, and usually flush left. They may contain a second unit (deck) of one to three lines in a smaller type size. Each deck is a skeletonized sentence that tells, as concisely as possible, the gist of the news that follows. And each may include a short line above or below the main lines to create some white space, but rarely is much extra white space used. Unlike magazine titles, headlines do not get a third-, half-, or full-page of space for display; and unlike magazine titles, they are often all from the same type family.

The following are helpful maxims for writing effective news headlines:

1. Headlines should be skeletonized sentences.
2. All headlines should include a verb, except when the verb would be a form of "to be" and is implied in the headline.
3. If possible, the verb should be in the first line in order to give action to that line.
4. Every line of a headline should be a complete thought unit; hence an adjective and its noun should be on the same line and a verb and its auxiliary should be on the same line.
5. It is possible, and sometimes preferable, to omit the subject in a headline (as in "Sues Partner for Contract Cancellation").
6. Headlines should be specific.
7. Headlines must be accurate; their condensation should not permit ambiguities or misleading implications.
8. Any abbreviations used should be well known to readers.

Correction and Verification

Editors have forever been faced with two truisms. One is that nothing does a publication more damage than errors, especially when they occur frequently enough to create an impression of carelessness. The other is that no matter how great the effort, errors sneak into copy, sometimes in the most surprising places. There is scarcely an editor alive who has not experienced the dismay of finding a *typo* (typographical error) in a title line in huge type after every remote detail of the body copy was carefully checked and re-checked. Sometimes the obvious is overlooked while minute detail is thoroughly scrutinized.

Despite the inevitability of errors (even *Time* and *Newsweek,* protected by armies of researchers and the most skilled of editors, must occasionally "eat" inaccuracies), the battle against them never ceases. Although absolute accuracy may be a holy grail always sought and never achieved, the continual effort to keep errors at a minimum has resulted in a high standard of accuracy among American magazines. Every procedure that can serve to ferret out errors, large or small, has been and continues to be a must for all magazines.

One of the best guardians against error is a knowledgeable editor. Editors who are well-read, who have stored away in their bank of knowledge great quantities of information, are going to be able to detect errors that would go unnoticed by less capable guardians of a magazine's reputation. The broad educational backgrounds required of modern journalism students, if backed up by a continuing search for knowledge, provides an indispensable quality for the making of a good editor. In the editing of specialized magazines, this broad background must be complemented by detailed knowledge of the magazine's specialized area. The editor of a farm publication must know farming; the editor of an oil industry periodical must be an expert in that field; and so it goes for any specialized subject. In highly technical fields, even the best-prepared editor may find it necessary to use the additional safeguard of an advisory board for the reading and evaluation of manuscripts.

Much more checking and re-checking with sources is required of the magazine journalist than the newspaper writer or editor, if for no other reason than that time permits it. It is much better to have sources verify the material they have provided before publication than it is to have them complain about inaccuracy after publication.

The "How" of Copy Editing

The copy editor of a daily newspaper no doubt envies the time between issues available to the editors of weekly, biweekly and monthly magazines. Magazine editors appreciate their time advantage; they realize that it represents the opportunity to give their copy the added dimension it must have to compete with other media. But this time advantage must be, and is, taken up with providing the additional depth and quality expected from magazines. It does not provide any opportunity for less efficient handling of copy.

Traditional Copy Editing

Consequently, as magazine editors work with a manuscript, they use every shortcut and efficient procedure available to them. Primary among these is a set of symbols for marking corrections of grammar, punctuation, spelling, and mechanics of style. These copy editing symbols, although they may vary slightly in their use from one office to another, are essentially standardized among all print media. As one can see in figure 7–2, they are based on common sense and the desire to be quick and efficient in relating changes to a printer. The beginner should be certain to avoid confusing these symbols with those used to mark corrections after copy has been set in type. Proofreading symbols are used for that purpose. The essential characteristics of copy editing symbols is that changes are marked at the point errors occur and not in the margin. All copy for typesetting should be typed double- or triple-spaced to permit use of these marks in the line and at the spot they occur. Figure 7–3 shows an article that has been corrected using copy editing symbols.

Computerized Copy Processing

As each day goes by, more and more copy editing is being handled via computerized devices. Word processing software varies among computers; the exact procedures vary according to the brand of the device being used.

Proprietary systems, designed by vendors offering their specialized wares to print media publishers, are highly sophisticated and have been geared to permit complex correcting and copy manipulation with very few key strokes. Some multi-purpose

Figure 7–2 Copy editing symbols.

COPY EDITING SYMBOLS

Desired Correction	Symbol to Use
1. Change small letter to capital	a̲
2. Change capital to small letter	A̸
3. Change form in numerals or abbreviations:	
3 to three	③
three to 3	⟨three⟩
Street to St.	⟨Street⟩
St. to Street	⟨St.⟩
4. **To start a new paragraph**	⌐Now is the
5. To put space between words	Now|is
6. To close up (remove space)	home ‿town
7. To delete a letter and close up	judgͤment
8. To delete words or two or more letters	to ~~fully~~ receive
9. To delete one letter and substitute another	beli̶eve
10. To delete two or more letters and close up	accommo̶dodate
11. To insert letters or words	not ^quite well
12. To transpose letters or words if adjacent	reci̶eve
13. To insert punctuation:	
comma ^ colon ⁝ apostrophe ᵛ	
period ⨀ exclamation ⎮ opening quote �...⟍	
question mark ? hyphen ＝ closing quote ("	
semicolon ⁏ dash — parentheses ( )	
14. To center material	⌐News Notes⌐
15. To indent material	⌐All the lines⌐ are indented
16. Set in boldface type	The news today
17. Set in italic type	The news today
18. To delete several lines or paragraphs, box in the material and X it out	⬚

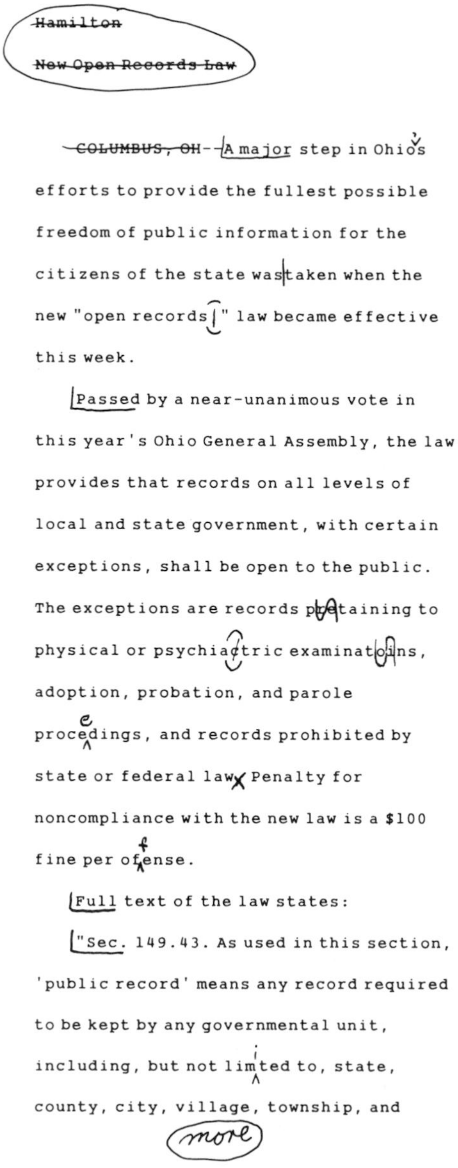

⟨Hamilton⟩

⟨New Open Records Law⟩

~~COLUMBUS, OH~~—⌐A major step in Ohio's efforts to provide the fullest possible freedom of public information for the citizens of the state was taken when the new "open records‿" law became effective this week.

⌐Passed by a near-unanimous vote in this year's Ohio General Assembly, the law provides that records on all levels of local and state government, with certain exceptions, shall be open to the public. The exceptions are records pertaining to physical or psychiatric examinations, adoption, probation, and parole proceedings, and records prohibited by state or federal law⨯ Penalty for noncompliance with the new law is a $100 fine per offense.

⌐Full text of the law states:

⌐"Sec. 149.43. As used in this section, 'public record' means any record required to be kept by any governmental unit, including, but not limited to, state, county, city, village, township, and

⟨more⟩

Figure 7–3 A page of a manuscript after copy editing. Note that all corrections are made at the point of error, not in the margin.

personal computers have more complex and less sophisticated provisions for basic copy editing, but there are principles that prevail for most systems.

As one can learn from experience with traditional copy editing, the corrections and changes made by editors range from minor, single-character changes to total rewriting of certain passages. Computerized systems have compressed these into five basic maneuvers: (1) delete, (2) add, (3) replace, (4) transpose, and (5) move.

To permit these maneuvers, copy is displayed in quantity on a video screen comparable to that of a small TV set, or in just a few words or a line on a very small screen. Access to the point of the change to be made is usually by way of a cursor (a light that can be moved from place to place by keys or other devices such as a pointer).

Function keys, usually grouped together, are used to make the necessary changes. A single stroke with a function key, often labled *delete* or *kill,* is usually sufficient to remove undesired material. The material is delineated by placement of the cursor, and is usually removed by a stroke of a *character, word, sentence, paragraph,* or *block* key, depending upon the amount of material to be deleted.

Material is easily added by placement of the cursor in the designated position. The material on the display opens up for the insertion of the new material as it is typed. The material inserted can range from a single character to a long passage. Replacement is usually just as easy. A single key stroke usually places the terminal in *overstrike* mode, thus causing the computer to delete each letter as another is keyed to that position.

Simple transpositions are usually handled by deleting and adding. With letters or words side-by-side, one of them is deleted, the cursor is moved to the new location and the deleted character or word is restored there.

Movement of copy from one location in an article to another is also easily done. All that is usually required is that the extent of the copy to be moved be designated by a key stroke (sentence, paragraph, etc.), the new location be identified by the

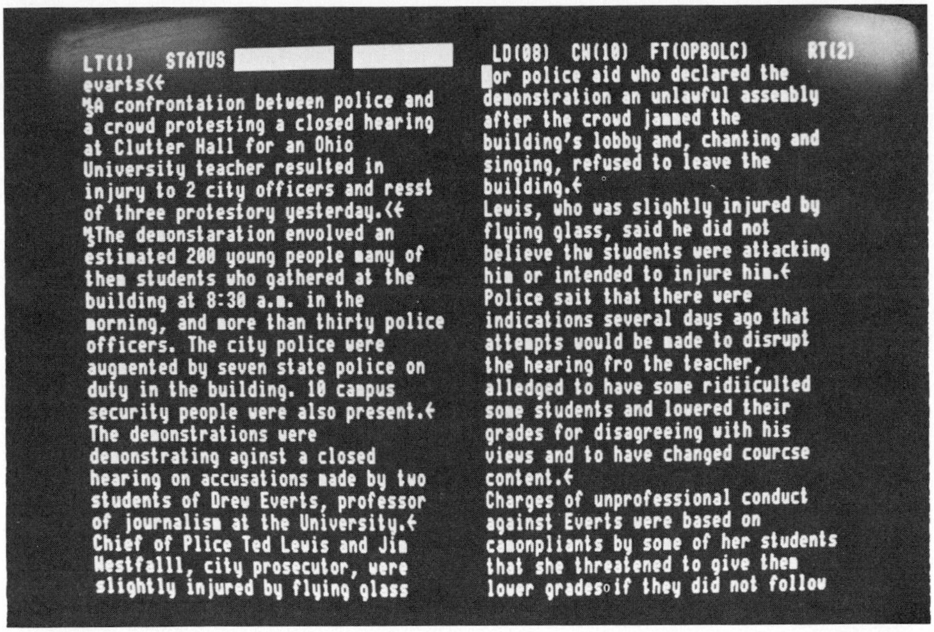

Figure 7-4 Split screen editing. With notes or one version of a story on one half of the screen, editors can work with a different version on the other half. Blocks of copy can be moved from one side of the screen to the other. (Photo by Ralph Kliesch.)

cursor, and a *move* key be struck. The most complex copy editing, traditionally handled by scissors-and-paste-pot rearranging of blocks of copy, thus, can be handled very efficiently by computers.

The use of a *split screen* is an example of the ultimate means for major changes (see figure 7–4). Specialized computer systems that provide for splitting the screen enable editors to look at rough material on one side of their terminals, while typing and viewing a new version on the other. Or it permits the display of two versions of an article side-by-side on the screen, with the capability of moving portions of either version from one side to the other.

Production-related aspects of copy editing also show the advantages of computerized editing. Fitting of copy to space and specifying printers' instructions are routinely handled by computerized systems, especially those that form complete front-end systems, from keyboard to type proofs. The fact that all parts of the system have been designed to work together makes communication among the parts simple and easy. Working with human printers is sometimes more difficult.

The necessity to prepare raw materials so printers can produce magazines efficiently points up the dual nature of magazine editing. As they attempt to make content match readers' needs, editors must also edit the material to meet the needs of their production partners, the printers.

Many of the production aspects of editing are looked upon as techniques, skills, or chores because they do relate directly to the manufacturing of the magazine. It is true that there are techniques and skills to be learned, but there is creativity involved also. We hope that a realization of the feeling of satisfaction derived from seeing an issue proceed from raw materials to finished product will emerge from later chapters devoted to the production aspects of editing.

Two other points should also be made here: (1) not all editing decisions can be based entirely on creative urges; cost of production is always a factor, and (2) research must be used to keep editors in tune with their readers. The next chapter shows how research can provide basic guidelines for creative decisions.

Notes

1. Lane M. Palmer, *Publishing Magazines To Meet Reader Needs and Interests* (Madison: Department of Agricultural Journalism, University of Wisconsin, 1971) p. 71.
2. Ibid, p. 20.
3. Ibid, p. 26.
4. For more thorough discussion of headlines, see Bruce Westley, *News Editing* (New York: Houghton Mifflin, 1980).

8

Magazine Research

"I'LL gamble a hunch against a statistic anytime," Herbert Mayes of *McCall's* often said. Ben Hibbs, while editor of *Saturday Evening Post,* wrote an article "You Can't Edit a Magazine by Arithmetic" for *Journalism Quarterly.* But even the best hunch can be checked against research data, though no one can guarantee that either a hunch or a research-based decision will pay off.

Research can provide important information and help editors make decisions, but it seldom can make a decision for an editor. Research is based in the past, telling you how readers responded to material that has been published. Research findings usually cannot tell you what future results may be, nor what to do to get better responses from readers. This inconclusive nature of research as a predictor irritates editors who prefer clear yes-no answers and puzzles many others.

Journalists believe in knowing everything possible before making decisions, so it is natural to use available research data and to foster additional research. A full-scale research bureau or department isn't necessary, nor is a continuing effort that always looks at the same situations or aspects of publishing. Public opinion and market research organizations can be retained to do occasional research projects that may be more productive and helpful than continuous research by a big, established research department within the publishing company. Results of other people's research can suggest approaches to editing as well as additional research studies to undertake.

Theodore Peterson told a group of editors how they can use research: (1) to make decisions about the mechanics of editing, (2) for guidance in choosing content, and (3) to put their jobs and goals into perspective by gaining insight into communication behavior generally.

Mechanics of Editing

Numerous studies have provided a wealth of information about how material presented one way is more effective than that presented another way. Titles, captions, illustration size, type size and leading, and subtitles have been studied. In many instances custom or common belief has been confirmed by research; in fewer instances it has been found erroneous.

Article Titles

Saturday Evening Post, Wallaces Farmer, Wisconsin Agriculturalist, Farm Journal, and other magazines have researched the effect of titles upon readers. The overall finding has been that readers do not like cryptic or unclear titles; they don't like being tricked into reading something they may not be interested in. Readers tend to react more favorably to dramatic words and titles they can identify with, including words like "I," "how-to," and "you."

Subtitles had been viewed by some editors as giving away too much of the article and thereby reducing readership. Research, though, found the opposite. Using subtitles increases readership, and the best location is beneath the title. This supports the finding that people will read what they are interested in, therefore telling them more about the article makes the title more recognizable, and sharpens their interest. If subtitles are placed above the title for variety, *Saturday Evening Post* found it most effective for them to read directly into the title, rather than be a separate unit of thought.

Captions

Photographers occasionally insist that a photo is too good to be ruined by a caption. But captions nearly always are needed to complete the story that a photo only begins—to set the location, the time, the sequence of events, the significance or outcome, and the identity of persons involved. Research has supported the case for captions, indicating that readers prefer full, informative captions placed near the picture they explain. Individual captions for each picture are preferred to a single block of captions describing several photos.

Wilson Hicks, first picture editor of *Life* and later its executive editor, so firmly believed that words and pictures have to combine into a single idea when neither is complete without the other that he titled a major address "One Word is Worth 10,000 Pictures." Words provide the corrective for camera distortion, translating a three-dimensional scene into a two-dimensional picture, or selecting only one representation of a sequence of events. The camera lies, often unintentionally, and words are needed to put the scene in its proper context.

Layout

Most layout studies have confirmed existing practices or beliefs, at least in essentially mechanical areas. For example:

1. Large illustrations generally draw more readers than small ones.
2. Unusually shaped halftones—tilted, football-shaped, jagged, silhouetted—tend to irritate readers. They prefer square finish halftones.
3. Photographs are more effective than sketches in illustrating articles. The most effective sketches are clear, realistic ones.
4. Four-color photos increase readership but black halftones are second, not duotones or black halftones printed on colored tint blocks.
5. Readers prefer (in a ratio of about two to one) conventional layouts in this order: picture, headline or title, deck or subtitle, body type. Placing the title beneath body type seems disordered or unnatural.
6. People are reluctant to read more than two or three lines of italic body type. Research does not clearly indicate that it is more difficult to read italics but simply that readers won't stick with it.
7. The standing head in the department or column should not overwhelm the head or title about this issue's specific topic. Constant readers will seek the standing head, but the fresh head can bring in readers who might skim over that department or column.
8. Readers usually see the lead picture and read its caption first, before reading the lead of the article, so the article lead should not be a repetition of the caption.
9. Pictures grouped together have greater reader interest than pictures scattered throughout an article. A group of pictures tends to function as one large illustration instead of several small ones.
10. A small amount of text and large picture on the opening page seems to increase readership; as, for example, about 20 percent text and 80 percent illustration.
11. Pictures should not be so small they are difficult to see. Something not worth showing large enough to see is not worth showing. [Editors who feel compelled to use pictures because they have them or have paid for them should develop the art of discarding anything marginal or questionable. Every time you add a picture to a layout, you increase the competition among the pictures for the reader's attention and decrease the potential readership of each picture.]
12. For titles, readers seem to prefer simple type faces that are familiar to them from a variety of publications.

Other studies have been unable to detect significant differences between readers' preferences for ordinary type design and design considered superior by a jury of graphic design experts. Such findings are disconcerting to art directors and designers who try to match the mood of the face to the content or emotion of the article. One operational principle is to avoid the monotony of using all simple, widely-used faces for titles, while also avoiding faces so ornate they are difficult to read or attract too much attention to themselves.

Some indications of type face legibility have been ascertained, but most of that research was conducted on books and may not be wholly applicable to magazine column width. Also the introduction and use of sans serif faces, such as Optima, that avoid the former monotone strokes may change reader reaction. Recent research continues to confirm that Roman type can be read faster than other faces.

In planning the break of the book, editors may want to consider that one-fourth of their readers start at the back and move to the front. Features at the back in one- and two-page units can capture attention and create something of an opening section for readers who begin at the back. Reader research also suggests it is wise to open the editorial section at the front of the book with the article that is expected to appeal to the largest number of readers.

Even reasonably clear research findings such as these are not something to be slavishly followed. Magazines would become dreadfully monotonous and dull if every spread looked almost like every other one because research suggested that a certain treatment was more effective. Obviously for one type of layout to be more effective than others it must be compared with others. Monotony of design might decrease effectiveness throughout.

One added observation here seems important. Some well-designed magazines use the same type face, size, line length, and number of lines for every article title. Often called "bookish" layout, this is used in think and opinion magazines and some news magazines where readers are expected to actively seek out the content they wish to read. Journalism students often turn automatically to the "Press" or "The Media" departments of *Time* or *Newsweek* and would continue to do so regardless of the typographic dress of those magazines. Readers of *New Republic* are accustomed to their magazine and know how to read it. They would be startled by dazzling graphics and probably would protest. An editor assimilating research data should not fall for just anything that tests well. Adopting it may change the magazine so much that it would alienate its readers and fail to attract new ones. When graphics become distractive and get in the way of reading, readers tend to rebel.

Choosing Content

Choice of content is an editorial decision, even when research results are available. A major finding is that articles of expected low readership combined with several of large readership can reach a larger total audience than an issue of all higher readership items. A study of 47 issues of *Saturday Evening Post* found that aiming one-half to two-thirds of the editorial content to majority readership and using the remainder of space for special or unusual features of low interest resulted in higher total readership because people who normally would not buy the magazine were attracted to an article that did not appeal to the majority of *Post* readers.

Farm Journal editors go out to check with their readers periodically. By nature, the dairy editor goes to dairy country and finds high readership of dairy articles. The hog editor goes to hog farming areas, with like results. They also report back to headquarters that general articles on schools and health are low in readership. The overall picture is, however, that the general articles that departmental editors find low in readership are consistently read across all farming specialties, which adds up to relatively higher readership. The hog farmers are not reading dairy articles, and the dairy farmers are not reading hog articles; consequently, the readership of these articles may not be as high as the more general material.

An editor may find it useful to visualize a core of the magazine, one-half to two-thirds, as being aimed at the general or overall readership and the remainder as an opportunity to serve special interests of both existing and potential readers. A book like *Farm Journal* or *Business Week,* of course, serves special interests with continuing departments, but some portion of each issue should be available for low-interest material that the readership is not expecting.

Related to this is the reader's intensity of interest, which often is difficult to gauge. Only 5 percent of the readers of an employee magazine may read an article on an employee speakers bureau, but those who do may be intensely interested in it, perhaps as part of the speakers bureau. The same holds for promotions and other personal items in some magazines. No one advocates giving the entire magazine to this type of content, but intense reader interest among a small number can contribute to greater overall readership of the issue.

An occasional survey can identify topics that deserve further or different treatment. When transferability of milk quotas was a complex issue in Wisconsin, *Wisconsin Agriculturalist* found that 72 percent of the farmers had not heard of the issue. More discussion of the issue was appropriate so farmers could vote on it intelligently.

Understanding of readers also helps to temper judgments that otherwise would be based on folklore. *Business Week* once ran pictures of bathing beauties to illustrate an article on the Jantzen company. Everyone knows that readers like pictures of pretty girls. Although the pictures were too large to be ignored, they were outscored in readership by four charts on the state of the economy, a picture of a new Cadillac, a picture of an old Rolls Royce, and two of "the worst pictures of a tunnel" the editor had ever seen. Businessmen read *BW* for business information rather than photos of models in swim suits.

An executive at *Life* already knew that pretty girls, babies, and animals on covers don't help sell magazines. Analyzing newsstand sales by cover illustration, he had found that pictures of children actually decreased sales and that one cover featuring a sexy pose of a motion picture star had the lowest single-copy sales of the year. More inquiry into why people buy a specific magazine and what content interests them could help to identify illustrations and covers more relevant to their interests and more likely to increase readership and sales. Some stars and public figures have noticeably increased newsstand sales of other consumer magazines.

Even an excellently designed research project will not necessarily tell the full story. Lane Palmer relates the time *Top Operator* ran a piece on record-keeping about forecasting "cash flow." Because the magazine had obtained 200 packets of information on cash flow from a bank, it offered them in a box at the bottom of a column. It was deluged with more than 2,000 requests. The title was effective, "How to Get the Cash You Need—When You Need It," and the spread was about 80 percent illustration, a drawing showing cash flow through the year. But further investigation showed that an outbreak of corn blight and drop in hog prices had hurt income so badly that farmers were having to borrow more than normal to make their new crop. Also, the new farm program had eliminated advance payments at the beginning of the year. Because farmers would not get full payment until harvest time, they had increased need for credit. Interest rates had dropped from 1970 peaks and farmers who had postponed purchases were now ready to buy. At the same time, banks had increased their promotion on the availability of credit. So—several unnoticed factors had combined to make an expected low-interest article on a dull subject a high-interest one.

Audience Research

Magazines find out about their audiences in varied ways. Commissioned research for individual magazines or publishing companies, industry-sponsored research, and combined research by one research firm for a number of magazine publishers all add to the data available to an editor. The bulk of magazine research is done to increase the sale of advertising, but some is done for the editorial department.

Readership surveys are made by going to readers' homes with copies of the magazine to find out what articles they read. Usually readership is gauged as "read all," "read most," or "read some." Over a period of time, an editor can determine the types of articles that score best and consider whether to use more of those types. He or she can find out what scored low and, if the survey is tabulated to indicate cross-tabulations, can find whether low-interest items were read by people who read little else in the issue.

An editor must consider whether readers get the magazine by action on their part—paying for a subscription—or as the result of some condition—as being an employee of a company. Readership tends to be lower in the latter instances and editors work hard to make such magazines more appealing. A study of employee magazines can combine an attitude or opinion survey with the readership survey to gain further insight into readership. One study found that about one-third of the employees' attitudes were "highly favorable," one-third "favorable," and one-third "unfavorable." Readership among the unfavorable group predictably was lower than among the other two groups. The President's letter on page 3 scored 59 percent among the highly favorable and 16 percent among the unfavorable. But an article on new machinery that would change production methods and possibly displace some workers was read by as many unfavorable as highly favorable and favorable, 32 percent.

If the magazine is part of the public relations or the personnel department, the survey may be tabulated by readership classifications for comparison—by job title or department, by length of service with the company, or by plant, if several plants are involved. Results then can furnish an insight into existing problems, potential problems, and areas with few or no problems—and give the editor information about how effectively the magazine is reaching its readers.

Mail surveys can be used to gauge readership of general content areas, departments, and some specific articles. A self-administered survey should contain background questions to help the editor evaluate readership results: how regularly the respondent reads the magazine, how he or she rates the magazine overall, and which items or departments he or she reads regularly, occasionally, seldom, or never. Intensity questions yield valuable data here, too.

Mail readership surveys are more economical than personal interview ones and can be helpful to the editor. These usually involve sending a copy of the magazine to a subscriber soon after the regular copy was mailed along with instructions about how to mark the survey copy. For example, the reader may mark an article he or she noticed with a check mark, one he or she read some of with a single line, and one he or she read most of with a double line.

Other surveys send a copy of the issue with a questionnaire or cards on which the reader checks his or her level of readership. One mails a miniature facsimile copy of the issue with a 12-page questionnaire booklet in which respondents can check boxes beneath each facsimile.

Samples usually are systematic or random and their sizes vary widely, roughly from 250 to 500, with readership results usually based on the first 100 returns. Because of differing methodologies, results from different services cannot be directly compared. Even results from different magazines using the same service cannot be directly compared.

Readership scores are not an absolute measurement of editorial effectiveness. The procedures in the mail surveys are especially prone to large error allowances, so an item read by 72 percent of the readers may not be significantly better read than an article read by 64 percent. Scores for a large number of articles over a period of time should cluster around certain types of content and give the editor an overall indication of what material is most popular and least popular as of the time of publication.

Because they take place after publication and require time to complete, readership surveys cannot give the editor immediate information.

The reader panel is another approach, which *Plant Engineering* has taken. To obtain reader reaction at modest cost, the magazine uses the panel to measure readership of all feature articles and to monitor editorial performance. Based on a pilot study, the size of each panel was set at 25, and nine panels are used on a rotating basis for the biweekly magazine.

READER RESPONSE

Each issue of NB Eye will carry a Reader Response Card. We'd like to know what you think of our magazine. Please let us know by answering the questions below, detaching the card and sending it to us either by interoffice or U.S. Mail.

Please rate the articles in this issue.	Great	OK	Dull	Didn't Read
Puttin' on the Ritz for 50 Years Now	—	—	—	—
The Merry Month of the Peanut	—	—	—	—
By Appointment to Her Majesty the Queen	—	—	—	—
New Products: Variety Is Spice of Recent Introductions	—	—	—	—
Profile: Calvin D. Ferber	—	—	—	—
Hail to the Chefs!	—	—	—	—
Recipes: The Peanut, More Than a Snack	—	—	—	—
INFO	—	—	—	—
Comments				

Subjects I'd like to see covered in future issues.

Fill in below *only* if you wish to be contacted about your ideas for NB Eye.

NAME _____ DEPARTMENT _____

PLANT/OFFICE _____ SUPERVISOR'S NAME _____

WORK TELEPHONE ( ) _____ HOME TELEPHONE (_____

Figure 8–1 Reader survey card bound into magazine solicits readership information and opinion. Each article is listed with Likert rating scale responses of "Great," OK," "Dull," and "Didn't Read." If the reader does not return it by interoffice mail, a postage stamp is required. That modest investment may skew results by decreasing response. Postage paid cards yield better results. (Courtesy NB Eye, *Nabisco Brands, Inc.*)

For each article, a panelist is given a form on which to rate on a four-point Likert scale whether the article was deficient, fair, good, or excellent on nine items. These include whether the article provides the information promised in the title, presents useful technical data or original ideas, the text is in logical sequence, the article reads easily, the length is appropriate, technical points are explained clearly and are easy to comprehend, illustrations, tables and charts help explain text and add value to the article, technical details in illustrations are easily understood, and the article is useful to the rater in his plant engineering duties and responsibilities.

Panelists are asked each year if they are willing to serve one year and are told they will be sent six articles four times a year. Articles are enclosed with the letter of invitation so the person can perform an audit before accepting.

The first 15 completed forms to arrive are used to compute the final score, because the pilot study showed that results from 15 to 60 persons were within a few percentage points of each other. Since it started full operation in 1969, the program has developed guidelines for interpreting scores, based on percentage of a perfect "excellent" score on all nine items. Below 65 percent is poor, 65 to 75 percent is fair, 75 to 85 percent is good, and 85 percent or higher is excellent. Fewer than six articles a year attain 85 percent or higher, and editors who write or edit an article that reaches this height are given a plaque and a check.

Articles that score under 65 percent are analyzed to learn why they were rated so low, and articles over 85 percent are studied with care to determine why they did so well. One finding was that subjects of limited interest routinely score lower than articles with broad scope. One example of a decision made from this research is that product case histories as feature stories were eliminated after they consistently scored low.

Panelists are not offered payment; the appeal is "help us do a better job for you." At the end of the year, token gifts such as framed prints and books of universal interest are sent to the panelists.

On occasion an item has been tested before publication. One was a new department, "FeatureFacts," which had a successful tryout with the panel before appearing in the magazine. The program also has made everyone on the staff more conscious of elements that contribute to high article readership.

Plant Engineering

Courtesy of Technical Publishing, a company of the Dun & Bradstreet Corporation.

EDITORIAL QUALITY AUDIT RATING FORM

For article titled:_____
(Please write in article title)

Nine desirable article characteristics are listed below. Please evaluate this article by circling the number that best rates each characteristic, USING THE SCALE BELOW:

	Deficient	Fair	Good	Excellent
1. The article provides information promised in the title.	1	2	3	4
2. The article presents useful technical data or original ideas.	1	2	3	4
3. Text is organized in logical sequence.	1	2	3	4
4. The article "reads" easily (considering relative complexity of subject).	1	2	3	4
5. The article length is appropriate to subject matter. (Should be: Longer ☐ / Shorter ☐)	1	2	3	4
6. Technical points are explained clearly and are easy to comprehend.	1	2	3	4
7. Illustrations, tables and charts help explain text and add to article value.	1	2	3	4
8. Technical details in illustrations are easily understood.	1	2	3	4
9. The article is useful to me in the performance of my plant engineering duties and responsibilities.	1	2	3	4

(If you circled (1) or (2): Is the subject of the article:

☐ Outside your job responsibility?
☐ No present problems on this subject?
☐ Not pertinent to your plant situation?
☐ Just a poor article?

NOTE: PLEASE USE REVERSE SIDE FOR COMMENTS ON ANY ASPECTS OF THE ARTICLE NOT COVERED IN THE ABOVE RATING-- (Optional But Valuable To The Editors).

Your Name:_____

Figure 8–2 Articles can be evaluated by a reader panel using a Likert scale on an instrument like this one from *Plant Engineering*. (Courtesy of Technical Publishing, a company of the Dun & Bradstreet Corporation.)

Computer models can be useful in assessing an overall situation or portion of it. *Playboy* used data from 52 issues to gain insight into factors that had greatest impact on magazine sales. For each issue, the number of copies sold, the number of competitors' copies sold, cover price, unemployment statistics, dollars spent on promotion, number of subscriptions serviced that month, number of copies distributed, number of full-cover displays, number of days on sale, and a score of several editors' estimates of the effectiveness of the cover, cover blurbs, and content of the issue were entered into the computer for a stepwise regression analysis that would point to the variables that combine best to produce the equation that equals total sales.

Variables influential in estimating sales were number of subscriptions, number of copies distributed, unemployment, competitors' sales, number of days on sale, and the qualitative index of appeal of the cover, cover blurbs, and content. One of the least influential items was the amount of money spent on promotion. The analysis also pointed to February and October as months when sales are somewhat lower than expected rather than the conventionally held July and August, and showed that seasonal variations were almost negligible, cover price changes only temporarily affected sales in an inflationary period, and the number of editorial pages in an issue had no correlation with newsstand sales or subscription sales. The most controllable factors, then, were the subscription list, the editorial content, and the cover.

Opinion or attitude surveys can develop an image of a magazine. In 1972 one question was asked of 1,200 women throughout the United Sttes: "Which one of the following women's magazines do you think is best?" Six magazine names were offered with these results: *Good Housekeeping,* 33 percent; *Ladies' Home Journal,* 21 percent; *McCall's,* 13 percent; *Family Circle,* 10 percent; *Redbook,* 7 percent; *Woman's Day,* 7 percent; *Cosmopolitan,* 3 percent; no preference, 6 percent. Results from a single question provide little enlightenment. More sophisticated and less obvious research techniques are needed. A detailed survey including questions about many items—food, fashion, decorating, remodeling, rearing children, fiction, etc.—can identify problem and strength areas.

A less obtrusive way to find how your magazine compares with one or more others is to use the semantic differential. The most widely used instrument checks 20 concepts in five areas:

1. Evaluative Factor
    Pleasant—unpleasant
    Valuable—worthless
    Important—unimportant
    Interesting—boring
2. Ethical Factor
    Fair—unfair
    Truthful—untruthful
    Accurate—inaccurate
    Unbiased—biased
    Responsible—irresponsible

3. Stylistic Factor
    Exciting—dull
    Fresh—stale
    Easy—difficult
    Neat—messy
    Colorful—colorless
4. Potency Factor
    Bold—timid
    Powerful—weak
    Loud—soft

5. Activity Factor
    Tense—relaxed
    Active—passive
    Modern—old fashioned

A respondent indicates his or her attitude toward the magazine by marking one of seven spaces between the opposites in each pair of words (example in Fig. 8–2). The median or mean scores on each factor for each magazine can be used to compare their relative standings, as can the overall score on the entire instrument for each magazine. This approach is more valuable than readership or demographic studies to get an overall view of the book's identity, personality, or image as seen by its readers. To obtain the most useful comparison, a study like this should make sure all respondents are familiar with all magazines being evaluated. Basing some evaluations on ignorance and others on intimate acquaintance will invalidate the overall results.

In another technique, Likert-type questions give the respondent a choice of four or five responses of varying intensity. The respondent is asked to check the one that most closely represents his or her opinion about the item. A median score for an item can be used to compare it with the same item asked about another magazine

SPORTS ILLUSTRATED

pleasant ___:__:__:__:__:____	unpleasant
valuable ___:__:__:__:__:____	worthless
important ___:__:__:__:__:____	unimportant
interesting ___:__:__:__:__:____	boring
fair ___:__:__:__:__:____	unfair
truthful ___:__:__:__:__:____	untruthful
accurate ___:__:__:__:__:____	inaccurate
unbiased ___:__:__:__:__:____	biased
responsible ___:__:__:__:__:____	irresponsible
exciting ___:__:__:__:__:____	dull
fresh ___:__:__:__:__:____	stale
easy ___:__:__:__:__:____	difficult
neat ___:__:__:__:__:____	messy
colorful ___:__:__:__:__:____	colorless
bold ___:__:__:__:__:____	timid
powerful ___:__:__:__:__:____	weak
loud ___:__:__:__:__:____	soft
tense ___:__:__:__:__:____	relaxed
active ___:__:__:__:__:____	passive
modern ___:__:__:__:__:____	old-fashioned

Figure 8–3 Magazine readers can sketch a multi-dimension image of magazines with which they are familiar by indicating their feelings on semantic differential instruments. Several magazines should be compared to get a clear idea of their relative strengths and weaknesses.

and, in some cases, can be cross-tabulated with related items to give a more sophisticated analysis of audience opinion of the magazine. The *Plant Engineering* rating form (Fig. 8–1) uses a Likert scale.

Respondents could be asked to rate an article as very interesting, interesting, uninteresting, or very uninteresting; or greatly important, moderately important, somewhat important, or unimportant; or very useful, moderately useful, slightly useful, or not useful. The Likert scale does not assume an equal distance of opinion between each adjacent pair of suggested answers, so answers can be tailored to the topic in question. That also is why the median rather than the mean is the appropriate score to use when making comparisons.

A reader could be asked to give a magazine an overall rating in broader terms, such as excellent, very good, good, fair, or poor. The scores for several magazines rated this way could give a general idea of how each magazine ranks within its competitive field.

The conceptualization and planning of research is the key to its validity and reliability. If questions or items are not prepared to make distinctions needed to obtain useful data, the research effort will be money wasted. Herbert Mayes, no man of research, underwrote the cost of a study of a half dozen previously published issues of *Collier's, Ladies' Home Hournal, Good Housekeeping, Saturday Evening Post,* and *Cosmopolitan* to find out what kinds of covers were most successful at selling copies on newsstands. The successful issues, the research firm reported, had covers with one large illustration, with red the dominant color, and three blurbs or cover lines. The unsuccessful issues had covers with one large illustration, with red the dominant color, and three blurbs or cover lines.

In magazine research, also remember the point Socrates made. When asked, "How's your wife Xanthippe?" he would reply, "Compared to what?" Research and evaluation always involve comparing one thing with another.

Focus groups can be used to test concepts for new magazines, proposed design changes, and changes in content. Small groups of six to twelve persons are assembled to discuss the topic and often also to evaluate competitors. Groups usually are selected in several cities to keep the results from being too narrowly tied to one city or geographic area. CBS Publications used focus groups in developing *Sports Score,* which eventually was market tested, but never fully launched. Time Incorporated filmed focus groups in preparing *TV-Cable Week* for publication and used some of that film of people criticizing competing TV magazines in a promotional film.

Market testing is the ultimate in introducing new magazines. Test issues are published and placed on sale in selected markets, often a dozen or so. If sales of the test issues, usually at least two, reach targeted goals, the magazine is fully launched. Even then, some magazines that succeed in test marketing fail.

Content Studies

Content analysis tells an editor how much of each type of material has been published in a given period of time. The results can be matched with content objectives, if they have been quantified. Some magazines do it with computers, others with pencil and paper, and many others not at all.

A formula book that has set rigid content goals for the year may plan meticulously to keep very near those projected goals throughout the year. Allowing for seasonal variation, by the end of March one-fourth of the goal should have been achieved.

Other editors check only periodically to make sure they are balancing content about the way they intend. Occasionally the analysis will reveal a mistaken memory or an erroneous hunch by showing overcovered and undercovered areas.

Content analysis categories should be tailored to the magazine. One study of employee magazine content used these categories:

1. Employee Content
   Wages, Hours, Benefits
   Health, Safety, Finance
   Employee Changes, Retirements, Promotions
   Management Changes, Promotions, Transfers
   Recognition of Employees
   Employee Recreation & Social Programs
   Family Features
2. Company Content
   Economic Issues
   Elimination of Waste Time & Material
   Develop Pride in Job, Loyalty to Company
   Company Policy News & Information
   Labor Relations
   Letters to Editor, Employee Participation
   General Company News and Features
   Political Issues
   Editorial Comment
3. General and Miscellaneous Content
   General Features (not company-related)
   Industry News (not company-related)
4. Advertising
   Company Advertisements
   Public Service Advertisements
   Employee Classified
5. Cover & Masthead

Better Homes and Gardens used these:
1. Building
   Architecture
   Materials, Modernization, Maintenance, Repairs
   Financing & Insurance
2. Children
3. Gardening & Flowers
4. Food & Nutrition
5. Home Furnishing and Management
   Appliances, Equipment, Housewares
   Tableware
   Decorating & Home Furnishings
   Homemaking and Home Management
6. Travel & Transportation
   Travel
   Transportation
      Automobile, Trailer (including Highways)

7. Business & Industry
8. Health & Medical Science
9. Sports, Recreations & Hobbies
10. Cultural Interests
11. General Interest
    Insurance & Savings
12. Miscellaneous
13. National Affairs
14. Foreign & International Affairs
15. Amusements
16. Beauty, Grooming, Toiletries
17. Wearing Apparel & Accessories
18. Fiction & Stories

Advertising Research

Demographic studies are used primarily to sell advertising, but their results show attributes of the audience that are worth examining. They may confirm some editorial hunches and correct others.

The statistics may be dizzying at first. After some reflection and realization that a number isn't as precise as it first seems, a general idea of the audience may emerge. For example, a skiing magazine found, through an independent research firm's study, that 47 percent of its readers considered themselves expert or advanced and 38 percent considered themselves intermediate skiers. Only 11 percent were novices. These figures confirm the obvious, that readers of a special interest magazine have more than casual interest in the subject.

Readers had skied an average of 21 days during the preceding season; 46 percent had taken a skiing vacation. After examining the ski equipment market in detail, the study delved into credit card ownership, private club membership, travel to Europe apart from skiing, beverages served when entertaining, camera ownership, TV and stereo ownership, auto ownership, motorcycle and motorscooter ownership, boat ownership, investments, age, education, and income.

Research done for the advertising department told the editor that his average reader was 27 years old and had a median income of $15,000, although 21 percent earned $25,000 or more a year. Nearly three-fourths were college graduates, 90 percent served alcoholic beverages, and 30 percent belonged to country clubs. One hundred other items were analyzed. The editor may have said, "This is the kind of person I've been editing to all along," or he may have found a few surprises in the data.

Demographic data standing alone are vague, but compared with those of similar magazines or national averages and viewed over a number of successive surveys, they can show where the magazine stands in relation to other magazines and how the audience is changing.

It is not uncommon for a magazine to begin with a relatively young readership, say nearly all in the 18–24 range, and 20 years later find that a big portion of the readership, perhaps one-third, is in the 35–49 age group. Numbers sitting there by themselves say little if one hasn't something to compare them with.

TABLE 8–1
Categories Typically Used in Demographic Studies

Age	Household Income	Education	Occupation
18–24	$25,000 or more	Graduated College	Professional/Technical
25–34	$20,000–24,999	Attended College	Manager/Proprietor
35–49	$15,000–19,999	Graduated High School	Clerical/Sales
50–64	$10,000–14,999	Attended High School	Craftsmen/Foremen
65 or over	$ 5,000–9,999	Did Not Attend High School	Other Employed
	Under $5,000		Not Employed

You may be editing to an intended audience and use demographic data to see how well the audience fits the objectives, or the other way around.

Demographic studies have been part of the advertising scene so long that they are almost unquestioned. But John O'Toole, president of Foote, Cone & Belding, asked if Grace Slick, the rock singer, and Tricia Nixon Cox, the former President's daughter, are one and the same person. Advertising researchers, he said, would classify both as being white women in the same age group, college graduates who work and have a family income in the same category, living in an urban area in a household of two to three members, and probably coming from an "upper-income family with professional or executive father who belongs to the Republican party." He said that the type of thinking that concludes that two so dissimilar persons are statistically equal is the type of thinking that has led to an erosion of public confidence in advertising. There's a message there for editors, too. If you can't see the person behind the numbers, it may be better to ignore the numbers.

Changing Nature of a Magazine's Audience

The editor must realize that the audience is not static, is not the same even from one issue to the next. The types of people interested in the magazine's content may not change drastically, or they may.

The magazine formula also may change by necessity or desire, fostering a change in audience. But only a segment of the audience—a majority for most magazines—is stable, even those people are changing as they grow older, and more or less affluent, and more interested or bored with the magazine's material. A very large minority do not renew their subscriptions upon expiration. So a magazine is appealing to a constantly changing overall audience that is homogeneous, but is made of sub-audiences with a variety of interests.

Demographic data can be helpful in showing audience shifts; reader surveys add to the depth of knowledge about readers and their changing interests.

Perspective from Communication Behavior

Understanding how people use mass media in their daily lives can place the editor's work in context and contribute to greater effectiveness. "Knowing the Reader" in chapter 4 has discussed the broad background of media use. People use a complex web of media to varying degrees, and no one medium can claim to be the cause of producing a given effect.

Because readers seek material they are interested in, the editor might as well make the appeal direct or straightforward, though not trite or dull. At the same time, the editor must recognize that it is tremendously difficult to change established beliefs. Once an opinion is formed, its holder will seek out material in the media that agrees with it. The editor's best chance at persuading a reader is to find an issue about which the reader has not formed an opinion. Given strong factual basis for the recommended opinion in this case, the reader may accept it.

Research Sources and Status

Opinion research firms that can do reliable, valid studies are readily available. An increasing number of magazines appear to be doing their research in-house, even if they have no research department. Large numbers of college graduates have sufficient backgrounds in public opinion and attitude measurement to help design and conduct such studies. And editors untrained in research who want to try a do-it-yourself survey can call upon university journalism schools and psychology departments for expert assistance.

A study by McGraw-Hill Research for *Folio* found that 65 percent of the 583 magazines responding conduct some kind of research. Of those conducting research, 57 percent conduct market studies, 55 percent do demographic surveys or reader profiles, 54 percent conduct surveys for editorial articles and features, and 44 percent perform studies to determine the editorial effectiveness of their magazines. Only

2 percent reported they were involved in syndicated readership studies, such as Simmons Market Research Bureau, and only 5 percent were involved in reader traffic studies, such as Starch and Readex, which gauge readership of advertisements in issues of magazines being studied. Simmons figures project total audiences for magazines in its studies, time spent with the magazine, and extensive marketing data by product category and magazine. The Simmons report requires about 40 volumes to contain its data.

Three-quarters of the magazines believed research is "very important" or "important" to the sales staff, and 58 percent said that studies determining the effectiveness of editorial content are "very important" or "important" to the editorial staff. Cost, time, and staff limitations were the three most mentioned problems with research. The cost problem was reflected in the techniques used to complete survey interviews, with 72 percent being conducted by mail. The other techniques were 7 percent telephone, 6 percent in person, 5 percent by a selected panel, 5 percent by a focus group, and 5 percent by other methods.

In the same issue of *Folio,* the vice president of research of McGraw-Hill Publications Company estimated that a single interiew by mail would cost between $5 and $25, one by telephone $15 to $50, and a personal interview $50 to $150. A focus group session involving eight to 12 persons would run $1,000 to $2,500, but a mail panel could be operated for as little as $5 per panel member responding.

About one-third (31 percent) of the magazines doing research had a research department within the company, but 48 percent were conducting their editorial research in-house.

Research No Substitute for Editorial Imagination

Research is not used more widely by editors partly because they quickly learn that it has limitations and cannot make decisions for them. Most research is based on the past, what has been published or what readers have experienced. For the most part, readers cannot visualize and evaluate something they have not seen or read, and thereby they cannot suggest bold new approaches, new subject matter, or new issues that should be probed.

Behind the statistical tests and mountains of data, people who understand research know it is only as good as the thinking, the intellectual conceptualization, and rigor that went into it. A statistic stands for something that has been conceptualized by a person, and if that concept is inadequate, the statistic is meaningless. The research project design is as important as the execution, and usually more demanding. Improper sampling, question wording, interviewing, coding, or tabulating can throw the results off enough to make them unreliable, but you have nothing if the design is faulty.

Research can be helpful in the ways that have been discussed: to find gaps in the reader's knowledge, to find how readers feel about the magazine, to find what they are reading and how intensely they are interested in it, and to find the most effective ways of presenting material. Research can cut down the risks, but it should not be used to avoid boldness or as an excuse to take the safe course.

The editor still must be the leader. Editors occasionally make misjudgments. But the great editors have been willing to gamble when they were sure they were right, and the great publishers have backed them.

9

Break-of-the-Book: Editorial Planning

ALLOCATING space within an issue of a magazine is called "breaking the book," and it is during this process that generalities must be translated into specifics. Broad concepts or formulas must materialize in the form of specific articles and departments; these in turn must then be converted into specific pages or spreads located logically among the other material being offered to readers. The "nitty gritty" of putting an issue together is usually the responsibility of managing editors, although they may be operating under some other title. For the purposes of this discussion, we shall simply call them "editors."

As they break the book, editors are concerned with such decisions as which articles merit two pages or more and which get only one, which article is the "lede" or cover article, which departments will be placed up front and which must go back, and what material will be produced in color. Careful, detailed planning and efficient procedures are required if these decisions are to result in the production of an issue that interests a maximum number of readers.

Although these are editorial decisions, they are complicated by factors stemming from advertising and production requirements. For example, except for some public relations and association magazines supported by sponsors, the sale of advertising dictates the size of an issue. Sale of ads to be printed in color also directly affects the potential use of color on editorial pages. And printers and their equipment sometimes seem to be total dictators of planning because they must work within precise mechanical limitations.

In real life, editorial decisions relating to break-of-the-book cannot be totally separated from advertising and production requirements. To clarify our discussion here, however, these aspects of issue planning will be held over for the next chapter. It will suffice here to know that those ramifications must ultimately be considered.

Editorial Issue Planning Starts Early

Editorial issue planning starts long before detailed work begins on an issue. One of the astonishing things to a newcomer in the magazine field is the amount of preliminary time that must be allowed for each issue. Except in the case of weekly news magazines, issues must be completely planned several months, or at least several weeks, in advance of publication. Some smaller magazines and newspaper Sunday supplements may require only five or six weeks, but six months is typical for most standard magazines. In the magazine field, editors must be accustomed to planning Christmas issues after rushing in from early morning rounds of golf in mid-July. And when the halls are decked with holly, they must think in terms of their readers' midsummer interests.

As the most preliminary planning for one issue gets under way, another issue is rolling off the presses, still another is in the typesetting stage, one is ready for layout, assignments may have just been made for another, and one or two more issues may be at some stage of preparation. Sound complicated? It is. To put together well-balanced, interesting issues regularly under such circumstances, an editor must establish efficient procedures for every step.

Figure 9–1 Each issue of a magazine starts with planning. Here senior editors at *Architectural Record,* a McGraw-Hill magazine, confer with Editor Walter F. Wagner, Jr., AIA (extreme left).

The First Step: Preliminary Planning Session

Planning and scheduling are, for a magazine editor, like the proverbial hen and the egg: both must be started at once. Planning starts with a schedule, but the schedule has to start with planning. For the moment let's look at necessary planning procedures, then turn our attention to scheduling.

The first step in the creation of an issue is preliminary planning. At this stage, an issue is discussed in only the most general terms. As a matter of fact, several consecutive issues may be discussed at the same time in order to build continuity from one to another. Sometimes more than one issue is needed to adequately explore a subject, and these issues must be coordinated. This coordination is established in preliminary planning sessions. The main goal of such sessions is to set a pattern for each issue that directly relates to the magazine's basic formula, character, or concept. The sessions serve as a bridge linking the subject matter of each issue to the long-range approach of the magazine.

As pointed out in chapter 5, preliminary planning goes on continually on an informal basis. For magazines with fairly large staffs these planning sessions may be somewhat formalized, and they should involve all staff members with executive positions. The advertising director can receive valuable guidance from these sessions, and he or she can contribute substantially to them. Cooperative ventures in which the advertising and editorial departments coordinate their activities should get their start at these early planning sessions.

Sometimes the central theme for an issue can originate in the advertising department, and sometimes considerable space can be sold when space salesmen know of pending editorial approaches that relate to their clients. Input from the research department is vital; readership and readability study results can guide editorial staffs to an improved product. Other departmental executives, including the circulation director, can provide valuable input as ideas are sought for subjects that will be on readers' minds half a year in the future. An art director can join the brainstorming by offering suggestions for potential visual approaches for subjects that come up for discussion.

Editors who must work alone or have only one or two assistants can proceed much more informally with their planning, but they cannot do without it. Neglect of long-range planning on even the smallest publication breeds disorder; unless a long-range course is charted, a magazine is almost certain to drift away from its basic goals.

Building a Theme

If preliminary planning is successful, whether it occurs in a formalized session or in an editor's mind as he or she meditates over a cup of coffee, it will produce a general thrust for an issue. This may be in the form of a single theme, or it may be only agreement on the subject for a lede feature backed up by one or two major article ideas.

The use of a single theme for an issue (or perhaps even two or three consecutive issues) has become widely accepted practice. A theme provides a handy organizing device for an editor; when all articles relate to the same subject matter, an issue is automatically going to emerge as an organized unit. The demand upon magazines for increasingly thorough treatment of subjects can best be answered with a thematic approach, too. Circulation and advertising departments find it advantageous for their promotional campaigns when they can point to themes that have been thoroughly presented in the past or are on the drawing board for future issues.

Any theme that is selected must, of course, be of direct interest to a majority of readers. It must be general enough to get interest from a broad range of readers, but not so general that it lacks unity or destroys potential future themes on related subjects. An editor of a company publication who chooses employee fringe benefits as a theme for an issue may regret the choice later as he or she realizes that retirement benefits alone would make a good theme. He or she is then faced with the prospect that, although his or her treatment of retirement was skimpy, devoting a full issue to that subject in the near future would appear repetitious. Or, in the case of a consumer magazine, an editor who has started with "American Education" as a theme may discover that it is too general a subject, and concentration on American universities would produce a much better issue.

Generating Ideas

The accent at all early planning sessions is on ideas, and the greater the input, the greater the potential for stimulating issues. The idea for a theme or an article can come from anyone or anyplace. Any of the departments whose representatives attend planning sessions can be a source. So can letters from readers; whether complimentary or critical, letters often provide a good gauge of the subjects readers have on their minds. So can an idea file. A wise editor follows carefully the content of other periodicals and clips and files articles or issues that might relate to his or her own magazine. Every day's newspaper is a potential source of editorial ideas. And general magazines explore subjects that the editors of specialized magazines might later find can be tailored to their specialized interests, and vice versa. A loaded idea file can start more action at an issue planning session than any other source, and a good editor is never without one.

The Second Step: Converting Ideas into Articles

With the theme or general direction of an issue already established, it is time for the editor and the staff to plan again, but this time the goal is to get going on specific, publishable articles. What were general subjects in the preliminary planning session must now jell into tangible features that will occupy prescribed pages in the issue.

At this stage of planning, it is important for the editor to work with the editorial assistants, such as artists and photographers. If the issue under consideration is to follow a theme, the theme must be broken into component parts that are then assigned to appropriate personnel for completion. The artist, with preliminary sketches, can help develop the slant or angle for each item. As work progresses, the issue begins to take shape. An issue intended to focus on the elderly in American society begins to shake down into articles on financial problems, health problems, psychological difficulties, institutions serving the elderly, and other elements within the general theme. The health program piece begins to take on a still more specific direction: the government medical program. As the editor, artist, and other staffers try to pin the subject down still more specifically, the artist may suggest an angle emphasizing difficulties with "red tape." Unwarranted delays in government payment for medical care, difficulties in qualifying for assistance, and other procedural problems appear to be at the heart of the problem. The suggestion for artwork showing elderly citizens in hospital beds and bound up in red tape as a title illustration is approved, and the writer and photographer are ready to develop the feature. Bit by bit, the other subjects gain specificity, and a full list of specific articles and assignments is completed.

The primary goal at this step is to narrow a subject down to its most precise point. Should there be any photos used? Should photos be the primary means of telling the story, or should they be secondary to text? Should an article rest basically on an opinion poll, or should it be translated in terms of one person or one family as a case example? Should the writer concentrate in an interview on what the source says, or should he or she prepare to do a personality sketch of the interviewee? How long should the article be? Will it probably get four pages, or is it more likely to be forced to fit into only two? These and other similar questions must be answered if assignments are going to materialize as an editor hopes they will.

Checking the Stockpile

At this stage of breaking the book, or earlier, the magazine's "stockpile" of manuscripts must be checked for any usuable material. Themes and approaches don't just materialize suddenly; they usually result from an accumulation of attention to several aspects of a problem. This accumulation often continues over an extended time period. During that time, staffers may have completed specific features or just done general spadework on articles that now fit a selected theme. Free-lance writers also may have provided some pieces that can be used as submitted or with moderate revision. Consequently, a magazine usually has a substantial backlog of manuscripts on file. This backlog should be carefully checked before final assignments are made for each issue, and a continuing effort should be made to maintain an adequate supply of material on hand.

Developing Continuing Features or Departments

A primary strength for many magazines is their standing features, such as a column, a special-interest department, or even cartoons. *New Yorker's* cartoons, *Newsweek's* columns, *Time's* book review section, *Family Circle's* money management, Burton Hillis's "The Man Next Door" page in *Better Homes and Gardens,* and *Playboy's* centerfold are well-known examples of hundreds of successful offerings of this nature. In the public relations magazine field such departments or standing features as job promotions or letter from the president have been mainstays for some magazines whose purposes can be furthered through such continuing offerings. Efforts to discover and promote standing features are worthwhile for any magazine, and they should be constantly under way.

However, the decision to create a topical department or to drop one must be recognized as having sufficient importance to require careful thought and research. The fact that any item is to run steadily in issue after issue is enough to force considerable attention to such an editorial decision. And once a decision is made to grant continuity to a feature or department, issue planning must take into account the readers who are accustomed to finding it in every issue. Some readers get strong feelings of attachment to particular offerings, and this should be considered when decisions are made as to the way in which such offerings are to be handled. Sometimes popular features can be used to bolster readership in a particular section of a book—the back, for example.

Reviewing the Complete Issue

The plannning for an issue begins in very general terms and then becomes very specific. Before the planning stage is complete, an issue should be subjected to another general overview. As part of this overview, the actual breaking of the book occurs.

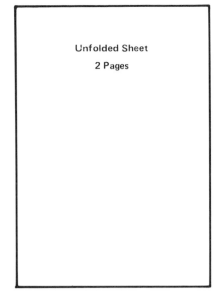

Unfolded Sheet
2 Pages

One Fold
4 Pages

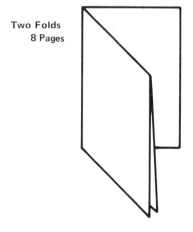

Two Folds
8 Pages

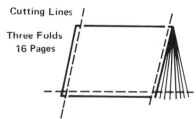

Cutting Lines

Three Folds
16 Pages

Figure 9–2 Folding a miniature dummy. Unfolded sheet, 2 pages. One fold, four pages. Two folds, 8 pages. Three folds, 16 pages. A folded sheet must be trimmed along all outside edges.

Use of a Miniature Dummy

In order to visualize the complete issue, most editors create a miniature dummy containing the number of pages set for the issue. An 8½ × 11-inch sheet of paper folded three times at right angles and then trimmed will form a handy 16-page section. The small 2¾ × 4¼-inch pages thus formed are easy to work with, and as many sections as are required can be put together to form a complete issue in miniature. Pages can then be numbered and brief notations can be made on each page as content is assigned to the page.

By thumbing through the miniature dummy, editors can begin to get a feeling as to how the issue is shaping up. Keeping both production and content requirements in mind, they now can make definite space allocation. As they do they mentally check out several requirements of a good issue.

Checking for Completeness

The first check is for completeness, or comprehensiveness. Does the issue, as a whole, deal with its theme or subjects in adequate depth? Sometimes as articles pick up their angles they leave some aspects of the subject uncovered or inadequately treated. Weak spots or complete omissions can be detected in an overall analysis of an issue, whereas they are easily overlooked when an issue is viewed in its individual parts.

Checking for Variety and Balance

Are there sufficient variety and balance in the issue to provide something worthwhile for every type of reader being served? There is some tendency for editors to prepare whole issues directed entirely toward the largest segment of their audience while neglecting smaller segments. Research has shown that a diversity of articles can result in greater overall readership than an issue full of features to please the majority. The old *Saturday Evening Post* discovered that it got peak readership if it directed about eight of its usual 12 to 15 articles per issue to the majority and used the remaining four to seven to lure smaller groups.

One of the failings of some research, as well as editorial intuition, has been the tendency to neglect the *intensity* of reader interest in some subjects. If, for example, only 10 percent of an audience may be interested in a subject, yet that interest is so intense that failure to include it loses that particular audience segment, it is obvious that the subject merits careful editorial scrutiny, to say the least. Besides, sometimes new readers for the "majority" content can be picked up through the use of editorial matter that appeals directly to their strong "minority" interests, thus providing an overall gain in readership and/or circulation.

A good issue will contain adequate variety to appeal to the special interests of all readers, but maintain a reasonable balance of material with broad appeal. In addition, the material should be distributed throughout the issue so the variety is apparent. An occasional "change of pace" is essential or an issue can seem to be monotonous. Longer articles should interspersed with shorter pieces. Subjects that are serious in nature should be broken up by an occasional light treatment. Picture stories get more impact if they are separated by interspersed presentations where the emphasis is on text. Pages that are framed with margins make those that employ bleed photographs pick up added impact. For the person who flips the pages of a magazine, checking the content, the impression should be one of variety and liveliness.

For some magazines with a specialized role to perform, the matter of content distribution becomes unusually important. For example, the editor of a company magazine for circulation to employees in a number of plants throughout the country may be forced to exercise special caution to avoid letting any one plant dominate the content. A feeling that "it never has anything in it from our plant" cannot be permitted to gain foothold among readers. *Republic Reports,* a magazine serving employees of many Republic Steel installations, has used a system of a definite percentage allocation of space to each plant in each issue to solve just such a problem. A fairly complex record-keeping system was devised to guarantee the desired space distribution. An engineering magazine might also find that care was needed to prevent content from becoming overloaded with material of interest to only one kind of engineer to the detriment of those with different special interests. In all such cases, it is wise to set distribution goals, and then establish a control method that will help achieve those goals.

Catering to the "Backward" Reader

All magazines have what can be called "backward" readers—those who do their flipping of pages from the back to the front. *Newsweek,* some years ago, explored the habits of its readers in this regard and discovered that almost as many scanned each issue from the back to the front as did from front to back. Quick observation in any periodical reading room will verify that finding; in some college classes we have even found the back-to-front viewers in the majority.

The traditional approach to allocation of space in an issue was to present all the editorial strength up front or in the middle and let the back of the book be a dumping ground for continuations that could be buried among fractional-page ads. Readership tests subsequently showed a substantial loss of audience for the material that was near the back.

Most magazine issues are now given two openings: one in front and the other in the back. The back opening, unlike the front, is usually restricted to a single page; we have not yet accepted the idea that pages should go in sequence from back to middle. But it is now common to use a strong, single-page feature on the left page facing the inside back cover to lure backward viewers into starting their reading quickly.

While checking over the miniature dummy for comprehensiveness, variety, and balance, the editor should also see if the back of the book has been given adequate strength.

Avoiding Pitfalls in Planning

With the planning steps completed, the editor is ready to proceed with the other steps involved in getting an issue together. If planning has been careful and complete, the likelihood of major crises occurring is reduced but not eliminated. Nature has a way of interfering with even the best laid plans. Interview subjects die or otherwise make themselves no longer appropriate subjects for planned articles. (A famous movie star was featured in a personal interview story regarding her "fantastically successful" marriage; before the ill-fated magazine hit the stands, newspapers were carrying a sensational story on her impending divorce.) Late developments bring on changes in reader moods, and what looked like good subjects in June might have to be scrapped just before an August copy deadline. Pitfalls emerge even with the most careful planning.

To keep pitfalls to a minimum, editors take on the roles of bookkeeper and expediter. They need adequate records to maintain a constant check on the state of affairs for each issue, and they must organize the staff's efforts so each necessary chore is completed in proper sequence on time. Obviously, the exact nature of the records an editor must keep varies considerably among the types of magazines, but in most instances they involve at least two functions: (1) scheduling, and (2) maintaining and recording copy flow.

Scheduling

A schedule is as important to the publication of a magazine as it is to the operation of a railroad. Each issue has a final publication date, its "end of the line." In order to reach its final destination on schedule, an issue must pass all way stations, and it must pass them on time. A schedule that can reasonably be met by everyone involved, and that is complete enough to provide checkpoints for all important stages (plus some allowance for unavoidable pitfalls), is an essential element of magazine editorial bookkeeping.

As we indicated earlier, every good schedule begins with planning. Unless it is scheduled, essential planning is likely to be neglected in the rush to meet other deadlines. Even the most preliminary discussions should be scheduled, with sufficient lead time provided to allow for reasonable completion dates for all other steps. A skeletonized schedule for the December (Christmas) issue of a monthly magazine might look something like this:

1. Preliminary planning session: June 15.
2. Specific planning session: July 15.
3. Assignments made: July 18.
4. Copy deadline: September 1.
5. Manuscripts edited and illustrations scaled and sent to printer: September 10.
6. Galley proofs from printer: October 1.
7. Galley proofs corrected and returned: October 8.
8. Page proofs from printer: October 23.
9. Page proofs approved and returned to printer: October 27.
10. Issue completed: November 10.

This schedule has been labeled "skeletonized" because it would have to be much more detailed for the actual operation of many magazines. In most cases sectional deadlines are scheduled, permitting some parts of the magazine to be held for completion close to the issue date while other sections will have earlier deadlines.

To be effective, a schedule obviously must be individualized. An example of a deadline schedule for a magazine with many pages and many color illustrations is shown in figure 9–3. This *Woman's Day* special interest magazine, *101 Craft Ideas,* eventually emerged as 100 pages, including ads, almost exactly six months and 23 deadlines later.

In figure 9–4 we see an adaptation of a schedule for the external public relations magazine for E. I. du Pont that includes a step necessary for most organizational magazines: approval by executives. Whether the organization being served is an industrial concern or a trade association, their basic public relations nature usually requires that content be approved by members of the administrative hierarchy. And if that approval isn't scheduled, the schedule is unworkable; approvals can take up as much issue-preparation time as any other production step (and sometimes more). We can note in this illustration also that the du Pont schedule is established for four issues; in many situations multi-issue scheduling of this type can be extremely helpful for long-term planning.

In sum, a written, precise schedule is required for efficient completion of each issue of a magazine. These schedules can be as different from all others as their circumstances dictate because a good schedule is tailored directly to an individual situation. They must, however, be complete; every step that involves time must be included on a schedule.

Keeping Track of Manuscripts and Illustrations

Manuscripts and photographs flow into most magazine offices continually, with the tide ebbing at times, perhaps, but always leaving enough material to create confusion unless it is handled efficiently. Some record must be maintained of all editorial material from the time it is received until it has been published or otherwise disposed of.

One of the first questions asked at issue planning sessions is, "What's on hand?" and unless a stockpile inventory is kept, an accurate answer may be difficult to get. Also, good relationships with free-lance writers requires an ability to respond fully and accurately to their queries about articles submitted at some prior time. And as deadlines approach, the stage to which all copy has progressed must be quickly ascertainable.

Record keeping, consequently, should ordinarily consist of the following:

1. A form recording all editorial material that comes from outside sources
2. An inventory form showing all manuscripts and illustrations in the stockpile

FROM: Nancy Kay DATE _____

TO: F. Bowers   F. Klein   L. Dugbee   B. Besten
     K. Bienstock (3) G. Allen   E. Reed   B. Bowen
     S. Lembo (2)   G. Disch   B. Gift   E. Friedhof (25)
     T. Marvel   M. Choma   R. Toner   S. Miller
     C. Lake   D. Mandolfo   J. Costa
     C. Friedlund   F. Devlin   B. Preye
     R. Mattison   H. Samuel   J. Rubessa
     H. Price   (2)   E. Frieden   B. Holman
     B. Matela (5)   J. Curcio   S. Ber

NUMBER ___2___   TITLE ___WOMAN'S DAY 101 CRAFT IDEAS___

SUBJECT ___WORKING PRODUCTION SCHEDULE___

COVER TO ART DEPT.	SEPT. 27
COVER ART TO ENGRAVER	OCT. 11 1st
COVER PROOF OK	NOV. 8
COVER FILM TO PRINTER	NOV. 15
COVERS 2, 3, 4 TO PRINTER	NOV. 15
4-COLOR ART DEADLINE	OCT. 11 1st
4-COLOR PROOFS OK	NOV. 8
4-COLOR FILM TO PRINTER	NOV. 15
FIRST COPY OUT	SEPT. 22
50% COPY OUT	OCT. 4
FINAL COPY OUT	OCT. 18
FIRST ART TO PRINTER	OCT. 18
50% ART TO PRINTER	NOV. 1
FINAL ART TO PRINTER	NOV. 15 FINAL
SHOP SECTION CLOSING	OCT. 18
SHOP SECTION DUMMY TO PRINTER	NOV. 8
SHOP SECTION ART & EDIT. MATERIAL DEADLINE	NOV. 8
AD CLOSING	OCT. 4
AD MATERIAL DEADLINE	NOV. 8
AD DUMMY TO EDITOR	NOV. 3
AD DUMMY TO PRINTER	NOV. 8
FINAL OK OF BLUES	NOV. 22
FIRST SHIPPING DATE	DEC. 15
ON SALE DATE	JAN. 9

Specifications to follow

Figure 9–3 A schedule as distributed to appropriate personnel for one of the special interest magazines of Fawcett Publications. (Courtesy Fawcett Publications.)

3. A copy control form for the current issue showing the status of all assigned manuscripts or illustrations
4. A production record noting completion of production milestones

As noted in chapter 5, a manuscript receipt record should provide for appropriate notations of all material received from outside sources. A centrally located record of the disposition of such material is essential; there is no purpose in maintaining a record of articles that can't be found when an article gets lost. If a record form must travel throughout the office with the manuscript, it should be a supplement to a central record.

An inventory record is also needed for most magazines. This record should provide all the information needed to enable an editor to assess quickly what material he or she has on file by subject and, perhaps, proposed issue date. Thus, when the question "what do we have on hand" pops up, an answer can be obtained quickly, whether the question relates to a particular subject, staff member, or issue date.

DUPONT CONTEXT				
	AUG	NOV	FEB	MAY
Copy (approved by story source) complete	Mon Jun 26	Tue Sep 26	Tue Dec 26	Tue Mar 27
Copy to editors	Tue Jun 27	Wed Sep 27	Wed Dec 27	Wed Mar 28
Copy out for departmental approval	Fri Jun 30	Mon Oct 2	Tue Jan 2	Mon Apr 2
Layouts, cropping complete	Fri Jun 30	Mon Oct 2	Tue Jan 2	Mon Apr 2
Color copy to printer	Mon Jul 3	Tue Oct 3	Wed Jan 3	Tue Apr 3
Copy approved by departments	Fri Jul 7	Mon Oct 9	Tue Jan 9	Mon Apr 9
B&W photos to printer	Mon Jul 10	Tue Oct 10	Wed Jan 10	Tue Apr 10
Copy to typesetter	Tue Jul 11	Wed Oct 11	Fri Jan 12	Wed Apr 11
Type galleys in hand	Thu Jul 13	Fri Oct 13	Tue Jan 16	Fri Apr 13
Corrected repros in hand	Mon Jul 17	Tue Oct 17	Thu Jan 18	Tue Apr 17
Random proofs in Wilmington	Wed Jul 19	Thu Oct 19	Mon Jan 22	Thu Apr 19
Dummy in Wilmington	Thu Jul 20	Fri Oct 20	Tue Jan 23	Fri Apr 20
Mechanicals in Wilmington	Mon Jul 24	Wed Oct 25	Thu Jan 25	Tue Apr 24
Dummy approved by company executive	Tue Jul 25	Thu Oct 26	Fri Jan 26	Wed Apr 25
Mechanicals to printer	Wed Jul 26	Fri Oct 27	Mon Jan 29	Thu Apr 26
Form proofs in Wilmington	Fri Aug 4	Mon Nov 6	Tue Feb 6	Fri May 4
On press	Wed Aug 9	Thu Nov 9	Fri Feb 9	Wed May 9
Advance copies in Wilmington	Mon Aug 14	Tue Nov 14	Wed Feb 14	Mon May 14
Ship to Eden Park	Tue Aug 15	Wed Nov 15	Thu Feb 15	Tue May 15
Distribution complete	Fri Aug 18	Mon Nov 20	Tue Feb 20	Fri May 18

Figure 9–4 Many magazines set editorial schedules for more than one issue at a time. This one, which establishes basic deadlines for four issues of an external company magazine, also introduces a new element as an essential item on the schedule: approval of various company executives. To be effective, schedules must be tailored to the local situation and incorporate all time-consuming steps involved with an issue. (Courtesy Dupont *Context*.)

What do we have on traffic safety? What do we have for a September issue? What picture stories done by Johnson and Murray do we have on file? The search for backlog material usually begins with one or the other of these types of questions.

A third handy record is what might be called a copy control sheet. It is designed to give an editor quick information about the status of every article or other piece of editorial material that is scheduled for inclusion in an issue. Has the assignment been made? Who has the assignment? Are photos involved? Are the text and/or photos complete? Has the material been copy edited? How much space is it going to occupy? A form set up so that a quick mark or a word or two is all that is needed to record this kind of information prevents costly miscues or misunderstandings. A quick glance can reveal problem areas and provide a base for follow-up action as needed.

Some record also is needed to provide a checklist of all the steps involved in getting material ready for a printer. The schedule for an issue outlines these steps, and a production checklist provides a means for insuring completion of all production steps on schedule. Because this information is of interest to the entire staff, it is often maintained in a form that is available for all to see. Many magazines have a tradition of putting an issue "on the board," a term used to describe the practice of displaying all pages (blanks) on a display board, a bulletin board, or around the walls of the office. As each production step is completed for a page or spread, it is entered or checked off. When check marks have been placed after steps beginning with "assignment made" and going through assignment completed, articles edited, galley proofs read, page proofs approved, and finally to "form closed," the job for that issue is completed. The posting of new page sheets signals the beginning of the day-to-day chores of another issue.

Two Dictators of Issue Planning: Publication Date and Printer

All the work in planning an issue must fall within confines dictated by a magazine's publication date and its printer. There may be some elasticity possible in other aspects of issue planning, but the publication date *must* be met, and the needs of the printer *must* be met. Good magazines meet their publication dates regularly; not to do so results in almost certain reader disaffection, trouble with postal authorities, and disaster in terms of advertisers. Every step in putting together an issue is related in time to the publication date; schedules start with that date and work backwards.

If a printer is to produce the magazine as expected, the schedule and the limitations of the equipment must also be adhered to in all phases of issue planning. A printer can do no more than the equipment makes possible; a press that has a maximum speed of 10,000 sheets an hour cannot be speeded up to 20,000 in order to make up for time lost by a magazine staff. If the press accommodates a form large enough for sixteen pages, the editorial staff must plan for forms that fit that press. And so it goes with all aspects of getting material into type, on the press, and into the hands of readers.

Good printers are cooperative, and they will adjust to emergencies as well as they can, but there is a point beyond which they cannot go. The following chapters deal with the procedures necessary to get a magazine issue through its production stages, starting with issue planning.

10

Break-of-the-Book: Production Planning

As EDITORS ALLOCATE SPACE in each issue to articles and departments, they must work within some unyielding restraints that stem from factors relating to the financing and production of magazines. The number of pages in an issue, for example, cannot be freely set to accommodate editorial needs; budget and mechanical restraints exert an influence in this instance and also seem to cast their shadows on editorial decision-making at every step.

If a magazine is supported by advertising, the total number of pages available for an issue will be determined on the basis of a ratio of advertising pages to editorial pages. Space rates and production costs usually require that more than half the pages be sold, and it is common to operate with a six to four ratio: income from six pages of ads being required to support four pages of editorial matter.

Some editors, especially those of specialized business magazines, feel the influence of advertising in another way: their front covers have been sold. Like it or not, this premium space has been set aside to provide income, with little or no space set aside on the cover to lure the reader to the magazine with editorial matter.

It is also common for an editor to find "position" sold; advertisers have purchased a particular place in the magazine, as well as a certain amount of space. Front of the book, back of the book, inside front or back cover, "next to editorial matter" are all common position requirements that editors may have to accept as they allocate space to editorial matter. Ads are placed first, before editorial, in most magazines.

Along with being told that an issue will contain "X number" of pages, of which certain ones already contain ads, editors are often limited as to the use of editorial color from the sale of ads. That is, ads may have been sold to be printed in black plus one or more additional colors, and, for efficiency in printing, these same colors on prescribed pages (those that fall within the same form) will be all that the budget will allow.

Another advertising-related problem that often presents itself at break-of-the-book time is a pre-printed insert. Often consisting of four pages, with only two pages (one side of the sheet) already printed with the ads, the other two pages must be "backed up" by the editor. Often these inserts are printed on special paper, so that working them into the binding can cause problems of appearance as well as complicate the pagination process.

Mechanical requirements also have an obvious effect on issue planning; novices who haven't yet given the mechanics of printing a thought quickly become aware of the fact that no printing system yields an uneven number of pages. True, we might print on only one side of a page, but the back of the page is always there, even if it is blank. Magazines are not printed one page at a time, however. They are either printed on large sheets that contain several pages or on a *web* (roll) of paper that also contains several pages after being printed and cut into sheets. Figure 10–1 shows a sheet emerging from a typical sheet-fed press, and figure 10–2 shows a web-fed press in operation. Both kinds of presses are in common use; the sheet-fed is for smaller circulation magazines; the web-fed is for those with large circulations.

Figure 10–1 These sheets are coming off a typical sheet-fed magazine press that is printing eight pages at one time on one side of the sheet.

Figure 10–2 A multi-unit web offset press.

Basic Press Operation

Printing presses, whether web-fed or sheet-fed, put an image on paper by way of some system for separating the image area from the non-image area so only the image areas carry ink to paper. In the most common printing system, *photo offset lithography,* the image area is receptive to greasy ink and the non-image area repels the greasy ink. Another common system for magazine printing, *rotogravure,* relies on depressed areas holding ink to form an image area, while the flat part of the plate carries no image. Regardless of the printing method, the printing presses are designed to print on common sizes of sheets or webs of paper.

A press's capacity can therefore be stated in terms of the size of sheet it can print, as well as the number of impressions per hour it can deliver. The size of the printing area corresponds to the size of the sheet and can be translated in terms of

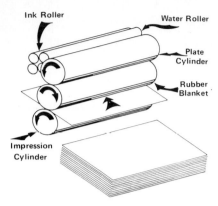

Figure 10-3 Diagram of an offset press.

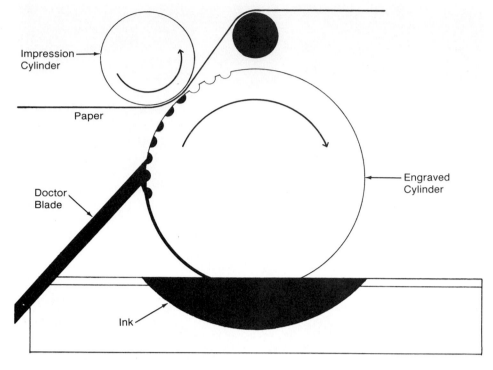

Figure 10-4 A diagram of a rotogravure press.

number of pages that can be printed at one time. Most magazine presses have image-carrying areas big enough to print either eight or sixteen pages "up." A sheet containing sixteen pages is usually printed eight-up (on one side of the sheet), and then the stack of sheets is turned over to have the other eight pages printed on the other side.

The page capacity of presses is of extreme importance to editors because the number of pages "up" (in one form or on one plate) is the basic unit for production planning. More will be explained about these planning units later.

Another fairly obvious point must be made here. Each impression of plate to paper carries an image in one ink, ordinarily black. Every additional color requires an additional impression. Multi-color presses essentially are nothing more than individual presses hooked together so one can print black, the next an additional color, and so on, up to four or more presses or units in line.

Presses also can be *perfecting,* meaning that they will print on both sides of the paper at one time. In essence, a perfecting press is the same as a two-color press; one unit prints a form on one side and the additional unit prints another form on the other side.

It must be kept in mind, however, that presses printing more than one color, or with the ability of perfecting the sheet, cost more than presses of the same size that are limited to one form. Even with multi-color presses, the basic goal of production planning is always to keep the number of required impressions to a minimum. Planning that wastefully requires a second press run, or a two-color press instead of one-color, is wasteful and unacceptable.

Magazines at any level of circulation, from the smallest to the largest, must be planned with production efficiency in mind. To see how editorial planning must take production requirements into account, let's look at basic production steps, relating them first to the smaller magazines using sheet-fed presses.

Signatures and How They Affect Editorial Planning

Signatures are the large sheets which, when printed and folded, are bound together to form a magazine or other publication. All aspects of issue planning are affected by the facts that (1) magazines are made up of signatures, and (2) the size of signatures is determined by the size of the printing press. Signature sizes vary, but the number of pages that are included in a signature must contain multiples of four pages. For magazine production, signatures usually contain at least eight and, more commonly, 16 pages.

Because it is most common for small magazines, the 16-page signature will be used here to show that such planning is necessary, and that it may involve half-signatures.

A typical flat-bed cylinder press for magazine production will handle a sheet big enough for 16 pages, eight on one side and eight on the other. That is, it prints "8-up." The plate carrying the image to paper will therefore accommodate eight pages, and the printer must arrange those pages on the plate so that (1) the correct pages will print on each side, and (2) all pages will be in proper sequence and right side up when the sheets are folded into signatures and bound into a magazine.

The arranging of pages on the printing plate so pages in the magazine will end up in proper order is called *imposition,* and it is a matter of prime importance for printers. Figure 10–5 shows the typical imposition of a 16-page signature with eight pages on each side of the sheet. This kind of imposition is called *sheetwise* or *work-and-back,* and it represents the preferred way to handle a signature. The required number of sheets is first printed with an 8-page plate on one side, then the press is cleaned, a second plate is put on, and the other eight pages are printed. Suppose a signature of only eight pages is needed, and the same press is to be used. With proper positioning of pages, the printer can put all eight pages on the plate, and print half the number of sheets needed. The sheets can then be backed up with the same eight pages, and then cut in half to form twin eight-page signatures, as shown in figure 10–6. This kind of imposition is called *work-and-turn* because the sheet is first *worked* (printed) on one side, and then turned over and printed with the same plate on the other side.

A 24-page magazine, for example, would probably be printed with one 16-page sheetwise signature and one 8-page work-and-turn signature. It should be noted here that most small magazines are what are called *self-cover,* meaning that the cover pages are part of a basic signature, not a separate four pages wrapped around larger signatures.

How Imposition Affects Issue Planning

Imposition affects issue planning because it has a direct effect on potential deadlines and the cost of color. Editors and printers both usually prefer to print magazines in pieces, or sections. In order for printing to take place, all pages on a plate must be completed. Therefore in figure 10–5, for example, pages 1, 4, 5, 8, 9, 12, 13, and

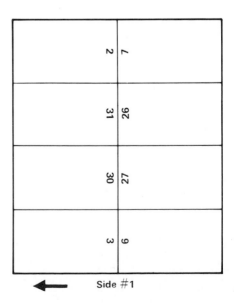

Side #1

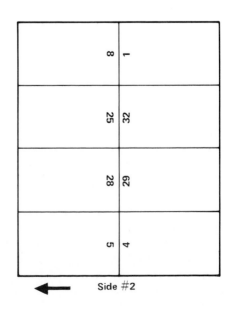

Side #2

Figure 10–5 A sheetwise imposition for the outside 16-page signature of a 32-page self-cover magazine.

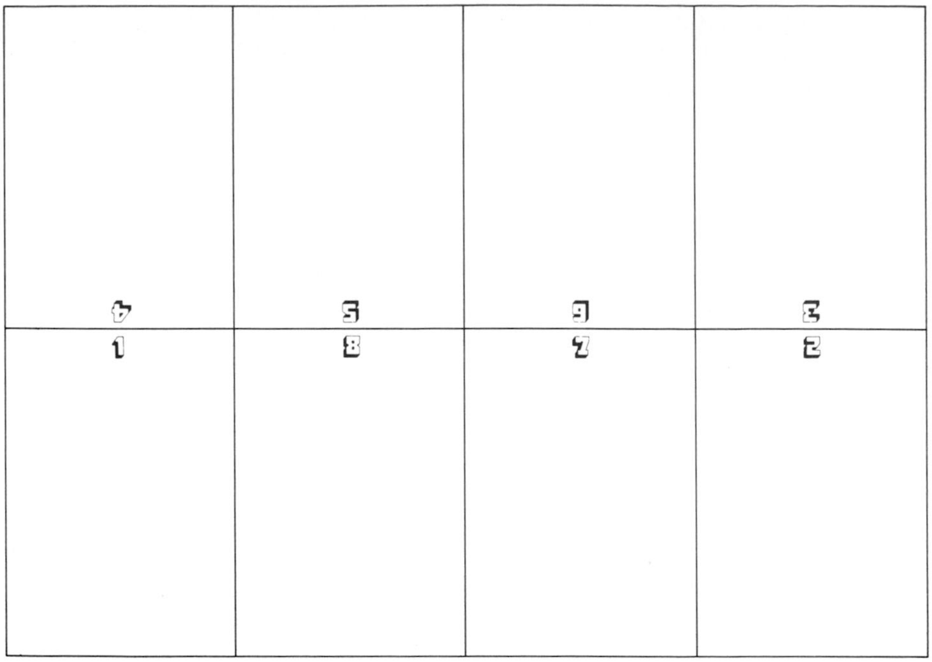

Figure 10–6 An 8-page work-and-turn imposition. After the sheet is printed, it is cut into twin 8-page signatures.

16 would comprise one printing unit, and pages 2, 3, 6, 7, 10, 11, 14, and 17 would be on the other plate (would print on the other side of the sheet). In figure 10–6, all pages from 1 through 8 would be on one plate.

Planning for deadlines and use of color must be geared directly to imposition. As shown in figure 10–5, the eight pages on one side of the sheet could be completed, sent to the printer, and actually be printed while work was being completed on the remaining eight. But, conceivably, 14 pages could be completed and printing would still be impossible because, for example, pages 1 and 2 were incomplete. With regard to color, consider the difference in cost of printing all the pages on one side of the sheet in one additional color, and that printing only two pages (such as 1 and 2) in the additional color when those two pages are in different forms. Twice the press time is required for the latter. More about planning by printing units will be presented later.

The actual location of each page on the sheet is determined by the imposition and folding of the sheet. In only one specialized printing technique (see *split roller* later in this chapter) is it necessary for editors to know these specific locations. But editors do need to know which pages are in each signature and, in sheetwise imposition, which pages fall on each side of the sheet. In order to have this information they must also know how sheets will be folded and which binding system is being used because they directly affect the pagination within signatures.

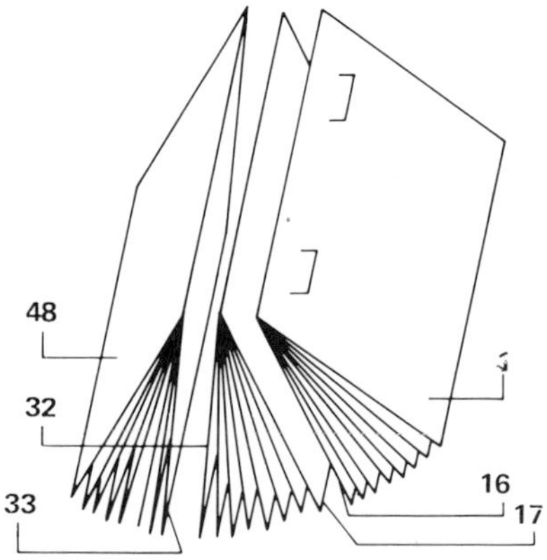

Figure 10–7 When three 16-page signatures are stacked as shown before binding, all pages in each signature are numbered consecutively. If staples are driven into the stack from the top through the bottom, the binding is called *sidewire*.

Folding and Binding

Magazine signatures are usually created with standard right angle folds: the first fold of the longest dimension produces a four-page signature; a right angle fold of the longest dimension produces a four-page signature; a right angle fold in the newly created longest dimension produces an eight-page signature, the next fold a 16-page one, and the fourth fold creates a 32-page unit.

Binding starts with the signatures folded but untrimmed. When bindery operations are concluded, the complete magazine is trimmed on the top, right, and bottom edges.

Bindery operations may be carried out by the printer, or by a specialized firm engaged only in binding. Most magazine binding today is either *perfect* or *saddle-wire,* although a few magazines are still *side-wire* bound (see figs. 10–7, 10–8, and 10–9). Most magazines that are thicker than a quarter of an inch (and such things as mail order catalogs, mass market paper-bound books, and telephone books) use perfect binding. With this method, signatures are stacked and clamped. The binding

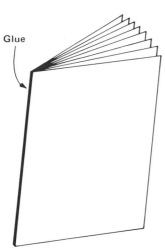

Figure 10–8 When glue is applied to the backbone of a magazine to bind the sections together, the binding is called *perfect*.

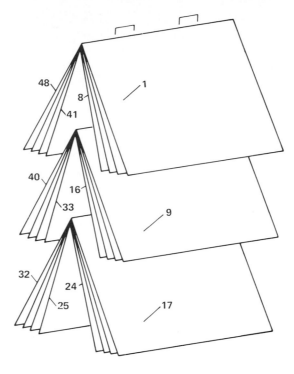

Figure 10–9 In saddle-wire binding, signatures are inserted rather than stacked, and for all but the center signatures, pages will not be numbered consecutively—half will be from the front of the magazine and half will be from the back. In this example, the outside signature contains pages 1–8 and 41–48.

edge of the stack is then roughed up, and a coating of highly-flexible glue is applied; a separate cover is wrapped around the stack and held in place by the glued edge, called the *backbone*. If staples are used to form the hinge function in this kind of binding (instead of the elastic glue) it is called side-wire binding. The staples are applied through the top of the stack to the bottom, about an eighth of an inch from the backbone.

In saddle-wire binding, the signatures are not stacked atop each other; instead, they are inserted within one another, as if each were a saddle. Staples are then driven from the outside to the inside of the centerfold. Most magazines are saddle-wire bound, unless they are too bulky.

Selection of the binding system is important. Generally speaking, saddle-stitching is efficient only for the thinner magazines that reach only about ¼-inch thickness. Leading magazines such as *Time, Newsweek,* and *Playboy* are bound by this method. As one can imagine seeing figure 10–9, the problem with the use of saddle-stitching for thick magazines is the effect that trimming the open edge has on page size and margins. The center pages, because they jut out more, lose more in trimming. Consequently, the thicker magazines such as *Popular Science, McCall's,* and great numbers of specialized business publications are bound by either of the other methods. The real importance of binding to the magazine production chief is, however, not related to selecting the right system of binding. Instead, it is the effect of binding on signatures and imposition that is of prime importance.

Putting Them All Together: Signatures, Folding, Imposition, and Binding

Most small magazines are put together with sheetwise imposition of 16-page signatures with standard right angle folds. Under these standard circumstances, it is quite easy to determine which pages go on each side of the sheet and, consequently, in each printing form.

The most common small magazine is composed of 32 pages, so let's use that as our first example. First, draw a horizontal line. On the top of the line at its extreme left, write the number of the first page in the signature. In this instance the number is 1. Then, working from the left, add numbers in pairs, alternating between the bottom and top of the line until you have added half the pages in the signature. Then work from the right in the same manner, starting with the number of the last page in the signature (page 32 in this case) and continue until the other half of the pages in the signature have been listed. This is the result:

1		4,5		8,25		28,29		32
	2,3		6,7		26,27		30,31	

In this same example, how would the pages fall on each side of the sheet that forms the center signature? The first page is 9, and the last is 24, so, following the same procedure, we get this result:

9		12,13		16,17		20,21		24
	10,11		14,15		18,19		22,23	

In each case, the numbers above the line are on one side of the sheet, and those below the line are on the other side.

Common sense planning in this case would provide for four deadlines—one for each set of eight pages in a printing form, and the same four units for color planning.

A 24-page magazine with the same equipment would be completed with three press forms—one for an 8-page work-and-turn signature, and the other two for the sides of a 16-page, sheetwise-imposed signature. Assuming that the 16-page signature is on the outside, the page forms would be as follows:

1		4,5		8,17		20,21		24
	2,3		6,7		18,19		22,23	

9,10,11,12,13,14,15,16

Working with a Miniature Dummy

As suggested in the previous chapter, a miniature dummy can be very handy in planning an issue. There is no better way for checking the break-of-the-book to see that content is as it should be *and* to make certain that no costly production errors are being made. For the novice, miniature dummies are also an effective method for learning the practical aspects of signatures, imposition, and binding.

To create a miniature dummy for the 32-page magazine diagrammed above, just use two sheets of ordinary typing paper. Fold each as the printer would fold the large sheet: break the 11-inch depth in half (makes four pages), then break the 8½-inch dimension (makes eight pages), then make the last fold by breaking the longer remaining dimension (5½-inch) to form the 16-page signature. Repeat the process for the second 16-page signature. Then, assuming that saddle-wire binding will be used, insert one signature into the other. Label the front of your miniature magazine with "page 1" and the back with "page 32." Numbering the remaining pages is somewhat difficult, but it can be done by opening the folds just enough to get the page number written.

Now you can unfold the sheets to know which pages are on each side of the sheet, and they will conform to the diagramming. To be able to turn the pages of your dummy, the top (or bottom, depending on your fold) must be trimmed along with the outside edge. By keeping two miniatures, one with the folds trimmed and the other without trimming, you can have one with "turnable" pages to check content and the other with untrimmed sheets to check for deadlines and color usage.

Miniature dummies for any number of pages and any folding or binding can be made in similar fashion, but variations in folding can present complications. Printing from a web rather than sheets makes all of production planning more difficult and complicated.

Web Offset Printing

Many magazines are printed on multi-unit web offset presses as shown in figure 10–2. As circulation and color requirements increase, the probability of moving from sheet-fed to web presses increases. There are so many alternatives for collecting and folding pages as they are cut from the web that only the printers themselves and skilled production managers can work out efficient impositions for these presses.

For one thing, web presses are perfecting; there is no way to print one side and then bring the paper back to the front of the press to "back it up" as we did in earlier examples. They are also composed of several units, can use varying widths of webs, and can use more than one web, making it possible to get a wide range of color possibilities. Only the cut-off point is fixed and unchangeable.

Web presses of a size suitable for magazines commonly print 16-page or 32-page signatures. To get just a basic idea of the versatility of web printing, look first at figure 10–10, with one web of paper receiving eight magazine pages in black on both sides of the web. This is the simplest use of the web. Figure 10–11 shows one web of paper going through two units, producing black plus a second color for the eight pages on each side of the web. Note that the colors can differ on the top and bottom.

In figure 10–12, a 4-unit press is receiving two webs, the top web being printed in black on both sides, plus red on the top and blue on the bottom. The bottom web is being printed in black on both sides, plus yellow on the top and green on the bottom, before merging into one 32-page signature.

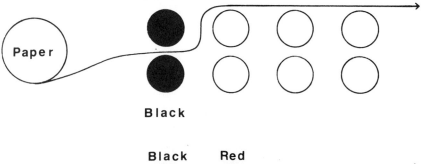

Figure 10–10 The simplest use of a web for magazine printing, eight pages in black being printed on the top and another on the bottom. A basic difference in web press operation is thus illustrated here; if the back side is to be printed, it must be done as the web goes through. Webs are not re-wound and returned to the feeding end of the press as sheets would be for a sheet-fed press.

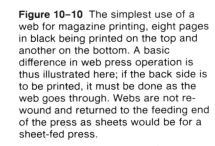

Figure 10–11 With the addition of a second unit, a second color can be printed on both sides of the web, and the color added to the top can be different from the color being added to the bottom.

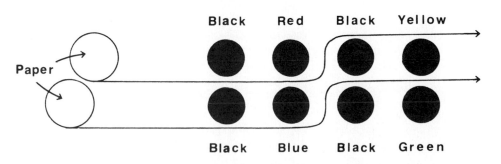

Figure 10–12 In this drawing a 4-unit press is receiving two webs, the top being printed in black on both sides, red on the top, and blue on the bottom. The bottom web is being printed in black on both sides and yellow on the top and green on the bottom before merging into one 32-page signature. Each of the four units applies ink to eight pages on each side of the web.

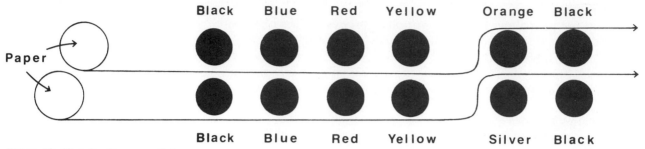

Black Blue Red Yellow Orange Black

Paper

Black Blue Red Yellow Silver Black

Figure 10–13 A 6-unit press with two webs, one being used to get process color on both sides of one 16-page unit and the other printing black plus an additional color on both sides of the other sixteen pages. The two sheets are folded together as a 32-page signature.

One of the most common problems of a magazine is providing process color for several advertisers, but only black plus one color for many others. Figure 10–13 shows a six-unit press with two webs: one printing process colors on both sides, and the other using the remaining two units to get black plus one color on each side.

These examples illustrate only a few of the complexities of imposition planning with web offset. When we consider the necessity for figuring which pages will fall on each side when multiple webs are being used and combined for folding, we can appreciate the need for production specialists on magazine staffs.

One example of the work of a production manager here can illustrate his or her role in relaying imposition requirements to any editors involved. The form in figure 10–14 was prepared by the production manager of *Medical Opinion* magazine as an imposition guide for the editorial staff. Four-color process ads from Campbell Soup, Roche Valium, and Merrill Tenuate were planned to be together, and other four-color ads from CIBA and SKF Stelazine were grouped together as shown. Blank editorial pages in those two rows were thus known to be available for any or all of the process colors; ads using only one of the colors were also placed accordingly.

Complexities of web offset also serve to point up the need for channeling all production decisions through one person, usually the editor in the case of a small sheet-fed situation or a specialized production manager in the web-fed situation. Efficiency of production is essential to avoid waste and increasing cost, and efficiency starts with the coordination of all aspects of production planning under one person. The title of that person is inconsequential—it may be managing editor, art director or something else—but ultimate authority in production matters must rest with that person.

The mere fact that more than one person works directly with a printer is enough to create a widening variety of production problems, including unnecessary cost. Advertising, editorial, and circulation departments are all involved with production, but an efficient operation is not possible if each department head works independently with the printer. If printers have the choice of blaming late delivery and overtime on the ad director for accepting an ad after deadline, or the editor for failure to provide illustrations on time, or the circulation manager for not being ready with address stencils, they have magazine staffs at their mercy. But if they deal directly only with one person, and that person has the power to force staff compliance with deadlines, as well as the power to negotiate printing contracts, they live up to their obligations or lose the contract. Normally they live up to their obligations in this situation because the staff's compliance with deadlines, thanks to the production chief's insistence, makes it easier for them to do so.

Although persons responsible for supervising production can come from any department, they must first of all be knowledgeable in all aspects of printing that relate to the magazine. They must also be able to see the complete, overall production picture so they can put the needs of all departments in proper perspective. They cannot be so imbued with the income-producing role of the advertising department that they fail to see the consequences of failure to meet production schedules in order to permit a special late closing for an advertiser. Nor can they be so involved with the editorial department that they permit that department any indiscretions that get in the way of production efficiency. In the final analysis, they are

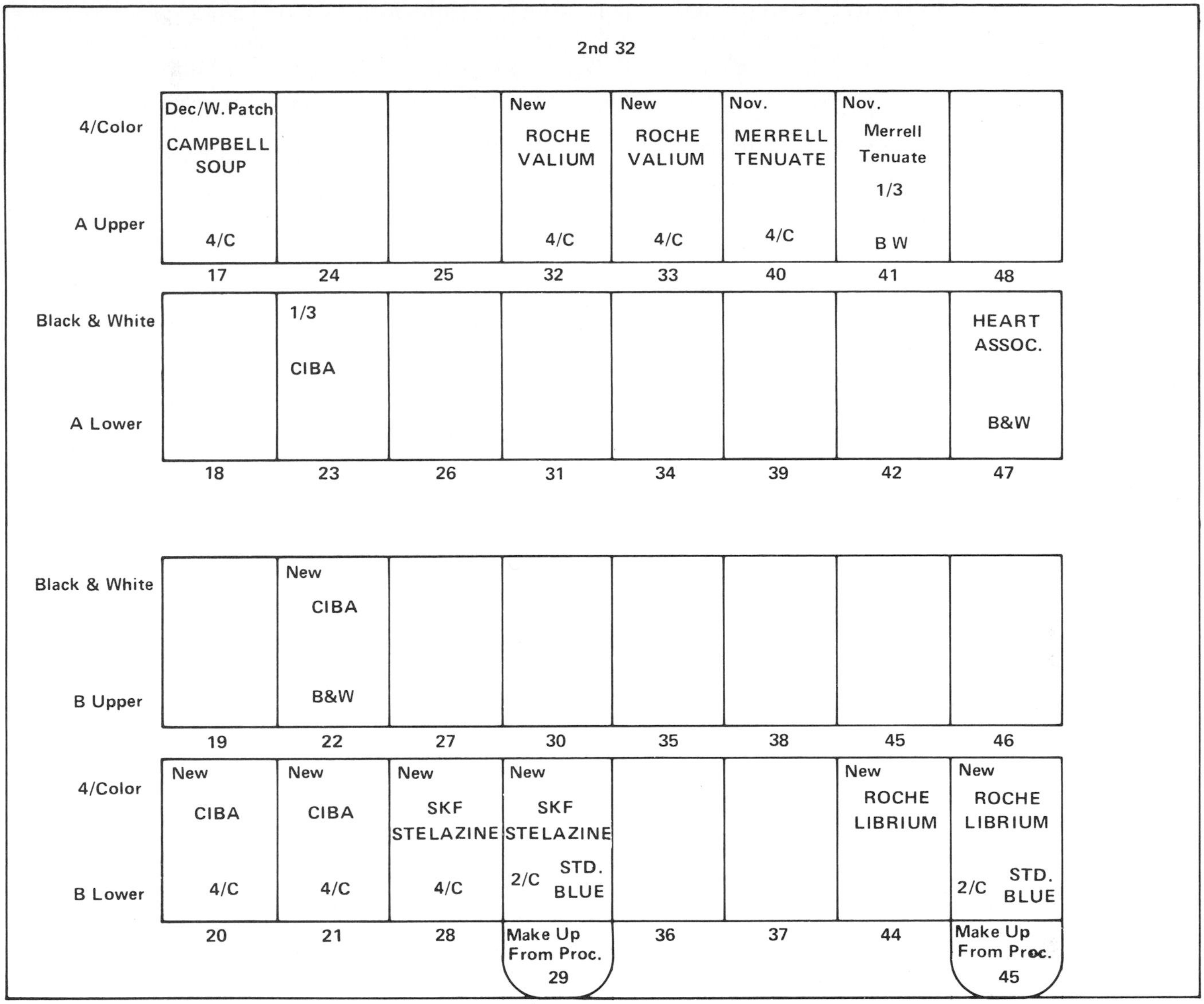

	17	24	25	32	33	40	41	48
4/Color **A Upper**	Dec/W. Patch CAMPBELL SOUP 4/C			New ROCHE VALIUM 4/C	New ROCHE VALIUM 4/C	Nov. MERRELL TENUATE 4/C	Nov. Merrell Tenuate 1/3 B W	

	18	23	26	31	34	39	42	47
Black & White **A Lower**		1/3 CIBA						HEART ASSOC. B&W

	19	22	27	30	35	38	45	46
Black & White **B Upper**		New CIBA B&W						

	20	21	28	Make Up From Proc. 29	36	37	44	Make Up From Proc. 45
4/Color **B Lower**	New CIBA 4/C	New CIBA 4/C	New SKF STELAZINE 4/C	New SKF STELAZINE 2/C STD. BLUE			New ROCHE LIBRIUM	New ROCHE LIBRIUM 2/C STD. BLUE

Figure 10–14 This diagram, provided by the production manager of *Medical Opinion* magazine to show the staff the placement of color ads, shows the planning necessary to keep the color pages together for utmost efficiency and economy of production. Two webs, each with eight pages on a side, were joined together and cut and folded into a 32-page signature. (Courtesy *Medical Opinion*.)

in charge of the manufacture of a product that several departments have contributed to, and they must have the authority to coordinate all their efforts once the manufacturing stage is reached.

They should start this coordination at the earliest stage of production planning. The printing process used and the printer hired to do the job should require their approval. Paper choice and paper buying should be under their control. They should constantly check the quality and delivery performance of the printer and correct any shortcomings through prompt negotiation with the printer.

But perhaps the most important of their contributions are in the planning and scheduling area. They should determine and enforce the production deadlines for all departments, basing their decisions on the contract requirements with the printer. An air-tight schedule of closing dates for all editorial and advertising sections that will guarantee delivery to subscribers on time is essential. The most tempting reason for breaking a closing date, especially with the smaller, specialized magazine, is the large, late-arriving ad that would give a nice boost to an issue's advertising space total. As enticing as a few hundred extra dollars may be, delay of a closing for this reason is usually a long-run liability. Printers whose schedules are thus disrupted cannot be expected to adhere as strictly to their future delivery commitments as they should. And once advertisers discover that a magazine will break its schedule in order to get a late ad, they are all inclined to expect the same treatment. The end result is delay in publication, a delay in collecting from all advertisers, and the creation of reader resentment that eventually makes the magazine a less effective advertising medium. All this for a few extra dollars which, in most instances, are forthcoming from the following issue anyway because, when pressed, the advertiser will usually accept the later publication. In most instances, especially when the ad's net revenue (after agency commission and other deductions) is considered, the added income wouldn't justify breaking the schedule under any circumstances.

Editing to Meet Production Requirements

Editorial departments like to stretch schedules, too, and reasons for doing so seem ever-present. But rarely can benefits outweigh the cost of schedule breaking. Cost is forever the handmaiden of content, and any decision to delay an issue for a late-breaking event must weigh the cost as well as the improved reader service. As a matter of fact, if a magazine's production is to be efficiently handled, all editorial decisions must be related to production procedures. Nowhere is this cooperation of editorial and production so obvious as in situations where a technique called *split-roller* printing is used.

Split-Roller Printing

Many contemporary magazines exploit split-roller (split-fountain) printing in order to keep color costs down. The technique is especially common among specialized business magazines with relatively low circulations but complicated color requirements. These complicated color requirements stem from the fact that specialized business publications are usually loaded with advertising, and the advertisers specify and pay for one or more colors to be added to black for their advertisements.

In split-roller printing the ink roller and the ink fountain on the press are divided so more than one color can be fed into the press for each impression.

To use a split roller effectively, an editor must know the location of each page in its printing form in addition to knowing merely which pages are in the form. Each segment of the roller will carry the ink from its segment of the fountain over the pages that are in a channel covered by the roller section as it moves across the form.

Figure 10–15 has been drawn to show how, with a 16-page work-and-turn imposition, a complicated color run necessitated by advertisers could be used to gain extra color for readers without added press time. When each of four advertisers stipulated that their ads be printed in one color besides black, and each one wanted a different color, the ad manager and editor cooperated with the production manager with this result. The red ad was assigned to page 2, the blue to page 6, the gold to page 8, and the brown to page 4, so that each would be in a separate channel. Pages 9 through 16 were to contain editorial matter, so the editor used the color from each channel to add reader appeal to those pages. Hence, with only two press runs, the first for black and the second with split sections of the roller, the editorial pages received four colors in addition to black.

The possibilities for wasting money in this situation are endless. The editor insisting upon a color not available from an ad, the ad manager insisting on special position for an ad that would take it from the appropriate color channel—each would require wasted cost for color. With split rollers, color *bleeds* (extending off the outside edge of a page) are restricted because for offset printing a 4½-inch gap is needed between the split sections. A bleed color page, because it reduces the gap area, will cancel out the possibility of using the adjoining channel for another color.

Although it would seem that splitting the rollers and ink fountains would make the technique costly, printers who specialize in magazine printing are prepared to offer split fountain printing at a very reasonable cost when compared with the cost of added runs or added units.

Wraps, Inserts, and Tip-ins

In spite of the most careful planning, there are cases in magazine production that call for printing and binding sections that are smaller than the usual signature. These

Figure 10–15 A diagram showing how, by splitting the ink roller and fountain, four different colors might be applied to one printing form with only one additional press run.

may be only a single sheet (two pages) called a *tip-in;* a four-page section wrapped around a signature before the signature is bound in place (a *wrap*); or a four-page section placed inside a signature for binding (an *insert*).

As a general rule, the smaller the number of pages being printed at a time, the higher the printing price will be per unit. Consequently wraps, inserts, and tip-ins are avoided in favor of 8- or 16-page signatures. A decrease in binding strength when using inserts and tip-ins also represents a disadvantage.

The most common reason for using the smaller page units is the demand from advertisers that their product be shown on a special paper stock or with some other special treatment. Occasionally an editorial section, such as a "late news" department, will be reproduced on a special stock and inserted in order to create an impression of unusual timeliness for the section.

As mentioned previously, advertisers often will print two pages of a four-page insert and leave the other two to be printed (backed up) with editorial matter. These instances, and the other uses of small page units, require careful planning to meet standard closing dates and to keep pagination in order.

Cost and Quality Go Hand-in-Hand

Much of the emphasis in this chapter has been on controlling cost—avoiding unnecessary expenses. That does not mean that the concern for quality expressed in the previous chapter is abandoned when one shifts attention from editorial content to production requirements. As a matter of fact, the two are interdependent.

The magazine graveyard is filled with the corpses of scores of magazines whose cause of death is simply listed as "cost." Like the proverbial housewife who explained her monthly checkbook deficit by saying simply that she ran out of money before she ran out of month, magazine autopsies often trace the cause of death only to the point of ascertaining that the victim ran out of income before running out of cost. Obviously this kind of verdict is oversimplified and much too general.

Setting aside the failures that might better be traced to editorial inadequacies, there are enough examples of success in fighting the cost battle to suggest that, in many instances, there are ways of controlling or overcoming the cost problem. An increase in the mailing cost, for example, can be fatal to one magazine while another, serving the same audience and facing the same new burden, can absorb the cost and remain alive.

The truth is that identical magazines, even though produced in the same plant, can show totally different cost pictures. These differences, and they can be substantial enough to be on a "life or death" level, stem from the ability or inability of a publishing venture to control its costs through efficiency of operation.

The importance of production efficiency becomes clear and apparent in such life or death situations. The efficient magazine survives, and the inefficient one dies.

But there are many instances in which inefficiency doesn't show itself so readily. In some situations, for example, favorable competitive advantages or special income potential permit a periodical to survive in spite of inefficiencies. There is a loss in such a situation, however, either by unnecessary profit reduction or, more probably, in a lower level of service to readers. Every unnecessary cost eliminates the possibility of adding pages, more color, or some other benefit for the reader. In the long run, perhaps these are the more critical situations, because the magazine industry as a whole is the loser. Magazines that die because of inefficient production usually deserve their fate, and are no longer around to plague the industry. But those that stay alive and hobble along providing only minimal reader services, tend to reduce the status of all magazines in the competitive mass communication industry.

As we shall see in later chapters, technological developments have placed control of production cost and efficiency more and more directly in the hands of magazine editorial staffs. Much of what formerly was production is now editorial, and the blending of the two presents the opportunity for better years ahead.

11

Steps of Production

WHEN Benjamin Franklin and Andrew Bradford started the first American magazines in 1741, there was no separation between their editorial and production operations. Both men were printers as well as writers and editors, and the thought of sending their material to outside printers probably never occurred to them.

Instead, it was the custom of the day for typesetting and even printing press operation to be "in-house"; that is, performed at the same place and by the same people who prepared the editorial content. Editors often put their thoughts into words as they stood at a printer's type case, picking up each metal casting of a letter or other character and lining it up in a printer's composing stick until their article was completed.

Such simultaneous writing and typesetting continued well into the 19th century, finally giving way to a separation of these functions when technology produced more complex machines and methods for printing production. Skilled machine operators were then called upon to produce, in type, the words of writers and editors.

Although much magazine production work is still done by contract printers totally separate from editorial staffs, an unusual cycle is now being completed that is bringing printing chores in-house once again. In a classical example of the cyclical nature of history, many magazine writers and editors of today are simultaneously writing and typesetting their wares, just as Franklin and Bradford did.

Obviously, they are not using the handset metal type and the stone make-up tables of Franklin's era. Instead they have at their command marvelous new machines that eliminate the need for separate human typesetters and page make-up persons. As they keyboard their words and instructions at a machine, today's writers and editors are also putting their words into type and perhaps even positioning their material on pages.

Without attempting to assign the production functions to either outside printers or in-house staff activity, let's first sketch the basic steps involved in magazine production. Some of these already have been shown to have a direct bearing on issue planning. The basic steps are:

1. Copy processing: getting words into type.
2. Illustration processing: converting illustrations from the original image to an image on a printing plate that can carry ink to paper.
3. Combining words and illustrations into pages: preparation of a mechanical, the camera-ready paste-up of type and illustrations. A separate mechanical is needed for each color to be printed.
4. Photographing the mechanicals to create negatives to be exposed on a printing plate.
5. Fastening the negatives (stripping) into opaque masks so material will be in correct page position when exposed on a printing plate.
6. Imposition: the positioning of pages in the mask so that, when they are exposed on a large printing plate and then printed on large sheets and folded, they will be in proper sequence.
7. Preparing a press plate by beaming light through the mask containing the page negatives.

8. Printing of signatures, the large sheets which, when folded, become sections of the magazine. For each color, the paper goes through a press or press unit one time (two colors, two impressions). Separate plates are needed for each color to be printed.
9. Folding: taking the large sheets and folding them into the desired shape and size (*format*).
10. Binding: putting the folded sections (signatures) together with glue, wire, or string.

These production steps are shown in figures 11–1 through 11–10.

Figure 11–1 Copy processing starts at a keyboard, such as the one being used at this video display terminal. If copy is first created at a typewriter, it may have to be rekeyboarded for type to be produced.

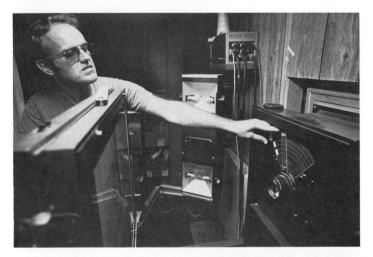

Figure 11–2 Continuous tone illustrations, such as photographs, must be photographed through a screen in a process camera. They may be enlarged or reduced at this step. Here the cameraman adjusts the lens. The camera extends into another room on the right and contains a vacuum frame holding a film screen tightly in place over the unexposed film. Exposures from lights (in center behind cameraman's forearm) create a dot pattern on the film as the light passes through the screen.

Figure 11–3 All line copy, such as type and line drawings, must be accurately positioned and fastened down on what is called a mechanical, which is then photographed with the process camera.

Figure 11–4 A vacuum copy board such as this one holds mechanicals or individual line drawings that must be photographed in the process camera. Here some line copy, which had to be reduced separately, is on the board.

Figure 11–5 Separate masks for line work on paste-ups and individual illustrations to be double burned in position must be prepared. Page negatives on the left have blank spaces for the illustrations; the mask folded back on the right contains the illustration negatives that are to fill the blank spaces. Each mask will be exposed (burned) in position on a plate. Negatives have been carefully positioned (registered) so the illustrations will appear exactly where they should.

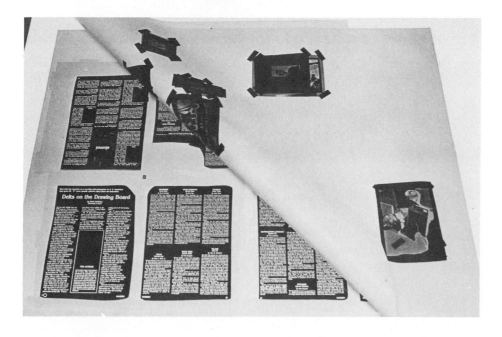

Figure 11–6 Imposition of pages in a mask. Eight page negatives are in position in the mask shown partially here. The half-tone negatives in the upper mask (folded to the right) must also be placed to fit the imposition of the pages.

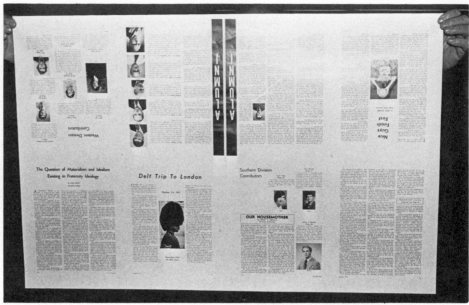

Figure 11-7 After the printer has painted (opaqued) out blemishes on any of the negatives (left), the plate (right) is burned. This plate contains 8 pages to be printed on one side of a sheet which, when folded, will form a 16-page signature.

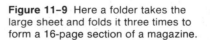

Figure 11-8 The printed sheet. Here the result of one impression from the press onto paper is checked. Note that the sheet contains several pages; it will be turned over and printed on the other side to form a signature.

Figure 11-9 Here a folder takes the large sheet and folds it three times to form a 16-page section of a magazine.

Figure 11-10 This saddle binder drives staples from the back to the center of the signatures that have been stacked like saddles, and are now ready to be trimmed as they emerge from the binder.

Selecting a Process and Printer

The steps described and shown in the illustrations in this chapter show the production of a magazine by *photo offset lithography;* the vast majority of magazines are produced in that fashion. Except for final platemaking, these steps are the same for other processes as well.

Magazines with larger circulation and extensive color requirements are printed on web presses containing several units, as described in the previous chapter. Magazines with primary emphasis on picture reproduction and multi-million circulations may be produced by *rotogravure,* a process that carries ink to paper from depressed areas in copper cylinders. Roto does an exceptional job of reproducing photographs, but the mechanics of the process make type reproduction less sharp than with offset.

Letterpress, the traditional process of printing from raised metal type and metal photoengravings of pictures, has virtually been eliminated from magazine production. In cases where letterpress is still used, it is likely that new platemaking methods have been adopted that make its production steps the same as those for offset or rotogravure.

Circulation, size, and basic production requirements virtually dictate the selection of one of the three processes for a magazine, but selection of a printer is a different matter.

Selecting a Production Partner: The Printer

For all magazines, including those with fairly complete in-house production facilities, the selection of a printer is an important decision. Even for magazines that go all the way to page paste-ups in the office, the printer is a vital part of a magazine production team. He or she is the manufacturer of the final, physical product. Printers often can cause more disappointment, create more confusion, destroy the budget more efficiently, and generate more frustration than anyone else a staff must deal with. On the other hand, they can be the fountain of all wisdom, the reliable right arm, the saviour of the budget, and the meticulous craftsmen that all magazine production people so desperately need. If only editors could have some extra-sensory means for perceiving how capable and compatible a printer might be, they could improve their odds considerably. But with no such magic method available, magazine editors and publishers must make their choice of printers with only the available facts plus good judgment as their guides. Good judgment requires consideration of quality and service, as well as cost.

Checking Quality

The time to determine whether a printer can produce high quality work is before a contract is signed, not after. A reasonable evaluation of a printer's capability can be made by carefully analyzing the work he or she is doing for others. Printers will provide samples of their output, and the more similar these samples are to your magazine, the better the analysis can be. Check carefully the three basic elements of a piece of printing: type composition, illustration reproduction, and page appearance.

One of the important factors of type composition is the availability of desired type faces. The printer's type catalog will tell you whether he or she has both body and display faces that will be adequate for your needs. If you want a type style that one does not have, he or she may order it for you but usually only at a cost beyond what you ordinarily would pay for typesetting. For offset magazines, it is important to know what kind of machine will be used for composition because of the difference in quality and capability among the many strike-on and photo-setting systems that are available. The system the printer will use should be capable of the quality and speed you need.

In any case, check the printer's samples to see if the equipment and its operators have produced composition that shows good spacing and correct hyphenation. Sloppy operators and/or unsophisticated machines can produce a disturbing variation in word spacing as they justify lines to make them flush on the right; and sometimes neither the machine nor the operator seems to know what a syllable is.

Where specialized typesetting companies are available, it may be wise to contract with one of them for your composition. In the larger cities, especially, there are type composition houses that offer the finest quality and service because they are specialists in this one phase of printing production. Their quality and service may more than compensate for the inconvenience of dealing with another supplier, and the possible additional cost.

The reproduction quality of photographs and other illustrations is controlled by the printer only in part. The original artwork may or may not have been good; but such things as inking and impression are indications of a printer's presswork and/or make-ready skill. Whatever the cause, any evidence of poor reproduction of photographs in any printer's samples should be looked into. Especially among offset printers, the skill with which halftone negatives are made can vary considerably. Any inadequacy in this department can be a primary source of frustration for the editor, art director, and entire production staff as they try to produce a quality publication.

General page appearance can reveal a lot about a printer's quality, especially in offset lithography. Such things as slight deviation in the placement (registration) of colors, some little specks of ink where they shouldn't be, and slight imperfections of alignment here and there can reveal a lack of care with the opaquing or stripping of negatives. A "washed-out" appearance in any or all of the printing area may indicate a failure to control the ink and water balance on an offset press as carefully as a first rate printer would control them.

For assistance in evaluating a printer's quality, consultation with one of the users may be in order and produce good results. Another editor who is working under contract with a printer can give insights into the printer's capabilities that an evaluation of samples may not disclose.

Checking Service

This consultation with another customer, plus a visit to the printer's shop, provides the best opportunities to check on the service you can expect from a printer. From one you can get a view as to how well a printer delivers on promises; from the other you can get an idea as to his or her capability to render good service. Generally speaking, it is wise to get a printer whose equipment obviously is capable of handling a magazine of the size in question. The printer who seeks your business on the grounds that your magazine wil be the biggest thing he or she handles, hence it will get top attention, should be checked out thoroughly. Such printers may not be able to deliver when breakdowns or other emergencies arise in their shops. It is usually safer to be one of several similar jobs that a printer turns out as a matter of routine because he or she is geared to handle a good volume of magazines of your size.

By checking with an editor of another magazine the printer produces, you might discover something about how well that printer keeps to a promised schedule. It is also important to know if the strippers or make-up persons follow your dummy specifications absolutely. Also, if the first proofs contain very few errors (are "clean") there is less possibility of errors getting into print. Some attempt should be made to be satisfied on all these points before signing a contract.

Ironically, the service performance of a printer may be the most difficult factor to determine in advance while, in many cases, it can be the most important aspect of a satisfactory relationship between a printer and a magazine staff. A few missed deadlines can soon destroy quality because of the rush they may cause, and production delays can cause all kinds of problems with distribution. It must suffice to say here that any advance checking that will reveal anything of a printer's level of service is well worth the effort.

Checking Cost

Although one might get the impression that printing costs are so standardized that shopping before buying is wasted effort, this is not the case. It is true that unionization tends to standardize wage levels in geographic regions, but there are other factors that produce some rather wide variations in pricing among printers. For example, the installation of a new piece of equipment by one printer may give him a decided price advantage over others who are using older equipment or doing a job by hand. Or, the need to keep expensive equipment busy may cause a printer to price his work low for jobs especially suited to that equipment. Pricing of printing is essential, therefore, when a magazine first is introduced and periodically thereafter.

Specifications. The difficulty with checking printing costs is that there are so many variables that it may seem almost impossible to make accurate comparisons. The only way to get a realistic basis for comparison is to provide a complete, detailed set of specifications on which prices will be obtained. These specifications should be based on common printing trade practices and expressed in terms and measurements used in the industry. Sizes of type, for example, should be expressed in points, with *body* types being those of the smaller sizes (under 14 points) and *display* types those of 14 points or larger. A point is considered to be 1/72nd of an inch.

Use of additional white space between lines (called leading) has an obvious effect on total amount of typesetting in any printing so it should be among the specifications for type. Other dimensions of printing are based on picas (12 points, 1/6th of an inch). Column widths, margins, and the white space breaks between columns are expressed in picas by printers.

Printing specifications should include at least the following items: trim page size, type page size, number of pages, number of copies, type composition, paper, cover requirements, illustrations, binding, proofs, production schedule, and distribution.

1. *Trim page size.* This is the dimensions of the magazine page after trimming; e.g. 8½″ × 11″.
2. *Type page size.* These dimensions represent the type area after margins have been deducted. The columnar structure of pages usually should be included here. The type area specification for an 8½″ × 11″ trim size might be: type page size 45 picas by 58 picas apportioned in three columns each 14 picas wide separated by 1½ picas with bottom margin of 4½ picas, top and outside of 3½ picas, and the inside margin of 2½ picas. The reasoning behind the variation in margins is discussed in chapter 14. The important point here is to realize that type page is a determinant of cost and should be part of the specifications.
3. *Number of pages.* For production efficiency, the number of pages should be a multiple of four or, preferably, eight or sixteen. Also be sure that there is no confusion by stating whether the number given here includes the cover. A typical page specification would be 48 pages, self-cover, if the cover is to be part of a regular section printed on the same paper as inside pages, or 48 pages, plus cover, if the cover is to printed separately in addition to the 48 basic pages.
4. *Number of copies.* The normal press run should be stated here with a request for the amount involved for adding or reducing that total by a hundred or a thousand copies. When setting the basic number, you must take into account the printing trade practice that permits a printer some leeway for unexpected waste. He or she may be permitted as much as a 10 percent under-run.

It is also important to get an understanding here of the amount that will be involved for adding or deleting a 4-, 8-, or 16-page section of the magazine. This is one of the variables that can cause difficulty; the low bidder may turn out to be the higher bidder when you turn out an unusually large or small issue unless you consider this cost at the outset.

5. *Type composition.* Every detail should be specified, including the size of body type, whether leading (extra white space) is to used, type designs and the methods of composition that are acceptable. Wherever special sizes or styles are to be used, as in the case of photo captions and blurbs, these should be specified. In dealing with offset printers especially, the stipulation of composition method is important because it might be desirable to rule out some methods of strike-on composition in the interest of quality. It is best to specify exact faces desired, because the choice of type faces can affect cost, as mentioned earlier. It is possible, however, to stipulate only that type design will be selected from among those stocked by any bidder. Ordinarily this is not wise unless the printers' catalogs of type faces have been checked before inviting them to quote a price.

It should be noted again here that a magazine staff may compose its own type for offset production; if such is the case the printer should be informed of the details of such an arrangement as they affect him. If you are using the services of a specialized firm for typesetting, this information should be given to potential printers.

6. *Preparation of mechanicals.* If pasting up mechanicals is going to be done by the staff, this fact must be relayed via the list of specifications. All production chores done in-house have an effect on printing costs and should be included (if titles are going to be hand drawn or prepared with paste-down letters, for example).

7. *Paper.* Here again the specification must be detailed. Paper is an important determinant of both quality and cost for a magazine. Its quality importance is perhaps reflected in a simplistic definition of the difference between a magazine and newspaper that was once given by a student: a newspaper is printed on poor paper and a magazine is printed on good paper. There are other differences, but there is no doubt that most magazines use a high quality paper stock. Paper buying in the graphic arts is a highly technical science beyond the scope of this presentation, but there are some principles that editors should be aware of. They must realize, for example, that several factors enter into paper selection. These are: technical requirements, the aesthetic "feel" or impression that is desired, and cost, including the effect of weight on distribution costs.

Technical requirements for paper vary with the process being used, and, obviously, the selection must take the method of printing into account. There are special papers for offset and special papers for gravure, for example, and the relationship of paper to quality of reproduction makes paper selection especially important. The smoothness of enamel-coated or supercalendered papers is often desired. Supercalendered papers are so called because they are extensively calendered (squeezed between rollers sufficiently to get a smooth surface).

In addition to the degree of smoothness, paper surfaces can vary according to a desire for special textures. Paper can be made to look like leather, linen, or textured material. The texture may be applied before or after printing; in letterpress printing it is ordinarily necessary for the printer or a special "pebbling" sub-contractor to run the paper through textured rollers after printing in order to get this effect. Offset lithographers may simply print on paper that was already textured before they acquired it. Although most magazines wisely use a basic paper finish selected with legibility in mind and leave special textures to other media, occasionally a "mood" paper may be desired. Any other special technical requirements, such as being suitable for special inks, gumming, varnishing, and the like must also be specified to the printer.

Papers also vary according to weight, and weight has a direct and an indirect bearing on cost. It has a direct bearing because paper is priced by the pound or ton. Thus, by ordering heavier sheets than are really needed, an editor can waste money because total poundage per issue will be higher. But the indirect effect of paper weight on postal charges is of even greater consequence. It is difficult for a beginner to comprehend the sums involved for postage in some magazine operations; some magazines have annual postal costs in millions of dollars. In fact, increases in postal rates have been a primary factor in the death of some magazines. Therefore, a specification that calls for paper that is any heavier than practicality demands can be extremely costly. Such waste could probably never occur with consumer magazines staffed with specialists in paper buying; nor would it be likely to happen in the publishing firms that produce several specialized magazines. They, too, have production specialists who are skilled enough to appreciate all aspects of paper buying. But with the company magazines produced by public relations departments, postal bills and paper bills are often permitted to get out of bounds because unneeded weight has been specified for paper.

The specification of paper weight is complicated by the fact that the method for describing weight is in terms of the pounds per ream of a standard-size sheet. Thus for the *book* paper usually used for magazines a standard sheet is 25″ × 38″, and if a ream of these sheets weighs 70 pounds it is classified as 70-pound paper. If the sheets being used are half that size (25″ × 19″), obviously, a ream will weigh only 35 pounds but it is still classified as a 70-pound paper.

8. *Color requirements.* Most modern magazines make liberal use of color, either to bring full-life color to photos or to get special emphasis for titles or other parts of a page design. Your specifications to a printer should indicate your normal color usage and request price quotations for the addition of one or more colors to a printed sheet, one or both sides. With all printing processes, the addition of color is a cost variable of considerable consequence. Other chapters will provide additional guidance in keeping color costs down while getting maximum utility with color.

9. *Cover requirements.* As the magazine's showcase, the cover is entitled to special treatment. Any such special treatment—added color, stiffer paper, slightly larger size—should be described here or elsewhere.

10. *Illustrations.* This specification, for an offset magazine, must indicate whether the use of screened photoprints on mechanicals is acceptable, what screen is to be used, and an approximation of the amount of space in each issue that will be occupied by halftones. Common screens used for magazines range from 100-line to 150-line for good quality of reproduction.

11. *Binding.* Unless a magazine's bulk prohibits it, saddle-stitch binding is usually preferred. Some side effects on production planning that result from binding selection are explained in other chapters.

12. *Proofs.* Mutual understanding about the number and kinds of proofs to be provided by the printer is essential at the outset of any editor-printer relationship. Both cost and efficiency are involved here.

Ordinarily, galley proofs of all type that is set, revised galley proofs made after errors have been corrected, and final page proofs, should be required. Reproduction and press proofs may or may not be required depending upon circumstances.

Revised galley proofs provide protection for the printer and the editor by permitting detection of errors made during corrections before material has been put into page form. It is more costly to make corrections after pages have been put together. Throughout the proofing process, the printer bears the cost of his errors, but the editor is billed for those he creates or causes, or for the revisions he makes in the proofed material.

Page proofs should be used for checking on any switching of captions and pictures or titles and articles, as well as such layout matters as alignment of elements. In offset, these proofs take the form of *bluelines* or *brownlines,* so named because of their color. They are replicas, in blue or brown, of all the pages in a section. Corrections involving placement of elements are not too difficult to make at this point; negatives can be pulled loose from their position in a mask and moved rather easily. But type corrections require resetting and/or the making of a new negative as well as reinsertion into a mask. Hence this is no time to be making type corrections; they should be caught in galleys or at least before paste-ups are photographed.

Not to be overlooked in any process are proofs of illustrations. Photoengravers provide letterpress users with proofs of their plates so quality of reproduction can be checked. Brownline or blueline proofs in offset should be used for checking the quality of illustration reproduction.

Reproduction proofs or their equivalent are needed for offset lithography in many instances. Type proofs that are "camera ready" are needed for pasting into page position, unless type is being provided in film form ready for stripping into a mask.

Press proofs, though they offer the only possibility for absolute checking of all potential errors, are usually not required because of cost problems. Once a form or plate is on a press, charges for time on the press begin. Unless an editor or production manager can be on hand immediately as the first copy comes off a press, time charges can rise to unacceptable levels very quickly because in this instance the charges are completely nonproductive.

13. *Production schedule.* The number of working days needed to get to galley proof stage and then on to final delivery should be indicated by printers as they price a magazine job. A printer's ability to provide faster service should be considered along with price.

14. *Distribution.* The printer's responsibility for any part of the distribution of finished copies must be specified. Are wrappers to be used? Must the printer do the addressing? Is delivery of copies to the magazine's office included? All such questions should be answered when a price is given or obviously the price can vary considerably according to the degree of responsibility for distribution a printer may assume is expected.

Importance of New Production Technology

Magazines have been facing stronger and stronger competition as each year goes by. Cut-throat competition from the other media, plus the competition among themselves, will continue to keep some magazines teetering on the brink of financial disaster. In order to survive, all magazines—large, small, general, or specialized—will have to take advantage of everything modern technology offers for their production.

The cost of production and the quality of content are obviously interrelated and directly tied to the technology that is used to put words and illustrations into print. The selection of the printing process to be used and the printer with whom a partnership is to be formed are preliminary planning decisions that have long-lasting effects. If these decisions are made knowledgeably, the day-to-day production decisions are easier to make and are much more likely to be wisely made. The degree to which production is brought in-house is also of importance and interest.

Some "Typical" Production Examples

Diversity of production systems is so great among magazines now that it is difficult to describe what would be "typical" systems, but some examples will at least show the extent of the diversity.

Traditional Staff-Printer Relationship

Many smaller magazines, especially public relations and association magazines, still mark the separation of where editorial work and production begins with the completion of words and illustrations on paper and edited with copy pencil and grease pencil. The raw materials are delivered, along with a layout plan, to a commercial printer who takes over with the setting of type, halftoning of pictures, and so on through binding and distribution.

Blending of Traditional and Computerized Production

In-house typesetting and page make-up have so many advantages, however, that small and specialized magazines are incorporating these activities into their editorial operations at an extremely rapid pace. Cost advantages, improved deadlines, and a more total control over quality can result from what is only a reasonable expenditure of capital.

An entry device or devices, a versatile typesetter, and basic layout tools such as drawing boards and T-squares are all that are needed to bring about these improvements.

A typical example of such a system is in use by *DIY Retailing,* formerly *Hardware Retailing,* a magazine published by the National Retail Hardware Association for those operating hardware, home center, and lumber yard retail centers. Like most such specialized publications, *DIY Retailing* is bulky, full of ads, and each issue is a major production effort.

As can be seen in the series of pictures in figure 11–11, production starts with typewriter copy from the editors and is edited for production in that form. A staff member then composes the type, both body and display sizes, on a computerized typesetter. At her screen and from her keyboard, she can use a wide variety of type designs very efficiently and while occupying very little space. Anyone who has worked in traditional systems with printers being located across town or in another city can appreciate the advantages of the close proximity of type composers. Correction of errors is much easier; after editors at *DIY Retailing* carefully read photocopies of proofs of set type, changes can be quickly made at the terminal keyboard.

After proofs are corrected, the staff person with graphics responsibilities follows editorial dummies to paste proofs in page position. The advertising production manager plans the ad and editorial positions in the book and provides the staff with forms and imposition sheets. When the pages are complete, they are delivered to the printer who completes the production of the issue.

A

B

C

D

E

F

Figure 11–11 *DIY Retailing,* a magazine for stores catering to do-it-yourselfers, does much of its production itself. (a) Step one is the editing of typewritten copy. (b) Next, type is composed at a video display terminal, and output comes from the compact but versatile typesetter just to the right of the staff member at the VDT. (c) Careful proofreading, with one staffer reading and the other checking the proof, can be done immediately. (d) Meanwhile, ads are placed and imposition sheets are prepared. (e and f) Page mechanicals can then also be done by the staff, leaving only final production steps for a printer. (Courtesy *DIY Retailing.*)

This kind of a system, without multiple computer terminals and large-capacity computers, can be the most cost effective for many magazines and is especially common among specialized business, public relations, and association magazines.

The "Total" System

Publishers of all print media are looking forward to a totally computerized production system that starts with keyboards for text and cameras for photos and ends with the printed page, skipping all re-keyboarding of copy, paste-ups, negatives, masks, and perhaps even the printing plates. Gone would be paste-up tables, photocomposing machines, film-processing dark rooms, and even traditional printing presses. In their place would be the computer: words and pictures would be entered into the computer, manipulated by keyboard into pages, and transferred to paper by computer-generated ink droplets.

Not all of these advancements are yet in place, but, as figure 11–12 shows, most of them are. Starting with the writer and his personal computer, it is now common in sophisticated electronic systems to be able to take words and pictures, blend them into pages, transmit those pages from place to place and computer to computer, with only platemaking and press work still functions of printers.

A

B

C

D

Figure 11–12 (a) The writer-editor at the video display terminal is the central figure in the *U.S. News & World Report* electronic production system. Original stories are fed into the computer from these stations and can be called from storage for editing on the same video screen. All typesetting and page layouts are done at the terminals.
(b) An illustration scanner electronically converts photographs to digital halftones in desired sizes and stores the information on magnetic tape and in the computer. From the computer the halftones and page placement information go directly to a CRT typesetter which produces full pages at the editorial location.
(c) Typesetter output in the form of completed pages with all body type, display type, and illustrations in place is developed on photo paper in this processor. These page proofs can be read and corrected at the editorial office. Because all page components come from the computer in digital form, the pages can easily be transmitted by wire or other means to printers anywhere.
(d) From this control center at *U.S. News & World Report,* completed pages are sent in digital form by satellite to three printing plants. At the printing plants, the pages are received on magnetic tape and then fed into typesetters. The typesetters produce full pages ready for platemaking. (Courtesy *U.S. News & World Report.*)

Perhaps the most mature and comprehensive computerized system in magazine publishing is at the *U.S. News & World Report* in Washington, D.C.. News weeklies, such as *U.S. News,* have been leaders in the introduction of such systems because of their size and frequency of publication. *Time, Newsweek, Business Week,* and *Forbes* all use similar in-house systems for all preliminary production steps.

U.S. News, beginning in 1974, pioneered systems that could handle complete pagination, including continuous tone photographs. Modified since its installation, the system is also typical of sophisticated systems in that it incorporates within it telecommunication transmission of pages to printing plants. As the pictures in figure 11–12 show, copy can originate from writers at any remote or on-site terminal, be blended with photos to form pages in the computer, and be transmitted in page form via Western Union's Westar satellite to printers at various locations.

Typesetters in such systems are digital CRT (cathode ray tube) typesetters whose output is complete pages. They are digital in that they are computer-driven and CRT in that the computer-generated images are projected onto paper by a television tube. Phototypesetters, on the other hand, expose copy letter-by-letter in line position. Page output from CRT typesetters is virtually instantaneous.

Advantages of such systems are relatively obvious. Much later deadlines are possible. Quality control is totally within the editorial department. Copy can be edited exactly to space requirements, hyphenation and justification can be controlled by experts as well as the computer, and extensive verification and correction are feasible. Computer-generated graphics have made illustration of complicated material much easier and more sophisticated.

Current Production Developments

In the current state of change that we see in magazine production, there is one thing certain. The evolution of in-house production systems will maintain a steady progression, with some magazines taking the first step by moving some basic typesetting chores into the office. Others with in-house typesetting will move from that stage to more versatile systems. Still others will be entering the "total pagination" group.

The old-line methods, with the printer taking over with typewritten copy and photos and doing all the production chores, are surely on the way out, but they are not yet a thing of the past. Factors of economics and editorial quality will continue to exert pressure on these methods, however.

As Robert Vereen, former editor of *Hardware Retailing* and now senior vice-president at *DIY Retailing,* put it:

In much the same way as the pocket calculator has broadened its market by constant and drastic price reductions, so too has electronic typesetting come into the pocketbook and budget range of an increasing number of publications due to sharp price decreases and improved (really meaning simplified) technology.

Today any publication, even one that spends as little as $500 a month, can afford in-house typesetting.

Equipment for direct-entry typesetting (all that's needed for a great many smaller trade publications) costs as little as $7,500 to $10,000. Chemicals, supplies, etc., are minor: maintenance negligible.

Vereen also points out that in-house production facilities provide much more than an economic benefit:

For trade publications particularly it affords a time benefit of immeasurable value. In-house typesetting permits the extension of closing deadlines by as much as a week or more . . . (And) in-house typesetting, in-house paste-up and in-house production are far simpler than dealing with outside sources who can misplace your copy, miss your deadline, fail to properly proofread your material, etc. Control is easy; production is simplified; accuracy is improved—and most importantly, speed is assured.

Benefits of the most sophisticated systems are such that magazines will strive to "move up" with their systems. When the *U.S. News* system was introduced, president John Sweet estimated that the system would reduce production costs by 50 percent and provide flexibility for advertisers as well. The advantage for advertisers can be a boon for the mass magazines who are competing with television for advertising dollars. As President Sweet said, in addition to helping magazines to hold space rates down and, thus, be more competitive, there were other ramifications. The long period between closing dates and publication has always been a disadvantage for magazines in competition with television because advertisers had no opportunity to make last-minute changes. Now, with the new production methods, this disadvantage can be removed.

The Meaning of It All

For those preparing for magazine writing and editing careers, what is the meaning of all this change in production methods? Obviously there is no change in the need for verbal talents and other qualifications discussed earlier in this text. In does mean, however, that a basic knowledge of printing production is one of the tools that will be needed now and in the future.

The emerging role of the personal computer means that, even for a writer at a remote location, there must be some concern for the production steps to follow because the writer is involved in the production process.

Understanding the basics of their computer systems, plus skill with a computer keyboard, are as necessary today as typing ability has been in the past. Some knowledge of typography is also essential, because the product is still composed of type, and communicating with a computer *or* with a printer will remain as basic necessities in the production of magazines as far as we can see into the future.

The Editor and Typography

12

Typography can be defined as the use and arrangement of type. It can be an art, but for editors it is more than that. It is an essential part of their communication role, a tool for getting words into the minds of their readers.

Type has many faces, and it can be said that it speaks with many voices. Type can speak boldly, delicately, quickly, or slowly. It can be high-pitched or well-modulated and deep. It can be old-fashioned or modern, active or passive. The many moods of type make typography a fascinating part of the magazine editor's role. It has its own technical language, too, that has developed through the centuries since Johann Gutenberg devised moveable type. Some of its language, though seemingly outmoded by new technology, nevertheless holds on and must be learned by any users of type.

Some Typography Terms

Type, itself, once easily defined as raised alphanumeric symbols on a metal body whose faces were transferred in ink onto paper by pressure, now requires a much more general definition. Type now is any alphanumeric symbols used for duplication in any printing process. It includes the old-fashioned *hot type* cast in metal, but also embraces a wide variety of *cold type* (any type not cast in molten metal). For example, typewriter-like machines place an image on paper by striking an ink-covered key against the paper (*strike-on* type). Adhesive-backed letters and numbers can be cut from sheets and placed into position for printing (*paste-down* type), or letters can be transferred to paper by rubbing the backs of sheets of what is called *transfer* type. Most common of the newer physical forms for type is *phototype,* letter images exposed in position on photo paper. A sophisticated variation of phototype is created via computer and cathode ray (TV) tube with the letters being stored in a computer and exposed in great quantity instantaneously when the image on the tube is exposed on paper.

A type's *face* is the image it leaves when printed on paper. Its *body* is the carrier of the face and must be large enough to carry every part of the face, from the *ascender* that rises to the top to the *descender* that drops to the bottom. Most of its letters are lined up to use only the center of the body and are called *center body* letters. The body can be artificially fattened without changing the face, thus separating the faces from each other by between-line spacing called *leading* (pronounced *ledding*).

Now, thanks to modern typesetting technology, the body can even be made smaller than the face through a technique called *reverse leading* or *back leading.* More about this later as we discuss type sizes.

Letters within a line of type can be squeezed together or spread apart; the first technique is called *minus letterspacing* and the second is called *plus letterspacing. Normal letterspacing* gives each letter its usual space. Spacing for letters is *proportional* to the width of the letter and not uniform as it is on an ordinary typewriter.

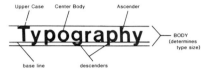

Figure 12–1 Type size is based on the normal body of a type face. That body must include room for ascenders and descenders as well as center body letters.

Type Measurement

Type is measured in *points,* a unit of measure that is 1/72nd of an inch. To understand type sizing, however, editors must do much more than commit to memory that there are 72 points in an inch. One of the thorny problems connected with type size stems from the fact that the *body* of the type determines the size, and not the *face* of any letter. Note in figure 12–1 that the body must allow for letters that go below a *base* line and rise above the *center body* area. Therefore, NO SINGLE LETTER OR CHARACTER IS EVER MEASURABLE TO DETERMINE TYPE SIZE. Or, to put it another way, when ordering type size in an effort to have it be equal to some hand lettering, one cannot measure any of the letters created by hand to determine the point size to order.

Various letter forms also can be in identical sizes but appear to be quite different in size, as shown in figure 12–2. When the center body letters (a, c, o, e, etc.) use up a large portion of the body, the type appears to be larger than when center body letters are small. The size of the center body letters is often referred to as the *x-height,* meaning the height of the small x of the type face.

Type measurement is further complicated by leading, the addition of extra white space between lines by expanding the type body without increasing the size of the letter faces. When type was cast in metal, the addition of a point or two of additional lead above and/or below a line of type in the casting process provided a helpful benefit for readers by forcing lines apart, thus adding white space between them. In cold type systems, although no metal is used, the term *leading* still prevails. Eight-point type put on a 10-point body then provides two points of white space between lines, and it may also be referred to as "8-point leaded two points," or "8 on 10."

Body Type and Display Type

Type that is in the smaller sizes typically used for the body of messages is called *body* type; type in the larger sizes typical of headlines is called *display type.* The exact point of separation is at 14 points; type 14 points or larger is display. The newcomer should keep the point of separation in mind because procedures for handling body types differ from those for display type. These differences will be pointed out as they arise in later discussions.

One must also be aware of a couple of "tricks" now available in typography and mentioned earlier: *reverse leading* and *plus or minus letterspacing.* Many photocomposition machines provide the opportunity for overlapping lines of type by exposing a line of type, then backing up and exposing another line in part of the space used for the first line as in figure 12–3. The technique obviously is restricted to the use of display type.

Figure 12–2 Although both of these are 36-point type faces, the difference in their design makes one appear smaller. The black square represents the x-height (portion of body used for center body letters).

Figure 12–3 Reverse leading can pull all-cap lines together.

In many situations reverse leading can provide better visual spacing for lines of display type (figure 12–4). For body type sizes, the area being occupied by type can be enlarged or reduced somewhat by having type characters crowded closer together or moved slightly apart. This *plus or minus word and letter spacing* often can be done without being apparent to readers. Various examples of this technique are shown in figure 12–5. At this writing there is no research to indicate what effect the technique has on reading ease.

The Pica and the Em

The length of lines of type is expressed in *picas,* a unit equal to 1/6th inch or 12 points. Printers' rulers, called *line gauges,* are a must for editors becasue they are marked off in picas, which are also used for expressing all other measurements used in printing: margins, column width, page size, and so on. A portion of a line gauge is shown in figure 12–6. Note that inches are shown on one edge and picas on the other; the smaller division within the pica represents six points.

An *em* is a unit of measure that varies with the type size being used, because it is a square in the type size. That is, an em in 9-point type is nine points wide, an em in 10-point type is ten points wide, and so on. For magazine editors, the main exposure to the term is in line spacing (the standard paragraph indention is an em) and when it is used imprecisely as a synonym for a pica (a 12-point square).

Plus or minus word and letter spacing are alternatives to normal spacing. This paragraph has been set in normal, plus one, and minus one to illustrate the different results. Spacing variations also available include plus or minus one-half unit. Units are based on the em and are usually one-eighteenth of an em. Note the effect of plus or minus letterspacing on total space in this example. In large amounts of body copy, spacing variation can be responsible for enlarging or reducing space demand about 5 percent in each direction.

Plus or minus word and letter spacing are alternatives to normal spacing. This paragraph has been set in normal, plus one, and minus one to illustrate the different results. Spacing variations also available include plus or minus one-half unit. Units are based on the em and are usually one-eighteenth of an em. Note the effect of plus or minus letterspacing on total space in this example. In large amounts of body copy, spacing variation can be responsible for enlarging or reducing space demand about 5 percent in each direction.

Plus or minus word and letter spacing are alternatives to normal spacing. This paragraph has been set in normal, plus one, and minus one to illustrate the different results. Spacing variations also available include plus or minus one-half unit. Units are based on the em and are usually one-eighteenth of an em. Note the effect of plus or minus letterspacing on total space in this example. In large amounts of body copy, spacing variation can be responsible for enlarging or reducing space demand about 5 percent in each direction.

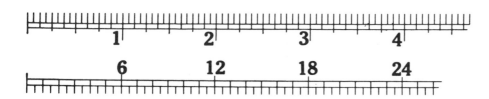

Take stock in America.

Figure 12–4 Using some of the blank space on the body reserved for ascenders or descenders can tighten up lines in capitals and lower case, sometimes with interesting results including better visual spacing.

Figure 12–5 This paragraph has been set with three different kinds of word and letter spacing: normal, plus one unit, and minus one unit.

Figure 12–6 A portion of a line gauge, the printer's ruler used to measure type size and other dimensions of printing. The top line is in inches and fractions; the bottom line is in picas, subdivided into nonpareils (6 points).

The Many Faces of Type

Type has many faces, many personalities. Letter forms range from simple to highly ornate, with thousands of variations available. Many basic type designs came into existence because they were copies of the work of calligraphers of a particular time and place. Others have been designed in modern times to achieve a mood or accomplish a specialized objective.

To bring some feeling of order to the study and use of type, these variations are classified first in broad *groups,* then *sub-groups, families, family variations,* and finally *fonts.* A quick look at basic letterforms will bring these divisions into perspective.

It should be recalled here that type faces rest on a body that determines their size. Looking again at figure 12–1, we can see that letters rest on a base line, with letters with *ascenders* (such as b, d, f) and capital letters (upper case) rising to the top of the body. Letters with *descenders* (such as g and y) reach to the bottom of the body. Basic letters (such as a, c, e) use only the center portion of the body. Non-capitals are called *lower case* to contrast them with capitals.

The Gothic Group

To form all letters of our alphabet in upper and lower case, only basic, uniform strokes are needed (figure 12–7). Such letters are *monotonal,* meaning no variation in tone that could be created by changes in thickness of strokes, and *skeletal,* meaning there are no unessential strokes. Faces of this type are usually called *Gothic* or *sans serif.* The latter designation means "without serif," and a serif is a short stroke running counter to the main stroke of a letter. By adding monotonal serif (figure 12–8) we can create a type design usually called *square serif Gothic.* These two sub-groups form a basic group with many variations, but all with a simple, strong character that makes them suitable for many uses.

The Roman Group

Letters designed with variation in thickness of strokes and distinct serifs (figure 12–9) form a group called *Roman,* using a letterform first used in the calligraphy of ancient Rome. The earlier Roman types, now called *Oldstyle,* were created with

Figure 12–7 The lack of unessential strokes and any substantial variation in thickness of strokes are characteristics of sans serif Gothic faces. Shown here is 30-point Futura Medium.

abcdefghijklmnopqrstuvwx yz&?! ABCDEFGHIJKLMN OPQRSTUVWXYZ $12345

Figure 12–8 This is 24-point Karnak, a square serif Gothic.

abcdefghijklmnopqrstuvw ABCDEFGHIJKLMNOPQR STUVWXYZ $1234567890

Figure 12–9 The Roman group is characterized by serifs and variations in stroke thickness. This 30-point Weiss Roman has moderate changes in stroke thickness, angular stroke thickness, angular stroke endings, and serifs that round into the stroke. These are common with Old Style Romans.

abcdefghijklmnopqrst ABC DEFHIJKLMNO $1234567

more angular strokes and less variation in thickness of storkes than those used for *modern Roman* faces (figure 12–10). Great variation on thickness of strokes, and thin, right-angle serifs are the hallmarks of modern Romans.

Script and Cursive
The flowing letters common to handwriting are produced in type through many script and cursive faces (figure 12–11). Script types generally resemble the precise, formal handwriting typical of a former era. Their letters are designed to join. Cursives, as a rule, are more informal, resembling hand lettering more than handwriting. Their letters do not join.

Text (Black Letter or Old English)
A rather specialized group of types forming a group called Text, Black Letter, or Old English is ornate and patterned after the calligraphy of German monks. It provided the pattern for type faces manufactured by the inventor of movable type, Johann Gutenberg (figure 12–12). Unnecessary and duplicate strokes, totally unessential for letter formation, are the primary characteristic of this group of type faces.

abcdefghijklmnopqr ABCDE
FGHIJKLMNOPQ $1234567

Figure 12–10 The stroke variation in this 30-point Bodoni, a modern Roman, is much greater than those of the Weiss. Note the hairline quality of some strokes. Serifs are thin and straight, not bracketed into the main stroke.

abcdefghijklmnopqrstuvwxyz
ABCDEFGHIJKLMNO
PQRSTUVWXYZ&?!

abcdefghijklmnopqrstuvwxyz $1234567890
ABCDEFGHIJKLMNOPQ!?

Figure 12–11 This 30-point Commercial Script (top) differs from the 24-point Mayfair Cursive in that the letters join in the Script. The Script is also somewhat more formal.

abcdefghijklmnopqrstuvwxyz
ABCDEFGHIJKLMNOP
QRSTUVWXYZ $12345678

Figure 12–12 This Engraver's Old English is typical of the Text group, used primarily for religious and related materials.

G.K.W.
COMPUTER
GOLD
RUSH
Gorilla
GOUDY
LOMBARDIC
GOUDY
ORNATE
Hobo
JIM CROW
JUMBO
Kabel Shaded
LETTRES
ORNEES
MADAME

Paper Clip
Pierrot
PINOCCHIO
PROFIL
RABBLE
Roberta
SACHER
STENCIL BOLD
STOP
Tempo
Black
THUNDER-
BIRD
MARBLEHEART
MEXICO OLYMPIC
Murray Hill Bold
Neil Bold
NEON

Figure 12–13 A few Novelty faces from a Zipatone, Inc., catalog illustrate the wide range of specialty types that are available from printers and suppliers.

Novelty

The above three groups came into existence as reflections of the handwork that antedated typography. Many other faces have been created to preform some special task or create a novel impression. These faces are without limit, as figure 12–13 should suggest; each year new faces are added to what appears to be an endless list. Types to suggest age, circus posters, the gay nineties era, computers, Broadway, and the like provide special designs for virtually every mood or purpose.

Type Families

Within each group, there are smaller groups of types that so closely resemble each other that if they were humans, they would likely come from the same family. These types are given a familial name and are said to be from the same family. Their names often are those of a designer, such as Bodoni, Garamond, and Zapf; they may also show the intended purpose, such as Commercial Script, News Gothic, or Dom Casual.

Family Variations

Just as with human families, type families have different personalities within them. Human families have tall and short members, fat and thin, upright and bent-over. Type faces present a parallel in that they can vary in size, posture, weight, and width. Unlimited sizes and letter variations for type families are available if cathode ray tube typesetters are being used. Slanting, expanding, and constricting of letter forms are easily achieved with such typesetters. But ordinarily the family variations are limited to four and normally-available sizes are 5½-, 6-, 7-, 8-, 9-, 10-, 11-, and 12-point for body types and 14-, 18-, 24-, 30-, 36-, 42-, 48-, 60-, and 72-point for display sizes.

For the Roman and Gothic groups, a standard family variation is posture, with the normal upright posture labeled as *roman* (note the absence of a capital) and the sloping posture called *italic* (figure 12–14).

The thickness of stroke—the resultant weight or darkness of a letter—can vary while other familial characteristics are present. Light, medium, and bold are basic for most faces, and extra bold variations are common also.

When the stroke and serif characteristics of a type face remain constant, but the relationship of height to width is changed, the type is still in the same family. Common variations range from condensed (narrow width) to expanded (more than normal width).

Letters in *outline* are also available in some families or as special designs.

Type Fonts

A *font* of type is one size of one branch of one family, such as 8-point Bodoni Italic. Therefore, type selection eventually must come down to the font, for only when they know what specific size, branch, and family are desired can printers set type to a customer's satisfaction. Selection of the type font, plus other factors associated with type choice, are important editorial functions.

Type Selection and Use

"Types are meant for reading," and selection and use of type should always be carried out with that maxim in mind. There are, however, substantial differences in what is expected of type in body sizes and large quantities as contrasted with display type in small quantities.

Hints on Use of Body Type

Type legibility—its reading ease—is the primary factor in selection and use of body types. For the body of articles throughout any magazine, use of a type face that is in any way difficult for readers to read would be an unpardonable sin. Presenting what would be a good type face in such a way that reading ease is impaired is equally deplorable. Research into body type selection has been ample enough to give us some general maxims that are useful:

1. Roman type faces, either modern or Oldstyle, have the edge over all other type styles when it comes to reading ease. The only competitor is the Gothic group and some specialty types that have been designed to be easily read. Some faces with variation in stroke width but without serifs are reasonable choices.
2. Upright (roman) posture is better than italic. Italic is an excellent contrast choice for small quantities, but is avoided when the basic body type is being selected.
3. Medium weight and width are usually most efficient of the selections. Designers place primary emphasis on their mediums; the extremes are then designed for special purposes. Bold types are useful for contrast, but also are effective for older and younger readers. Condensed widths provide benefits in space use.

Factors involved in the use of type can influence the ease of reading as much as the actual selection. Some accepted principles involving type use include:

1. White space is so important that most type faces can be improved with a point or two of leading between lines. Margins and white space between columns must also be adequate to provide contrast to type. Nonwhite backgrounds should be used with care or they will not provide adquate contrast.
2. Type size must be correlated with line length, but larger sizes are of benefit for older and younger readers. For magazines, 9-and 10-point sizes provide a happy compromise between the desire to make material as legible as possible and the

Futura Light

Futura Light Italic

Futura Medium

Futura Medium Italic

Futura Medium Condensed

Futura Medium Condensed Italic

Futura Demibold

Futura Demibold Italic

Futura Bold

Futura Bold Italic

Futura Bold Condensed

Futura Bold Condensed Italic

Futura Extrabold

Futura Extrabold Italic

Futura Extrabold Condensed

Futura Extrabold Condensed Italic

FUTURA INLINE

Futura Display

Figure 12–14 These variations in the Futura family are typical of those usually available. Missing from this assortment are the extended variations that are often offered in a family.

abcdefghijklmnopqrstuvwxyz

Figure 12–15 This lower case alphabet in 10-point Bodoni Book represents a minimum line length for that size and face; double this length would be the maximum unless leading is used.

This is 10-point Century type. It has a relatively large x-height and, consequently, tends to need some leading between lines. The ascenders and descenders of letters in Century tend to be shorter than in many other types.

This is 10-point Baskerville type. It is designed to have a smaller x-height and longer ascenders and descenders. It looks smaller because of its design and seems to have adequate white space between lines.

Figure 12–16

Volenikowa, a 39-year-old mill operator, fled with her family from their native Czechoslovakia during the Soviet invasion of Prague in the Spring of 1969. "We fled because we did not want to live like slaves," says Volenikowa. She went to work in the factory rather than continuing her career as a nurse because she felt that an error on her part resulting from language problems would be less serious in the shop than in a hospital.

Having never been in a factory before, Volenikowa had a lot of adjusting to do.

It is not only space, but time which dramatizes Iowa: In open prairie landscape, in its wooded valleys along its many streams, in its pure air (which can still burn you in summer and blast you in winter), its quiet small towns, its belief in hard work and in decency to your neighbor, its willingness to be taxed for top-level education, its cheerful conviction (in spite of some evidence to the contrary) that work and honesty will always produce the good life, Iowa keeps the good qualities of the 19th century. In excellence of its industries, which are,

Figure 12–17 Justified type (top) and ragged right (bottom).

necessity to put as much material as possible into restricted spaces. They also correlate well with common line lengths. A common rule of thumb for legible maximums of line lengths places the shortest line length at one lower case alphabet and the longest at two alphabets. The alphabet of 10-point Bodoni Book type in figure 12–15 measures 10 picas; line lengths should therefore be no less than 10 picas and no more than 20 picas. This rule of thumb is especially good because it takes into account the setting characteristics of the individual type face. Another guide suggests that the minimum line length should be, in picas, the same number as the point size (8-point type minimum length would be 8 picas, the 10-point type minimum line length would be 10 picas) and the maximum should be double that figure. In both cases, the midpoint represents the optimum line length. Also, the maximum in both cases can be enlarged a pica for each point of leading. Line length importance should not be underestimated when considering type legibility; anyone can see enough bad examples in print to see how difficult reading becomes when lines are extremely long or extremely short. Selection of type size also must be related directly to its design. If one were to analyze the various type faces it would be noted that there is a wide variety of perceived size impressions that can be gotten from different types that are all actually of the same size. This fact stems from the differences in design relative to the vertical height of letters that have no ascenders or descenders. This is referred to as the "x-height." Compare the letter x in one 10-point face (Century, for example) with another (Baskerville) and you will detect quite a size difference (figure 12–16). Century looks much larger than Baskerville because the ascenders and descenders in Baskerville are so long, leaving less vertical space for the x-height. One must view a sample consisting of at least a paragraph or two before being able to logically settle on size and style. Or better yet, by seeing potential types in use in other magazines one will be getting a better sample.

Viewing a sample containing a reasonable amount of type also permits one to detect any tone or feeling the type may seem to create when it is used in quantity. Words like *coarse, fine, rough* and others often come into the minds of designers as they look at a type area, because the overall pattern created by a type face can form an impression. This impression should be considered as the type design is being selected.

3. Setting of type in *justified* columns (each line is flush to the left and flush to the right) seems to have no legibility benefit over setting *ragged right* (figure 12–17). Cost may help make the decision between the two; some computerized systems can produce type that is hyphenated and justified (h&j) more efficiently than ragged right because they are programmed to do so; in other instances, elimination of h&j may be more efficient.

4. Capitals and lower case obviously are more legible than all capitals; consequently one doesn't see magazines with body type in all capitals.

Hints on Use of Display Type

Although reading ease is an important factor in selection and use of display type, *suitability* of the type to its subject and audience is perhaps even more important. The fact that display type is often used as an attention-getter also makes a face's ability to carry out that function an important factor. Both of these points— suitability of the type face to its subject and its capability to attract attention—are always in editors' minds as they use display type to create strong titles.

The first step in creating effective visual presentation for titles is to allow sufficient space for them. Titles demand large amounts of white space, and allowance of a third to a full page of space for a title is routine (see fig. 12–18); anything less permits only a prosaic headline treatment.

The second step is to give type adequate size for attracting attention. Whereas a news headline as large as 72 points is rare, the type in magazine titles routinely exceeds the size. Especially in situations where one or two key words with abundant white space are given primary responsibility for luring readers, those key words should get heavy display (see fig. 12–19).

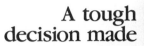

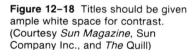

Figure 12–18 Titles should be given ample white space for contrast. (Courtesy *Sun Magazine,* Sun Company Inc., and *The* Quill)

The third step is to dress titles typographically so they fit the occasion and create the desired impression. Type can speak, not only through the words it conveys, but also through its form.

It is worth re-emphasizing here the point that type faces can reflect moods and motifs. Some types are delicate; some are strong. Some are modern; others are old-fashioned. Some have class and tone; others are brash and bold. Some are formal; others informal. Some are masculine; some are feminine. If a type face doesn't exist to match a specialized purpose, designers can create such a face. For complete collections of these faces see a good type specimen catalog from a large type composition company, or look at catalogs of graphics products suppliers, such as Zipatone, Chartpak, Formatt, and Prestype (figure 12–13 shows a few of these faces).

When used most skillfully, type form can speak in harmony with its message, reiterating or reinforcing its verbal message. Particularly when assisted by art work, the typography of a magazine article title can be as much a part of the message as the words themselves. Figure 12–20 shows this principle in practice; in each case, some graphic aspect of the title has been designed to say, visually, what the words are saying verbally.

Figure 12–19 Large sizes of display type—much larger than those used by newspapers—are often used in magazine titles. (Courtesy *The Elks Magazine*, *Sojourners* Magazine, and *Measure*, Hewlett-Packard Company.

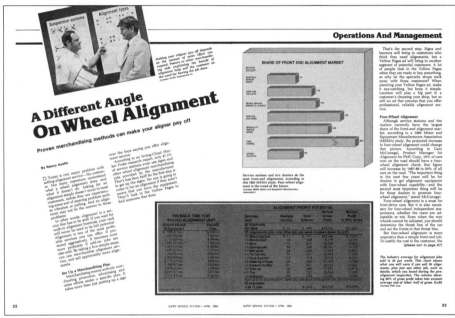

Figure 12–20 Type can be made to graphically portray the words of a title. Note in each of these examples that this goal has been achieved. (Courtesy *Aramco World* and *Super Service Station*.)

Although it is hoped that title type will reinforce its message by visually reflecting the words, it must at least be in keeping with its subject and readers, not discordant.

Variations in size and style of display type can also create necessary emphasis for certain portions of titles. For example, one word can be made to stand out if it is given italic posture and a size that is greater than that used for other words. Readers only pause for a few seconds as they view magazine pages, and emphasis for a key noun or gerund in a phrase or sentence in a title can make the difference in capturing reader interest. Irregular patterns of display type, visually interesting because of the shapes they form, can also stimulate interest. Figures 12–21 and 12–22 show these principles in practice.

The final question to be answered when selecting and using display type for article titles is "where should the title be placed?" The answer is simple: *anywhere*. Whether it be for a page, a two-page spread, or a fraction of a page, the placement of a title should be permitted to follow the dictates of attractive and efficient design, as discussed later in Chapter 15.

Figure 12-21 Variations in size and style of display type can create necessary emphasis for certain portions of titles. (Courtesy *America Magazine*, reprinted with permission from the Fall 1982 *America,* © 1982 by 13-30 Corporation, 505 Market St., Knoxville, TN 37902, and *American Film Magazine.*)

Some Final Hints

Regarding design and placement of titles, a final word of caution is in order here. It must be remembered that titles, by their nature, are way stations for the reader, not destination points. Hence, a basic guideline dictates that title type selection and placement cannot confuse the reader on the way to the next way station. It would be foolish to get a reader's attention only to lose it because he or she does not know where to proceed after reading the title, or is not encouraged to continue because of poor type selection. In all aspects of creating titles, from rhetoric to typography, success is finally measured in terms of how high a percentage of readers are stopped, and then encouraged to read on. Attempts to be "different" with type can create bizarre and undesirable results. The suitability of a type face for a particular purpose should suggest itself, and not be forced. Straining for special effects can be worse than monotonous type dress. Therefore caution should be used when selecting types for mood and character. Don't mix a hodge-podge of faces; chaos results.

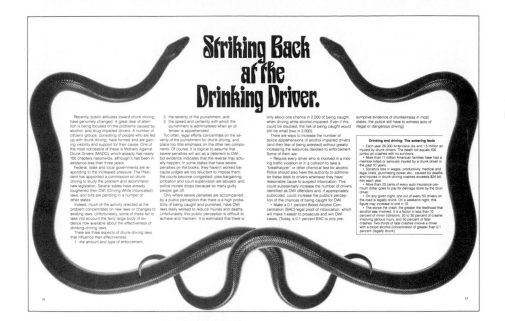

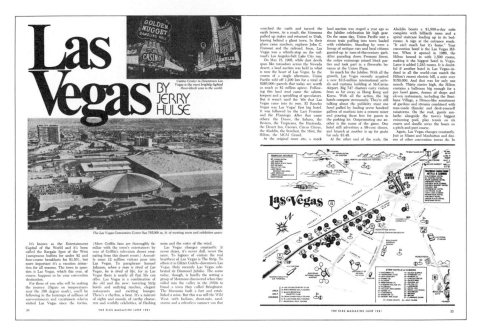

Figure 12–22 Words grouped to form irregular shapes and patterns are also a characteristic of the use of display type in magazines. (Courtesy *Aide Magazine* and *The Elks Magazine.*)

A reiteration of the maxim that "type was made for reading" is also in order here. Graphic designers rarely use type upside down, because that obviously creates a problem for a reader. Many will, however, use type on its side or in other abnormal patterns that are also difficult to read. Readers do their reading from left to right, and type should be displayed in that fashion. Also, avoid using delicate faces on textured papers; hairlines are lost on rough papers.

Readers are also accustomed to the contrast of black on white for type on paper, and variations should be used with care. Type can be reversed to be white on black or dark gray; it can also be used in color on gray or in black on color. Such uses can be effective, but care must always be exercised lest the reader find the presentation to be too difficult to read and move on to other things. All type decisions should be made with the reader in mind.

13

Images: A Visual Typography

MODERN magazines exist in a visual age. With television in the forefront, the mass media have been converting Americans from *readers* to *viewers* who rely on images for their receipt of information and entertainment. This reliance on images seems destined to increase.

Image communication seems to be everywhere, not just bouncing across the television tube. Highway signs, once almost totally verbal, have been revised to become almost entirely pictographic. Textbooks at all levels have changed from sparsely illustrated word collections to visual delights loaded with helpful illustrations. And magazines have come to rely more and more on illustrations to get their particular communication job done.

As a matter of fact, one might even go so far as to paraphrase Marshall McLuhan and say that for magazine editors "the image is the message." Magazine editors of the present and the future must be expert in something called *iconography,* the art of communicating by means of pictures or other images, because readership and understanding often depend on the iconicity of a presentation. The skillful wedding of words with illustrations for effective communication has long been admired and sought; now the increased passivity of the recipients of communications simply makes the expert use of illustrations even more important.

Types of Illustrations

The photograph is undoubtedly the leading image form for magazines, but the term iconography was deliberately introduced to make the point that all forms of illustrations have a place on magazine pages. We therefore shall be concerned in this chapter with all types of artists' drawings, from the simplest line drawing whether in pencil or ink or some other medium and whether reversed or shaded, to the most beautiful watercolors and other paintings. We also will include all kinds of photographic illustrations, from black and white, through duotones and process color to the elaborate line conversions or other gimmicks involving the photograph. And of course charts, bar graphs, maps, or any other illustrative device are also included.

The Editor and the Illustrator

Although editors may have had some direct experience with photography or other illustrations, they are usually not as skilled or talented in these areas as the professionals who work for them. For that reason, the successful relationship begins with a feeling of mutual respect existing between the editor and the illustrators that will give the illustrators maximum creative freedom. Editors, with their knowledge of reader interest and their grasp of a magazine's direction can and should make assignments and evaluate the work of their photographers and artists. But once they have established the guidelines for the work they want done, they should let the talent of their illustrators take over for the actual execution of an assignment. Otherwise the true potential of the artist cannot be realized, and all editors certainly want their photographers or illustrators to produce something better than what they, the editors, could themselves produce. They want something that demonstrates the special talents for which they are paying.

Toward that end, an editor should provide adequate support in time and money. For example, it is unwise to seriously limit a photographer's film and supplies budget, especially if salary or travel expenses for an assignment are substantial. The same is true of drawing variations; the wider the selection from which to choose, the better the final quality. Ideally, the illustrator should provide full input during the selection process, also. Final selection must rest with the editor, but cooperative effort from the illustrator and the art director should enter the selection process.

Functions of Illustrations

Illustrations should be evaluated according to their functions. The photograph or other illustration is usually expected to accomplish one or more of these five purposes: (1) attract attention, (2) illustrate a point made in text, (3) tell a story itself with the aid of only a caption, (4) tell a story in sequence with other illustrations, and (5) give visual relief to a design.

Attracting Attention. The great picture magazines of the 1930s through 1960s set the style for use of a dominant picture as the key element on a page or on a two-page spread, and designers and editors have been adapting that idea ever since. In trying to tell stories with pictures, these magazines needed "key" or "lede" pictures just as text articles needed strong beginnings. These pictures were selected to symbolize an article's theme and were given prominent position and size. Their role was to stop the readers' eyes in the hope that they would continue to read into the caption, title, and text (fig. 13–1).

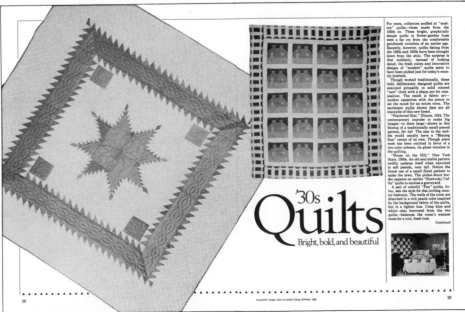

Figure 13–1 A photo or other illustration can actually be the lede of a magazine article. Here editors used a reproduction, in color, of colorful paints and quilts to perform the lede role in admirable fashion. (Courtesy *Sun Magazine,* Sun Company, Inc., and *Country Home,* © Meredith Corporation, 1983, all rights reserved.)

A quick glance at a stack of contemporary magazines also provides immediate examples of how large photos are used to attract attention to a magazine's cover.

Photos are not alone in working to attract attention. Other kinds of illustrations are used for the same purpose. In the chapter on titles, the point was made that titles should be treated as illustrations. Here it can also be said that illustrations can be treated as titles (as in figs. 13–2 through 13–4). Actually, the term "title illustration" is the most accurate description of the lede photos mentioned above. Usually working in combination with a few words, illustrations frequently play the title role in magazines.

Any photo or drawing assigned this top billing should be given adequate display to perform its attention-getting task by means of greater magnitude, added color, or a special finish (such as outlining).

Illustrating a Point. The simplest role of the illustration is typified by the head-and-shoulder portrait, the "mug shot" as it is called. An article is about a person or perhaps just mentions a name, and the illustration is called upon to show readers what the person looks like, an assignment for which words alone seem inadequate. Or, in the case of travel articles, the photographs or drawings may be called upon to show what a place looks like, again filling in where words lack capability.

Figure 13–2 Illustrations can serve as the major element of titles as these Figures 13.2 through 13.4 show. (Courtesy *BFG Tempo.*)

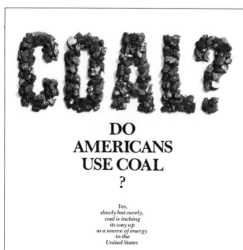

Figure 13–3 (Courtesy *Exxon USA.*)

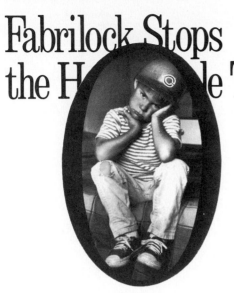

Figure 13–4 (Courtesy *BFG Tempo.*)

Illustrations take on increased importance when they are used to explain a textual point involving action; an illustration of a wood carver that shows his technique with a cutting instrument, as well as what he looks like, naturally carries a greater responsibility.

Charts, diagrams, bar graphs, maps, and other visual devices (see fig. 13–5) are especially effective in "explanation situations." Figures are confusing, and reinforcement with iconistic devices is often needed by readers trying to grasp statistical material.

The familiar pie chart, however, has reached "tritehood" because it was so effective in such explanation situations. Editors of company magazines, trying to give meaning to budgets and annual reports, have used pie charts to the point of indigestion.

Sometimes simple bar graphs can do a job well. But most effective in many situations is the use of a pictorial symbol to represent large quantities, such as one apple to represent each thousand bushels of production in a specific area. With such self-explanatory symbols, an illustration can get meaning across more quickly and with fewer words of explanation than might be needed with a chart or bar graph. Four apples in a row contrasted to one apple, for instance, drives a four to one ratio of apple production home better than a four-inch bar next to a one-inch bar. A state map showing apple production by counties with such a pictograph is probably as concise and effective a device as one can find for explaining the pertinent figures.

For pictographs, the variation in the size of an object is less effective and more confusing than a variation in the number of objects. One can readily see difficulties that could arise from using an apple four times as large as another apple to show production differences. Does the bigger apple mean that better or bigger apples are being produced? Is it four or five times as large as the smaller one? Also, care should be taken to avoid trying to show too much in a single pictograph; a single comparison can be made quickly and accurately, but a pictograph becomes confusing when it is used in more complex situations.

Skillful editing requires thorough analysis of the illustrative needs of any article. What points call for an image to explain them? What type of illustration will make the point most effectively? What kind of production treatment, such as added color, will an illustration need for clarity? These questions should be carefully considered while all verbal material is being processed.

A Single Image

Magazine readers have been well trained by way of heavy exposure to cartoons to get a message from a single illustration with only a minimum of verbal explanation. One drawing or one photograph (witness the photo of a crippled child and

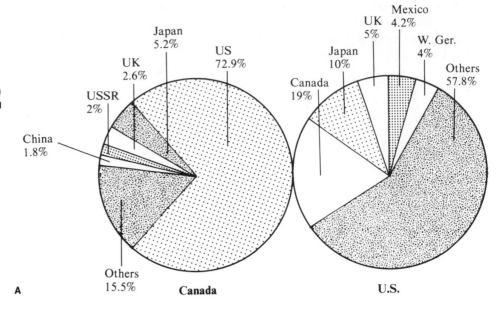

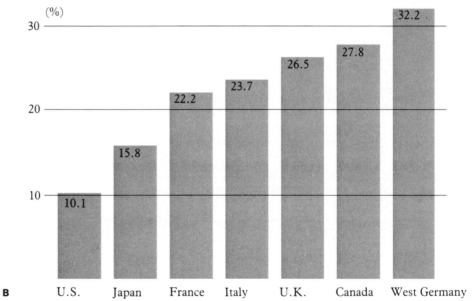

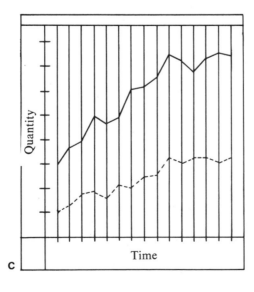

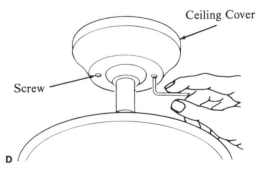

Figure 13–5 Charts and diagrams can serve useful explanatory roles: (a) pie charts show relative sizes of portions of a whole; (b) bar charts and pictographs show comparative amounts; (c) line graphs show trends over time; and (d) schematic diagrams can show how to carry out complex tasks.

a caption, "Buy Easter Seals") can effectively tell a story or arouse a reader's emotions. A wise editor will recognize these single-image situations and resist any impulse to add unnecessary text or superfluous illustrations that can actually detract from the impact that one illustration can give.

However, it should perhaps also be pointed out here that the possibility of a single photograph telling a story or making a point without the aid of any words is so rare as to merit elimination from the list of possibilities. If for no other reason, a few words in a caption are needed to reinforce what the readers are convinced that the image is telling them. Readers translate a graphic image into a verbal one, and they need reassurance that their translation is accurate. The caption gives them this reassurance.

The Picture Story

The use of a series of pictures to tell a story, aided only by a minimum of words, has been a common and effective magazine technique since the birth of the picture magazines in the 1930s.

Life and *Look,* the two giant general picture magazines, made the picture story a dominant form as their spectacular successes created a new approach, called photojournalism, and a new breed of glamorous photojournalists. Then came the death of both the giants in the early seventies and some resultant speculation that perhaps the picture story was also dead, another casualty of the television invasion. Such speculation would appear to be short-sighted, however. As the discussion in earlier chapters of this text indicates, the overall decline of general magazines was based primarily on economic factors. Although the moving images of television must certainly have some ultimate influence on uses of still photography, the picture story is alive and well.

One of the obvious uses of the picture story is in the "how to" area. One cannot imagine a more effective way for telling how to redecorate a room, remodel a home, or build a dune buggy than through a series of pictures. Nor is there a better way for taking readers with you on a tour of a scenic attraction or to show the customer readers of a company magazine how a product is made. Regardless of the subject area of a magazine, whether it is a house and home, travel, customer relations, science and mechanics, or a specialized business interest, the picture story remains a viable form for effective communication. When the primary goal is to "show" readers something, rather than "tell" them, the role of the illustration becomes dominant, and words are secondary. In all cases, however, success comes through a skillful merging of both.

The potential for telling a story through a series of drawings should not be overlooked. Long before the existence of picture magazines, Americans were avidly following their favorite comic strips, which are nothing more than stories told with a series of panels (drawings). In some instances, drawings can even be more effective than photographs; some "how to" instructions just don't lend themselves well to the eye of a camera, but they present little problem to the artist.

Perhaps the best example of the effectiveness of drawings in this sense is the "Wordless Workshop" of *Popular Science.* This feature has entertained and enlightened *Popular Science* readers by successfully showing how to complete a home workshop project without a single word of explanation.

Illustrations as Decoration

The weakest reason for using illustrations is for decoration, but there are instances when this motive alone provides adequate justification. Mention has already been made of the fact that we live in a visual age—that we have become passive receivers of communication. Reading does take effort, and editors must accept the idea that many readers will have a low threshold of tolerance for masses of words. Consequently, situations do arise in which it is wise to relieve a verbal message with illustration, or perhaps provide an illustration only to decorate a page. In the first instance the illustration is aimed to refresh the readers and help them continue reading. In the second instance, it is hoped that the attractiveness of the presentation will create a favorable impression. Just as Americans hang paintings and photos on their walls for aesthetic reasons only, so can editors use illustrations on their pages.

Obtaining Good Illustrations

Potential sources of good artwork and photographs are rather obvious: (1) a staff specialist, (2) a free-lancer, (3) a syndicate, (4) a public relations outlet, and (5) the editor.

For most situations, these sources have been listed in the order of their desirability, but the wide range of magazine staffing capabilities makes it necessary to mention all of them. Some staffs are large and loaded with talent; others consist of an editor alone. Editors who can call on an art director and staff are fortunate; they can get skilled advice on the use of artwork as well as the preparation of finished illustrations. And if they are assisted by one or more skilled photographers, they can assign the picture coverage they need and get professional results. In the foregoing situations they can concentrate on sharpening their judgment of visual needs while employing the supervisory qualities necessary for getting the most from talented members of their teams. They usually will also have the option of buying the offerings of free-lancers in situations that are beyond the capabilities of their staff or that present some financial advantages.

Many editors of smaller magazines must operate without full-time staff photographers or artists. They then prefer the output of skilled free-lancers whose services are contracted for as needs arise. Sometimes (as is the case with editors of some organizational publications) they must settle for the submissions of amateurs and readers who might produce material meeting minimal publication standards.

Syndicates can provide photos and artwork that are technically of the highest quality. Material from these sources (often called "canned" material) usually has the disadvantage of not being tailored to a publication's need. Such stock material might turn up simultaneously in other periodicals, but there are situations in which even the prestigious newsmagazines, *Time* and *Newsweek,* rely on the output of the good photo syndicates.

Magazines of all sizes get photographs, and, occasionally, other artwork, from public relations outlets. Skillful public relations directors or agencies know the values of illustrations and will provide media with technically excellent material. The problem of editorial judgment relating to wise use of publicity material applies to illustrations as well as to verbal copy. Often, however, in small-staff, low-budget operations good illustration becomes an "in" for the use of copy from public relations sources because the editor has few other illustrations available.

The last source of illustration is the editor himself. Although even Norman Cousins was known to use some of his own pictures while he was editing *Saturday Review,* editors usually lack the talent or experience to produce illustrations on a par with those of professionals. Editors are more inclined to recognize their shortcomings when it comes to drawings; they turn quickly to a free-lancer or a syndicate because the amateurishness of their work is instantly recognizable. Too often, however, they are willing to settle for their own photographs (everyone gets an occasional masterpiece), and the results are not at the quality level they should be. Unless they have come up from the photographers' ranks, editors should be as hesitant to use their own photos as they would their own etchings.

Selecting Illustrations

Whether they are selecting drawings or photographs, editors usually work with "rough" miniatures, usually produced in rough and miniature form so that large numbers can be made available with an economical expenditure of time and money. Free-lancers, when not operating on assignment, often produce finished work for selection, for obvious reasons.

The selection of drawings is somewhat easier than the selection of photographs because of the ability of the artist to modify miniatures to meet any desire of the editor. If none of the drawing miniatures represents exactly what is desired, the one that is closest to the desired image can be altered precisely to meet the need.

Photos can, of course, be modified to an extent. As editors view their proof sheets of scores of views, they can select a portion of any view for emphasis. They may even, in some instances, be able to ask for further shootings in order to get exactly what they want. But usually they are working within the limitation of what the photographer's skills brought through a camera's lens and onto film.

What Makes a Good Photograph?

Magazine editors, scanning their contact proofs with the aid of a magnifying glass, are searching for the photograph (or photographs) that will do a particular job for them. Consequently, they will base their selection primarily on whether a photo will perform its particular function. They also want a photo that is artistically pleasant, technically correct, and void of any unnecessary distraction.

Function

Photos are called upon to do different things, from attracting attention to a magazine's cover to illustrating a particular point in a "how to" article. The essential basis for selection, therefore, is the ability of a photo to perform its function.

The photo that is to be pulled from a group and given the responsibility that goes with cover position must have some special qualities. It needs an instantaneous impact, an impact that will carry with it some arousal of curiosity. It must have more communication ability than most photos; there may be a caption with it, but the photo must stand on its own sufficiently to cause a reader to direct attention to the magazine. It should be somewhat symbolic of the issue's best content. It ordinarily will be given large size, so it should be especially good technically.

A photo that is to serve as the "lede" illustration of a major article needs many of the same qualities as a cover photo. It must get instant attention and be representative of the article's subject.

A photo that is to illustrate a point must clearly make its point. If it is to show how to apply a canvas canoe cover, its beauty is secondary to its clarity in showing how to hold the canvas and where to first apply it. And the photo that is to stand alone with only a caption and title line must be selected with that function in mind; others with more impact but lacking story-telling completeness would have to be set aside.

In other words, content is king. It is the meaning that counts. Form and technical considerations, though important, cannot substitute for content.

Research and instinct have combined to give us some general guidelines for the kinds of content that have reader appeal. These are: people, emotion, and action, with the emphasis on people. One need only think for a moment about favorite magazine photos, especially covers, to come up with examples of each of such appeals: babies, women, old men, famous, familiar or unknown; tear-streaked faces, bright smiles, or a flag-draped coffin; sports action, crashes, animals in flight, and the much overdone use of glamour girls, bathing beauties, and other "sex images."

Pictures without people, emotion, or action are rare because editors make a conscious effort to include one or the other of the three elements in any photo; in most instances, the function of the photograph is accomplished more efficiently because of that effort.

Composition. Magazine photographers are artists in their own right. Consequently they should be given the freedom and encouragement necessary to produce artistic photographs.

An editor's primary responsibility to a photographer is to make it clearly known what functions a set of photos is to accomplish. Operating within the limit of function only, the photographer can proceed to turn out pictures that are artistically composed.

Good photographers will see to it that their prints contain aesthetic beauty; then the role of the editor is simply to select those that best perform their editorial function. They must also, of course, be given the display they need for proper impact to avoid destroying their artistic quality through editing.

Technical Qualities

Photos for magazine publication must be suited for reproduction by the printing process a magazine uses. Some photos that would make excellent salon exhibits might be inadequate for magazine reproduction.

In general, photo prints intended for printing reproduction should contain a wide range of tones from very dark (but not black) to very light (but not white). Some salon prints are too dark, and after being screened and reduced to a smaller size, lose significant detail. Prints that tend to be contrasty, but with a full range of middle tones, provide the best copy for reproduction.

Engravers and lithographers also usually prefer glossy prints rather than matte finish, and they would rather reduce than enlarge from the original copy. Good craftsmen will work wonders even with small snapshots, but it pays to provide large (8″ × 10″ or 5″ × 7″) glossy prints when possible.

Improving Photographs

As they prepare photos for inclusion in a magazine, editors have two techniques at their disposal for improving them. One of these is *cropping;* the other is *retouching.*

Cropping is the figurative cutting away of portions of a photograph. Rather than use scissors or a razor blade to cut off a piece of the photo that contains disturbing background, the editor uses little marks to set off new dimensions (see figure 13–6).

Elimination of undesirable background is the most apparent improvement of photos through cropping, but not the only one. The placing of emphasis on the center of interest that results from effective cropping can improve a photograph immensely. Note in figure 13–7 how tight cropping has added impact and "telling power" to the photo. By such cropping the editor is doing the same thing for a photograph that good word editing does for a story—eliminating the nonessential, concentrating on the central theme, and adding to impact by dramatic presentation.

Retouching, too, can improve photos by eliminating undesirable background; it can also contribute to emphasis on a center of interest, though not so dramatically as cropping. Retouching is best left to the artist or engraver, but an editor should be aware of its potential (figure 13–8). Skillful airbrushing can change a harsh, disturbing background to a pleasing, neutral backdrop that serves to highlight the

Figure 13–6 Marks made with a grease pencil serve to delineate the borders of the portion of a photo that is to be reproduced. These crop marks may be placed in an effort to eliminate unnecessary detail and improve a photo.

Figure 13–7 After cropping, the photo in Figure 13.6 does a much better job of emphasizing the central subject.

Figure 13–8 Airbrushing can make a reproduction better than the original photo by eliminating disturbing elements of background and focusing attention on the central subject.

central subject. Isolated blemishes can be removed, as in the case where the letters of a sign behind a portrait's subject seem to be coming out of the ears. The letters can be subdued or eliminated through retouching.

Some additional story-telling power can be added by retouching. The addition of dotted lines, arrows, or other identifying or directional marks often will clarify the point a photo is intended to make. In all retouching, however, the work should be done by a skilled artist, one who also knows the capabilities of the reproduction process being used. Amateurish retouching is usually infinitely worse than none.

Color and Images

One of the most amazing things about printing is the fact that, with only black ink on white paper, images that are in full color around us can be communicated to readers. We look at pictures of blue skies and red roses and instantly recognize the sky and the roses for what they are.

But anyone viewing the status of mass media today must be impressed with the increasing use of color for images. Newspapers like *USA Today* and magazines of all kinds are loaded with larger and larger amounts of color. Television also has jumped from two-dimensional black-and-white to full, life-like color. Along with the increased color has come the increased use of visuals called *graphics,* themselves in multi-colors. Generation of such graphics via computer has helped increase their use and will continue to promote more and better visual images.

Functions of Color in Magazines

In magazines, color has many of the functions of illustrations, whether it is being used to form the illustration or is operating independently. At the beginning of this chapter, we pointed out the role of photos and other illustrations in attracting attention; color is at a par with photos in that regard.

Color in photos enhances their attention-getting value, of course, but color can also do the job alone. Color can assist in clarifying the message of a drawing; it can develop associations and psychological moods; and it can simply provide decoration.

Potential Use of Color

Virtually anything that can be put on a magazine page can be provided in color, including the body type. But color for the sake of color alone often is worse than no color, so the successful use of color requires correlating the use with the objective.

Body type in color, for example, is rarely as good as it is in black on white. Contrast is the source of reading and identification of images, and most colors pale in contrast to black for small type. The lighter the color, the less potential it has for use, and, in this case, a light color such as yellow is totally unusable. Brown on buff sometimes can be effective, as can blue or green on some shades of off-white. But, essentially, the use of color for body type is limited to occasional captions or other small areas that require special contrast with surrounding black and white areas.

Display type in color can be especially effective. Giving contrast to certain words in titles by using them in color can add to the attention value and communication value of the words.

Rules and borders in color can separate and draw attention to panels of text, such as staff listings on contents pages or author blurbs with or near title type.

Typographical *dingbats,* such as initial letters, stars, and bullets, can get special attention through color. Singling out items in a listing of a magazine's contents by placing a colored check mark in front of them is an example of such usage.

Overprinting of type in color over illustrations provides a means of getting necessary contrast when black would not be suitable in many such situations.

Conversion of black-and-white photos into two-color reproductions, called *duotones,* sometimes can help set a mood for the illustration. Blue-and-black outside snow scenes, brown-and-black desert scenes, and green-and-black forest scenes are common uses for duotones. The effect is achieved by simply making two negative reproductions of the original photo, then putting one of them on the plate that applies black to paper, and the other on the plate carrying another color to paper.

Reproduction of original photographs or paintings in full-color is perhaps the ultimate use of color in printing, but it is also very expensive. Original prints, paintings, or slides are reproduced in amazing fidelity in print. Full-color, called *process color* because it requires the process of separating colors out of the original before making separate plates to blend the primary colors again for full-color reproduction, does more to enhance the presentation of pictorial images than anything else. When budgets permit, magazines use abundant amounts of process color because of its ability to show scenes exactly as we view them.

Color enhancement of graphs and charts can be especially helpful. Added dimensions can emerge from bar graphs and line charts when colors can be added to black-and-white presentations.

Tint or tone blocks are also available for use in color as well as black-and-white. As panels underlaying type (fig. 13–9) or on their own, they can draw attention to what might otherwise be weaker areas of a page. Also effective in only black-and-white for some situations, tone blocks can be solid (meaning that they carry 100 percent of the tone to paper), or in any other percentage from 90 down to 10 percent, as shown in figure 13–10. Tone blocks have a singular advantage in that they are available at virtually no cost. Printers maintain a supply of film sheets that will yield the various percentages, and, unless the sheets must be specially cut, they can be used repeatedly.

Figure 13–9 Tint blocks can form effective backdrops for body type or, as in this case, of a subtitle. (Courtesy *BFG Tempo.*)

Figure 13–10 Uniform tonal areas in ten variations of tone can be obtained for little or no cost. The first block shown above is 10 percent of full tone and the last is 100 percent (solid).

A Word of Summary

All images, especially those in color, require special care in production, and, in the case of process color, they can be a major budget item. Therefore they should be used in a cost-effective, as well as a functional manner. Editors should be well-grounded in the production aspects of image use that are presented in chapter 17.

14

Designing A Visual Personality

As pointed out in earlier chapters, much of a magazine's success is determined by its ability to find its specific audience and to direct its objectives and content to that audience. It obviously follows that the design (the appearance) of a magazine must correlate closely with this kind of editorial planning.

A magazine planned for an audience of doctors must be different in appearance from one planned for homemakers. One whose editorial thrust is to relate technical information would seek a different visual personality from one whose goal is to attract and hold the interest of professional and amateur bowlers from across the country. Scores of other examples could be cited, but the point is rather obvious that magazine design must be appropriate for its audience and objectives.

Some primary audience factors that must be considered are such basic reader characteristics as age, sex, occupation, and education level, plus an intangible—the probable intensity of interest. Although there has not been much research that is helpful in correlating magazine design with these audience factors, what has been done generally reinforces the intuitive practices developed by magazine designers over the years. The conservatism that comes with age is usually catered to with a layout approach that emphasizes stability and order. On the other hand, a periodical for teens suggests a design with action and "splash" loudly selling its wares. A magazine that caters to an audience of high educational level can take a classical approach to its basic design. And a women's fashion magazine that itself isn't visually fashionable certainly would be out of synchronization with its audience.

But intensity of interest is perhaps of most importance in layout planning. In this case, the importance of visual elements in a layout varies in inverse proportion to interest level. A physician or a scholar seeking out vital information, thus having a maximum interest level, would find decorative visual elements unnecessary and perhaps even distracting. Periodical design in this instance is extremely "low key." But for the magazine at the other extreme, such as one a company might distribute to its customers, a dynamic physical appearance might be essential to get reader attention, to keep readers interested in the material, and to create an impression of company dynamism.

Hence, the audience and objectives of a magazine tend to direct magazine managers toward decisions that set up a continuing visual personality for each magazine. The factors contributing to this visual personality are many. How much color and in what manner color should be used is one such contributor. So is the amount and type of illustration; an all-type scholarly journal has a different character from that of a sports pictorial weekly magazine. Even the type of paper selected (although there are production factors that are important, too) is based on personality considerations. Magazines are sometimes even classed (as "pulps" or "slicks") according to paper stock because even so technical a decision helps set up a personality.

The layout personality of a magazine is a management decision because it is an element that must remain constant. To change from a picture magazine to one with a primary emphasis on text, or from conservative layout practices to the bizarre, or from pulp paper to glossy stock are all changes that cannot be made from issue to issue. To change these and other basic elements of design is to change personality; changes in personality tend to destroy a magazine's identity with its readers and to reduce the readers' feelings of identification with *their* magazine. Such personality change decisions are primarily made by management; basic design elements are changed only after a careful analysis of the changes that might have occurred in the periodical's audience, or in the magazine's basic objectives.

Format

Another constant in magazine layout is the *format,* or basic size and shape of the magazine. Although the term is often more broadly used to include other continuing make-up characteristics, format is more precisely used here to describe only size and shape.

Magazines, though they come in all sizes and shapes (fig. 14–1), rarely *change* format. When a change is made, it, too, is a management decision based on the same factors that usually enter into the original decision.

Factors influencing this decision are usually functional. One of the first matters of concern, for example, is that the format be one that can be produced with little or no waste in paper or press capacity. Consequently, formats tend to be somewhat standardized to fit common paper sheet sizes and printing presses.

In addition to production efficiency, ease of handling is also considered, as well as other pragmatic factors. Is it essential that the magazine fit into a standard filing cabinet? Must it fit into a standard bookshelf? Should it be small enough to fit into a man's pocket? The answer to one or more of these questions may direct the choice of format.

But other factors related to content and goals of the magazine are important, too. For example, if one of the magazine's goals dictates that a primary part of content be comprised of large, dramatic photographs, one of the larger formats may be mandatory.

These are the most common formats, although their exact dimensions vary considerably.

> Miniature: 4½″ × 6″
> Book: 6″ × 9″
> Basic: 8½″ × 11″
> Picture: 10½″ × 13″
> Sunday supplement: 11″ × 13″

Most common of these formats is the 8½″ × 11″. It is most common, perhaps, because it can be cut without waste from standard paper sheets, and as far as layout is concerned, it represents a compromise. It is easy to handle, it permits fairly dramatic sizing of photos and other layout elements, and it has the plus of being the same size as standard typing paper. Hence it fits nicely into files or piles of paper, whichever is its final destination.

Figure 14–1 This photo of a bookstore magazine rack shows the wide range of magazine formats, from the large *Rolling Stone* at the bottom left to the small pocket-size *TV Guide,* with most of them in the standard size, about 8-1/2 inches by 11 inches.

Perhaps least common is the miniature, which has experienced some popularity for consumer magazines relying on newsstand sales, but creates many design problems because of its extremely small pages. The book size has been popular for digest magazines (perhaps because they give the impression of condensing much into a small package) and for academic and professional quarterlies. The fact that this format's dimensions are also common for textbooks might explain the latter use.

The two larger formats (10½″ × 13″ and 11″ × 13″) owed their original popularity to their ability to exploit the impact of photos and other illustrations. Pictorial magazines, home magazines, and fashion magazines used these formats, but most of these have bowed to economic factors and have reduced to the basic 8½″ × 11″ format. Mailing cost was one of the important factors in the decline of these larger formats.

Number of Pages

The relationship of number of pages to page size merits discussion here. For magazines without advertising support, the number of pages can be a semipermanent management decision just as format is. In such cases the two decisions are closely related. For magazines relying on advertising, the number of pages usually is based on a ratio of advertising pages to editorial pages that will provide for a profitable operation. In such instances the number of pages in an issue varies directly with the number of ad pages sold.

For the nonadvertising magazine, the decision to be made may be between 16-pages, 8½″ × 11″, or as an alternative, a 32-page pocket size. In this case, the flimsiness of 16 pages in the larger size might be justification to go to the greater heft of the smaller dimensions.

The Cover

A magazine's front cover is its most important page. It is the magazine's face; it creates the all-important first impression. Like a person's face, it is the primary indicator of a personality. Consequently, it should remain relatively constant in appearance. Human beings can smile, or frown, or otherwise "make faces" that will slightly change their facial features from minute to minute or day to day. But only disease, serious injury, or malformation would ever force a person to undergo plastic surgery for transformation of facial features. And a magazine cover, while it can tolerate minor changes, it not subject to major layout surgery unless equally serious layout problems demand such surgery. In that case, a complete reshaping of the editorial personality usually takes place.

The basic design of the front cover, therefore, is of great importance, although it is usually created only once or twice in a magazine's lifetime. Before the artist or editor even begins design work, however, some basic decisions relating to the cover must be made.

Self-Cover Versus Separate Cover

First, it must be decided if a *self-cover* or a *separate cover* is to be used. As explained in the previous chapter, magazines are printed on large sheets that are folded into signatures (sections) that are usually 8, 16, or 32 pages in size. A self-cover is part of one of these signatures. It is printed in the same press run as a part of the large sheet.

A self-cover, being printed on the same paper as the inside of the magazine, possesses what may be an inherent disadvantage. If the basic paper stock is pulpy or especially thin, this disadvantage, reflected in the cover, may be of considerable detrimental consequence. If, on the other hand, the interior stock is high quality and has reasonable weight, the self-cover can be an advantage. In either case, however, printing on the large sheet rather than on a separate 4-page cover sheet can be a very real production economy. Also, if only the cover is to be printed in more than one color, self-cover can serve to provide the extra color for all other pages on the form at virtually no cost.

Advertising Versus Editorial

For magazines with advertising, there may be strong competition from the advertising department for use of the cover, especially on specialized business publications. The premium price that can be commanded for the front cover is an attraction that is difficult to combat. The intangible benefits of a strong editorial cover—one that brings the readership that, in turn, brings in the advertising revenue—must be weighed against the quick return from sale of the space. The other cover pages (inside front, inside back, and outside back) can provide an adequate amount of premium space for advertisers.

Laying Out the Cover

A good magazine cover has several jobs to do. In the first place, there is no other page that has as much responsibility for setting the tone, or personality, of the magazine. Secondly, the cover must be dynamic enough in appearance to draw readers to the magazine. Thirdly, it must provide some continuing characteristics that will identify it from issue to issue. But it must also be flexible enough so that each issue can be readily identified as a different issue—to let the reader know instantly which issue he or she is viewing. And finally, it should lure the reader into the magazine.

Primary factors in setting the tone of a cover are the nameplate's type dress, the use or lack of illustration, and the overall design. Aside from the fact that it must be large enough and clear enough to quickly identify the publication, the nameplate has no typographic restriction. It usually is designed and created by an artist so it can be tailored to suit the tone of the magazine. Flowing scripts, bold sans serifs, ornate texts, common Romans, and any novelty types might be used, depending upon the appearance that is desired. The nameplate design may call for the type to be printed in black or one or more colors. Or the type may be reversed to be white against a black or colored background. Even if the front cover carries advertising, the nameplate has its role to play.

Most magazines use a combination of illustration and type on the front cover, but some use type only (fig. 14–2). The fact that type only is used, in and of itself, helps set a tone for the magazine. For a newsmagazine, or perhaps what one might call a "newsy" magazine because it deals in short, timely items of information, the all-type cover can be appropriate. But if photographs are a primary, basic or important part of the content, this fact virtually dictates that one or more photographs be included on the cover. Otherwise the cover doesn't accurately portray the character of the contents.

A look at the accompanying illustrations should also reveal that the overall design of the cover contributes to the impression it creates. By jamming a lot of elements on a cover, a feeling of life and action may be obtained. By concentrating on a minimum of elements, and perhaps placing those elements so that absolute balance or equilibrium results, the feeling of restraint, dignity, or conservatism may prevail. A design that calls for a single, large photograph has a different impact from the design that uses a number of smaller illustrations.

Figure 14–2 Although virtually all these magazines are computer magazines, their covers vary considerably. Some have all-type covers, and some contain advertising, but most of them rely on a strong photograph and heavy type display for their nameplate to attract attention. Almost all have some type devoted to a sales pitch for material contained inside.

To draw attention to the magazine, most designers rely on photographs. If there is such a thing as a basic cover design, it is one that employs a single, striking photo to catch the eye. Color and/or type can also do the job, but only if adroitly used. Type blurbs are most effective in drawing the reader inside the magazine, and, in the final analysis, perhaps this is the most vital function of a cover. Consequently, a cover that carries only a nameplate, photo, and date can be failing to fulfill one of its primary missions. One of the cover trends in the seventies has been toward the use of more type—more blurbs to sell the content to the reader. Note in the accompanying illustrations how some of the covers direct readers to the issue's most important features by way of type messages.

Because it has to stand the test of continued use, the cover design must be flexible enough to take care of the specifics of individual issues without losing its continuing identification. A design created to include a photo, but requiring that the photo must always be emphatically vertical in shape, would soon reveal that it is too restrictive. A design that provides for a distinctive nameplate to serve as the constant for the continuing identification and a spot for issue identification, plus a large open area for use of a photo with blurb can be both effective and flexible.

Design of Continuing Pages

In addition to the cover, most magazines will have at least one other page that remains relatively constant in design from issue to issue. If there is no other, at least there is a table of contents page in a magazine. But many will have letters pages, editorial pages, or other features of a continuing nature. These pages should get the same design attention that a cover does.

The table of contents page, for example, should be professionally designed so that it has a constant form—a form that is different from the usual monotonous list of titles that represents the curse of many magazines (see fig. 14–3). It is generally wise to "beef up" the contents page by the addition of at least one other feature with substantial reader interest. Letters, a publisher's message, a column of interesting anecdotes and the like can be used to prevent the page from becoming an interest graveyard. A design that deliberately calls for the use of one or more pictures to illustrate the contents listing can add some life to the page. Further help can come from the adoption of some device for drawing attention to the leading features in the listing: using a photo for each, varying the type size, or using a check mark, arrow, or other type ornament.

Mailing information often is used on the contents page; postal regulations call for its use up front in the book, and the contents page is the likely page for it. Masthead information also often finds its way to this page. All such information should be subordinated (buried might be a better term) in favor of more interesting material. Such material should be placed so that it can be found by those who seek it, yet without getting in the way of material that might interest most readers scanning the page.

Establishing a Page Grid: Traditional Approach

Establishment of a page pattern, a *grid,* is another important policy step in magazine design. The traditional approach to a grid is simply to determine margins, column widths, and any other typographical limitations set in advance to establish a consistency of appearance from page to page. The result is an appearance resembling traditional books.

Grids may also break the page into modules that set a geometric pattern for page design that is assymetrical and non-traditional. The horizontal and vertical lines that establish the modules provide a great variety of options that can reflect the tastes of the designer and objectives of the periodical.

Layout sheets containing all the grid lines are printed and serve as guides for page layouts. Working with grid sheets assures a magazine of page designs that are consistent with the personality set by design policy, whether it be traditional or contemporary.

First, let's look at the traditional approach to developing a page grid.

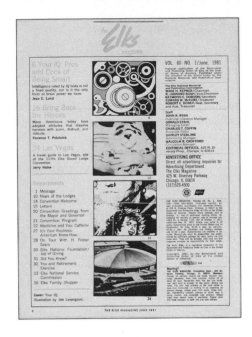

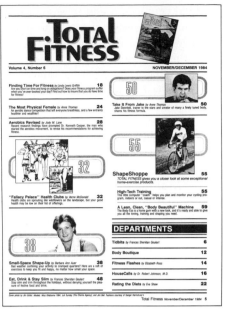

Figure 14–3 Table of contents pages, by virtue of the kind of content ordinarily used there, can be visually dull. But most magazines, such as these examples, use illustrations and other visual aids to create interesting pages. (Courtesy *The Elks Magazine;* Total Fitness Magazine, © 1984 by National Reporter Publications, all rights reserved; *Aide* Magazine; *Super Service Station;* and *Sohio* Magazine, the Standard Oil Company [Ohio].)

Type Page Size, Margins, and Columns

A traditional grid establishes standard margins and a vertical division of space into two or three columns; there are no other modules formed by horizontal lines. The space inside the margins is referred to as the *type page size.*

Although there are no absolute rules to guide magazine editors and designers as they prescribe margins and column widths, there are some general principles relating to design and type legibility that can be helpful.

Margins are important to the design of a page because they constitute the frame that holds the page together as a unit. Consequently, margins should be large enough to overpower any normal internal lines of white space that might otherwise divide the page into undesired segments. For books it is not uncommon for margins to comprise 50 percent of the page area, but for magazines 20 to 30 percent would be more common. For example, an 8½ by 11-inch magazine with margins of one inch at the bottom, one-half inch on the outside and top, and one-third inch on the inside is devoting 20 of its 93.5 square inches of space to margins.

In the foregoing example it can be noted that all margins are not equal, and such is usually the case. The inequality of margins stems from the fact that the optical center of a design is somewhat above the geometric center. You can affirm this principle very quickly by drawing intersecting lines from each of two adjoining corners of a page to their opposite corners, as shown in figure 14–4. A mark at the point of intersection (the geometric center) appears to be below center. By raising the mark slightly above the intersection, you achieve the appearance of having it at the center. The type page area, therefore, must be located somewhat above a centered position if it is to avoid the appearance of sliding down the page. Consequently, the bottom margin is always the largest.

Location of the type page within its margins is further complicated by the fact that readers always view two pages at a time when a magazine is opened before them. This means that the two inner (gutter) margins are side by side, thus forming a single gutter of white that is twice the inner margin's dimension. In order to keep this gutter of white under control—to avoid separating the two pages so completely that they cannot be tied together—the inside margin is made smaller than the others (see fig. 14–5).

In traditional book margins (called *progressive* margins), the outside and top margins are not the same, either. The outside is larger than the top. The margins progressively grow smaller from the bottom to the inside working in a clockwise manner for left pages and a counter-clockwise manner on the right pages. Many magazines, however, use identical margins for the outside and top edges of both facing pages.

Before applying these principles to the selection of exact dimensions for margins, it is necessary to consider the amount of white space needed to separate columns of type. Although a few magazines have used black lines as column separators when that seemed to be the fad, white space consistently serves as the more efficient means for separating columns. These column dividers must be of adequate size to

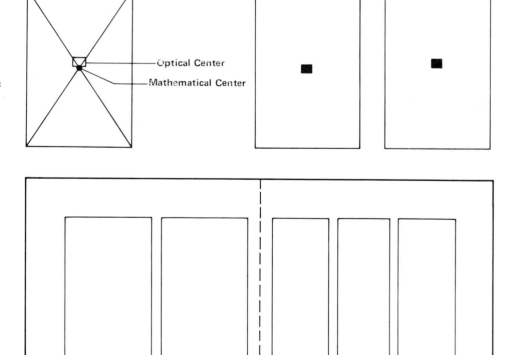

Figure 14–4 The optical center of a page is slightly above the geometric center. A spot located at the geometric center visually appears to be a little low; consequently the optical center is usually used as the center for a type page, thus making the bottom margin larger than others.

Optical Center

Mathematical Center

Figure 14–5 The establishment of margins, column widths, and the amount of space to use as column breaks are the basic considerations in setting up a traditional grid.

give the reader a pronounced starting and stopping point. On the other hand, they cannot be so large that they break the page into design segments. Once again, only a common sense principle is available to serve as a guidepost: these column dividers cannot be as large as even the smallest margin.

By applying our principles we can come up with a usable set of margins and column dividers, if we start with either the smallest or the largest of the white space areas. As an example, let's assume that the minimum amount of white space that will serve as a column break is one pica, and the maximum for that purpose should be two picas. Our smallest margin might then be set at three picas. If the gutter margin is three picas, the top might be four, the outside five, and the bottom six if we wanted progressive margins. Or we could make the top and side both four and the bottom only five picas.

After making these decisions, the only remaining one would be with regard to the number of columns on a page. The decision as to column width actually is an important one because it has a direct relationship to the ease of reading. Type style and size, as we shall see shortly, also enter in the decision. It should suffice to say here that, for most commonly used type styles and sizes, the use of either two or three columns to a standard magazine page is acceptable and common. As a matter of fact, many magazines will use a two-column design for some sections and a three-column approach for others. To come up with a uniform type page in this instance we might settle on the following:

Bottom margin: five picas
Outside margins: four picas
Top margin: four picas
Inside (gutter) margin: three picas
Column divider on a 3-column page: one pica
Column divider on a 2-column page: two picas
Type page dimension for an 8½ by 11-inch trim size magazine: 44 picas wide and
    57 picas deep
Column width: 21 picas and 14 picas

Although this example is quite typical for an 8½ by 11-inch magazine, it is only one of countless possibilities for that size or any of the other common sizes. The important elements here are the relationships that should exist among the margins and column breaks so that the end result will be a unified readable product, not the exact dimensions. Dimensions can vary considerably.

Establishing Typographical Policy

Traditional magazines, like books, are inclined to adhere to rather strict typographical guidelines. Body types are usually consistent for any magazine, being selected in a size and style that assures reading ease. Column widths, because they set line lengths for body type, have a bearing on size and style selection. Basic principles of body type selection are covered in chapter 12.

Along with newsmagazines, other magazines of traditional design often restrict display type to one or only a few styles used in patterns that also have little variety. Some, however, use all varieties of display type in order to tailor the type display to the content of individual articles.

There are a number of other minor but consequential visual devices that should be a matter of typographical policy. Decorative typographical devices, called *dingbats,* can serve some useful purposes. One of these, the large initial letter, can be an especially helpful device if properly used. If used indiscriminately, it can contribute to a cluttered appearance. Misuse can be prevented by setting the policy that large initials will be used, but only to signal the start of the text of an article. Continuity can be achieved by deciding in advance on the sizes to be used and whether they are to be dropped into their text or ride above it. A "drop-in" initial letter (see fig. 14–6, except top example) requires special marking on body copy so that more than one line will be set to a shorter measure (or partially blank) to make room for the initial. A stand-up initial (see fig. 14–6, top) needs room only at the beginning of the first line. Either is acceptable, but usage should be uniform.

Nearly 200 years ago a group of statesmen met in Philadelphia, the principal city of British North America, to protest England's oppressive colonial policy.

At the same time the general mood of the colonists began

At its spacious, breezy headquarters beside the Amman airfield, the academy's classrooms are a 30-second walk from its fleet of Cherokees. There are six single-engined Cherokees, a twin-engine Piper and six full-time flight instructors, in addition to ground instructors. The

When Columbus pushed his vessels into the waters of the New World, almost 200 different Indian cultures were flourishing in Mexico. Countless others had come and gone by then, leaving towering and breathtaking records of their presence: mas-

Although some historians say Syria's capital is the oldest continually inhabited city in the world, the fragments of the city's walls still standing don't reflect this great antiquity. The most picturesque section of wall, a mile-long stretch of stone and clay fortification

Figure 14–6 Initial letters, raised and dropped. Note the special effects in the second and fourth examples.

it can also be helpful to readers if a graphic symbol is used to indicate the end of articles. Some kind of a typographical device can become, through usage, recognized as an end mark that can prevent some readers from leaving an article when coincidence causes the end of a section of that article to fall at the end of a page, perhaps leading the reader to think the article has ended. A bullet (large dot), one or more stars, some asterisks, check marks, or other devices are used with considerable success. Selection of the device and provisions for its use in a way that ensures uniformity should be a policy decision.

Even so small a matter as the *folio* (page number) requires a policy decision because it is a continuing aspect of the magazine's typography. Should the folio be spelled out or used as a numeral? Should it be centered or flush to either side? Should the word "page" be used with the numeral? It is surprising how many questions can be asked about so minor a point, and uniformity demands that some decision be made and followed. About folios it will suffice to say that their use should be in keeping with the other typographical practices that are adopted. Although their placement on outside bottom corners seems practical from the standpoint of the reader's ability to locate them quickly, any folio policy, so long as it is consistent, seems to be acceptable.

Applying the Principles

Many magazines with a consistent traditional approach to design have created visual personalities that have developed and maintained reader loyalty for years. One of the best of these examples is *Smithsonian* magazine, whose book-like design has been welcomed and appreciated by readers for fifteen years.

The original design for *Smithsonian* was worked out fifteen years ago by Edward K. Thompson, the founding editor, and Bradbury Thompson (no relation), the noted designer. Editor Thompson wanted a magazine that was clean and straightforward and reasonably dignified, as a magazine representing the Smithsonian Institution would be expected to be. The success in meeting these basic goals can be seen in figures 14–7 to 14–12.

From its cover to the single-page opening feature at the back of the magazine, *Smithsonian* shows conservatism, dignity, and class. Founding editor Thompson had been a longtime managing editor of *Life,* and disliked rules, cookie-cutter graphics,

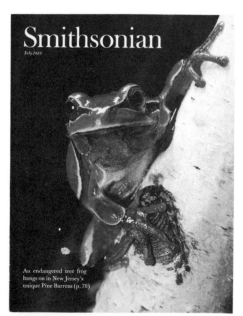

Figure 14–7 The traditional book design of *Smithsonian* starts with a cover devoted to nameplate and bleed illustration. One dignified block of type usually sells the main article of the issue. (Courtesy *Smithsonian Magazine.*)

Figure 14–8 White space opens up and gives plenty of air for the listings on the table of contents page which resembles such pages in books. (Courtesy *Smithsonian Magazine.*)

Figure 14–9 Departments carry out the functional and tasteful use of traditional typography by using a working title along with a departmental label and ample white space. (Courtesy *Smithsonian Magazine.*)

"and other such razzmatazz," in the words of current editor Don Moser. Moser, who shares his predecessor's belief in letting good pictures speak for themselves, continues to guide *Smithsonian* in its traditional design. Moser gives these specifics about *Smithsonian* design:

The design is very simple. All the type (except in front and back matter) is 10/12 Baskerville. We use only two or three headline styles, and either a two- or three-column grid of 19.6 or 13.5 picas. There is a generous use of white space: wide margins, a sidehead breaking every full column, and a *Smithsonian* trademark, the "Thompson Corner," named after Brad Thompson. This is an 18-line block of white space in the upper left-hand corner of a spread, and we usually use one to three of them in a story. I think that all of this gives the magazine an airy, inviting look, and although we run some pretty long pieces, I think that the appearance of the stories says to the reader: This isn't something you're going to have to slog through.

The magazine's design is so simple that we don't even have an art director in the conventional sense. Laying out an issue is essentially a matter of picture selection and placement; the job is done by the editor, the picture editor and a representative from a local design firm.

Although the design is certainly conservative, I find it significant that I have never received a single letter of criticism about it from our readers—and they are quick to complain about anything they don't like. And so we must be doing something right.

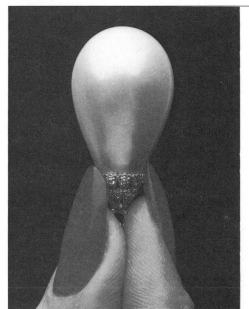

By Nigel Sitwell

The 'queen of gems'–always stunning, and now more cultured than ever

Figure 14–10 These spreads show the attention paid to strong photos and white space to attract and hold attention. (Courtesy *Smithsonian Magazine*.)

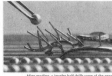

Figure 14–11 The rectangle of white space dropped in at the upper left at intervals as articles develop has been a hallmark and tradition of *Smithsonian* design for years. (Courtesy *Smithsonian Magazine*.)

Figure 14–12 Like many other magazines, *Smithsonian* takes care of readers who might start at the back of the magazine by using the first left-hand page for a short feature of high interest. Design of this page carries the visual personality started with the front cover and carried through to the end of each issue. (Courtesy *Smithsonian Magazine*.)

Look again at figures 14–7 to 14–12. The desired personality is evident on every page. Traditional framing of pictures is evident, but when a full-page bleed is warranted, it is used, often as the climax to an article. Generous white space, strong photographs, and legible type make the *Smithsonian* both interesting and easy to read.

The Smithsonian Institution is unique, and the readers of the magazine are special, so what is successful there might not be so successful in other situations. It does illustrate the principle, however, that a magazine's design should be tailored to its editorial content and its reader interest.

Establishing a Page Grid: Nontraditional Approach

Magazines giving special emphasis to design often are inclined to create contemporary visual personalities, breaking away from the traditional book approach to design.

Page grids in these cases usually move away from standard column structure, often using half-columns, and create geometric patterns that are unusual but standardized enough to provide a continuing nature to the design. They usually divide the page into rectangles, often taking this division down to a small unit, such as those framed by horizontal lines that are one line of type apart and vertical lines that are the same or perhaps a pica apart. Larger rectangles are overlayed on these small units, and provide compartments for location of titles, illustrations, or other display units. White space can then be allocated in geometric patterns conforming to these compartments. These rectangles or "mods" as they are sometimes called, reflect the design skills of the creator of the grid, with no real restrictions applying otherwise.

An example of use of a non-traditional grid and another example of a magazine's design personality being tailored to its editorial content and its readers' interests is *Enterprise* magazine of the Southwestern Bell Corporation. This public relations magazine is published quarterly for the company's employees and retirees. As a public relations magazine with goals to accomplish for the company, it must rely on design and graphics to generate interest among its readers.

Established in 1984 when the Bell companies were separated from AT&T, it is an excellent example of the planning and partnerships that are necessary for success of a corporate magazine. With the breakup of AT&T, the newly independent Southwestern Bell Corporation wanted to signal to employees the change in corporate identity through a new quarterly magazine replacing a monthly magazine called *Scene*. Editor Peter J. Faur's statement of objectives and procedures involved in creating a new visual personality for *Enterprise* best shows the planning that was involved:

The new magazine would help foster a sense among employees that they in fact are proprietors of the business and should treat their jobs accordingly. By encouraging this new, entrepreneurial attitude, the company hoped to provide a more rewarding workplace while simultaneously reaping the benefits of increased employee contributions to the business.

The magazine also wanted to signal to employees that, even though the company has been separated from AT&T, there is no reason to be seen as one of 'Ma Bell's homeless, pitiful orphans.' Instead, the magazine's design would help capture the truth that Southwestern Bell Corporation is a dynamic, powerful leader in telecommunications, residing in the top 50 of the Fortune 500 companies.

Enterprise, it was decided, had to be far different from its folksier predecessor.

Design planning began with the establishment of goals and objectives for the visual personality of the magazine:

The magazine's visual impact has to convey 'controlled excellence,' that is, it has to have a clearly stated appearance, consistent from page to page and structured to make the publication easy for the reader to follow. The concept has to be structured enough so that we can apply it consistently but not so rigid that it looks academic or literary. We want a look that will stand up to passing design fashions yet will consistently appear contemporary.

Design consultants were invited to offer proposals for the new magazine, and Hawthorne/Wolfe of St. Louis developed the winning design. As seen in figures 14–13 through 14–18, the design was based on a three-column format with a floating half-column. Editor Faur cites these advantages of the grid:

The half-column offers tremendous flexibility. It can be used to carry art and cutlines. It can separate a sidebar from a main story. It can be coupled with a full column or multiple columns when art requires an unusual display area.

Hairline rules lend a structured, business-like look to the publication. Four-point rules accent the tops of all short columns and provide contrast to the hairline rules.

For display faces, the magazine uses the Bodoni and Futura type families. Depending on the needs of a particular spread, various sizes are specified. Settings are upper case or upper and lower case as necessary. Italics are used on occasion to provide a more active look to the page. With the wide range of options available in Bodoni and Futura, *Enterprise* can maintain a consistent typographic style without becoming visually tiresome.

The partnership of editor and designer was in place right from the start, and publication of each issue has carried that partnership forward. Hawthorne/Wolfe was retained to work closely with the editor and art director on each issue because it was believed that "as the magazine and its design evolve, the creator of the design should be involved in the process."

Figure 14–13 *Enterprise* magazine of Southwestern Bell is an excellent example of emphasis on contemporary design, from front cover throughout. (Courtesy *Enterprise,* Southwestern Bell Corporation.)

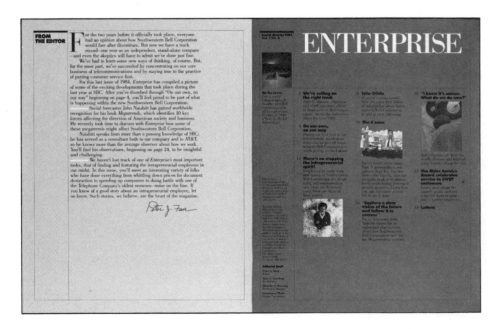

Figure 14–14 The inside cover is a letter from the editor to his readers, and the page design plus the facing table of contents page begin to set the modern, sophisticated design personality planned for it. (Courtesy *Enterprise,* Southwestern Bell Corporation.)

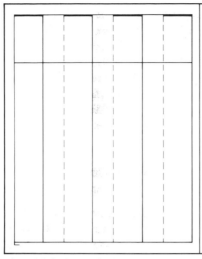

Figure 14–15 One of the key parts of the page grid developed for *Enterprise* is the half-column that can float according to the needs of any page or spread; another is the use of rules for column dividers. (Courtesy *Enterprise,* Southwestern Bell Corporation.)

Figure 14–16 These opening two pages of a four-page article show the use of a strong illustration to open the article, the half-column of white space, large initial letter, vertical and horizontal lines, subheads, and an arrow to lead the reader on, all as elements of design interest. (Courtesy *Enterprise,* Southwestern Bell Corporation.)

Designing A Visual Personality   **182**

Figure 14–17 The second pair of pages for the article in Figure 14–16 uses the two half-columns in the gutter for an illustration, providing a definite change of pace. A small dingbat marks the end of the article. (Courtesy *Enterprise,* Southwestern Bell Corporation.)

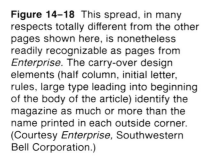

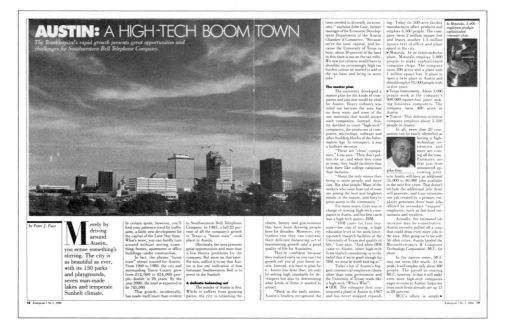

Figure 14–18 This spread, in many respects totally different from the other pages shown here, is nonetheless readily recognizable as pages from *Enterprise.* The carry-over design elements (half column, initial letter, rules, large type leading into beginning of the body of the article) identify the magazine as much or more than the name printed in each outside corner. (Courtesy *Enterprise,* Southwestern Bell Corporation.)

Editor Faur describes the issue-by-issue procedure in this fashion:

Each issue of *Enterprise* begins with the editor's story lineup. The editor, the art director and Hawthorne/Wolfe discuss each story and make preliminary decisions about which stories will be handled with illustration and which with photography.

After stories are written, freelance illustrators and photographers are chosen. Their work is supervised either by the art director or Hawthorne/Wolfe, depending on who recommended using a particular individual.

As the text and art come together, Hawthorne/Wolfe creates a rough layout for the art director's approval.

As successive issues developed, subtle changes were made. Initial caps sometimes were screened back or colored to soften their impact. Headline treatments were experimented with to reflect more closely the tone of articles. Also, we've continued to explore new ways to use the floating half-column.

Although *Enterprise* and *Smithsonian* have totally different visual personalities, they both represent excellent design and procedures for establishing a magazine's personality. In each case, the needs of their organizations and their readers were paramount in development of the design, and editorial and design personnel worked in partnership to meet those needs.

Page Layout

15

ONE of the most interesting and challenging aspects of magazine editing is the process of putting all the components of a magazine into an attractive, effective package. Layout of pages is the final stage in this process, and it requires both artistic and editorial skills and knowledge.

In the ideal situation, the staff will include a specialist, usually called an *art director,* who has primary responsibility for the creative aspects of design. In some larger operations, the art director is assisted by a fairly sizable staff. But often, because of budgetary or other considerations, the assistance of a free-lance designer on a part-time basis is the only help provided for an editor. There are also many instances in which the editor must operate without the assistance of an art director or of an artist. Unfortunately, this latter case is typical among the smaller magazines that so often provide the training ground for the newcomers in magazine editing.

Working With, and Without, an Art Director

There is no doubt that a talented art director is one of a magazine's most valuable assets. From art directors can come the innovation that lifts appearance out of the commonplace. Their visual presentations can add a vital dimension to editorial material. The history of contemporary magazines is full of examples of the impact art directors can have on their own publications and on magazines generally, as well. Alexey Brodovitch, the Russian born designer who became art director of *Harper's Bazaar* in the early 1930s, gave his own publication a fresh visual appeal and influenced many of the people and magazines of his era. Willie Fleckhaus, from his office in Munich, designed the pages of *Twen* magazine so effectively that his new ideas set the pace for design of other magazines all over the world, including some of those in the United States. Allen F. Hurlburt's work with *Look* magazine, Henry Wolf's and later Samuel Antupit's with *Esquire,* and Otto Storch's with *McCall's* set standards of excellence that have provided inspiration for other designers. They and others who provided new concepts of magazine design also established the art director as a top-level partner in the editorial-management team of consumer magazines.

The partnership of art director and editor was not an easy one to establish, nor is it an easy one to maintain. The relative importance of form and function provides ample fodder for continuing debate and potential antagonism. The excesses of "screaming graphics" that made some magazines almost impossible to read in the 1960s, though also deplored by many designers, unfortunately served to fuel the prejudices of editorial types who place visual presentation at the bottom of their importance scale.

The de-emphasis of content by some designers to the point where they seem to be designing for the sake of design alone also presents some difficulty. So does the tendency of many to imitate the innovations of the creative pacesetters to the point that fads sweep through the magazine industry, making look-alikes of periodicals whose varied functions logically demand varied design approaches. Regardless of the difficulties, the maintenance of a partnership relationship between editor and art director is essential if our magazines are to be at their best.

Basically, the editor's job in working with an art director is to keep design within some limits of function. At the same time, the art director should be given the freedom to provide the creative spark that results in the bright and unique presentations needed to attract and hold readers despite the great competition for their reading time.

For editors who must work alone as they join pictures, artwork, and white space together to form magazine pages, it is best to let form follow function. Design that has been created expressly to carry out a communication function is usually acceptable. Attempts at spectacular design by the untrained or untalented can produce disastrous results. If, as editors lay out the pages of their magazine, they consider the editorial "why" for their actions, the pages should at least be unobtrusive in design. At best they may even give added visual appeal to their content.

It is beyond the scope of this book to attempt to provide any student with the background for art direction of a magazine. For that matter, considerable additional reading is recommended to gain a full appreciation of the role of the art director of mass circulation magazines.

There is no doubt that the minimum for art direction should at least include establishing the visual personality as described in the previous chapter with the development of page grids. Beyond that, it may be necessary for editors to make design decisions on a day-to-day basis, applying sound editorial judgment and some basic layout principles as pages are laid out. Fortunately, there are some principles which, if applied well, will result in functional and attractive page layout.

Working in Miniature

One of the most helpful aids in page layout is a miniature dummy. The miniature can show at a glance how an edition is shaping up visually. Checking on the issue's adherence to the magazine's visual personality and/or the need for changes of pace in layouts is easy to do in miniature. Availability of color and any other production requirements can also be shown on a "minny."

Pre-printed sheets with facing pages outlined in miniature size can permit layout "doodling" that will produce alternate ideas quickly and efficiently.

While doodling miniatures, editors should be preparing to specify display type because it ordinarily will be lettered on the final page layout and be typeset from the layout, not from a typed sheet of paper. If design policy has not precluded it, the editorial content should be reflected in the title typography. A magazine ordinarily is intended as a storehouse of many different articles, each with its own flavor and substance. Titles, through their type dress, should convey these differences. As suggested in chapter 12, many type faces do seem to be especially suitable for certain subjects, certain feelings, and certain moods. The *tone* and approach of a magazine page can be matched by type also. A page that is heavy in design, with large pictures and strong lines, will accommodate bold and heavy type styles. On the other hand, a page with a delicate and balanced group of components might call for just the opposite kind of type selection. In any case, suitability should be a basis for type selection and use. Figure 15–2 illustrates this point well. The "wild west" flavor of the type, and the circular treatment of the illustration work together to give visual meaning to the layout. The special treatments given to type and illustration here have definite design purposes. The use of type designs just for the sake of being different can have disastrous results; wild display and bizarre arrangements are as unsatisfactory as dullness and monotony.

Order and Structure

While trying for suitability of design, an editor or designer of magazine pages is also concerned with order and structure because these are, in fact, the foundation of design. A primary determinant of order in design is *balance,* a relative feeling of equilibrium with respect to a vertical axis in the center of the area. The easiest way to insure this equilibrium is to place elements directly on the axis, just as if they were being placed directly over the fulcrum on a teeter-totter (fig. 15–3). Complete

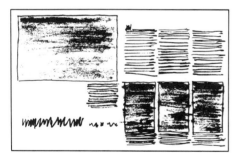

Figure 15–1 Possible page designs roughly sketched in miniature are a helpful first step in page layout. With little effort, several possible variations can be visualized before full-size layouts are started.

FLAGSTAFF'S CIRCLE OF WONDERS

A multitude of parks, natural phenomena, monuments, and historic places are crowded around this famous Arizona city

Figure 15–2 An article on Flagstaff, Arizona, uses type dress and page design to enhance the content. The ''wild west'' type design and page layout are appropriate and visually reflect the content of the article. (Reprinted from *Friends Magazine* of General Motors.)

Historian at the Stove

A collector of cookbooks and utensils and no slouch in the kitchen himself, William Woys Weaver is exploring the origins of Pennsylvania German cookery

by Ruth Hoover Seitz

SYNCRUDE ON STREAM

The risk and reality of oil in the tar sands

BY GORDON DONALDSON

PHOTOGRAPHS BY ALEX MACDONALD

The people who dropped from heaven

The Miccosukees, a unique tribe of native Americans, are Exxon's neighbors in Florida's Big Cypress Swamp.

Figure 15–3 A feeling of equilibrium on a magazine page can be achieved automatically by placing the dominant elements on the center line. (Courtesy *Americana,* © Americana Magazine, Inc., all rights reserved; *Imperial Oil Review;* and *Exxon USA.*)

symmetry is thus obtained, guaranteeing a feeling of stability. Absolute symmetry also can be obtained by placing equal elements at equal distances from the axis (fig. 15–4). Relative symmetry can be obtained by varying the distance from the axis according to the weight of the elements. Heavy elements can be balanced by lighter elements when the heavier ones are placed close to the axis and the lighter ones farther away (fig. 15–5).

Another basic contributor to order on the magazine pages is *grouping*. Especially in situations involving several items—perhaps five photos, five captions, a title, and an authur's blurb—grouping is essential. The smaller the number of display elements, the greater the chance for order. If the five photos can be grouped to form one visual element, and the captions are visually tied to the photos, the potential for order has been increased and the tendency toward clutter and disorder has been decreased.

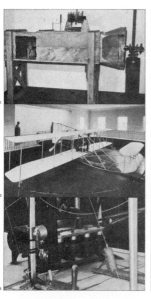

Figure 15–4 Relatively equal elements positioned on both sides of the center line also provide a feeling of equilibrium. (Courtesy *America* Magazine, reprinted with permission from the Fall 1982 *America*, © 1982 by 13–30 Corporation, 505 Market St., Knoxville, TN 37902.)

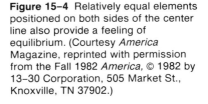

Figure 15–5 Placement of heavier (larger, darker) elements closer to the fulcrum to balance them with lighter elements placed farther from the center. (Reprinted from *NCR World* of NCR Corporation.)

Alignment

Alignment of elements can also be especially helpful in giving order to magazine pages. A good question to ask when placing any visual element on a layout is, "what can this line up with?" Instead of floating in space, captions should be lined up with the edges of photos, photos should line up with column dividers, title type should line up with an adjacent illustration, and so on. Figure 15–6 shows how alignment prevails between elements and within elements, such as titles. It also shows that alignment can sometimes tend to aid a reader's eye movement as he or she views the page or spread.

Visual Syntax

The fact that a layout has order and structure does not mean that it is static. Some motion that correlates to normal reader eye movement can be a vital charactertistic of well-designed pages. To make pages effective in this regard, two things must be considered: (1) what pattern will reader eye movement take, and (2) in what order should elements be placed along any eye movement path if readers are to be able to extract meaning from the presentation?

With regard to point one, there are some generally accepted assumptions that are reasonably substantiated by research. For example, the upper left quadrant of a page or spread is considered the normal starting place, with readers tending to read to the right and then down. Two commonly accepted movement patterns are those that resemble a question mark or a letter z. But even if these patterns are valid, successful communication is not assured unless elements are placed in a sequence that is meaningful.

An analogy with verbal syntax is in order here. We know, for example, that as a person reads a line of type from left to right, the words must be in proper order if they are to convey meaning. Journalists are taught that, for many basic news stories, the simple declarative sentence with the standard order of subject, verb and object can be most effective. Complicated sentences can fog meaning, and incorrect word order can give totally erroneous meaning. It seems reasonable to assume that the order of presentation for graphic or visual elements can have the same results. There is, in effect, good and poor visual syntax.

Armed with photos, title, captions, body copy, and white space, how can an editor place them in proper order for reader viewing? There is at least one technique that can help: the careful selection of a dominant element, such as one of the illustrations or the title. This element can then be given visual dominance, made to be the starting place for a reader. Placement of this element in the upper left takes advantage of the reader's normal inclination to start there. We can think of this as an analog of placing the subject first in a simple declarative sentence—in most cases it is the easiest, most effective way to communicate. But it should be noted that

Figure 15–6 Note the alignment, horizontally and vertically that is evident among the elements on this spread. (Reprinted from *NCR World* of NCR Corporation.)

good writers don't use only simple declarative sentences, and good magazine designers don't always put the starting element in the upper left. As pointed out in the chapter on titles, there is nothing wrong with placing titles any place on a page or spread, provided they are given sufficient strength to get reader attention. In verbal syntax, when sentence structure becomes more unusual or more complicated, more care must be given to the arrangement if meaning is to remain clear. And so it is with the visual; the more designers vary from the normal, the more careful they must be to make sure their graphic presentation is strong enough to guide readers through the layout in a meaningful order. The creation of lines through placement of elements is perhaps the best way of directing reader eye movement.

Working with Spreads

Placement of elements to direct eye movement must be done with the realization that readers are ordinarily viewing two pages as a unit, and not a single page. As a matter of fact, except when looking at the front cover or back cover, readers will always have the horizontal area created by two pages spread out before them. Consequently, spreads, rather than single pages, should be the basic layout area.

As indicated in an earlier chapter, margins are usually set so the inside (gutter) margin is no more than half the size of the largest margin. This practice is intended to help hold the spread together, rather than let it visually become two separate page units. Other techniques are also employed to maintain a horizontal directional flow that will bridge the gutter and tie two pages together. An obvious and straightforward line can be used (fig. 15–7). Placement of photos in horizontal groupings can also help. Titles can be designed to carry across the gutter, too. Figures 15–8 and 15–9 show some of these page-linking devices at work.

Perhaps equally important is the necessity to give vertical eye movement to a page that must stand independently from the one facing it. An article that opens on a right hand page, for example, should be designed to be completely separated from the end of an article on the facing page. Placement of white space, vertical shapes for titles, vertical alignment of photos, and similar devices are helpful in this instance. Some pages that were designed to stand apart instead of forming a unit that includes the facing page are shown in figure 15–10.

Importance of White Space

This short discussion of white space is not included at the end of our discussion of layout because it is of least consequence. In fact, the reverse is true. Although we tend to think of the black type, the dark photos, or the color blocks as we create page layouts, the apportionment of white space that results from the positioning of other elements is of utmost importance.

For anyone who has worked with a camera, the importance of white space should be obvious, because we know that a camera sees only white space. Place a type proof in front of a camera and black type will reflect no light to the film but the white background will fully expose the film. Human eyesight relies on the reflection of light also, and this point should be remembered when any graphic design is created.

White space can be a powerful unifying factor. It can also destroy a design as effectively as huge black lines. For the beginner, there is this helpful maxim: *place excess white space to the outside of a layout.* If that is done, the effect will be to unify the spread or page. Interior white space can be destructive.

In this context it should be remembered that margins are only intended to be limits for type. The urge to push outward (thus leaving inner white space) in order to form neat marginal lines should be resisted.

In the placement of photos, however, the restriction of white space may be undesirable. Rather than confine the action of photos with borders of white, it is often better to bleed them in order to add to rather than restrict their magnitude.

Figure 15–7 Sometimes obvious lines are used to bridge the gutter and help unify two pages. (Courtesy *Modern Maturity* and *Lines*, Reliance Insurance Company.)

Mechanics of Page Layout

All of the attention to good design, the positioning of elements for maximum impact, and all other factors of appearance go down the drain unless elements fit their designated locations and printers understand exactly where these locations are.

At some point, the content and the layout must be made to match. The length of the body copy, the words of a title, and the content of illustrations might be made to dictate layout; that is, the design would be forced to conform to material intended for use. Or, on the other hand, an art director might design the page or spread, and the writers and illustrators must make their product fit the package. Or, even more likely, form and content are juggled simultaneously as page layouts are executed. The extent to which production stages are completed in-house or by outside specialists also complicates procedure.

Figure 15–8 Alignment of elements horizontally across a spread wipes out the normal division created by the gutter margins. (Courtesy *Modern Maturity* and *Imperial Oil Review*.)

Figure 15–9 Pictures, titles, and white space, jointly and separately, can serve to unite two pages. (Courtesy *Sun* Magazine, Sun Company, Inc.)

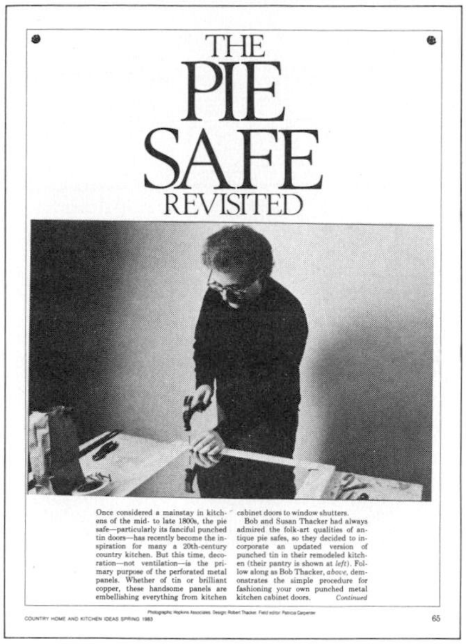

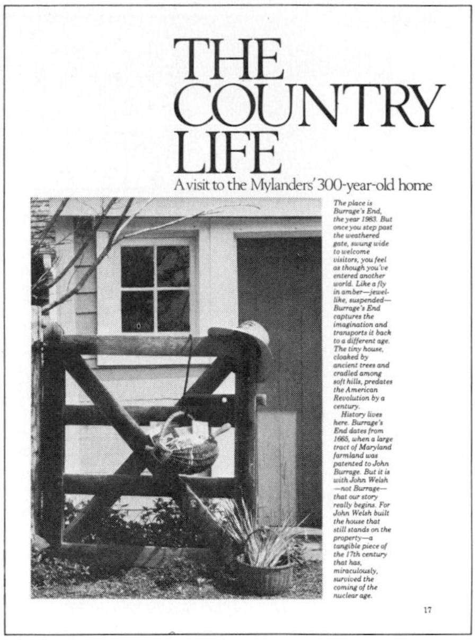

Figure 15–10 Single pages must be made to stand apart by putting adequate white space toward the gutter, and arranging elements in vertical rather than horizontal lines, as on these right-hand pages. (© Meredith Corp., 1983. All rights reserved.)

Basic Steps in Page Layout

Starting with a miniature layout showing the number of pages and the rough apportionment of space among title, illustrations, and body copy, plus full-size grid sheets, these steps must be completed:

1. Determine the exact amount of space that will be used by the text of the article.
2. Determine the amount of space for any illustrations.
3. Position body type and illustrations.
4. Design and position display type for title.
5. Place type specifications on layout for all display type.
6. Show in color all elements that are to be in color, or designate color usage.
7. Specify any typographical requirements that would not accompany the article manuscript, such as border rules or shaded areas.

After the above steps are completed, the final product should be a plan that a printer can follow precisely to create a finished page or spread that will be exactly as planned. The exact sequence of the steps just listed can vary considerably, and they also tend to blend together, but we will present them in a sequence here that can work in most situations.

Fitting Body Type to Space. Casting body copy (determining how much space the manuscript will occupy) often is done first because the text tends to be least flexible of the elements. Type size, leading between lines, and line length are usually constants that cannot be changed, thus making expansion or contraction of edited copy impossible. Using the technique described in the next chapter, it is relatively easy to determine the total depth of type, in picas, of any article.

Assuming, for example, that we have decided that two facing pages will be needed for an article, have made the calculations, and know that the article (when set in our type specifications) will use sixty-four picas of space. That is too long for a single column in a standard magazine, so we have the choice of dividing it into two, three, or whatever larger number of columns would be available.

In making this allocation of column space to the body type, we must have in mind what illustrations are available, what shapes they are, and how strong they are. We might, for example, want to use one as a full-page bleed to open a two-page spread, or we could be aware of the fact that three photos are vertical rectangles that could be lined up to form a horizontal panel across one full page.

To create a working example here, let's say we have four photos and we will use one of them (a horizontal shape) to dominate the left page, and we can use the other three together or independently. After some doodling, we came up with the miniature in figure 15–11. By dividing our 64 picas of body type into three columns,

Figure 15–11 One miniature of the many that may be tried is selected as the basis for a final page layout.

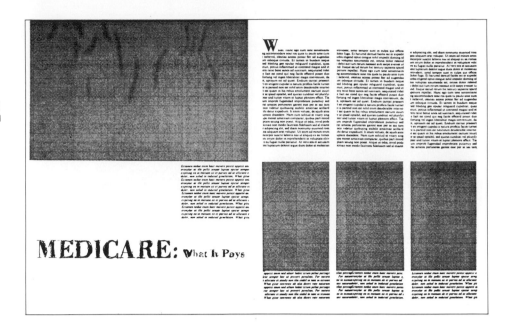

Figure 15–12 After tone sheets have been placed in areas to be occupied by photos, and bogus type has been placed to show the space occupied by body type, the title can be assigned. Hand lettering to size is the best method for insuring a good fit, and tracing from type books guarantees exact fit.

it will go across the top of the second page (fig. 15–12), and the three pictures will line up across the bottom with captions directly under each.

These three photos, plus the one we will position on the left page, must go through a process called *scaling* or *proportioning* so that we will know their dimensions after enlargement or reduction for use on our spread. The specifics of illustration scaling will be presented in chapter 17.

It will suffice here to say that our dominant photo will occupy space as shown in figure 15–12, and the other three will be placed as shown there. The remaining open space will accommodate the title.

After some rough lettering on scratch paper, we might present our title, MED-ICARE, Its Pluses and Minuses, as lettered in position in Figure 15–12. We know the title will fit there because we have lettered it by tracing from a type book, and our type specs for it are from the book. Techniques for fitting display type to space are also explained in the next chapter.

Figure 15–12 now represents a blueprint for the printer to follow in putting these pages together. If we have typesetting facilities in our own offices, we could set the type and paste photocopy proofs in position. Or, as shown here, we can use bogus type to show the location of body type. Note that photos are indicated by tone sheets in figure 15–12. We might just draw rectangles with Xs to show the location of photos, numbering each to insure proper placement, but use of tone sheets and bogus type permits good visualization of what final pages will look like. A contrasting bogus type has been used for captions. Bogus type and tone sheets can be purchased at art stores or made to order.

Note that there are no instructions on the layout for body type; the person setting this type never sees the layout and must have full specifications on the type-written sheets, not here. Note, however, that the display type specs are here; usually display type is set from the layout, thus permitting the setter to follow any special spacing that might be desired and shown on the layout.

The layout shown in figure 15–12 may be the only one needed. If properly done, positioning of the elements is exact, and each will be placed exactly as shown. In some situations, a layout is not made until the type has been set, and the type proofs are in position, instead of bogus type (fig. 15–13).

Assuming that we might want our key title word (MEDICARE) to be set in red, lettering it in red on the layout communicates that fact to the printer. Verbal designations of color are also acceptable, but they do not permit visualization in advance of the effect the use of color will have.

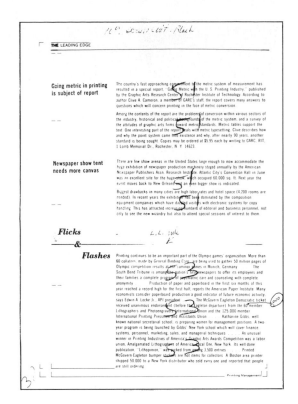

Figure 15–13 In addition to the dummy as executed in Figure 15–13, or as a substitute for it, a paste-up using the actual type proofs may be required. The letters and numbers on the type proofs on this page from *Printing Management* identify the type that should be positioned there. (Courtesy *Printing Management.*)

Regardless of variations in procedures that prevail, these functions must be accomplished by a layout:

1. Show the locations of all visual elements exactly.
2. Guarantee that each block of body type, each word of display type, and each illustration will fit as placed on the layout.

Page Layout by Computer

Computers are ideally suited for layout of magazine pages, and they are increasingly being put to work for this task. As illustrated in chapter 11, publications such as *U.S. News & World Report* are able to paginate totally by computer, including storage and placement of photos. The large amount of storage needed for photographs (the many scan lines and many tones to be recorded in digital code add up to tremendous numbers) continues to make that aspect of page layout a manual process for most magazines, but other aspects of layout are routinely done electronically.

Computer pagination can vary from partial pages (*area composition*) up to full pages. In area composition, display and body type are joined together to form rectangles that will cover major sections of a page, and thus reduce the number of elements to be pasted in position to a minimum. Designation of type specifications and number of *legs* (columns) is usually done from a keyboard.

Full pages may be put together through *templates* (set geometric patterns or grids that are programmed into a computer). Upon specification of a pre-determined template, the computer will arrange the material, and a typesetter will produce the full page, with or without photos or other graphics. Designation of X and Y coordinates is another way of keyboarding placement instructions in computer pagination systems.

Specialized terminals even provide screen viewing of type in exact style and size, thus permitting good visualization and the opportunity for modification of position and reduction or enlargement of space requirements for elements.

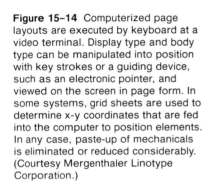

Figure 15–14 Computerized page layouts are executed by keyboard at a video terminal. Display type and body type can be manipulated into position with key strokes or a guiding device, such as an electronic pointer, and viewed on the screen in page form. In some systems, grid sheets are used to determine x-y coordinates that are fed into the computer to position elements. In any case, paste-up of mechanicals is eliminated or reduced considerably. (Courtesy Mergenthaler Linotype Corporation.)

Preparation of Mechanicals

Magazines without the capability of pagination by computer are involved directly or indirectly with preparation of mechanicals (the finished, camera-ready paste-ups of pages). Traditionally the domain of the printer, preparation of mechanicals is now more likely the responsibility of magazine staffs. Even if mechanicals are prepared by printers, however, the knowledge of the basic techniques involved is essential for editorial and production staff members.

Function of a Mechanical

The word *mechanical* is short for *photomechanical,* the term which properly identifies the camera-ready paste-up as the first step in the photochemical printing process.

As the beginning phase of production, it requires mechanical skills and strict attention to detail during preparation. A good mechanical will reduce to a minimum the work that follows; incomplete or sloppy mechanicals cause additional work when negatives are being made or stripped into a mask for platemaking.

If a mechanical is incomplete, extra stripping is required, and it is much more difficult to fasten negatives into a mask than it is to apply paper proofs to grid sheets. Any blemishes will require extra brush work when opaquing negatives. Fortunately, such blemishes can be removed from the negative, but, again, the time and cost involved for opaquing are greater than what is involved in keeping a mechanical clean.

A good mechanical will also have all elements positioned exactly, and absolutely square and true. It will, in addition, contain any instructions necessary for later production steps.

A separate mechanical is needed for each color involved in printing, and sometimes extra ones are needed even if only one color is involved. Overprinting of type or line illustrations over photographs may involve separate mechanicals, for example. In any case, one of the mechanicals is considered the *key* and is usually made on board or paper; the others are called *overlays* and are usually made on transparent or translucent film.

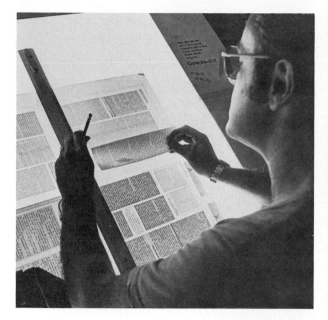

Figure 15–15 Working at a light table with T-square and ruling devices, a staff member pastes proofs in exact position to create a usable mechanical.

Figure 15–16 An overlay is used with a key paste-up to assure correct positioning of material that is to be in any additional plate burning. The key and the overlay are photographed separately, put into separate masks, and exposed to separate plates if they are to be printed in separate colors. They are exposed on the same plate when the overlay is used only to get precise positioning of elements for printing in black only.

Positioning of elements is controlled by *register marks,* small marks with a cross enclosed in a circle, much like a gunsight. With transparent overlays placed so their register marks fall exactly over the register marks on the key, exact positioning is assured from that point on.

Register marks are, therefore, a part of the communication from the preparer of the mechanical to the stripper who must take the negatives made from mechanicals and strip them into position in a mask.

Content of Mechanicals

One must know the difference between what printers call *line copy* and what they label as *continuous tone copy* to know what can be placed on a mechanical. Line copy is any copy composed of only pure whites and pure blacks, such as body type, display type, and line drawings. Continuous tone copy is all material that contains images ranging in tones continuously from light to dark, such as photographs, watercolor paintings, and oil paintings. For best results, continuous tone copy is han-

195

dled separately, going through the halftone screening process, and then being stripped into a separate mask. The process of exposing light through a second mask onto a plate is called *double burning*.

To avoid double burning, it is possible to convert continuous tone copy into screened photoprints that can become a part of the basic mechanical containing line copy. Screened photoprints, often called Veloxes because of the brand of paper used in making them, suffer some slight loss of quality in the converting step, but they are used by many magazines.

Tools and Materials Needed

To prepare mechanicals, tools needed include:

1. A grid sheet, pre-printed with all critical lines in place.
2. Cutting tools, such as X-acto knives or razor blades, for precise cutting of proofs.
3. Adhesives, such as rubber cement or adhesive wax, for fastening proofs in position. Glues that cause paper to wrinkle are not satisfactory.
4. Guides for alignment, such as drawing boards, T-square, and triangles.
5. Red, blue, and black pencils and pens for drawing lines and writing instructions.
6. Paste-down borders, rules, and other typographical symbols.
7. Transparent red film with adhesive backing for designating continuous tone areas.
8. A light table that provides lighting from underneath.
9. Masking tape for fastening sheets to table surface.

Preparing the Mechanical

The first step in preparing a mechanical is to fasten the grid sheet to the working surface with masking tape, using T-square and triangle to be certain that margins and columns are lined up.

Lines are blue on the grid sheet because, for lithographic film used by printers, blue is the same as white: it will expose film totally when light is reflected from it. On the other hand, red lines are just like black lines, and will not expose the film because it absorbs the rays of light. You should remember that lines that do not reflect light to film will remain clear on the film and will, therefore, allow light through to a plate resulting in the line being printed.

A non-reproducing blue pencil is essential for working with mechanicals; using it to draw lines can provide guidelines that will not show up in print. Care must be taken not to use dark blue lines; the darkness comes from black within the blue, which can cause such lines to reproduce.

By reserving black lines for material that is to be reproduced, and red lines for material that is to carry through to the negative but then be blacked out, some confusion can be avoided. Red lines reproduce as well as black, but if their use conveys the notice that the material should not be in the final reproduction, they can provide very helpful placement lines for the stripper.

The second step usually is the drawing or placement of any rules, borders, or other lines that are to print. Most borders or rules are available in rolls of pressure-sensitive tape that can be easily positioned and cut. Drawing of these lines is best avoided; good ruling pens and undercut line guides are absolutely necessary if that is to be done.

Next, trim all type proofs and illustrations, including screened Velox prints, usually leaving about ⅛th inch of space around them. The fact that the proof is raised above the surface can cause a shadow, and the edge allowance usually causes any shadow to be far enough from the image that it is hidden behind the mask after stripping.

This edge allowance interferes with accurate alignment of type columns, but this difficulty can be eliminated by cutting a slit about a quarter-inch long at the top left edge of the proof and another at the bottom left. The cut then forms small tabs that can be lifted up to permit lining up the proofs with the grid line below.

Illustrations can be most accurately placed if they are positioned before final trimming. Crop marks or grid lines can be followed for the final trimming.

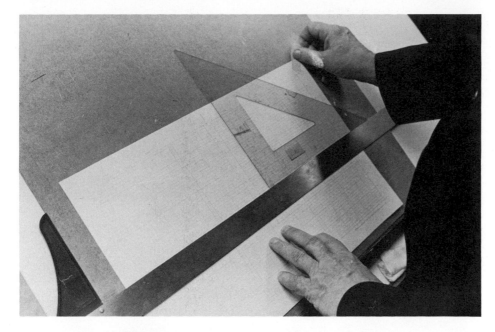

Figure 15–17 First step in preparing a mechanical is to fasten grid sheets into a squared off position on the drawing board or light table.

Figure 15–18 Border tape is used to form column rules or outlines for boxed areas. It is available in various styles and is pressure sensitive.

Figure 15–19 Type proofs, with adhesive wax or rubber cement, are positioned on the grid sheet.

Figure 15–20 Areas being set off for halftones are covered with pressure-sensitive red transparent film. The red film results in a clear window on the negative, thus permitting the placement of a screened negative beneath it. Screened Velox prints may be used on the mechanical instead of the film.

Preparing Overlays

An overlay is usually required for each color in addition to black and/or for any double burning that is required. It is possible, however, that printers will prefer that they break for color from a single mechanical. For example, if everything on a page is to be black except a title line in green, one mechanical including the title as well as other elements, could be used to make two negatives. By blocking out the title on the one negative, the black plate can be made. Then, by blocking out everything but the title in the other negative, the color plate can be made for applying the green ink.

When starting preparation of an overlay, the register marks must be placed to coincide exactly with the marks on the key mechanical under the overlay. Then any material positioned on the overlay will be as exactly located as it would be if it were being placed on the key.

Double Burning

To get the highest quality of reproduction for photographs, they will be separately exposed on a printing plate. The technique used for positioning them on the key mechanical is to cut and position transparent red film in their place. Pressure sensitive red tone sheets are available from art stores for this purpose. The result is a clear window in the negative made from the key mechanical.

The halftone negative can then be stripped into exact position in a separate mask that will be double burned on the same plate with the material from the key.

The best and most positive means for identifying illustrations for a stripper is to use a photostat of the illustration behind the red tone sheet; it will not appear in the negative, but it will be seen there on the mechanical as the stripper fastens halftone negatives in the mask.

Tint Screens and Special Illustrations

Tint screens and special finishes for illustrations can be handled on mechanicals, but in general it is wiser to let printers do this work at the negative stage.

A tint screen glued to a mechanical can be distorted or marred before the mechanical is photographed, but if a negative for a tint screen is stripped in position, quality of reproduction is guaranteed. The same is true of using red film to form a mask to outline a shape in a photo or to get a reversal of tones. Unless a staff is especially skilled in mechanical preparation, all these techniques are best left to the printer and his or her strippers.

16

Copy Processing: Editing for Production

As editors apply their creative talents to improving words and pictures and putting them together as functional and attractive pages, they must be constantly aware of production-related aspects of editing.

They are creating a product that must be manufactured, and the limitations or capabilities of the manufacturing process (and the personnel involved) cannot be forgotten or ignored. Open communication, always in the language of the producers (printers), is essential through all the steps of copy processing.

These steps include marking instructions for typesetting, insuring that all material is properly positioned, correcting the typesetting, and making certain that all material fits into the allocated position.

In some circumstances, the actual preparation of pages for the creation of negatives and plates by the printer is also an editorial responsibility.

Marking Instructions for Typesetting

The copy editing symbols presented in chapter 7 are used to tell printers of any changes in typewritten copy; they represent an efficient shorthand for deleting, inserting, and changing typewritten copy. On video terminals, the cursor and keystrokes provide for even more efficiency in copy changing.

Specifications for how the body type is to be set are usually placed at the top of the manuscript, and the instructions for display type are usually put on the layout. There are many variables in typesetting, and absolute understanding between printer and editor is necessary if the printer is to deliver an acceptable product. Specifying all these variables would be somewhat complicated except for the fact that many of them, because they are the norm, can be assumed.

For example, a printer really needs eight specific bits of information before typesetting can begin, but most of these can be skipped under normal circumstances. Complete type specifications would include:

1. Size of type (such as 8-point)
2. If there is to be additional white space between lines (usually created by adding space to make lines taller than the size of type, such as 8-point type set on a 10-point line)
3. Family name of the type style, such as Bodoni, Baskerville, Vogue, etc.
4. The particular variation within the family, such as bold, condensed, etc.
5. The posture of the type (roman [upright] or italic [slanted])
6. Letter composition (all capitals, capitals and lower case, capitals and small capitals, etc.)
7. Appointment of space (flush left and right, centered, letter spacing, etc.)
8. Length of line (usually expressed in picas)

Although all these items are rarely included, a full set of instructions thus might be written in this fashion: *8/10 Bodoni Bold ital. c/lc, flush left and right × 18 picas.* The expression of the type size (8 pt.) and the thickness of line (10 pt.) as a fraction is a common short form as are the abbreviations for italic and capitals and lower case. The "× 18 picas" is also an accepted brief way of denoting line length;

Polychrome purchases plant to expand plate production

Polychrome Corporation, manufacturer and distributor of lithographic printing products, announces the purchase from Celanese Corporation of a manufacturing plant on a 10½ acre site in Clark, N.J.

Purchase of the recently constructed plant will enable the company to increase lithographic plate manufacturing to augment its present production facilities in Yonkers, N.Y. The new plant also will enable Polychrome to expand both production and research and development activities of many printing products the company markets including a new photopolymer relief plate for flexography, letterpress and dry offset.

Figure 16–1 The typewritten sheet of copy as edited produced the galley proof shown here. Note the typesetting instructions, plus slug (guide) lines. (Courtesy *Printing Management.*)

Printing Management News National
Nov. Drahos
9755

Set body 8/10 Times Roman on 12 picas

Polychrome purchases plant
To expand plate production   Set 14 pt Spartan Bold Cond c/lc fl lf on 12 picas

Fl lf   Polychrome Corporation, manufacturers and distributors of lithographic printing products, announces the purchase from Celanese Corporation of a manufacturing plant on a 10½ acre site in Clark, N.J.

¶ Purchase of the recently constructed plant will enable the company to increase lithographic plate manufacturing, to augment its present production facilities in Yonkers, N.Y.

The new plant also will enable Polychrome to expand both production and research and development activities of many printing products the company markets, including a new photopolymer relief plate for flexography, letterpress and dry offset.

some editors designate line length as the bottom element of a fraction: $\dfrac{\text{8/10 Bodoni Bold Italic.}}{\text{18 picas}}$

Because of mutually accepted assumptions, only a few of these specifications need to be written on each piece of magazine copy. For body copy, it is assumed that there is no difference between type size and line thickness unless specified, the family version is standard, posture is upright, letter composition is as typed, and appointment of space is flush left and right and letter spacing is normal. Thus a more typical set of instructions might simply be *8 pt Bodoni × 18 picas*. The more "unwritten" (but clearly understood) communication that exists between editor and printer, the more efficient the operation. In some in-house operations (the print shop is operated by the magazine's publisher), it may even be possible that no instructions are needed for most copy. If type specifications, including column width, are standard, only exceptions, such as cutlines, need to be marked.

Type specifications should be clearly written at the top of each piece of copy; they usually are circled to indicate that they are not part of the material to be set in type.

Computer Specifications

Computer video terminals can handle type specifications very efficiently. Terminals usually are on line (wired directly) to a typesetter, and instructions can be keyboarded to the typesetter.

To avoid the necessity of transmitting the eight points of specific information listed above, computer systems are usually programmed to designate fonts by number, a font being the specific designation of one size of one branch of one family of type. Font 1 might be 8-point Century Condensed, for example. Other details, such as leading and line length, are usually programmed into *format* keys. In this case,

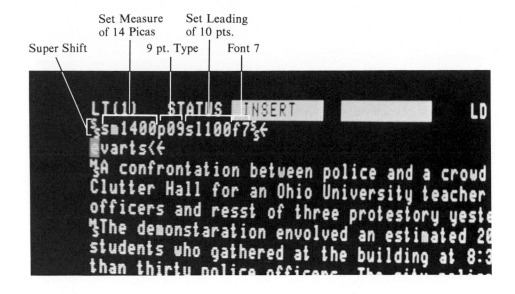

Super Shift | Set Measure of 14 Picas | 9 pt. Type | Set Leading of 10 pts. | Font 7

Figure 16–2 Note the line of typesetting instructions on the terminal, identifying the line length, size, leading, and face of the type to be used. The first keystroke (SS) stands for *super shift* and it simply alerts the typesetter to the fact that instructions follow. The sm is for set measure, line length, of 24.0 picas. Point size of type is 9, and the sl (set leading) of 10 provides for one point of white space. The face is identified by number, and the instructions end with the super shift. With formatting, this line of instructions is in the system memory and can be called into place with one format key.

formatting is the term describing the use of a single keystroke to specify complicated typesetting instructions. By prior programming, one key stroke might designate the specifics of display type to be used as a headline, as well as all necessary specifics for body type that goes with it.

Keying Copy for Location

No article is fully marked with instructions until it contains the information necessary to get it (1) to the proper publication when it is set in type and (2) to the correct location within the publication.

A *slug* of some kind is necessary, usually including the name of the magazine, the issue date, and the page number. This information is set into type and becomes the first line or two on the type proof. In figure 16–1, "Printing Management" tells the printer which magazine the copy was set for, "November" indicates the issue, and "News National" tells the department where it is to be included. The same slugging systems prevail when working at computer terminals. The first line of type on the screen should identify the story; the page layout will then show where the story is to be placed.

Reading Type Proofs

Printers are responsible for the errors of their typesetters and will correct such errors free of charge provided they are detected and clearly marked on a galley proof. They will also correct any "author's" errors at any time, but will charge for the labor time involved.

Corrections on type proofs are made with a uniform set of proofreading symbols (fig. 16–3). Application of these symbols involves marking the error at the point it occurs in a line of type, sometimes drawing a guideline to the nearest margin, but always writing the proper symbol in the margin. A sample of corrected proof is shown in figure 16–4.

The admonition is worth repeating here that *all* type corrections should be detected and marked at the earliest possible stage of the type checking cycle. Corrections missed on galleys become costly as they are made on page proofs because they require undoing work already done.

When working with a computerized system, editors should make all corrections before type is *dumped* into the typesetter. Corrections made after proofs are made tend to lead to considerable re-setting or sloppy work. Patching-in small sections of a column of type, once the type is exposed on the photopaper, can result in misalignment or shifting of the patches. Obviously, all errors cannot be avoided even with constant vigilance, but proofing of copy while it is still on the screen must be as thorough as possible.

Figure 16-3 Proofreading symbols.

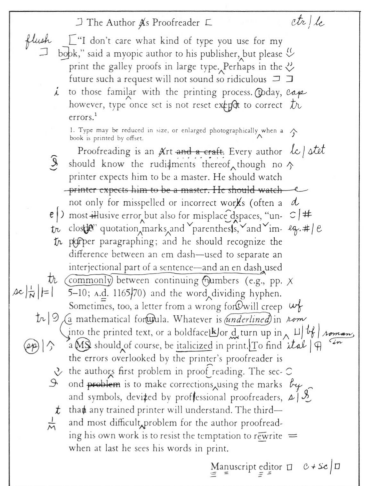

Figure 16-4 A corrected proof. Note that the correction symbols are in the margin.

Figure 16-5 In a computerized system, proofreading is done on the video screen. Here the cursor is placed in the fourth line to delete a character. The fact that the editor is actually serving as a typesetter places greater responsibility at this stage of correcting copy in computerized systems.

Fitting Body Copy to Space

As in the case of the proverbial two pounds of sugar that won't fit into a one-pound bag, it should be obvious that only so much copy in a given type size will fit into a column, a page, a signature, or a magazine. It should also be obvious that the feeling that would arise when an editor discovers he or she had underestimated the material would be dismal indeed. Blank pages, or pages with gaping white holes that should have been filled, just don't sell magazines or give editors satisfaction. The consequences of having too much copy are just as bad, although they may not be quite as obvious to the beginner. In either instance, quality and cost are both likely to be affected. Under-writing can destroy appearance, and rushing to fill unwanted holes at the last minute often adds overtime costs or causes delay. Over-writing also can destroy appearance, and there is a direct and measurable cost that comes from *overset,* type set by the printer but not used. Printing contracts are based on a normal amount of typesetting, and printers rightfully charge for excessive overset.

Careful planning during copy editing is necessary, therefore, in order to have material fit space that has been allotted to it or to allot sufficient space for material that has already been processed. Most magazines try to fit copy with an accuracy that permits no more than a line or two of variation in a column; they also like to have a system that is as simple as possible in its computations. With only a line or two of variations, a shortage can be compensated for with slight additional white space between paragraphs. On the other hand, a line or two of extra length can usually be squeezed into an area without destroying page design; at least any resetting would be minimal. Some magazines, such as *Life* and others that copied it during its lifetime as a weekly, carried copyfitting to an extreme by insisting that the last line in a block of copy fill out to the right in spite of the fact that some resetting was often needed.

The copyfitting system used for body copy by virtually all magazines is based on the number of characters in a specific type face that will fit into a given line length. A character is any letter, space, number, or piece of punctuation; no allowance is made for obvious variations in width among characters. In small type sizes and relatively large copy blocks, variations in character width are expected to average out.

The character count system does take into account the variations resulting from design differences in type faces, and consequently is much more precise than systems based on average type designs or on words rather than characters. To use the system, an editor must be provided with information about the type face he or she is using. This information is furnished by the printer or type manufacturer either in the form of figures denoting the number of characters in a pica of line length (fig. 16–6) or the number in a given line length, such as 20 picas (fig. 16–7).

When working with information presented as it is in figure 16–7, the line length (in picas) must be multiplied by the number of characters in a pica to find the number of characters in a line. For example, a line of 10-point Baskerville that is 20 picas

Face	Point Sizes				
	8	9	10	11	12
Baskerville	3.22	2.96	2.64	2.46	2.3
Caledonia	3.12	2.87	2.63	2.44	2.26
Caslon	3.39	3.27	3.16	2.76	2.38

Figure 16–6 Characters per pica.

Face: 10-point Bodoni

Length of line in picas:	12	14	16	18	20	22	24	26	28	30
Characters per line	37	43	49	55	61	67	73	79	85	91

Face: 10-point Bernhard Modern Roman

Length of line in picas:	12	14	16	18	20	22	24	26	28	30
Characters per line	43	50	57	64	71	78	85	92	99	106

Figure 16–7 Characters per line.

long would contain 52.8 characters (20 × 2.64). For ease in computation, this figure can be rounded off, preferably to the lower whole number, 52. It is better to be slightly short of copy than over because type cannot be squeezed into a smaller space, but it can be spaced out without difficulty.

A magazine operating with columns that are 20 picas wide would therefore be copyfitted on the basis of 52 characters in each line of type if the face chosen was 10-point Baskerville. To facilitate copyfitting, most magazines would then standardize manuscript typing to 52 characters per line so a line of typewritten material would be, on the average, equivalent to a line of type. The printing of ruled copy paper with the space between rules accommodating the desired number of characters is a common aid for copyfitting. Manuscripts typed on the ruled paper, if lines are typed so that those that go beyond the right margin are balanced out by those that are short of the right margin, will contain lines each the equivalent of a line of type.

When the characters per line are known, the only other dimensions involved in copyfitting are the number of lines and the thickness of lines. For an example, let's assume that our magazine uses 10-point Baskerville leaded two points (10/12 Baskerville) in columns that are 20 picas wide. A manuscript that has been typed with 52 characters per line contains a total of 36 lines. We would know immediately to allow 36 picas of space in a column for the manuscript because each typewritten line is the equivalent of a line of type, and each line of type is 12 points (one pica) thick.

Eliminating the shortcuts taken in the above example, the procedure for finding the amount of space an article will occupy involves:

1. Finding the number of characters that will fit into a line of type (from printer's information).
2. Finding the number of characters in the manuscript being edited (facilitated by typing manuscripts in standardized fashion).
3. Dividing the number of characters per line into the number of characters in the manuscript to find the number of lines of type needed.
4. Multiplying the number of lines of type needed by the thickness of the line to find how many points of column depth the article will occupy. Because dummying is ordinarily done in picas, divide the points by 12 to find the number of picas of depth.

Although at first glance copyfitting seems to be complicated, for magazine editors it really is not. The fact that type styles and sizes and column width are standardized takes care of much of it for them. After fitting a few articles to space, it becomes a matter of simple routine. For the beginner, practice can bring the same skill and confidence. Figure 16–8 shows the steps involved "by the numbers" as an aid for practice.

Copyfitting with computer systems can be virtually effortless, depending upon the sophistication of the system. Major news weeklies have systems that show the equivalent of a type proof on a screen instantly, permitting additions or deletions by keyboard to make the copy fit a specific space. Other systems may require input of basic type instructions and font specifications before computing the length of the column that would be formed by the copy.

Fitting Display Type to Space

Computerized systems also make fitting of display type relatively effortless. After the words or lines are on the screen, input of the type specifications via the keyboard will result in the computer's determining the number of picas per line needed for the material as specified.

In traditional copy processing, the common procedure for fitting titles is to write and design the title, and specify an appropriate type that will fit the space. Hand lettering of the type to correct size (often called *comp* lettering) will reveal which

Figuring to determine depth of space needed on layout:

1. Find characters per pica or characters in line from printer's type catalog. If using characters per pica, multiply by picas in line of type to get characters per line.

2. Determine total characters in article by multiplying characters in a typewritten line times number of lines in article. All lines count as full lines.

3. Divide total characters in article by the characters in line of type to find the number of lines of type that will be produced when article is set in type. Round up to next line if answer is in fraction.

4. Multiply the lines of type by thickness of lines (type size plus leading if any) to find the space needed (in points). Convert to picas by dividing by 12 points in a pica. You can now mark off that total depth on your layout knowing the article will fit.

Finding how many characters to write to fill space on layout:

1. Find characters per pica or characters in line from printer's type catalog. If using characters per pica, multiply by picas in line to get characters in line of type.

2. Measure depth of area on layout in picas and convert to points by multiplying by 12 points in a pica.

3. Determine number of lines of type that will fit in area by dividing points of depth by thickness of type line (type size plus leading if there is any). Round down to lower number if answer is in a fraction.

4. Multiply the lines of type by the number of characters in a line of type to find the total number of characters to write. You can now proceed to write an article of that length knowing that it will fit the layout.

Figure 16–8 Copyfitting at a glance.

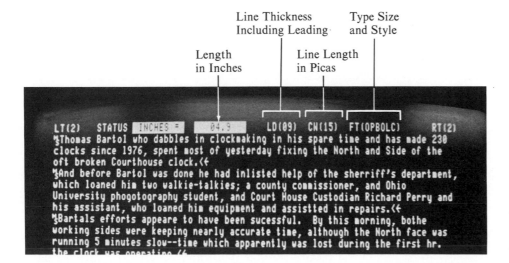

Line Thickness Including Leading

Type Size and Style

Length in Inches

Line Length in Picas

LT(2) STATUS INCHES = 04.9 LD(09) CW(15) FT(OPBOLC) RT(2)

Thomas Bartol who dabbles in clockmaking in his spare time and has made 230 clocks since 1976, spent most of yesterday fixing the North and Side of the oft broken Courthouse clock.

And before Bartol was done he had inlisted help of the sherriff's department, which loaned him two walkie-talkies; a county commissioner, and Ohio University phogotography student, and Court House Custodian Richard Perry and his assistant, who loaned him equipment and assisted in repairs.

Bartals efforts appear to have been sucessful. By this morning, bothe working sides were keeping nearly accurate time, although the North face was running 5 minutes slow--time which apparently was lost during the first hr. the clock was operating

Figure 16–9 Identifying the style of type, size, and leading plus the line length results in instant copyfitting when the proper key is pressed. Here the length is given in inches.

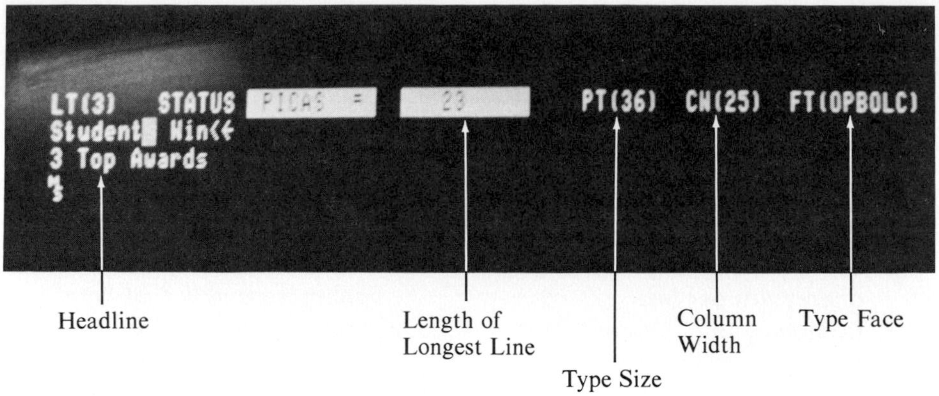

LT(3) STATUS PICAS = 23 PT(36) CW(25) FT(OPBOLC)
Student Win<←
3 Top Awards
M3

Headline   Length of   Column   Type Face
                            Longest Line   Width
                                      Type Size

Figure 16–10 This system will tell how many picas a line of display type will occupy if it is told the size and style of type.

Hand Lettering

Figure 16–11 The best way to assure the fit of display type in most magazine situations is to letter the type exactly to size by hand, as shown here. To have the type set in the size as lettered, one must be certain to allow for descending letters, even if there are none in the line.

Many Men Want
Equality Also

**Many Men Want
Equality Also**

Figure 16–12 These lines, as shown here, were typed at a typewriter without proportional spacing and appear to be equal. When set in type, the lines are quite different in length.

size or sizes to specify. Some trial and error effort may be involved, but if a type catalog in complete fonts is available, tracing of letters guarantees an absolute fit.

When specifying size based on hand lettering, the novice must remember to allow for descending strokes. Figure 16–11 shows how guide lines for the center body letters (such as a, c, and e) and the tips of the ascenders will assure accurate sizing and fitting to space. Remember, no letter will ever measure out to be the point size needed, not even capitals. Size of type is based on the body, which includes space for the descenders on letters such as y and p, even if all capitals are used.

In some instances, the use of transfer and paste-down letters can be the most efficient methods of all. With only reasonable care, the title can be presented on a layout exactly as it will be when it appears on a finished page.

If some means for enlarging or reducing is available, such as a photostat machine or process camera, manipulation of title sizes becomes easier than by trial and error. Sophisticated typesetting that permits reverse leading, letter distortion, and limitless size with its internal enlargement or reduction makes title design much more flexible, also.

Newsmagazines and other magazines with book-style design usually simplify title design and type fitting through the use of *headlines* and *headline schedules*.

Use of a Headline Schedule

Headlines and headline schedules are really a product of newspapers, but they have a natural application to magazines with standardized title treatments. Assuming that one one or, at most, three type families are to be used, it is relatively easy to establish acceptable size, depth, and width restrictions for a variety of headline patterns.

First, the type faces to be used must be determined, including the number of sizes and family variations to be available. Second, the display patterns must be selected; flush left and/or right lines are common. The third and last step is to establish a headline schedule that is based on these selections and provides the method for fitting the headlines to space.

The first and second steps outlined above are really design considerations and should be a part of the creation of a personality for the layout and page grid of the magazine. Selection of conservative, old-style type faces or new, modern faces obviously help establish the visual character of any publication.

The mechanics of setting maximum or minimum lengths for headlines are relatively simple. We should recall here that typography is based on variable letter spacing, not equal spacing as with typewriters (Figure 16–12). This variable letter spacing, plus the fact that there are only a few letters, each with large size, in most headlines make the use of character counting too inaccurate for fitting headlines to space. Instead, we would have to make allowances for thin letters, such as *Iliftjr* and wide letters such as *m, w* and capitals. A *unit count* system with reasonable allowances for such variations is usually used.

Unit Count System

In order to simplify the fitting of headlines to space, a simple unit count system with only four variations is usually used, considering letters to fall into one of these four categories: thin, medium, fat, and superfat. With one unit for medium, the thin letters are considered to be one-half, the fats one and one-half, and the superfats would be two. The task then is to determine which characters should be in each of the four divisions, with these assignments often being accepted:

One unit: All normal letters, such as *a, b, c, d, e, g, h, k, n, o, p, q, r, s, u, v, x, y, z,* spaces between words, all numbers except one (1).

One-half unit: These narrow letters: *I, l, i, f, t,* and perhaps *j, r,* depending on the particular type face being used.

One and one-half units: All capitals plus the lower case *x, m,* and *w.*

Two units: Capital *M* and *W.*

It is important to note here that whatever unit assignments are made in determining counts for the headline schedule must be used as the headlines are fitted to space. If *j* and *r* are normal letters in the original count they must be given a full count as headlines are written.

For every specific headline included in a schedule, a sample should first be set. One example here should suffice to show the procedure. Assuming that we have a headline to be formed by flush-left lines of 36-point Bodoni stretching across two 13.5 pica columns with one pica of white space between them, we can set lines with a random assortment of letters to fit that space, 28 picas. Figure 16–13 shows such a line, along with the assignment of unit values for each character. It indicates that the maximum number of units possible for such lines is 21. Figure 16–14 shows a line from a headline written to conform to that maximum, with the unit count conforming to the one used for the sample. Unit counting assures that this line of 20 units will fit the space allowed for it.

It is possible to establish a much more accurate counting system for display type based, for example, on the subdivisions of the *em* that prevail in many display typesetters. Most typesetters divide the em (the unit of measure equal to the square in the type size, or what usually is the width of a lower case *m*) into eighteen units, thus allowing much wider variations, with separate values for *i* and *f,* for example. But such a system would make counting of headlines too complicated and time consuming. The "half to one and one-half" variations provide sufficient accuracy so headlines, properly counted, seldom fail to fit.

Because type families vary according to their manufacturer, it is best to use output of the typesetters that will be used for production as a basis for a headline schedule. Use of paste-down letters in creating a schedule when a phototypesetter will be used for production would put unnecessary inaccuracies into the system.

Mdlirep Cenwitf Ghitile

2   1   ½ ½ 1   1   1   1   1½   1   1   1½   ½ ½ ½ 1   1½   1   ½ ½ ½ ½   1 (21)

Figure 16–13 An assortment of letters in 36-point Bodoni by 23 picas.

Roads Suffer Damage

1½   1   1   1   1 1 1½   1   ½ ½   1 1 1 1½   1   1½   1   1   1   (20)

Figure 16–14 A line written to conform to maximum for 23 picas.

17

Processing Illustrations for Production

GETTING original illustrations ready for production is even more involved than the marking, correcting, and fitting to space of body copy. The steps are fundamentally the same—illustrations must be marked for the printer, errors must be corrected, and they must fit the space allocated to them—but the fact that they must be re-photographed compounds the procedures.

Any illustration, from a bar chart to a full-color photo, can be enlarged or reduced for reproduction, and the figuring involved for these enlargements and reductions is puzzling to some beginners in editing. Part of the problem stems from the fact that this figuring does not take place in a vacuum; the content of the photo or other illustration is an important and ever-present consideration. To make the process as clear as possible, let's consider it step-by-step and in terms relating directly to magazine usage.

Marking Printers' Instructions

No illustration is ready for production until it contains four crop marks to set its original dimensions and provide the printer with reproduction dimensions. In special circumstances, special descriptions of the reproduction techniques must be given.

Let's look at the photo in figure 17–1. You may recognize it as the same picture used in chapter 13 to show how it was cropped to emphasize the main subject. Note that there are four crop marks; the two across the top are establishing the original width, and the two on the right side are establishing the original depth. Any additional crop marks would be confusing and misleading for printers, but these four are essential. The top pair could be used across the bottom, and the side pair could be moved to the right side, but in no case would we use more than those four. As far as printers are concerned, the photo has now been cut off at these marks, just as much as if it had been cut with scissors or a razor blade.

Look also at the weather map in figure 17–2; it also contains the four crop marks. Without the crop marks, the dimensions are not established, as far as a printer is concerned. In this case, the marks allow the full outline of the map to be included in the reproduction.

Figure 17–1 This photograph, used in Chapter 13 to illustrate cropping to improve a photograph, shows the crop marks necessary for a printer: two to set the width and two to set the depth.

It is best to keep all dimensions or other marks off the front of the photo; they, also, would only create confusion. Crop marks also should be in the border, if possible, and made with a china marker (grease pencil) so they can be rubbed off if need be. Any lines drawn on the face of the illustration also would be a source of potential production problems, often finding their way into the reproduction at some points.

With crop marks placed, the next step is to give the printer directions for making the reproduction. This can be written on the back (preferably on a sticker, so the writing does not press into the photo) in terms of inches (for example, 4 × 3 inches) or picas (24 by 18 picas), with the width always expressed first. For the photo in figure 17–1, we would also have to specify a screen to be used in the reproduction.

Continuous tone illustrations are reproduced in printing by being re-photographed through a screen in a large *process* camera, a camera equipped with a vacuum back to hold a film screen tightly over film as light is reflected from the

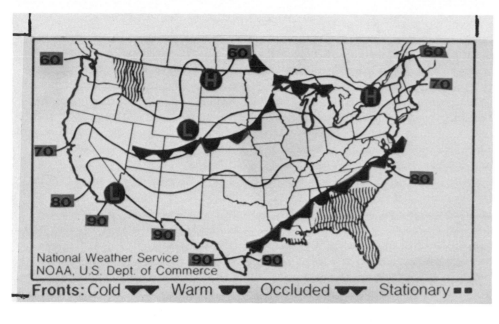

Fronts: Cold ▼▼ Warm ▾▾ Occluded ▾▾ Stationary ▪▪

Figure 17–2 No illustration, including line drawings like this weather map, is ready for production without the four crop marks as shown here.

copy board to the film, as shown in chapter 11. The screen used is made of intersecting black lines, and the area between the lines forms a small opening for light to go through to the film and expose a dot. The formation of these dots provides the means for capturing the various tones of the original on film and then on the printing plate.

The more intersecting lines per linear inch of a screen, the finer the dots will be and, generally, the finer the reproduction that is possible. The common screens for magazines contain 110, 120, 133, or 150 lines per inch, all of which provide reasonable fidelity of reproduction, but one of them must be specified. Therefore, to complete our marking for the photo in figure 17–1, we might order (on the back of this photo) a 4 by 3 inch, 150-line halftone reproduction.

With the map in figure 17–2, the marking could be complete with dimensions (such as 4 inches by 3 inches) and *line illustration* as to the type of reproduction desired.

Marking of illustrations, therefore, seems simple enough—just set the dimensions of the original with four crop marks and specify reproduction dimensions and the type of reproduction desired.

There are several complications, however. If drawings are to be reproduced in more than one color, overlays should be made containing the portion of the drawing to be done in each color. If special treatments, such as silhouetting a portion of the photo, are required, an overlay containing visual and verbal instructions to show exactly what portion is to be outlined must be included. But the biggest complication is related to the enlargement and reduction of the originals.

Reductions and enlargements are made photographically, and reproduction dimensions *must* relate to the original dimensions. The fact that we ordered a 4 × 3 inch reproduction in figure 17–1 does not guarantee that a printer could deliver a reproduction in those dimensions. As a matter of fact that would be impossible here because the original shape is a vertical, and 4 × 3 would be horizontal. The work involved in relating original shapes and sizes to reproduction dimensions is called either *proportioning* or *scaling*. Photographs rarely come from photographers with the same dimensions an editor eventually will set for them. If such is the case, they can be cropped and marked to be reproduced *same size* (SS). Otherwise, some proportioning or scaling must be done.

Proportioning and Scaling

Although this aspect of illustration processing is relatively simple, it seems to be difficult for some beginners to grasp; rather than understand the procedure they attempt to learn a handy formula only to find that their lack of understanding often makes the formula, or any other helpful device, useless.

To clarify, let's look at this technique from two directions, each suggested by one of two names given to it. Proportioning, for example, refers to shape, and shape is set by the relationship of the sides of a rectangle. A rectangle that is 4 inches wide and 4 inches deep is a square shape; one that is 4 inches wide by 8 inches deep is a vertical shape; and one that is 10 inches wide and 5 inches deep is a horizontal shape (refer to fig. 17–3). In processing illustrations we must remember only that the enlarged or reduced shape will have the same proportions as those of the original. Therefore, our square (4 × 4) can be enlarged or reduced to any other square (2 × 2, 8 × 8, 1.5 × 1.5, and so on) because the relationship of 4/4 equals 2/2, and 4/4 equals 8/8, and 4/4 equals 1.5/1.5.

Our vertical rectangle (4 × 8) will reduce and enlarge only to other vertical shapes with the same relationship of sides, such as 2 × 4, 3 × 6, and 5 × 10. For all these rectangles the width is one-half the depth.

The horizontal rectangle can enlarge or reduce only to shapes with the same proportion of 10 to 5 (such as 4 to 2, 12 to 6, and so on).

The proportions in these examples are deliberately obvious, and the potential enlargements or reductions can be seen without any computation. For shapes that are not obvious, computation can be carried out in this fashion:

$$\frac{\text{Original Width}}{\text{Original Depth}} \text{ equals } \frac{\text{Reproduction Width}}{\text{Reproduction Depth}}$$

When three of the dimensions are known, the fourth can be found quickly:

$$\frac{8}{10} \text{ equals } \frac{4}{x}$$

In this case our photo is 8 inches wide and 10 inches deep and is being reduced so it is 4 inches wide, but we do not know the depth. By cross multiplying we find that 8x equals 40. Dividing both sides by 8 then tells us that x equals 5. We then know that an 8 × 10 will reduce to a 4 × 5. Any problem in which editors know three dimensions and must find the fourth can be solved in this manner. They are simply finding dimensions of a rectangle that will have the same proportion as another rectangle, the dimensions of which they already have.

On the other hand, if one thinks of this process as *scaling,* one is concerned with an area being enlarged or reduced so that it is to *scale* with the original, just as maps are to scale (i.e. one inch equals 10 miles). Now we must keep in mind the fact that if one side of a rectangle is reduced, the other side will be reduced to the same degree. Therefore, if we consider our 4 × 4 square on this basis, we think in terms of the width, 4 inches being reduced to 2 inches, and the depth being subjected to the same reduction, 4 inches to 2 inches. For our earlier example of a vertical rectangle, if the 4 inch width is reduced to 2 inches, the 8 inch width must also be reduced to half its dimension, 4 inches.

Setting these up as we did before, we see that the original width will reduce to a reproduction width as the original depth is reducing at the same rate to a reproduction depth:

$$\frac{\text{Original Width}}{\text{Reproduction Width}} \text{ equals } \frac{\text{Original Depth}}{\text{Reproduction Depth}}$$

Figure 17–3 Understanding the figuring of proportions of photo enlargement or reduction involves an appreciation of the basic rectangular shapes: square, horizontal, and vertical.

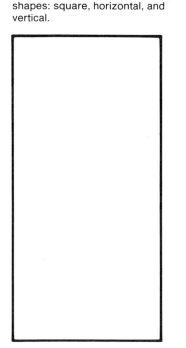

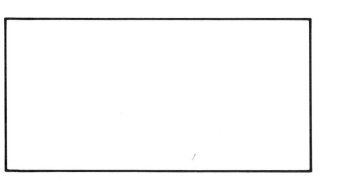

All problems that an editor might have can easily be computed in this manner. For example, if the 4 × 8 rectangle is going to be reduced to a reproduction that is 2 inches deep, the editor will want to know the width of the reproduction:

$$\frac{4}{x} \text{ equals } \frac{8}{2}$$

$$8x \text{ equals } 8$$

$$x \text{ equals } 1$$

The reproduction of the 4 × 8 photo therefore will be 1 × 2.

Whether one thinks in terms of illustration proportions or their scaling is relatively immaterial. Printers, because their camera settings are based on the percentage of reduction, are concerned with scaling. For them, the problem immediately above is simply a matter of the 8-inch depth being reduced to one-fourth of its original size, thus this is a 25 percent reduction (meaning that it is reduced to 25 percent of its original size). The important point for beginners here is simply that they should understand either method of computation. If they do they can efficiently use one or the other of two common shortcuts.

Mechanical Aids for Figuring Enlargements and Reductions

Editors who must figure enlargements or reductions for scores of illustrations each issue would do most anything to avoid figuring their problems as shown above, and rightly so. They are interested in speed and accuracy for getting the job done. It must be noted, however, that ability to make the arithmetical computations is necessary for emergencies, and for an understanding of how any device used operates.

The most common scaling tool (fig. 17–4) contains a rotating circle that is calibrated in fractions of inches on its edge. This circle is matched on the fixed background surface by another circle calibrated in the same fashion. The figures on the outer (fixed) circle line up with the figures on the rotating circle and represent fractions, all of which are equal around the circle. The scaler shown in figure 17–4 has been set so the 8-inch original width is aross from the 10-inch original depth. By looking to the left on the outer circle until we find the new width (4) we can locate the new depth (5) because it is directly across from the 4.

This scaler can also be used to figure the percentage of reduction that is involved in any problem. When either original dimension on the inner scale is lined up against the reproduction size of that dimension, the percentage of reduction shows under the arrow. In figure 17–4, because the 10 is lined up with the 8, the arrow points to 80 percent. With the circular scaler, pictures can be proportioned or percentage of reduction can be figured in only a second or two.

Use of the Diagonal

To avoid working with figures while editing pictures, editors can also use a geometric method that requires only the use of a diagonal line and a ruler to measure dimensions.

This system is based on a geometric principle: any larger or smaller rectangle formed by right angle lines drawn to meet at the diagonal is in proportion to the original. This principle is illustrated in figure 17–5, which shows square, horizontal, and vertical rectangles with diagonals drawn on them. The dotted lines are the sides of some of the new rectangles that would be formed by the right angle lines; all form rectangles that obviously are the same shape as the original. Therefore, when three dimensions are known, the fourth can be found by simply measuring the appropriate dotted line. Here's how some editors use the system. First they place a transparent overlay sheet on the face of the photo. If in this case they know the width of the reproduction and want to find the depth, they first draw a diagonal from upper right to lower left. Next they measure the known reproduction width to the right of the upper left corner and mark that dimension. By measuring the distance from that point to the diagonal they determine the reproduction depth.

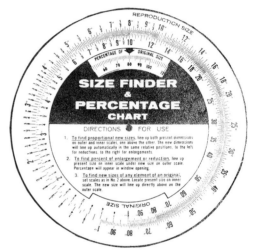

Figure 17–4 This circular scaling device contains a stationary outer circle and a rotating inner circle. By turning the inner circle, you can line up original dimensions, one over the other (8 over 10 in this case) and all ratios around the wheel will be of that shape. If the reproduction width is to be four inches, we can tell that the depth will be 5 because it is directly under the 4. As will be shown later, the wheel can also be used to find percentage of reduction.

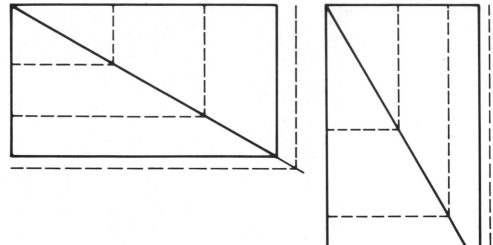

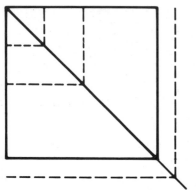

Figure 17–5 On any rectangle, lines drawn at right angles from adjacent sides to the diagonal as shown will form another rectangle of the same proportions. All the shapes made by the dotted lines in the square are squares; those in the other rectangles are the same shape as their original.

A word of caution: lines on the overlay must be drawn very lightly to avoid damaging the reproduction surface of the photo.

Some Typical Examples

Now let's get back to some examples that are typical of the normal day's routine for magazine editorial staffs. In one of them, we will first crop the photo and then do the proportioning. In the other, we will have to make the proportions of the original conform to the shape of the reproduction.

Let's start out with the easier example. We'll use an 8 × 10 inch original glossy photograph of the head and shoulders of a man as this example. As we look at the image of the man, we place two crop marks across the top, cutting off a little unnecessary background as we do so. Those crop marks measure 7 inches between them, and that is now our Original Width. Next we place two crop marks at the left, one slightly below the top and the other up a bit from the bottom. The distance between these crop marks is 7.5 inches and that is now our Original Depth. This picture must reduce to fit into our column width, which is only 14 picas. With three dimensions known, it is easy for us to do our figuring based on proportioning:

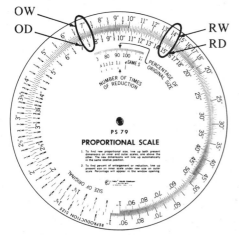

Figure 17–6 When the 7-inch original width lined up over the 7.5-inch original depth, we can look to the right for 14 and find that the depth will be 15 picas. The fact that one set of numbers is in inches and the other in picas is immaterial to the scaling wheel.

$$\frac{\text{Original Width}}{\text{Original Depth}} \quad \text{equals} \quad \frac{\text{Reproduction Width}}{\text{Reproduction Depth}}$$

or

$$\frac{7}{7.5} \quad \text{equals} \quad \frac{14}{x}$$

$$7x \quad \text{equals} \quad 105$$

$$x \quad \text{equals} \quad 15 \text{ picas}$$

Notice two things of importance here: the fact that the original started out as an 8 × 10 inch photo does not enter the figuring because (1) the original dimensions are always within the crop marks, and (2) we did not bother to convert picas to inches or vice versa because that would be wasted effort. As we do the figuring, we are concerned merely with figures (ratios) that set shapes. We assign picas to our answer of 15 after the figuring. The only trick is to know if the answer in such problems is in picas or inches. The fact that photos are often measured in inches, and layouts are always designed in picas, makes it handy to be able to figure as we have here, without converting dimensions. It works with the wheel, too (see fig. 17–6).

If, however, we want to figure percentage of reduction, we must divide one original dimension into its counterpart reproduction dimension, and both figures must be in the same unit of measure, either inches or picas. We could convert the 7 inches into 42 picas (remember: 6 picas to an inch), and divide that into 14 to find that the percentage of reduction would be 33⅓ percent, as we can see in figure 17–7.

It is important to understand that in this example we are concerned with ratios that set shapes; 7 by 7.5 is slightly vertical, as the reproduction must also be, and 14 by 15 does represent the same shape. Incorrect answers will be readily discernible if this correlation of shapes is kept in mind.

This example is probably the most typical proportioning problem facing magazine editors, and it is by far the simplest. Cropping is dictated totally by content, and the one reproduction dimension is dictated by the column width.

Cropping for Shape

But sometimes cropping must be done to change the shape of a photo, hopefully without weakening the content, and preferably also improving it. The situation arises when layouts are completed, and content is made to adhere to the layout. In such cases, the dimensions of the reproduction of a photo are set, and the photo must be made to conform to them. Any of the above proportioning and scaling methods must then be used to determine how much to crop from the original photo to get it to the right proportions. It should suffice to say here that such problems merely involve taking one of the original dimensions as the unknown; the other photo dimension joins the two reproduction dimensions as known figures. The visualizing of shapes tells an editor which original dimension becomes the unknown; if a horizontal is to be reduced to a vertical, the width becomes the unknown, and if a vertical is to be reduced to a horizontal, the depth becomes the unknown. If the change in shape is not obvious, it becomes more difficult to visualize.

Such is often the case with the most common instance involving cropping to shape: the marking of a photo to become a full-page bleed reproduction. In some respects, this also represents the most difficult problem for students to understand.

One of the complications is the fact that photos that bleed off the edge of a page must be reproduced slightly larger than the page, so when the page is trimmed the chance of any irregularity with the edge will be eliminated. The *bleed allowance,* as it is called, is usually 1/8th inch or one pica; this is sufficient to compensate for irregular folding or binding that otherwise might leave a slight sliver of white along a portion of an outside edge. Bleed allowance prevails *only* for the *trimmed* edges, so a full-page bleed would be trimmed top, bottom, and outside. Thus, for an 8½ × 11″ magazine, we would add two picas to the depth and one to the width, making it 52 × 68 picas.

Supposing then, that we have an excellent photo of basketball action for the cover of a sports magazine and it is, before cropping, 8 inches wide and 10 inches deep. Can an 8 × 10″ photo be reproduced as a 52 × 68 pica photo?

$$\text{Does } \frac{8}{10} \text{ equal } \frac{52}{68} ?$$

$$10 \times 52 = 520, \text{ and } 8 \times 68 = 544$$

Obviously, 520 does not equal 544, but they are reasonably close. Some cropping must be done to make the photo's shape exactly the same as 52 × 68 picas without weakening the photo. The simplest way to do that is to crop the photo's width slightly, so the product of Original Width × Reproduction Depth will drop from 544 to 520. Our ratios would be:

$$\frac{x}{10} \text{ equals } \frac{52}{68}$$

$$68x \text{ equals } 520$$

$$x \text{ equals } 7.64$$

This figuring and the wheel in figure 17–8 tell us that we must crop the 8-inch width to 7.64 inches and, by studying the photo's content again, we determine that such cropping would do no damage to the picture. What would happen if we wanted

Percentage of Reduction

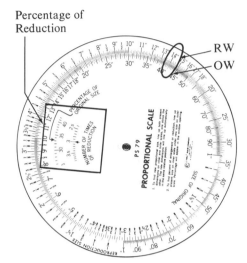

Figure 17–7 To figure percentage of reduction, one original dimension is divided into its counterpart reproduction dimension, and the wheel will figure this by having the reproduction dimension below the reproduction dimension. If 42 picas is to reduce to 14 picas, we put the 42 picas beneath 14 and look into the opening in the scaler for the percentage (33⅓).

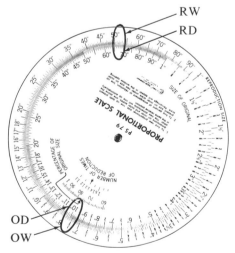

Figure 17–8 If a photo is to be reproduced as a full-page bleed (52 picas by 68 picas) we can set that ratio and look across from our known original dimension (10 inches) and find the missing original dimension (7.64 inches). Remember, in this and other similar cases, the reproduction dimensions are absolute and one of the photo's dimensions must be changed.

to get rid of some of the depth of the photo? The amount to crop from the width would increase, and that could be troublesome.

Finding the percentage of reduction or enlargement in the previous example could be done most simply by dividing the Original Depth in picas (60) into the Reproduction Depth (68); we find that the reproduction would be a 113 percent enlargement.

The use of a circular scaler eliminates all the calculations in these examples, but practice is essential before newcomers can know with certainty which way the wheel is to be set, and where the pertinent ratios are located.

Production Techniques for Illustrations

Our examples of the photograph and the map illustrated the two common divisions of reproductions for illustrations: halftones and line. There are many variations possible for both of these reproduction divisions, as well as combinations of the two. Let's look at all these possibilities, starting with the simplest line illustration and working through combination reproductions. All have some value for magazines and should be understood by anyone responsible for processing illustrations for any printing process.

Line Drawings

The simplest form of illustration is a line drawing (fig. 17–9). An artist creates a line drawing, usually with pen, but perhaps with pencil or brush, without any middle tones. Where a pen makes a mark, the full tone (black) is created; the background (nonprinting areas) carries no tone.

For offset or rotogravure reproduction, the drawing can be pasted in position on its page layout, unless it has been prepared so that the special enlargement or reduction is required. If enlargement or reduction is needed, the lithographer will make a special *line negative* to be put into position in a mask along with other elements on the page.

There is no charge for line illustrations in offset lithography or rotogravure unless a special negative is needed.

Reverse Line Drawings

Printers can convert line drawings so the background becomes the printing area, and the drawing becomes the nonprinting area. In other words, the black areas in the drawing become the white areas and vice versa. This necessitates the making of a second negative by the exposure of light through the original line negative onto another piece of film. Figure 17–10 shows a reverse line illustration.

Benday Shading

The impression of middle tones in a line drawing can be created by artificially applying shading to the desired areas as in figure 17–11. Although printers can apply the shading patterns as they etch a plate, it is now much more common for the artist to apply patterns directly to the drawings. At any rate, the production of a bendayed line illustration is no different than a standard line illustration in offset lithography.

Benday patterns are available in many varieties, including dots, stippled effects, slashes, hashmarks, and many others. Transparent patterned sheets, with adhesive backing, are usually used by the artist for applying the shading to drawings. Any art supply store can provide them.

Continuous Tone Illustrations: Halftones

Photographs, oil paintings, watercolors, and any other original illustrations containing continuous tones require special production handling. As pointed out earlier, illustrations of these types must be photographed through a screen in order to produce a negative that will, when it is transferred to a metal surface, produce an image

Figure 17–9 The simplest reproduction is called a line reproduction; it has no middle tones, only the extreme light and dark.

Figure 17–10 A reverse line illustration produces opposite tones from the original.

Figure 17–11 The appearance of middle tones can be added to line illustrations by applying screen patterns where desired. This process is called Benday.

Figure 17–12 The halftone on the left was made with an 85-line screen; the one in the middle was made with a 133-line screen, and the one on the right, with a 150-line screen.

that will reproduce the various shades of tone. Figure 17–12 shows a photo reproduced with an 85-line screen, a 133-line screen, and a 150-line screen for comparison. The reproduction as shown is referred to as a *square-finish halftone,* the basic rectangular presentation for a continuous tone illustration.

Many special finishes are available, each involving some added cost because of added production time. Any halftone illustration in letterpress is somewhat expensive because of the need to etch a zinc or copper plate. There is an added halftone cost in offset lithography also because the special screened negative must be prepared in exactly the same fashion as for letterpress printing. However, it is a considerably smaller cost than for letterpress because no special plate is etched.

Figure 17–13 A silhouette or outline halftone.

Silhouettes

Any halftone can be given a *silhouette* (outline) treatment (fig. 17–13). Even a standard mug shot (head and shoulders picture) can be made so the subject is silhouetted against the white background of the paper it is printed on. The treatment is especially effective in emphasizing the central subject of a photo; elimination of the background provides for maximum contrast. Partial silhouette treatment also is effective in such instances as an athlete in action silhouetted from the feet upward but with the turf given square finish at the bottom. A building with a distinctive roof line may be silhouetted at the top but squared off at the bottom in order to retain a well-landscaped foreground. To get a silhouette finish, an editor usually uses a tissue overlay to serve as a diagram specifying the background that is to be eliminated. The engraver or lithographer eliminates the dot structure from the appropriate background by painting that area on the negative with an opaque fluid. The extra charge depends on the time involved in opaquing the background; the reproduction dimensions are those of the rectangle that would have included the opaqued background.

Vignettes

To create a feeling of age, beauty, or softness, a halftone may be given a *vignette* finish (fig. 17–14). Rather than have the subject silhouetted or on a square-finished background, it is given an irregular border that simply fades into the paper. Portraits of delicate beauties, "old-time" subjects, or any scene calling for a soft or sentimental treatment are often vignetted.

The vignette effect is achieved by gradually eliminating dots from the background area of a negative in an irregular border surrounding the subject. It, too, involves a time charge beyond the normal price of a square-finish halftone.

Ovals and Other Special Shapes

Another standard way of creating an "old-time" impression for a portrait is to present it in oval shape (fig. 17–15). Any geometric shape can be reproduced, provided only that an overlay sheet shows the engraver or lithographer how the treatment is to be carried out. Providing him or her with line artwork that can be made into a line negative that will serve as a mask to create the special shape is also helpful.

Figure 17–14 A vignette finish on a halftone.

Figure 17–15 An oval is only one of unlimited special shapes that can be ordered for halftones.

Mortises and Notches

Areas within the border of halftones, or areas from the outer edge of halftones, may be eliminated to provide open space for type or other material. If the cut-out is within the halftone, it is a *mortise* (fig. 17–16) and if it is from the outer edge inward, it is a *notch* (fig. 17–17). The shape and dimensions of mortises and notches are shown on tissue overlays. Beginners must remember to allow for any enlargement or reduction of the photograph as they note the mortise or notch on the overlay.

Figure 17–16 A mortised halftone.

Figure 17–17 A notched halftone.

For letterpress printing, the areas are literally sawed out of the metal surface and wood mounting of the engraving plate. For lithography, the area need only be masked out when the negative is stripped into a mask.

Mortise and notch areas can be handy for inserting captions or titles; they also are sometimes used to make a spot for insertion of another illustration. Their added cost is usually negligible.

Combination Plates

The opportunity to have a line illustration and a halftone in the same area without running a sheet through a press two times is provided by *combination* plates. As the name implies, these plates combine halftone and line material on the same plate surface. Because the reproduction of type constitutes line material, combination plates provide the opportunity to run titles or legends across a halftone surface.

If the line material is to appear in black on the surface of a halftone printing in black, the treatment is called a *surprint* or *double-print* combination (fig. 17–18). The name comes from the fact that two photographic exposures (printings) are needed to get the two images on one plate surface. To get a surprint combination finish, an editor must provide the halftone copy (usually a photo) and the line illustration (often a proof of type). An overlay must be used to show the location for the line illustration on the face of the halftone. The production steps involved would include the making of a normal halftone negative and line negative. The halftone negative is then exposed on the plate surface; when it is removed, the line negative is exposed in position. When the plate is then developed, the line illustration is in position on the halftone.

It should be obvious that if a page is being printed in more than one color, the halftone can be printed in black and the line illustration can be printed in another color over it without the use of a combination plate.

Should it be desirable to have the line illustration appear in white on the halftone surface, a *reverse combination* treatment is required (fig. 17–19). In addition to the line and halftone negatives required for a surprint combination, a reverse line negative must be made for this treatment. The halftone and reverse line negatives can be exposed on a plate simultaneously because the background area of a reverse negative is transparent.

Figure 17–18 A surprint combination places line copy on the face of a halftone.

Figure 17–19 A reverse combination places line copy in reverse on the face of a halftone.

Some Special Effects

Interesting and unusual special effects can be given to illustrations through what might be called *gimmickry*. Especially during the late 1960s and early 1970s, designers were making maximum effective use of such techniques as *line conversions, magnified screens, special screens,* and *posterization*. Most of these effects are best shown in multicolor reproduction, but a few can be illustrated here in black-and-white.

A line conversion is the reproduction of a continuous tone illustration as a line illustration (fig. 17–20). It is designed to create an impression similar to a pen or brush drawing of the subject. Addition of color and combination with tone reproduction produces dramatic effects.

Magnified screen illustrations result from another distorting device for the reproduction of continuous tone illustrations. The dot pattern that is normally present in halftone reproductions is so magnified that the pattern becomes an integral part of the illustration (fig. 17–21). Special screens, in which the pattern may be made by straight lines, wavy lines, circles, pebble grains, wood grains, mezzotints, or any custom design that might be wanted, are available and can be used in similar fashion.

Figure 17–20 A continuous tone illustration reproduced as a line illustration is called a line conversion.

Figure 17–21 As shown here, halftone dots can be enlarged for special effects.

They are intended to add style or a mood to a continuous tone illustration. Some special screens are shown in figure 17–22.

In posterization, negatives made from a continuous tone illustration are manipulated to get the solid applications of color that create a poster look.

These special treatments are only a few of those available; there is virtually no limit to the design effects that can be obtained. Combinations of the above also present different and interesting results.

The talent and imagination of art director, the skill of the lithographer or engraver, and the editorial judgment of the editor, if mixed in proper dosages, can produce striking and effective results.

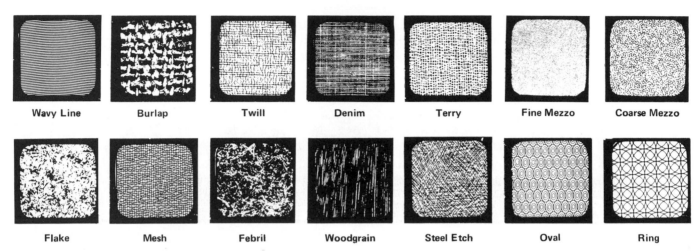

| Wavy Line | Burlap | Twill | Denim | Terry | Fine Mezzo | Coarse Mezzo |

| Flake | Mesh | Febril | Woodgrain | Steel Etch | Oval | Ring |

Figure 17–22 Special screens of many kinds are available to create special "mood" effects when reproducing photographs.

Magazine Circulation

18

MAKING it easy for readers to get their favorite magazines, whether at the newsstand or by mail, isn't as simple as one may imagine. A large magazine's circulation department may be the most complex operation within the organization.

Circulation means the distribution of periodicals to readers and also the number of copies of a given issue sold or distributed. Some editors believe in separation of editorial from other departments to the extent that they are unconcerned with circulation, but many find that sharing information with the circulation department can help them in the editing process.[1]

All magazines make basic policy decisions about circulation at the outset of their publishing venture and then review these from time to time as they continue publication.

Circulation Policy

The editorial idea for starting a magazine is itself a circulation policy decision. A plan to edit a magazine for homemakers about food, beauty, fashions, home furnishings, gardening, appliances, and housewares has implicit in it a policy of circulating to homemakers interested in this content. The target audience may have to be defined more specifically, but this is a starting point.

In the business magazine field, basic circulation and editorial policies are determined when a company decides, for example, to begin a magazine for tire dealers.

Sometimes the general policy may be specific enough. A travel magazine may want to reach *everyone* interested enough in travel to pay the subscription or single-copy rate. A business magazine, however, may want to restrict its audience to a field limited by a certain criteria, such as job title, number of employees supervised, annual budget administered, size of company in which subscriber is employed, or whether the subscriber is licensed within the field. *Purchasing,* for example, considers as qualified recipients "vice-presidents in charge of purchasing, purchasing directors, purchasing managers, purchasing agents, assistant purchasing agents, procurement managers, buyers, material directors and/or managers, plus a limited number of titled individuals who perform the purchasing function."[2]

Some consumer magazines have attempted to zero in on targets, such as people in the top 60 markets or A and B counties.[3] Both *Saturday Evening Post* and *Look* announced policies along these lines before they ceased publication,[4] but most consumer magazines are not selective about who can subscribe.

Base circulation policy to be determined includes whether circulation will be primarily paid, primarily controlled, or a mixture of paid and controlled; whether it will be audited; and what its desired demographic qualities are.

Paid Circulation

Consumer magazines usually are distributed by paid circulation, which is one criterion for determining who is sufficiently interested in the magazine to receive it. Basic standards for paid circulation have been established by the Audit Bureau of Circulations. The ABC regulations are complex, but the two principal factors are that at least 70 percent of a magazine's circulation must be paid to qualify it as a paid magazine, and a purchaser must pay at least 50 percent of the basic price for a copy or subscription and not buy it for resale. A magazine with a $9 a year subscription price can count as paid subscriptions all that are sold for $4.50 or more. A magazine with a $3 single-copy price similarly can count as paid all copies sold for $1.50 or more. Special offers and the number sold must be reported on the publisher's ABC statement.[5]

Paid circulation has some advantages besides determining who will receive the magazine:

1. Paid circulation periodicals qualify for second class postal rates, which are lower than other rates.
2. Paid subscriptions provide revenue to the publisher in addition to advertising revenue.
3. Paid lists can be "cleaner" because nonrenewals and cancellations are eliminated from the list.[6]
4. Subscription renewal can be measured[7] and is an indication of the reader's interest in the magazine.[8]

Controlled Circulation

The majority of business magazines are distributed by controlled circulation, which refers to setting specific qualifications and sending the publication to anyone who requests it and meets those qualifications. Qualifications usually are specified in terms of the field served and the types of persons who will receive the publication.

Magazines with controlled circulation save much of the cost of promoting and selling subscriptions that paid publications must undertake and, although they must periodically check on readers' qualifications, they save the cost of promoting renewals. This is especially beneficial in the business publications field where the definition of the target audience severely limits the number of persons eligible to be subscribers.

Some advantages advanced for controlled circulation include:

1. Controlled publications can reach all the significant personnel in a field.
2. Broader coverage of the field can come to paid publications only through the time-consuming process of building circulation by selling subscriptions. Controlled publications can build rapidly.
3. Paid circulation may be developed through promotional devices such as discounts, premiums, aggressive subscription sales personnel, or low rates like $1 or $2 a year. A subscription does not necessarily mean interest.
4. Controlled publications avoid the high cost of promoting subscriptions and the extra record-keeping and collection problems involved.[9]

Controlled circulation usually is linked to business publications, but some consumer magazines are distributed by this method. Other nonpaid magazines include the airline inflight magazines and magazines distributed in rooms by motel chains.

Combination Paid and Controlled

Most magazines have some paid and some controlled circulation, but are predominantly one or the other. A few approach a 50–50 split. The mixture of paid and controlled may change for a given magazine as conditions change. Natural expansion of its field made it advisable for *Automotive Industries* to increase its circulation to 30,000 from 20,000. The publisher made careful estimates and decided the advertiser would be best served by going part paid and part free, building the additional circulation on a tailor-made basis. It would have been too costly and time-consuming to add 10,000 paid subscriptions on a quality-controlled basis. As time passed and the field expanded further, *Automotive Industries* became an almost totally controlled circulation magazine, its 65,000 circulation 97 percent nonpaid and 3 percent paid. Another Chilton publication, *Motor/Age,* had a circulation of 132,000 that was 51 percent paid and 49 percent nonpaid.[10]

Auditing Circulation

Verification of circulation figures became a crucial issue in the early 1900s. Advertising rates were based on circulation, and exaggerated or false circulation claims were widespread. At that time, advertising agencies were mainly space brokers, buying space in publications and selling it at profits of 25 to 75 percent. In this situation, unscrupulous operators had an unfair advantage over honest publishers.[11]

The Audit Bureau of Circulations was established in 1914 to set standards of definition and reporting for paid circulation. Growth of controlled circulation, primarily in the business publication field, eventually resulted in formation of the Controlled Circulation Audit in 1931, renamed in 1954 the Business Publications Audit of Circulation, Inc., or BPA.[12]

Both ABC and BPA are tripartite organizations with voting power divided among advertisers, advertising agencies, and publishers. They audit only member publications. Membership dues vary according to class of membership and other characteristics of the member firm. Beginning October 1981, for example, national advertisers paid $90 a year for ABC membership while regional advertisers paid $20. Advertising agencies paid according to their billings, from $50 for billings under $250,000 to $6,600 for billings over $125 million. Business publications paid from $50 for circulation under 5,000 to $475 for circulation over 250,000, and magazines and farm publications paid from $95 for under 10,000 circulation to $1,760 for over 15 million. In addition to membership dues, publishers pay the full cost of their audits based on a uniform hourly rate for the field auditor's time.[13]

A third auditing agency, the Verified Audit Circulation Company (VAC) is a profit-making organization that audits all types of publications, regardless of field served or method of distribution, and verifies the validity of circulation by surveys to random samples of subscribers.

For a magazine that sells advertising, the value of being audited is apparent. The standards established by the auditing agencies and the verification of figures through the audit itself certify to advertisers the exact circulation, permitting advertisers to make more meaningful comparisons in selecting their media.

Auditing may be more important to magazines with large circulations. Most reported circulation is audited even though most magazines are not. An ABC circulation study found that 3,379 magazines, farm publications, and business publications in the United States reported total average circulation of 477 million per issue, and that an additional 454 did not report their circulations. Of these publications, 1,489 were audited, and 716 ABC members accounted for 69 percent of the total reported circulation.[14]

The large-circulation magazines are paid, audited, and members of ABC. ABC lists 62 consumer magazine and farm publication members with circulations exceeding 1 million, not including comic books and magazine groups.[15]

One also can sense that a subscriber to one magazine is not necessarily equal, in the eyes of the advertiser, to a subscriber to another magazine. The fact that hundreds of magazines can sell advertising without reporting circulation figures suggests that even an unknown quantity of readers in a given field has value to certain advertisers.

For many years there was a significant separation between paid and controlled circulation publishers and auditing groups. As the promotion and renewal costs increased, fields grew, and magazines wanted to reach them quickly and at low cost, multiple publishers issued some paid and some controlled magazines, and the situation changed.

BPA audited only controlled circulation until 1947. It now audits controlled, paid, and any combination of the two.[16] ABC audited only paid circulation publications until 1970, when it changed its rules to admit business publications whose circulations were at least 70 percent request circulation in the field served, or a combination of paid and direct request totaling 70 percent of total distribution.

Auditing standards and definitions help to standardize classifications to facilitate comparisons, even though no two publications or their audiences are identical. Besides total circulation, reports tell advertisers where the readers are and, for business publications, something about their dispersion within the field served.

Both ABC and BPA publisher's reports list thorough breakdowns of the average circulation per issue for a six-month period. Total qualified circulation is shown by paid and nonpaid, and also broken down by subscriptions, single-copy sales, and subscriptions paid for out of association dues. They also list circulation for one issue by nine geographic regions and by individual states, and, in Canada, by provinces. For business publications, circulation also is shown by types of firms and persons served within the industry.

Publisher's reports also indicate the duration of subscriptions sold, prices for which they were sold, whether sold with premiums or not, and channels of subscription sales—mail, salesmen, association memberships, and other channels. Supplemental Data Reports may list circulation by county.[17]

A large number of magazines that are not audited report their circulations on sworn (notarized) statements. For these, Standard Rate and Data Service defines the terms "paid," "non-paid," and "unpaid" or "nonqualified" the same as ABC and BPA to standardize figures reported in its publications.[18] Many respected publications use sworn statements rather than audit reports.

Quality of Circulation

In the business magazine field, some readers are more valuable than others to advertisers. A purchasing director of a company with hundreds of outlets obviously is more important to an advertiser than a buyer for a single retail store in a small city. Beyond circulation figures themselves, publishers attempt to demonstrate that their readers are more valuable to advertisers than readers of similar magazines. This is done through the use of demographics.

Demography is the statistical study of human populations, especially with reference to size and density, distribution, and vital statistics. Magazines spend much time and money to gather demographic data about their readers in many areas: income; marital status; ownership of property, automobiles, or other durable goods; consumption of goods; occupational status; and the like.[19]

Demographic data for constructing reader profiles often come from group studies supported by several magazines. All the magazines get the data, then each can emphasize the facts that look best in selling its advertising space. In effect, each can counter the others' arguments and each knows the strengths and weaknesses of all the magazines in the study.

To give one example, an advertisement in *Consumer Magazine and Farm Publication Rates and Data* proclaimed *U.S. News & World Report* superior to both *Time* and *Newsweek* in terms of percentage of readers in 27 of 29 demographic characteristics listed, including household income, individual income, income from stocks and bonds, college graduates, managerial/professional/technical occupations, own a second home, own a vacation home, own three or more cars bought new, bought five or more replacement tires in the last year, and took three or more foreign trips in the past five years.[20]

In the same issue *Newsweek* was advertising that the same Simmons report showed that an average issue of *Newsweek* reaches 13,465,000 individuals age 18 or older and that 8,442,000 are members of households with annual incomes of $10,000 or more, 6,554,000 attended college, and 4,119,000 are in professional or managerial occupations.[21] *Newsweek* emphasized numbers of readers while *U.S. News,* with a smaller circulation, emphasized its percentage superiority. *U.S. News* also pointed out, based on another study, that 73 percent of its subscribers do not subscribe to either *Time* or *Newsweek.*[22]

Business publishers' reports give a business analysis of circulation by classifications agreed upon by member publications within that field. These can be very detailed. *Engineering News-Record,* for example, reports circulation by 16 classifications within the construction industry then by seven levels of personnel within each classification for a total of 112 separate circulation categories.[23]

A simpler example is *Discount Store News,* which reports circulation in four classifications: (1) retailers, including (1–1) multi-unit independent headquarters executive corporate officers, merchandising and buying personnel, regional/district managers and supervisors and (1–2) chain store management personnel, store managers, and other supervisory personnel; (2) wholesalers, jobbers, and distributors; (3) manufacturers and manufacturers' representatives; and (4) others allied to the field (including financial institutions, investment firms and industry associations).[24]

These reports give the advertiser important information (especially when it measures the data against the size of the industry as a whole) about both the sizes of the businesses reached and the position within the firms. These figures can also serve to remind editors of some characteristics of their audience.

Coverage of the firms within the industry is called horizontal coverage. Or, horizontal coverage can also refer to coverage of a given position or function across several industries—purchasing agents, for instance, regardless of the specific industry in which they are employed. Vertical coverage refers to coverage of persons at various levels within a firm or field. In a retail field, vertical coverage may reach executives in headquarters offices, corporate buyers, departmental buyers, and sales and promotion personnel.[25]

Probably no magazine could achieve or survive 100 percent coverage of a field; there is a point of diminishing returns. One axiom some business magazine people use is that 20 percent of the firms in a given field do 80 percent of the business in that field. U.S. Census figures indicate that 17 percent of the total retail units in the United States account for 67 percent of all retailing volume.[26] Advertisers are interested in reaching the major firms who do most of the business because they constitute the most worthwhile audience from a business-producing standpoint, hence the most profitable.

One business publication developed a marketing brochure pointing out that there were 35,647 retail outlets in its field, but that 21 percent of the stores did 71 percent of the total sales volume. Obviously these 7,483 stores were more valuable to the advertiser and to the publication than the other 28,164.

Limiting horizontal coverage, therefore, can maximize efficiency and economy in reaching the most important units in a field. Controlled circulation publications with broad horizontal coverage can sell subscriptions at a price that approximates printing and postage costs to smaller units that do not represent good prospects for the advertiser. One weekly publication with 99 percent controlled circulation charges its 1 percent paid subscribers $30 a year.[27]

Relationship of Circulation to Advertising Rates

There is a direct relationship between circulation and advertising rates, expressed as cost per thousand or CPM. It refers to the cost of one page of advertising in 1,000 copies of the magazine and is calculated by dividing the advertising rate for one page by the circulation and multiplying by 1,000. A magazine having a page rate of $500 and a circulation of 100,000 has a CPM of $5, for example ($500/ 100,000 × 1,000 = $5).

Separate CPMs can be figured for black-and-white advertising pages, four-color advertising pages, and even the cost of reaching consumers interested in a specific product. In the latter case, the advertiser can use Simmons or other market and readership data to determine how many readers of a given magazine are prospective automobile buyers, for example, and the cost of reaching each 1,000 of them. This figure is much more meaningful than the gross cost of reaching 1,000 readers, most of whom are not interested in buying a given product.

The burden on the circulation department in relation to advertising is to maintain the circulation guarantee upon which advertising rates are based. Subscriptions are expiring daily, and new ones must be sold to maintain the needed number. Selling too many new subscriptions can be bad, too, because the magazine is not receiving advertising revenue for the bonus circulation beyond the guarantee, but has the expense of printing and delivering it. Some leeway is allowed in setting advertising rates, of course, because the magazine does not want to fall short of its guarantee. Circulation promotion and sales must be a continuous operation to avoid an erratic circulation pattern.

Because the CPM is not the same for all magazines, demographic data are important. Three sports magazines show CPMs of $8.85, $14.00, and $18.90, a difference that should be explained in demographics. In the women's field, six magazines have CPMs of $6.16, $6.40, $7.00, $7.00, $7.38, and $7.94.[28] All are fairly close together, except for the one at $7.94, which may try to show a better demographic position or less duplication of circulation with the other five. Each magazine, however, needs to use demographic information to show prospective advertisers how it differs from the other magazines so close to it in CPM. In other words, circulation and CPM are starting points, not decision-making points.

Circulation of Public Relations Magazines

Public relations magazines, because they are circulated to advance the sponsoring company or institution, have a different approach to circulation. First, they must determine who will receive the magazine, and, second, they must determine the most effective way to deliver it.

Audience

The nature of a magazine selects much of the audience. An employee magazine usually attempts 100 percent coverage of a company's employees. A customer magazine, though, may restrict its coverage to customers who do a certain amount of business with the company or to those who have made purchases recently, say within the last two years. The cost of printing and distributing the magazine is substantial, so copies should not be wasted.

Auto companies generally require their dealers to pay the cost of distributing their magazines to customers. This keeps the lists up-to-date, because a dealer who is paying for the magazine is less likely to keep a poor prospect or former customer on that list.

The magnitude of waste also is illustrated by the experience of *Cascades,* award-winning magazine of Pacific Northwest Bell Telephone Company, Seattle, Washington. Offering its readers some of the most beautiful color photography found anywhere, with articles about the Pacific Northwest, its free distribution grew to more than 50,000 by the end of 1970. However, nearly half the circulation was outside the company's territory of Oregon, Washington, and northern Idaho, and those readers received a letter in March 1971:

We're sorry to disappoint you, but we can no longer offer CASCADES to readers outside the Pacific Northwest.

Ten years ago, CASCADES began publication as a regional magazine for readers in Oregon, Washington and northern Idaho, the area Pacific Northwest Bell serves. Today, the magazine has subscribers throughout the United States and in a great many foreign countries. The number of readers has doubled from 25,000 to more than 50,000.

The increase in circulation has been flattering, but rising production costs and our budget limitations dictate a change in our policy.

We hope you'll understand.

A public relations magazine needs to define its audience so that it will achieve adequate coverage with minimum waste circulation. Besides its primary audience—employees or customers or stockholders—it should select other recipients who may benefit from the magazine and from whom the sponsoring company may in turn benefit. Examples of this latter group are:

1. Employees on leave—military leave, sick leave, educational leave. Employees temporarily away from their employment like to keep in touch.
2. Potential employees—students in professional schools (engineering, pharmacy, journalism), college libraries, and other places where potential employees can be reached.
3. Retired employees—people who like to talk about their former place of employment and will do a good job of presenting its story if kept well informed.
4. Business publications in the company's industry—occasionally will produce valuable publicity for the company through reprints of articles and condensations of news items.

5. Other company publications—because editors like to see each other's work, get ideas, and keep each other apprised of what they are doing.
6. Civic and political leaders—to keep key persons in company communities in touch with what the company is doing.
7. Doctors and dentists—to make the company's message available in waiting rooms of professional persons. Employees also may take some pride in seeing their company's publication on display in these places. The size of the community and the nature of the publication will determine whether such circulation is desirable.

Mail Distribution

The 1979 International Association of Business Communicators' survey, although it does not represent all public relations magazine distribution, reported that 58 percent of the participating magazines' distribution is by mail, 7 percent in-house, and 35 percent a combination of the two.

Advantages of mail distribution include:

1. Family readership—there is greater potential for other members of the family to read the magazine if it is mailed to the home, and many editors are particularly interested in reaching the employee's spouse with the company story, knowing that if the spouse is satisfied, the employee tends to be satisfied also.
2. Leisurely reading—the reader is likely to be more relaxed and willing to read the magazine at home after a day's work.
3. Certainty of coverage—by mailing to each recipient, the editor can be sure that each person in the intended audience is receiving a copy.
4. Reasonable cost—although in-house distribution has no postage expense, it often requires larger press runs to offset waste from extra copies employees pick up, and those copies required to be sent out in bulk to cover a number of distribution points within the company; so the cost difference is not so great as one may originally estimate.

In-house Distribution

Advantages of in-house distribution also tend to be disadvantages of mail distribution. They include:

1. Less competition with other magazines—the public relations magazine won't arrive in the mail with *Time, Newsweek, Sports Illustrated, McCall's, Better Homes and Gardens,* or other consumer magazines.
2. Reader receptiveness—because employees are thinking about the company at work, it is better for them to receive the magazine at work than at home, where they may prefer to forget the day's work. Reader receptiveness probably varies from company to company and from type of work to type of work, so no single generalization appears to be applicable. Research into the most receptive time and place may be beneficial to an editor.
3. Reaches home anyway—most employees who are at all interested will take the magazine home, and those who are not probably would throw away a mailed copy as just more "junk mail." So mail distribution is not automatically more effective at reaching the family than in-house distribution.
4. Low cost—in many businesses, distribution can be inexpensively handled by distributing them with pay checks, at the time clock when employees punch out, or through supervisors who hand them out. The nature of the sponsoring organization as well as the audience will determine which is the most effective and least expensive method.

An editor or public relations director designing an efficient distribution system will analyze all the aspects of the company and the magazine's objectives as well as those beliefs about distribution effectiveness. Editors have contended that in-house distribution gives a check on reader acceptance, because the more copies that are thrown away at work, the less well accepted is that issue. But they don't know whether the employee reads the issue before discarding it, and they don't know the discard rate of mailed copies, so they are still guessing, for the most part.

Especially with stockholder and other external magazines, a business reply postal card can be inserted every year or two asking the recipient if he or she wants to continue to receive the magazine. External magazines often tell the reader they will discontinue mailing to him or her if he or she does not mail back the card. Others simply ask whether they should continue sending it without mentioning cancellation. The approach may depend upon budget and whether the company is willing to pay to reach marginally interested readers.

Although the public relations magazine has a different circulation situation than paid and controlled circulation consumer and business magazines, its circulation should be handled just as professionally and carefully if the magazine is to be effective in achieving its objectives.

Selling Circulation

Consumer magazines need to screen out some potential subscribers just as do business magazines. The criteria may not be so readily obvious nor so vigorously applied, but there are ways magazines can be selective in reaching households of above-average income and with heavy users and heavy buyers of products and services.[29] Selling circulation is a very specialized facet of the magazine industry.

Considerations in circulation strategy include the magazine's circulation guarantee to advertisers, its desired demographic makeup, the economics of selling subscriptions by direct mail, and the feasibility of selling single copies on newsstands.

Single-Copy Sales

Magazines that successfully sell the majority of their copies on newsstands claim superiority of circulation because they say it proves the reader is willing to pay the full single-copy price and is making the decision every issue, unlike some subscribers who buy a discounted subscription and fail to read the magazine when it arrives in the mail.

Few magazines are outstandingly successful at single-copy sales. One is *Penthouse,* which sells 95 percent of its circulation as single copies. *Cosmopolitan,* long having required subscribers to pay as much as if they bought each issue at the newsstand, is selling 96 percent of its circulation at the newsstand. Depending on how you look at it, the single-copy champion is *TV Guide,* selling 9.3 million or 54 percent of its 17.2 million circulation as single copies, or *High Society,* 100 percent single-copy sales at 381,000.[30]

Most magazines, however, rely mainly on subscriptions, and Karyl Van points to a danger in overselling a concept:

Sometimes circulation and advertising people, in a desire to promote current advantage, wake up a few months later to find that the exploited advantage no longer exists and that we have burned our bridges behind us. . . .

As an example, newsstand sales soared at the close of World War II. Almost all of us sold this great voluntary circulation like crazy. It was, we said, a great demonstration of voluntary purchases by readers. Newsstand circulations declined, and we went back to looking for that bridge to get across on safe ground. It wasn't there.[31]

As an example of changes in newsstand sales, *Life* was selling 2.5 million single copies per issue in 1947 and only 210,000 in 1971. *Look* sold 1.4 million single copies per issue in 1947 and 240,000 in 1971.[32]

Another consideration in single-copy sales is the logistics of getting the right number on each of the 138,000 newsstands each issue. Paul Young, then in charge of single-copy sales for Time Inc., once said, "No newsstand man ever sold a copy of a magazine. It is circulation's job to get the right number of magazines in the right place at the right time, properly displayed. The magazine must sell itself."[33]

H. Carlisle Estes says that the "only salesman for single copies is the editor," and "most important to sales is the proper cover." The magazine is an impulse item, and the customer makes the decision on which magazine to buy at the newsstand. The magazine needs an attractive cover to get attention, then cover lines which describe the contents "in such a way as to grab the customer's interest. . . . I don't think anything is as important as choosing the proper cover lines."[34]

Estes pointed to the need for minimizing waste in a print order. He noted that a copy of *Family Circle* cost 147 percent its cover price just for printing, paper, and distribution. After giving the normal markup to retailers and wholesalers, the publisher got 53 percent of the cover price. So each copy costs nearly one and one-half times the cover price, whether or not it is sold, and must generate more than twice its cover price to break even.[35] If a wholesaler gets too many copies and returns proof of the unsold copies, the publisher refunds the money and absorbs the loss. The same thing happens if the wholesaler does not distribute the copies properly and move them around from slow-selling outlets to those approaching sell-outs during the sales period.

A certain number of unsold copies (*returns*), though, is desirable. Estes calls them "growth allowance." If the magazine sells out, the opportunity for growth is restricted, especially if it's a hot issue that might induce some new buyers to come back issue after issue. A newsstand with an average volume of 100 copies an issue may be given 120 to allow it to build up an increase in sales. A small dealer averaging two copies per issue may be given three to allow for growth. These figures represent 20 and 33 percent growth allowances, showing that dealers must be watched so copies are not wasted. Although growth is needed, the cost of growth must be controlled.[36]

Dealers, too, don't want sell-outs; they want merchandise on hand to sell. Many stores have established several points of purchase for magazines. *TV Guide* may have as many as 20 displays in one store, *Reader's Digest* 10, and *Newsweek* 3. This added factor of multiple displays affects the return or growth allowance policy.[37]

Publishers' growth allowances vary. *Family Circle* operated on a 12 percent allowance; other magazines have as much as 40 percent. Each publisher's economic structure determines the return rate.[38]

The rapid turnover in magazines makes them a profitable item for the retailer. A study of drug stores in five metropolitan areas by Wholesalers Project Development found for every $100 worth of inventory in the average drug store magazine department, $732 worth of gross profit is produced in a year. Turnover amounts to 24.4 times a year.[39]

Single-copy sales are important to the consumer magazine publisher. Even though the publisher receives only 50 to 55 percent of the cover price from a newsstand sale, that is far more than the 10 percent received from a subscription sale by a direct-mail subscription agency. A $2 monthly magazine yields $1. Over a year that is $12 compared with $1.80 if it is sold as an $18 subscription by a direct-mail agency.

Magazines usually use one of the dozen national distributors to reach the 550 wholesalers who service the 138,000 retailers. A few publishers bypass a distributor and work directly with the 550 wholesalers.

The distributor instructs the printer, who ships copies to the wholesalers. That takes about a week to 10 days. Another week is required for the wholesaler to get the magazines to the retail outlets.

Nearly all magazines are sold on consignment. A monthly magazine is kept on sale for 30 days; then unsold copies are returned to the wholesaler for credit. Eventually reports from all wholesalers will be combined by the national distributor into a record of sale for each issue. This record, which may be six months old, is used by the publisher's single-copy sales manager and the national distributor's account executive to determine the number of copies of the next issue to distribute.

The distributor generally will advance 10 to 25 percent to the publisher after shipping an issue. On a 25 percent advance contract of a 300,000 draw magazine with a $2 cover price, the publisher will get $82,500 ($1.10 × 75,000 copies). The distributor also will advance shipping costs to the wholesaler.

Final settlement for an issue usually comes 90 days after off-sale. The November issue, placed on sale October 15, will be collected for about February 15. If the magazine sold 50 percent, which is the average in the industry, there would be 150,000 returns, which would be destroyed or recycled by the wholesalers, and the publisher would receive a second payment of $82,500 less shipping charges and special allowances. The national distributor's share will run 6 to 8 percent of the cover price of sold copies.

The new publisher often is at a disadvantage in single-copy sales. A small dealer with a poor credit rating, for example, may deal with the wholesaler on a cash basis. Such a dealer may reject new magazines for which there is no sales experience. Or the dealer may return them for credit before the sales period has ended.

The national distributor bills the wholesaler for the copies sold (draw less returns) at 36 to 40 percent off the cover price. The discount usually is split with the retail dealer.

There are about 2,000 newsstand magazines, but even large retailers display only about 200. Most display only a small portion of the cover, hiding the cover lines. The largest, most aggressive magazines with large field staffs get full display at checkouts—*Family Circle, Woman's Day, TV Guide, People,* and *National Enquirer,* for example.

New magazines often pay dealers special allowances for full display, usually 10 percent of the cover price. But not all dealers live up to the agreement and it is difficult and costly to police.

Nontimely magazines could use the "rollover" system of distributing copies in one region of the country, and, after three weeks or so, taking unsold copies to the next region. In West Germany, which has been divided into four regions, newsstand sale reaches 95 percent. Dell used this method in the United States nearly 80 years ago, trimming the magazines so they had clean, crisp edges when placed on sale in the new location.

The date on an issue usually indicates when it goes off sale. A monthly magazine that goes on sale September 15 for one month, for example, will be dated October. A weekly magazine, such as *Newsweek* or *Time,* published April 9, will be dated April 16.

Business magazines, of course, generally do not want single-copy sales because it would dilute their control over the audience they sell to advertisers.[40]

Subscriptions

Most magazines do not lend themselves to single-copy sales. Only 15 of the 50 top circulation magazines sell more single copies than subscriptions. So the circulation department must obtain subscriptions to meet the circulation guarantee on which advertising rates are based and keep it there or continue to increase it. But it also must avoid too rapid growth that pushes the cost of printing and distributing the magazine up more rapidly than advertising rates can be increased to cover it.

Two basic areas of subscription sales are "new business" and "renewals." Decision areas under new business include the number of new readers wanted, and the number wanted through commissionable sources (agents, salespersonnel, etc.), space advertising, and promotion, such as Christmas gifts. Rates, terms, types of readers desired, how much can be spent on achieving the circulation goal, and how fast the readers must be added also are major considerations.[41]

Renewal business justifies the money spent on getting new subscribers if the reader continues reading and paying for the magazine long after the trial subscription expires. Often a magazine will lose money promoting new subscriptions and attempt to make it back through renewals of those subscriptions.

Each magazine, depending upon the audience it is attempting to build, will find its own best sources of prospects and promotion techniques. Women's magazines obviously have different successful strategies than men's magazines, confession magazines different than *haute couture* magazines. Some generalizations apply to most paid circulation magazines, though.

Direct Mail Strategy. List brokers specialize in maintaining and selling or leasing names and complete addresses of people who can be approached by direct mail advertising. They can provide numerous *mail-order lists* of people who have already responded to someone's mail-order solicitation, either by making a purchase or requesting information. They also can supply *compiled lists* of people who share some common interest or description, such as PTA, campers, physicians, boat owners, florists, and teachers. Compiled lists don't identify who has responded to direct mail and, generally, are less productive than the mail-order lists. The cost of mailing to compiled lists is likely to exceed total income from all the subscriptions they buy.[42]

Mail-order lists are not always preferable to compiled lists, but they usually are preferred and are in plentiful supply for consumer magazine use. A business magazine, on the other hand, having defined its field of service, is in effect restricted to the equivalent of compiled lists of building contractors, architects, engineers, building material dealers, and the like within its field.

Lists should be keyed so their productiveness can be measured in terms of subscriptions, deadbeats, cancellations, and renewals.

Some things are so essential in selling new subscriptions they are almost axiomatic:

1. A reduced price or introductory price is essential to significant production of new readers. The editor abhors those reduced-price offers. And yet, they are essential to really significant production.
2. If your offer includes significant savings, then emphasize these savings within the copy. Give them dramatic position. For example, "half-price offer," abhorrent as it may be to an editor, is good for extra subscription orders.
3. Credit privileges are most important today for a maximum return. Extending credit is economically sound today. We do live in a credit economy, and most people do pay their bills.
4. Emphasis in mailing should be on short terms to encourage the prospects to try the magazine without a long-term commitment. Certainly, you have your crack at those people for renewals on a long-term basis, but at first, offer modest terms.[43]

Subscriptions expire every day and new ones must be sold, but there are better times of the year for renewals than others. Experience among magazines varies, but some publishers say January, February, July, and August are the four best months to obtain new subscribers by mail.[44]

In selling new subscriptions, a 10 percent rate reduction may bring in more dollars, but a 50 percent or half-price offer is dramatic and easy to grasp and usually will bring in many more subscriptions, opening the way to potentially more renewals.[45]

Because direct mail promotion is so extensive and expensive, it is imperative to test the mailing piece and its approach. Gordon Grossman said *Reader's Digest* would test mail 10,000 pieces costing $2,000 to reach decisions about mailing 20 million pieces at a cost of $2 million.[46]

Cost is an important factor in direct mail. The letter that sells the most subscriptions may be uneconomical because of its higher production cost than the letter it is tested against it. In a two-way test where letter A pulls 20 orders per thousand mailed (2.0 percent) and letter B pulls 24 orders per thousand (2.4 percent), B pulled better. But if A is black-and-white and costs $80 per thousand to mail and letter B is four-color on high quality stock for $120 per thousand, A's orders cost $4 each and B's cost $5 each. If cost per order is the important factor, letter A is the choice. If total orders regardless of cost is the major consideration, letter B is the choice.[47]

Subscription Agencies. Subscription agencies are a tremendous source of new readers. Orders cleared through agencies originate in numerous ways: through individual agents, catalog agencies, department stores, telephone solicitation, mail agencies, cash field selling, sponsored sales, newspaper agencies, school plans, and paid-during-service (PDS).

Individual agents are salespersons who report directly to the magazine publisher, sometimes selling for premiums or prizes rather than cash commissions. Catalog agencies are similar, but the agent has a catalog of many magazines—maybe hundreds—and clears orders through the one agency rather than directly with individual publishers.[48] Two or three catalog agencies sell to 30,000 libraries of schools, government agencies, and large corporations. The publisher receives 10 to 15 percent, plus a good source of renewals and very large pass-along readership.

Department stores have sold subscriptions for years in the store and through inserts with billings, mailings separate from billings, and telephone solicitation. Telephone solicitation also is used by publishers and agents.

The WATS (Wide Area Telephone Service) line has made it economical in some instances to solicit from a single city, like New York, across time zones from a single location (called a *boiler room*). Solicitors can call from, say, 9 A.M. New York time through 10 P.M., which is 7 P.M. in California, keeping the line in use 13 hours a day. An installation and effort like this may be used only one or two months a year.

Mail agencies were developed when the high costs of mailing made it desirable to offer several magazines in one mailing piece. The first attempts were through department stores, and some are still handled that way. Other agencies have been started, including a huge one that offers 40 to 99 magazines at a special introductory price that must be at least as good as any offer the publisher will make directly. Because these offers usually are for shorter terms as well as lower prices, some major publishers do not use this source.[49] Sweepstakes often are used to promote response to these offers.

Direct-mail agencies pay publishers in advance for subscriptions, even though that is only 10 percent of the subscription price. Publishers can pinpoint when they want to receive their subscriptions. The cancellation rate is comparatively small, but renewals are a problem because the customer wants a good deal again and another chance to win the sweepstakes. The demographics of readers buying this way usually are lower than those gained through the magazine's own direct mail efforts.

Cash field selling is done by trained professionals who work in crews traveling from city to city. They collect the full subscription price in cash before transmitting the order. They may collect only a down payment at the time of the sale, but their agencies will not transmit orders to the publisher until they are paid in full.

Sponsored sales were developed to overcome some of the problems of fly-by-night magazine solicitors during and following the economic depression. A local organization, such as a church, volunteer fire department, or hospital organization, is booked to sponsor the sales drive and provide local identification for a professional crew or even individual agents, for which the organization gets a commission from each sale.

Newspaper agencies sell one form of paid-during-service subscriptions. The usual approach is an annual sales campaign that permits a newspaper subscriber to receive three or four magazines for a small weekly charge added to the price of the newspaper. This is a good source of quality business at a moderate cost, and the subscription term usually is two years or more.

School plans involve student sales of subscriptions from lists of 150 or so magazines to provide commissions to the school for activities, projects, or materials. Individual or team prizes may be awarded to student salespersons as incentives in the campaign that normally lasts a week to 10 days. The fact that a subscriber chooses from a list of 150 magazines indicates significant interest in that magazine and its editorial content.

Paid-during-service operations are much like the newspaper agency, but without the newspaper. Typically, salespersons are residents of the community and offer a choice of magazines from a card for a weekly amount that is payable monthly. A contract is signed, and after the sale is reported, the branch office vertifies it by telephone, mail, or personal visit before the order is processed. Subscribers usually mail the monthly payments to the agency. More than half of the 30 PDS agencies registered with the Central Registry are owned by publishers. It is estimated that PDS sales account for the largest number of all subscriptions sold by magazine agencies. PDS is a relatively low cost source of new business. Most PDS agencies block out certain groups or areas in a community where they will not operate because experience has shown an unacceptable rate of collection. PDS subscriptions have a greater tendency to be canceled before expiration than those paid in advance.[50]

Renewals. Magazines make more money on renewals than on new subscriptions, and renewals provide some stability to circulation. Circulation managers analyze circulation on an annual basis, considering two six-month introductory subscriptions as one circulation (or *circ,* pronounced sirk) and one two-year subscription as two circs.[51]

In overall circulation strategy, renewals are tremendously important. By analyzing the number of cancellations (both by subscribers themselves and by the magazine for failure of subscribers to pay) and the percentage of first renewals, second renewals, third renewals, fourth renewals, and so on, a circulation manager can form a basis for algebraically determining the number of new subscriptions needed and the renewal promotion techniques likely to be successful.[52]

An introductory offer may result in 10 percent cancellations and 30 percent renewals after the 10 percent shrink, but those 30 percent renewals the second time around may be good for 65 percent renewals and only 5 percent cancellations, and it may continue at about a constant rate for the second, third, fourth, and subsequent renewals.[53]

Renewals are less expensive to sell because the list used is live customers who have already purchased. Even the 30 percent renewals for an introductory offer is very good compared with the 2 percent or so subscription rate from a direct mailing to prospective new subscribers. Also, renewals are more likely to send cash with order than new subscribers, cutting down billing costs. Obviously, editorial content is tremendously important in securing renewals.

Advertising

Publishers often trade off advertising on a circulation basis. If one magazine has 600,000 circulation and another 300,000, the second will run twice as much advertising for the first as the first runs for the second. Newer magazines making concerted efforts to increase circulation are more likely to trade off than are more established magazines.

Radio and television commercials are an expensive way to sell magazine subscriptions. Using a toll-free number to take orders gets results, but a lot of these subscriptions have to be cancelled for nonpayment. Radio and television are most effective at promoting newsstand sales.

Fulfillment and Records

Fulfillment

Essentially, fulfillment is getting the magazine to the reader for the term of the subscription, including promptly placing the name on the mailing list when the order is entered and making address changes as they are necessary. It may encompass other services to the reader, editor, research manager, circulation sales, advertising sales, and operating management in some companies.[54]

Fulfillment involves record-keeping and adequate staff and machinery to maintain the services to keep records up-to-date. Equipment may range from simple stencil or metal plate addressing machines to sophisticated computers, depending upon the magazine's or publisher's size. Most large-circulation magazines contract with one of the large fulfillment houses to handle this for them.

Records

Circulation records may be classified by three types: working records, forecasting and projection records, and budgeting and planning records. The editor need not be thoroughly familiar with these, but should understand their necessity.

Working records include renewal results, billing results, bind-in results, agency production, direct-mail results, other miscellaneous promotion results (as clubs and reader service inquiries), and the single-copy draw and sales results.[55]

Examples of forecasting and projection records are renewal percentage and trend, billing percentage and trend, expire inventory and its structure, and agency production and renewability. The direct-mail potential with lists, pull of lists, list record forms, and single-copy sales promotion test results also relate to forecasting and projection.[56]

Budgeting records include the expire inventory by source, the renewability of expires by source, the record of direct-mail pull by volume mailed, extension percentages in direct mail, extension percentages in agency production, and single-copy sales history of draw and sale.

The forecasting and projection records grow out of and are refinements of the working records. Budgeting records are refinements of the forecasting and projection records. By using the history of various subscriber groups, lists, promotion strategies, payment records, and the like, the circulation department can forecast trends and establish budgets to provide for growth in subscriptions and single-copy sales.[57]

Magazine publishing is a tripartite operation—editorial, advertising, and circulation. Some magazines get along without advertising, but none exists without some kind of circulation operation.

Notes

1. See for example, John Mack Carter, "Reader Profiles—One Dimension or Two?," in *Modern Circulation Methods,* eds. S. Arthur Dembner and William E. Massee (New York: McGraw-Hill Book Company, 1968), p. 11.
2. "Publisher's Statement for 6 Month Period Ending December 1971, Business Publications Audit of Circulation, Inc."
3. Of 3,073 counties in the United States, 406 (13 percent) containing 68 percent of the population, are classified as A and B counties.
4. William L. Rivers, Theodore Peterson, and Jay W. Jensen, *The Mass Media and Society,* 2d ed. (San Francisco: Rinehart Press, 1971), p. 175; and "New Bundle of Hope for Ailing Post," *Business Week,* May 25, 1968, p. 42.
5. Provisional membership is available to magazines with at least 50 percent paid circulation. They have three years to achieve 70 percent paid. *Bylaws and Rules,* (Chicago: Audit Bureau of Circulations, 1980) pp. 10, 11, and 26.
6. Under ABC rules, a nonrenewal can be carried up to three months beyond expiration and still be counted as part of the circulation.
7. ABC does not require renewal percentages in its magazine reports. Many large consumer magazines do not report their renewal percentages.
8. Russell N. Baird and A. T. Turnbull, *Industrial and Business Journalism* (Philadelphia: Chilton Company, 1961), p. 282.
9. Baird and Turnbull, p. 283.
10. *Business Publications Rates and Data,* December 24, 1984, pp. 175 and 189.
11. Edwin Emery, Phillip H. Ault, and Warren K. Agee, *Introduction to Mass Communications,* 3d ed. (New York: Dodd, Mead & Company, 1970), p. 190; and F. Fraser Bond, *An Introduction to Journalism: A Survey of the Fourth Estate in All Its Forms,* 2d ed. (New York: Macmillan Company, 1961), p. 320.
12. Baird and Turnbull, pp. 286–7.
13. *ABC Bulletin, Bylaws and Rules,* September 1981.
14. Analysis based on "United States and Canada Periodical Circulation Study," (Schaumburg, Ill.: Audit Bureau of Circulations, December 16, 1980).
15. *ABC Fas-Fax,* December 31, 1980.
16. *All About BPA in Brief* (New York: Business Publications Audit of Circulations Inc., (n.d.) [received by author February 1972].
17. ABC *Bylaws and Rules,* 1980, pp. 12–60.
18. *Consumer Magazine and Farm Publication Rates and Data* 55 (February 27, 1973):23–24, and *Business Publications Rates and Data* 55 (March 24, 1973):37.
19. Richard Loyer, "Specialized Subscription Sales," in Dembner and Massee, *Modern Circulation Methods,* p. 85.
20. *Consumer Magazine and Farm Publication Rates and Data* 53 (December 27, 1971):235.
21. Ibid., p. 227.
22. Ibid., p. 236.
23. *Business Publication Rates and Data,* December 24, 1984, p. 608.
24. Ibid., p. 341.
25. Baird and Turnbull, p. 279.
26. Ibid.
27. *Business Publication Rates and Data,* August 24, 1977, p. 251.
28. CPMs calculated from data in *Consumer Magazine and Farm Publication Rates and Data,* June 27, 1981, pp. 232, 422, 425, 499, 511, 551, 553, 556, 558, 560–61, 563–64, and 577–79.
29. Karyl Van, "Audited Circulation and Advertising Sales Business," in Dembner and Massee, p. 14.

30. ABC *Fas-Fax,* June 30, 1984.
31. "Audited Circulation," p. 14.
32. Chris Welles, "Can mass magazines survive?" *Columbia Journalism Review,* July–August 1971, p. 13.
33. H. Carlisle Estes, "Single-copy Sales," in Dembner and Massee, p. 74.
34. Estes, "Single-copy Sales," pp. 76–77.
35. Ibid., p. 79.
36. Ibid.
37. Ibid., p. 81.
38. Ibid., p. 79.
39. "Mags earn big profit on investment," *American Druggist,* July 14, 1971, p. 75.
40. Estes, p. 74.
41. John Millington, "Circulation: Strategy and Tactics," in Dembner and Massee, p. 7.
42. William S. Campbell, "Prospecting by Direct Mail," in Dembner and Massee, p. 19.
43. Ibid., p. 20.
44. Ibid., p. 23.
45. Ibid.
46. Gordon Grossman, "Direct-mail Testing," in Dembner and Massee, p. 27.
47. Grossman, "Direct Mail Testing," 57–58.
48. Robert M. Goshorn and William A. Eyerly, "Magazine Subscription Agencies," in Dembner and Massee, pp. 100–101.
49. Ibid., p. 103.
50. Ibid., pp. 109–12.
51. Halbert F. Speer, "Renewal Analysis," in Dembner and Massee, pp. 115–16.
52. Speer, "Renewal Analysis," pp. 116–23.
53. Ibid., pp. 116–18.
54. Bernard P. Dangelmaier, "Business Publication Fulfillment," in Dembner and Massee, p. 165.
55. Walter Mills, "Circulation Records," in Dembner and Massee, pp. 142–51.
56. Ibid., pp. 150–51.
57. Ibid., pp. 153–54.

19

Pressures and Responsibilities

IF a public relations man who would like favorable treatment of his company in your magazine asks you out for a drink, do you turn him down? If not, at what point do you say no? After the dinner? The Broadway play? The weekend in Bermuda?

The catalog of ethical problems is long and persistent and easier to talk about in the third person, the other person. Pressures on editors come from many directions: business, government, special interest organizations, staff members, individual readers. Editorial integrity is a prized attribute that can easily be eroded, and once erosion starts, it tends to snowball.

A situation involving a photographer looking for scenic pictures in a state park is described by William Rivers and Wilbur Schramm.[1] The photographer notices an interesting pattern of leaves and rocks along a stream but thinks it would be more attractive if he moved two leaves and added another. A class of 30 graduate students, after considering the situation, decided the picture was artistic and would not preclude arranging leaves. They were unanimous, though, in criticizing a veteran press photographer who recommended that a photographer carry a broken tricycle in his car trunk to provide foreground interest when covering fatal accidents involving children. Rivers and Schramm observe:

One of the most damaging aspects of photojournalism is that too many of the men who make pictures for the mass media treat the truth casually. They become accustomed to arranging pictures and do not know when to stop. The time to stop is at the beginning—with the innocuous little scene of the leaves.[2]

The analogy extends to other areas of editing and writing, although it is more difficult to avoid arranging in words because all writing is arranging words. The editor must determine what is "truth" and insist that it be served in the magazine.

With such variety in the magazine field and with emotion and entertainment often foremost in an individual magazine's appeal, there always will be publishers and editors out to make a fast buck rather than to report the truth. An argument can be made that diversity among magazines makes slanted reports, one-sided reports, and advocacy pieces desirable. In the typical community there may be three or four daily newspapers, counting ones that come in from neighboring cities; a dozen or so radio stations near enough to provide regional or local service; and two to eight television channels. But a newsstand may have 50 to 150 different magazines on hand at any time. There the reader has much greater selection and may opt for what serves him or her best. So why should the editor be so concerned about ethics as long as he or she does not knowingly or unknowingly spread falsehood?

Although it is tempting to insist on a prescribed ethic for everyone, ethics and "social responsibility" are largely matters of individual integrity, honor, and choice. Journalists are not licensed and cannot be disbarred, so the individual, operating with support and pressure from colleagues, ultimately makes his or her own decisions.

Social Class Pressures

The company editors keep is usually not typical of their magazine's readership, and most realize it. In all media of communication, the people at the top were well paid and move in a social circle higher than the typical reader's or viewer's. Editors socialize with publishers, business persons, entertainers, and prominent persons in many other areas. William Allen White called it the "country club complex" and noted that persons in these positions soon "get the unconscious arrogance of conscious wealth."

Concerns of business probably come across clearest to editors because they have more contact with business people in their professional and social activities. Magazines, too, are part of business, and editors can be expected to think like business people.

If the publishing company suffers from lack of integrity, the editor must make a personal decision about his or her future. One may have the opportunity before becoming an editor, if one joins the staff in a lesser position. A. J. Liebling spoke of more than newspapermen when he wrote, "Newspapermen are quick to get the idea of what the boss wants, but those who get it first have usually had similar ideas right along. The publisher chooses some staff members as his instruments and ignores others (or, if they are obstreperous, gets rid of them)."[3]

Editors of public relations magazines have the added burden of being advocates of business and part of management. If their magazines are effective, they must remember the needs and interests of their readers and strongly identify with them. The overzealous advocate of management's viewpoint may have an unread magazine and do no one any good.

Simply recognizing the existence of class bias will not eliminate it, but it is a start. An editor who consciously considers personal biases when choosing content, angles, and play usually will arrive at better decisions than one who does not. Better, though still not perfect, is a feeling of professionalism, the desire to do a job that will be respected by one's peers. The growing number of journalism reviews has a salutory effect. Published criticism, which usually has some basis, may be answered, but it will serve to nudge the editor to better or more professional performance next time.

This feeling of professionalism is important because magazines will not stop being a business, editors will not discontinue their business luncheons and social activities, and letters from readers threatening to cancel subscriptions will keep arriving. But those letters cannot carry much clout unless there are great numbers of them and the magazine is in such financial straits that it is endeavoring to please all pressure groups and therefore pleasing none. An editor should consider the point a reader makes in a letter, but he or she cannot afford to be constantly intimidated by threatened or actual cancellations of subscriptions.

Advertiser Influence

Influence upon editorial decisions by advertisers goes along with social class pressures. The threat seldom has to be made directly and overtly; pressure is more subtle than that. Over the years, it may permeate the editorial office. "He's one of our long-time advertisers; let's jump a good article next to his ad," has been heard even from seasoned editors. This kind of influence is virtually impossible to pin down and prove. One staff member may insist it exists while the person at the next desk believes there is nothing but fair play involved.

Important here is that advertisers and their agencies attempt to select the most effective media for their messages. When one advertiser is obviously favored, others will justifiably be irate. And there can be a backlash against the favored advertiser, because a competitor might insist on a better deal. Editors tell how *Collier's* and *Saturday Evening Post* sold editorial favoritism to advertisers before going out of business.

Editor Ben Hibbs of *Saturday Evening Post* said of *Collier's:* "Someone from the business office was always looking over their [editors'] shoulders. Things often were done editorially solely to attract advertising—always a vain procedure and usually a fatal mistake."[4]

Otto Friedrich tells how Martin Ackerman promised advertising executives at Ford Motor Company that Henry Ford's picture would be on the cover of the October 5, 1968, *Saturday Evening Post* to save $400,000 worth of Ford advertising in that issue. But editorial employees insisted that the other auto makers would object and that immense damage would result. Since Ford had not been offered exclusive display on the cover, someone suggested featuring the heads of all four auto makers.[5] The obvious problem arising if the magazine sells out to one advertiser is that there is no stopping as the word gets around. Price beomes the only question.

Editorial integrity is much easier to maintain if the book is in solid financial condition and does not need to desperately woo advertisers. But the price of selling one's integrity is more likely to be loss of advertising pages rather than gain.

The question of whether editorial content, especially bold content, will lose advertisers from the magazine frequently arises. John H. Johnson said *Ebony* has to have advertising, and in some cases he thought the magazine was going so far that advertisers would reject it. He was fearful of the possible consequences of publishing "Was Abraham Lincoln a Segregationist?" and later an entire issue devoted to the "white problem" in America. But in each case, after thinking about it and weighing the circumstances, he said, "I've got to go forward with this."[6]

Articles that directly relate to advertisers are no different, as Herbert Mayes, former editor of *McCall's* and *Good Housekeeping,* noted:

To set out deliberately to antagonize advertisers would be senseless. But when there was reason to investigate and expose, there was no hesitation. Disclosures of unfair airline practices ('Going to Fly? Another Look at the Airlines'), or of the diamond monopoly ('Diamonds Are a Girl's Most Overpriced Friend'), or life insurance sales methods ('Let's See What the Insurance Companies Offer'), meant we might never get the advertising of the companies named; such possibility never deterred us.[7]

In the history of American journalism, honesty and integrity have been proved necessary for economic survival. Dishonesty in advertising and circulation claims around the turn of the century led to the formation of a number of professional associations to ensure the truthfulness of these claims. Editorial integrity and strong independence from advertisers also have been found to be sound business practices.

A magazine in financial difficulty often finds that some of the advertising it has been carrying was placed by whim or hunch rather than on the basis of sound business. The psychology of advertising in such situations is summed up by the trite saying attributed to advertising agency executives: "No one wants his ad to appear in the last issue of a magazine." So when rumors make the rounds about a magazine's problems, ad pages decline, hastening the magazine's demise.

Separation of Advertising from Editorial

One long-standing principle of editing decrees that advertisements be clearly differentiated and separated from editorial matter. Postal regulations require that ads that do not clearly look different from editorial matter be labeled "(Advertisement)." In recent years, though, more and more ads that copy a magazine's page layout style and use its editorial type faces have found their way into print. However, since the policy of differentiation is not primarily an editorial policy, but an overall publishing policy and an advertising policy, the advertising department has the option of rejecting ads that look like part of the magazine's editorial content. Ads that have come under fire for being virtually indistinguishable from editorial content have included a full-page insurance ad in *Look,* a Delta Air Lines ad in *People,* and ads for Oil of Olay in *Reader's Digest, Saturday Evening Post,* and several other magazines.

Another criticism of advertisements is lack of taste. Although the editorial and advertising departments should be completely separate, an editor certainly is concerned with whether the advertising department accepts ads that may be objectionable to some readers or that may promote dangerous products or services. Does advertising policy permit the acceptance of advertisements for products and services that have not been checked?

Advertising layout also has taken some strange turns. Magazines that formerly had handsome, colorful ads began to have a sprinkling of ads with layout that is intentionally cheap and cluttered looking. These ads jump out at the reader with their unsophisticated, irritating appearance. And they diminish the reader's overall impression of the magazine. A magazine has the right to accept and reject ads, and the advertising department should insist upon a standard of visual taste in keeping with the visual appearance of the rest of the magazine.

Irregular sized and shaped ads can be bothersome to the editor. The ad that takes the shape of a dust mop or soft drink bottle creates an awkward editorial hole to fill. And some magazines accept ads that take up most of the page, but leave a column narrower than standard down one side and only enough room for a headline across the top of the page. This is hardly the way to present editorial matter properly, or to have a pleasing page.

Undue advertiser influence may be implied when the magazine publishes an article written by an advertiser's public relations department or the ad agency's PR department. The line of demarcation here becomes thin, almost invisible. It is more dangerous if the reader is not informed that the article was written by a PR agency and is left with the impression that it is a staff-written piece.

Magazines frequently create special sections, even special editions, to generate additional advertising. The editorial staff will be expected to provide related features that will be informative, helpful, or entertaining to readers. As long as the staff maintains its editorial integrity and standards of quality, there should be no problem. But if transparent puffery of advertisers' products or services, whether mentioned by brand name or not, is used, there is disservice to both readers and advertisers.

Each issue of *Columbia Journalism Review* contains a short listing of "darts and laurels" covering all media. Newpapers and television stations get most of the darts, but the January–February 1972 issue was heavily magazine, including:

Laurel: to the dozens of companies that must have shunned the *Reader's Digest's* widely advertised special section on the environment, in the September, 1971, issue. Only eight companies responded to the *Digest's* invitation to place environmental apologetics in the magazine in the *Digest's* unique "articlad" form. . . .

Dart: to *Editor & Publisher,* weekly of the newspaper business, for running, in its issue of Sept. 18, an eighteen-page promotional insert by the American Forest Institute—without identifying the insert as paid advertising. . . .

Dart: to *Philadelphia,* a leader among the new city magazines for tarnishing its crusading reputation in the recent Philadelphia mayoralty campaign. It ran an invidious article on the Republican candidate, Thacher Longstreth, but killed its prospective article on the Democrat (and eventual winner), Frank L. Rizzo. Even granting the editor's premises–that 1) there was no pressure from Rizzo or his friends; 2) the manuscript was unsuitable for publication; 3) the magazine is not obligated to give equal space to candidates, and 4) it had run earlier articles on Rizzo—there was still a vacuum of expectations. *Philadelphia's* past efforts had led its public to expect that it would deal with equal toughness with both candidates. Its silence on Rizzo must have given its readers that hollow feeling.[8]

Gifts, Favors, Junkets, and Moonlighting

Whether a journalist should accept small gifts, favors, junkets, and positions on boards of public bodies will forever be debated. The best answer is to avoid all offers that may influence or be construed by readers to influence any writer or editor, or that may undermine the magazine's credibility with its readers. Publishers, editors, and writers don't always see it that simply.

Many writers, of course, are working on several manuscripts at a time, offering them to different magazines or publishers. Their editors need to know more about them than is included in the manuscript.

If an editor believes a writer's work is so good that it must it published in spite of entanglements, allegiances or obvious business connections, the least he or she can do is to be totally fair to all ideas and sides, to make the piece balanced, to have researchers check it for both factual inaccuracies and omissions. And an editor's note with the piece should state that the writer does public relations for the firm involved or that the writer once worked for this candidate, as the case may be. Readers never should be surprised to learn later, from some other source, that the article they enjoyed was written by a person with a vested interest in the subject.

The number of companies that can find reasons to fly writers and editors to Europe, the Bahamas, and other comfortable places is astounding. Only the number of writers and editors who accept is more astounding. It may seem petty to insist that media pay their writers' way wherever they go, but it may be the small difference between editorial independence and potential allegiance.

Hypocrisy is not unknown, either. A corporate vice-president for public relations was awaiting the arrival of a magazine writer. He asked an assistant to be sure to take the writer to dinner and offer to pay his hotel bill. "The last magazine writer who was here," he said, "opened by telling me it was against his magazine's policy to accept favors, entertainment, or travel expenses. Then in the next breath he said, 'Do you belong to a private club where we could have dinner tonight?' " That writer was wined and dined as he requested.

Five-dollar cigarette lighters and occasional lunches may not be enough to mar the integrity of a professional writer or editor. But there can be a cumulative effect if there are enough small gifts, and there is no reason to open one's self to that eventuality. Even if such items do not affect the judgment of a writer or editor, the reader may suspect that they do. The appearance of such influence is as much a concern as any real influence. The reader may question, if not doubt, the magazine's integrity.

Image or Reality?

When news was conceived largely in "man bites dog" terms, editorial judgment was relatively simple. Significance, importance, intellectual stimulation and worth have long since complicated the matter. The staged event, publicity stunt, press conference, and news release have made it tougher to distinguish material of legitimate public interest from self-serving promotion. Historian Daniel Boorstin discusses this at some length in his popular book, *The Image*.

The pseudo-event, Boorstin writes, "is not spontaneous, but comes about because someone planned, planted, or incited it. Typically it is not a train wreck or an earthquake, but an interview." The objective of a pseudo-event is to be reported. "Usually it is intended to be a self-fulfilling prophecy," leading to the general belief that something said to be true is true.[9]

Experience and research tend to indicate that you can't fool all of the people all of the time in regard to truth about events and product performance. The realm of ideas is more difficult to assess. An individual may develop a favorable attitude toward a company or candidate based upon inadequate or one-sided information and hold that attitude until strong contradictory data demolish or alter it. Packaging ideas and persuading people is more challenging than reporting an observable event. Social security was attacked as socialism in the 1930s but accepted as a normal governmental program within 20 years. "Socialized medicine" was vehemently fought in the 1950s, but partially accepted as "Medicare" for the aged in the late 1960s. Others continue to insist that proper health care is a human and civil right that should be made available to all by the federal government.

Public relations practitioners will continue to advance their interests, whether they are pseudo-events, one-sided position statements, or idea pieces offered as balanced presentations with a hope that readers may side with the advocates' interests. All these tie into another problem editors frequently face: ghost writing. Prominent persons, from the President of the United States through cabinet officers, corporation executives, university presidents, and even university professors, have writers who "know" what the employer wants to say, who offer some additional ideas, and who mix them together into speeches that can be given and articles that can be published.

We usually can assume that the person whose byline appears on the piece has at least approved it, but we don't know who wrote it or whose ideas really are being expressed. In many cases, neither the editor nor the readers can judge a public figure by what is published under his or her name.

One step toward honesty is the use of *with* or *as told* to in addition to the principal's name: "Mickey Mantle's Decision" by Mickey Mantle with Gerald Astor (*Look*) or "Arnold Toynbee Talks of Peace, Power, Race in America" with J. Robert Moskin (*Life*). This at least suggests to the reader that the principal's ideas were used but refined and embellished by the writer.

Writers frequently find that they must submit questions in writing before an interview and then limit themselves closely to the questions and prepared answers. In developing a special report on the environment for the second issue of *DuPont Context,* Editor John J. McCafferty submitted his questions to Russell E. Train, Chairman of the President's Council on Environmental Quality. He felt that obtaining the five-page cover article was well worth the effort he put forth.

Editor McCafferty also interviewed Christian A. Herter, Jr., Special Assistant to the Secretary of State for Environmental Affairs and Director of the State Department's Office of Environmental Affairs, for the same issue. His piece was so much Herter that he checked back with him to get permission to use Herter's byline, to which Herter agreed. Whether the article was so close to what Herter had more or less dictated was a decision for the editor first and Herter second, based on their experience in the interview and review of the article that resulted. Many editors would have preferred adding an *as told to* or *with* line to the government official's byline.

Editorial Bias

Bias within the magazine staff itself is frequent and not always bad. A denominational religious magazine can be expected to support its sponsor's positions on moral issues, although it may find the occasional offer of contradictory ideas by other writers to be advantageous. A magazine of critical opinion, like *The Nation,* may well make clear its own position and admit its bias. Balance does not always mean giving the other side or sides equal space or impact. If something is obviously wrong, there is no need to publish material advocating the wrongdoing.

Stopping short of sensationalism is recommended, although opinions vary about where that point is. Robert Root told of a National Health Forum where a physician asked why *Look* had used a sensational heading, "Why Hospitals Lock Out Doctors." The *Look* editor replied, "What is sensational about that? They are colorful words. . . . We are competing for his [the reader's] attention." An emotionally involved reader, or a reader within the industry or profession being discussed is usually more sensitive and more critical than the average reader. Editors must make their best judgment and prepare to take the flak that comes their way from such readers.

Inaccuracy

News reports sometimes become garbled in news magazines and on wire services. More often than not the mistakes are made by an editor who had not covered the event and who was not given a clear enough report of it by the writer. Sometimes it occurs when tightening writing. The conventional advice is to avoid making mistakes by carefully checking everything, but when mistakes are made, to publish clear, carefully worded corrections. The belief that printing corrections creates suspicions about everything else in the publication has given way to one that corrections create a greater feeling of credibility, that when errors are made they will be acknowledged.

Big Government

Government seldom exerts a direct threat to magazines, but the people who operate its many bureaus often hinder the free flow of information, and public officials use the press for their trial balloons. Writers and editors often sense that they are being used to advance proposals that are not being made whole-heartedly, and that can easily be shot down by public reaction. Whether to permit such use of a periodical is a decision that the editor must make by individual case. In a free marketplace of ideas, a cabinet officer's article on a proposed new federal program, revision of an existing agency, or elimination of an ineffective one can add greatly to public discussion that is part of the legislative and administrative process. Editors are delighted to publish pieces by articulate cabinet officers, senators, and other officials, especially if they might add prestige or readership to the magazine.

Social Responsibility

Freedom of the press is guaranteed by the First Amendment to the United States Constitution and by articles in or amendments to the several states' constitutions. This establishes what is called the libertarian philosophy, that there shall be no prior restraints upon what people may publish in periodicals. Over the last 40 years, dating particularly from the 1947 report, *A Free and Responsible Press,* by the Commission on Freedom of the Press, a concept called social responsibility has developed. The Report insists that the press should publish balanced reports that reveal the truth about the fact as well as the fact itself, that significance should be indicated, and that meaning should be stated to flesh out the reporting of the facts.

Because costs today prohibit everyone from starting his or her own publication, some insist that every reader has a right to space in established publications to express his or her ideas or views. As a practical matter, access cannot be guaranteed to everyone because there just is not enough space in periodicals for everything readers would like to have published. A guarantee like this to readers would result in an infringement on a free press, forcing editors to publish items that their editorial judgment says should not be published. In other words, a guarantee to readers abridges the publishers' and editors' freedom of the press. But the social responsibility concept emphasizes to editors that their readers' broad interests must be carefully considered as items are accepted for or rejected from publication, that there is a responsibility to the public interest beyond what will sell.

Balance does not always mean giving equal play to two or more sides of an issue. When it becomes known that Vietnamese prisoners were placed in tiger cages, there should be no compulsion to find someone who favors that action. If mistreatment of mental patients is uncovered, one needn't find a spokesman who favors such mistreatment. The positive, social responsibility in these cases requires the editors to stand for what is right for society as they see it.

Reporting Techniques

Magazines that deal in news and reportage face the same ethical questions as newsgathering organizations in other media. They must decide whether to obtain information by deception or misrepresentation in some cases, whether to permit sources to remain anonymous, whether to use composite characters in articles, and whether to let interviewees check an article before publication. The answers to these vary according to the specific situation, the field the magazine serves, the principals involved, and the ethical standards by which they operate. All of these ethical problems are discussed at much greater length in other works, as they deserve to be.

Editors frequently pay sources for information. Many journalists oppose all such "checkbook journalism" and many others accept it as long as convicted criminals are not paid for their stories and are not given undue publicity. The National News Council found *Life* fell short of the highest professional standards in paying $8,000 ($1,000 each) for pictures of Bernard Welch, the burglar accused of killing Dr. Michael Halberstam for an article on the careers of both in the February 1981 issue. *Life* obtained pictures of Halberstam from his family and the Harvard University Archives. The National News Council reiterated its position of 1975 on checkbook journalism:

If compensation beyond actual expense is made to any person for news in the form of an interview (published or broadcast), or for information to be used in a news story or broadcast, or for an article by a person in the news, that fact should be disclosed. A prefatory note or on-the-air statement immediately preceding the article or program should be published or broadcast.

Such notification to the reader or viewer is not intended for the publication of articles or photographs or radio and television productions actually written or produced by an individual or supplier and marketed to the news organization through commonly accredited practices that do not deceive the public.

The council further recommended that news organizations not pay criminals for news materials.[10]

Relations with Outside Writers

Editors maintain a trust with outside writers that is enhanced by complete communication. Occasionally a writer will simultaneously submit an article to two or more magazines. If the writer admits this to each editor, he or she runs the risk of immediate rejection. An established writer may get immediate attention and a quick offer, start a bidding war, or be rejected by all editors involved. If the writer does not admit the simultaneous submission, two or more editors may schedule the piece for an upcoming issue until the writer informs them of the problem.

Because editors recognize that their magazines seldom can be any better than their writers, they temper their reactions to a writer who has simultaneously submitted an article to several magazines with restraint and diplomacy. While the first reaction may be to reject the writer and ban him or her from the magazine, that writer may develop into a first-rate source of material for the magazine. Editors cannot dictate the ethics of all their free-lance writers. They can be open and honest in their communication with them and encourage the same in return.

Writers sometimes use the same material but write it from different angles for different magazines. Editors generally appreciate knowing that an article with a different angle and preferably with no or very little duplicated information has been submitted elsewhere. The editor wants a distinctively different article, really a unique one, and does not want to be surprised by a nearly identical article by the same writer in a competing book. Editors may find it advisable to tell writers this when contracting with them for an article.

Editors usually will edit an article as much as necessary to make it meet the magazine's requirements. It is generally accepted that the article, as the work of the bylined writer, should have no substantive changes made by the editor without permission of the writer. Changes for purposes of style, grammar, conciseness, or arrangement may be made by the editor so long as they do not change the intent or sense of the article.

A writer may be obliged to rewrite a piece upon an editor's request, according to the code of the American Society of Journalists and Authors, but the writer also is entitled to withdraw the manuscript and offer it elsewhere. A writer also may consent to having the piece rewritten by someone else. Staff writers may have to adhere to other practices. As employees, they are expected to write to the employer's standards and practices.

Code of Ethics

Journalists have long debated whether codes are of real value, citing their vagueness and lack of enforceability as major weaknesses and their usefulness as general guidelines as a strength. Journalistic codes generally stand for and discuss truth, accuracy, responsibility, independence, impartiality, fair play, and freedom of the press. The definition and application of these precepts are left largely to individual journalists and especially to editors. When the codes become specific, as in the Society of Professional Journalists, Sigma Delta Chi's statement that "nothing of value should be accepted" or that journalists should protect themselves "from conflict of interest, real or apparent," large numbers of journalists disagree.

Codes nevertheless are useful guides to most journalists, who need to be reminded of basic precepts and what others in the profession say about them. The Association of Business Publishers has framed a Code of Professional Research Ethics and Practices as well as a Code of Publishing Practice. The ABP Code of Publishing Practice is one example in the magazine field:

As a condition precedent to membership and as a condition for the continuation of membership, each member of the Association of Business Publishers, Inc., agrees:

1. To hold uppermost the interest of its readers, firm in the knowledge that devoted service to readers is the key to effective service to advertisers.

2. To publish no editorial material either as a consideration for advertising or in return for monetary or other consideration; and further to publish no advertising material which simulates the publication's editorial content without clearly and conspicuously identifying such material as a message paid for by an advertiser.

3. To maintain absolute editorial independence from advertisers, from government, or from sources other than the publisher.

4. To vigilantly and forcefully fight for the constitutional right of freedom of the press.

5. To practice and encourage the highest standards of journalistic and publishing ethics; to strive constantly for honest and effective presentation of all news and articles; to refrain from infringement of the trademarks and copyrights of others.

6. To submit each publication to regular circulation audits conducted by an independent, non-profit, tripartite auditing organization, and to encourage similar auditing practices by all publications of whatever type.

7. To make available to advertisers, advertising agencies and other interested persons or organizations, a complete listing of all the prices which a publication charges for all units of space, including but not limited to preferred or specified positions, colors, bleed, inserts, etc., as well as the terms of payment thereof; and to afford no advertiser an opportunity to purchase such space at a rate more advantageous than is available to any other advertiser.

8. To refuse knowingly to accept advertising which is untruthful, misleading, deceptive or in bad taste, or which unfairly disparages or attacks the goods, prices, services or advertising of any competitor or any other industry.

9. To promote and sell its own publications solely on their merits.

10. To employ no advertising or personal selling methods on its behalf which are untruthful, misleading or deceptive, or which unfairly disparage other publications or advertising media.

Notes

1. William L. Rivers and Wilbur Schramm. *Responsibility in Mass Communication,* rev. ed. (New York: Harper & Row, 1969), pp. 140–41.
2. Ibid., p. 141.
3. A. J. Liebling, *The Wayward Pressman* (New York: Doubleday, 1948), p. 109.
4. *Advertising Age,* February 16, 1959, p. 8.
5. Otto Friedrich, *Decline and Fall* (New York: Harper & Row, 1970), p. 374.
6. " 'Failure is a word I don't accept', an interview with John H. Johnson," *Harvard Business Review,* March–April 1976, p. 88.
7. Herbert R. Mayes, *The Magazine Maze* (Garden City, N.Y.: Doubleday & Company, 1980), p. 102.
8. *Columbia Journalism Review,* January/February, 1972, pp. 6–7.
9. Daniel Boorstin, *The Image,* (New York: Atheneum, 1962) pp. 10–11.
10. " 'Life' criticized for paying accused killer," *Columbia Journalism Review,* May/June 1981, p. 91.

20

The Editor and Law

Legal problems that confront a magazine editor usually stem from inadequacies in editing—failure to check accuracy or authenticity, acceptance of facts from untrustworthy sources, or recklessly disregarding the truth in a rush to publish. Libel is not a great threat to a magazine that is carefully edited. Nevertheless, magazines of any size should budget for legal counsel and be prepared to be sued.

It should be pointed out that anyone can file a civil suit against anyone else, so even the most carefully edited magazine needs a libel lawyer. The big cost may be attorney fees rather than court judgments. And congested court dockets, delays, and appeals can extend the duration of a suit to unbelievable lengths.

Libel

Communication that exposes a person to hatred, ridicule, or contempt, lowers him in the esteem of his fellows, causes him to be shunned, or injures him in his business or calling, is known as defamation. Libel is defamation by written or printed words, by its embodiment in physical form, or by any other form of communication that has the potentially harmful qualities characteristic of written or printed words.[1]

One of the celebrated cases in the latter days of the *Saturday Evening Post* stemmed from an article, "Story of a College Football Fix," in the March 23, 1963, issue. It charged that Wallace "Wally" Butts, University of Georgia athletic director, gave information to Paul "Bear" Bryant, University of Alabama football coach, before an Alabama-Georgia game and was based on information obtained from an insurance man who reported that he had been cut in on a long distance conversation between Butts and Bryant.

Butts immediately sued for $10 million in Atlanta Federal Court, claiming the *Post* had "willfully, maliciously and falsely" libeled him. Bryant sued for $5 million in Montgomery Federal Court.

The Butts case came to trial in August, and on August 20 the jury awarded $60,000 in general damages as compensation for his loss of reputation and $3 million punitive damages for callous disregard of the injured party. The *Post* filed for both a new trial and reduction of judgment. The federal judge in Atlanta ruled the punitive damages excessive and gave Butts the choice of accepting a reduced judgment totaling $460,000 or going through a new trial. On the advice of his lawyers, he accepted the reduced judgment. However, the *Post* again filed for a new trial, and Butt's lawyers countered with a motion to restore the original judgment.

Finally the judgment was affirmed by the United States Supreme Court in 1967. Justice Harlan wrote in the court's opinion:

The evidence showed that the Butts story was in no sense "hot news" and the editors of the magazine recognized the need for a thorough investigation of the serious charges. Elementary precautions were, nevertheless, ignored. *The Saturday Evening Post* knew that Burnett [the source of the article who was "cut in" on the telephone conversation] had been placed on probation in connection with bad check charges, but proceeded to publish the story on the basis of his affadavit without substantial independent support. Burnett's notes were not even viewed by any of the magazine's personnel prior to publication. John Carmichael who was supposed to have been with Burnett when the phone call was overheard was not interviewed. No attempt was made to screen the films of the game to see if Burnett's information was accurate, and no attempt was made to find out whether Alabama had adjusted its plans after the alleged divulgence of information.

The *Post* writer assigned to the story was not a football expert and no attempt was made to check the story with someone knowledgeable in the sport. At trial such experts indicated that the information in the Burnett notes was either such that it would be evident to any opposing coach from game films regularly exchanged or valueless. Those assisting the *Post* writer in his investigation were already deeply involved in another libel action, based on a different article, brought against Curtis Publishing Co. by the Alabama coach and unlikely to be the source of a complete and objective investigation. The Saturday Evening Post was anxious to change its image by instituting a policy of "sophisticated muckraking," and the pressure to produce a successful expose might have induced a stretching of standards. In short, the evidence is ample to support a finding of highly unreasonable conduct constituting an extreme departure from the standards of investigation and reporting ordinarily adhered to by responsible publishers.[2]

Bryant had earlier sued the *Post* for $500,000 over an article that linked him with college football brutality. On February 3, 1964, he settled both suits out of court with the *Saturday Evening Post* for $300,000.

A former football player at the University of Oklahoma won a $75,000 judgment against *True* magazine for a paragraph dealing with alleged dispensing of pep pills to athletes. The Supreme Court upheld the judgment in 1964.

When an editor is sued for libel, the best defenses are truth, privilege, and fair comment and criticism. If he or she can prove the truth of the published statement, and that it was published with good motives for justifiable ends, the editor usually has a "complete defense." The second defense is based upon the assumption that under a republic form of government, free and open discussion in public and official bodies must be protected. Statutes vary widely from state to state over what is both public and official, and journalists often are mistaken in thinking some information they have procured from a government agency, such as facts from a police blotter, is privileged. Further, because the journalist is not publishing the full text of courtroom testimony or a legislative session, his or her defense becomes qualified privilege, qualified by the publication of a fair and accurate summary of the proceedings.

In many instances the most effective defense is fair comment and criticism. Many statements that are not privileged and whose truth cannot be proved can be made as statements of opinion. The test for fair comment and criticism revolves around an honest opinion based upon observed fact and lacking malicious intent. The requirements for fair comment and criticism have been summarized into six statements: (1) The published material must be an intellectual appraisal or evaluation. (2) It must be founded on facts. [One cannot honestly pan a book he or she has not read.] (3) It must be free of any imputation of sordid or corrupt motives. (4) It must be the result of *honest* opinion. (5) It must be free from malice. (6) It must be on a subject of public interest. Ridicule and sarcasm come under fair comment and criticism as long as they meet the six tests.

Another defense originated with the *New York Times* v. *Sullivan* case in 1964, and has been used more frequently than any other defense in libel cases since then. Under it, a public official or public figure must prove actual malice on the part of the publisher in order to recover damages. Actual malice is defined as knowledge of falsity or reckless disregard for the truth.[3]

The defense does not necessarily apply to every case involving a public official. Public officials are required to prove actual malice only "when the defamatory comments or statements concern (1) their *official conduct,* that is, actions taken in an official capacity or actions while they undertake their public official role and (2) their general fitness for public office."[4]

The *Rosenbloom* v. *Metromedia* decision (1971) extended the public figures portion of this defense for a while to all public or private persons who were libelled in a discussion of an event of interest to the public. But that was narrowed in 1974 to two types of persons who are "public figures" in *Gertz* v. *Welch*. Although active in civil rights disputes in Chicago, Gertz was ruled not a public figure in this case which did not involve civil rights. The Supreme Court, in the opinion by Justice Powell, described two kinds of public figures:

In some instances an individual may achieve such pervasive fame or notoriety that he becomes a public figure for all purposes and in all contexts. . . . More commonly, an individual voluntarily injects himself or he is drawn into a particular public controversy and thereby becomes a public figure for a limited range of issues.[5]

It is useful to note that the Gertz case involved a magazine, and Rosenbloom involved radio, a spot news medium. This is one of many indications that magazines have less leeway than spot news media.

A person on a public payroll or who receives public funds is not necessarily a public official or a public figure. The director of research of a state mental hospital who had successfully applied for nearly a half-million dollars in federal funds for research on aggression in animals was ruled not to be a public figure in *Hutchinson v. Proxmire* (1979). "Hutchinson did not thrust himself or his views into public controversy to influence others," and his position did not invite public scrutiny.

The *Gertz* decision also established a new requirement that a plaintiff cannot win punitive damages in a libel suit unless there is evidence of negligence on the part of the publication in not discovering the falsity of the published statements.[6]

The question of whether the material is in the public interest or is of interest only to the magazine personnel, possibly arbitrarily selected by them for publication, arises in the *Gertz* case. Gertz is an attorney who represented the family of a young man who was slain by a Chicago policeman in a civil action for damages after the policeman was convicted of murder. *American Opinion* magazine, published by Robert Welch, attacked Gertz, falsely charging that he was a Communist fronter, a Leninist, and an architect of the frame-up against the police officer, and alleged that he had a criminal record. Gertz had been only a peripheral figure in the circumstances surrounding the death and the murder trial, and being found not a public figure did not have to prove actual malice.

In *Firestone v. Time, Inc.* (1976) the court affirmed *Gertz* and pointed out that a controversy of interest to the public, in this case a divorce proceeding, is not the same as the "public controversy" cited in the Gertz opinion, even though the plaintiff was a prominent member of Palm Beach society and held several press conferences during the 17-month legal proceeding.

New York magazine called Tex Maule the worst writer on *Sports Illustrated,* and said most of his stories were rewritten. The court determined him to be a public figure because he had taken an affirmative step to attract attention through publication of his books and articles (*Maule v. New York Magazine,* 1980). The criticism was directed toward Maule's writing, the area to which he had attracted attention to himself.

A California case further illustrates that magazines are expected to maintain a higher level of accuracy than media reporting "hot news." Carol Burnett won a libel suit against the *National Enquirer* for a 1976 item that portrayed her as boisterous and loud and traipsing around a Washington, D.C., restaurant. As a public figure, she had to show that publication was made with knowledge that it was false or with reckless disregard for the truth. The trial judge ruled that the *National Enquirer* is a magazine rather than a newspaper and therefore is not protected by a California statute that limits libel judgments against newspapers that print retractions. (At Burnett's request, a retraction had been published.) The jury's award of $300,000 in general and $1.3 million in punitive damages to Burnett was cut by the judge to $50,000 in general and $750,000 in punitive damages. The *Enquirer* announced it would appeal.[7] The District Court of Appeals retained the $50,000 general damages verdict, but cut the punitive damages to $150,000. Burnett finally settled in December 1984 for an undisclosed sum rather than exercise her option to seek a new trial.

A libel judgment against *Look* won by former San Francisco mayor Joseph Alioto over an article published in 1969 was upheld by the U.S. Supreme Court in 1981. "The Web that Links San Francisco's Mayor Alioto and the Mafia" was published with reckless disregard for the truth because, according to the Court of Appeals (9th Circuit), there were "obvious reasons to doubt the veracity" of the source who had supplied the authors with much of the information for their article.[8]

Plaintiffs often lose their cases or have them dismissed. In dismissing a libel suit filed by a biochemist against *Consumer Reports,* the court stated that he had not demonstrated actual malice and further stated: "It is clear that *Consumer Reports* made a thorough investigation of the facts. . . . The unquestioned methodology of the preparation of the article exemplifies the very highest order of responsible journalism."[9]

A suit for libel must be filed within the statute of limitations, which varies from one to five years and in most states is one or two years. About half the states accept a later sale of the issue in question as an additional publication that reactivates the beginning of the time period covered by the statute. The other states have ruled that each entire edition is a single publication and subsequent sales do not constitute republication.[10]

The date on a magazine usually is not the date it was published, but rather an off-sale date. Courts have ruled that the statute of limitations begins on the date the magazine is distributed to a substantial portion of the public. *Time,* which is published a week before the date on its cover, was sued in New Jersey on February 17, 1981, over an article in the February 18, 1980, issue. Because a substantial portion of that issue's circulation had been distributed to subscribers and newsstands before February 18, 1980, the United States district court ruled that the statute of limitations had expired (*MacDonald v. Time,* 1981). A similar suit by Donald Wildmon, a minister, over an article in the November 1978 *Hustler* magazine was dismissed because the October 9, 1979, filing date was more than one year after the issue went on sale October 3, 1978 (*Wildmon v. Hustler,* 1979).

Occasionally an error slips past everyone into print. In these cases a retraction is in order. If a suit is filed, the retraction will tend to decrease the amount of damages by showing lack of actual malice. But a libelled person often will accept a properly worded retraction as sufficient settlement, especially since few people want to expend the time, funds, and energy to undergo the rigors of a trial and its attendant publicity.

Right of Privacy

A person's right to be left alone, to keep his or her name and picture out of the mass media, is the right of privacy. This right varies from state to state and is judged by the court in each case. Privacy statutes have been passed in eight states (New York, California, Massachusetts, Oklahoma, Rhode Island, Utah, Virginia, and Wisconsin) and privacy has been recognized in common law in 37 states and the District of Columbia.

When newsworthiness can be proved, a person generally cannot collect damages for invasion of privacy, but if the material in question was used without his or her consent for advertising or commercial purposes or in fiction, a person's privacy generally has been invaded. Part of an opinion by Justice Shientag of the New York Supreme Court gives useful guidelines, even though it is based on the New York statute:

The rules applicable to unauthorized publication of photographs in a single issue of a newspaper may be summarized generally as follows:

1. Recovery may be had under the statute if the photograph is published in or as part of an advertisement, or for advertising purposes. . . .
3. There may be no recovery under the statute for publication of a photograph in connection with an article of current news or immediate public interest.
4. Newspapers publish articles which are neither strictly news items nor strictly fictional in character. They are not the responses to an event of peculiarly immediate interest but, though based on fact, are used to satisfy an ever-present educational need. Such articles include, among others, travel stories, stories of distant places, tales of historic personages and events, the reproduction of items of past news, and surveys of social conditions. These are articles educational and informative in character. As a general rule, such cases are not within the purview of the statute.[11]

In a 1950 opinion, Justice Van Voorhis wrote, "These classifications apply, with some possible distinctions, to books and magazines."[12]

Although "newsworthiness" is broadly construed, consent of persons depicted in photographs is advisable. Most cases involving the right of privacy have centered on misused photographs.

A 10-year-old girl was knocked down by a careless motorist, and a news photographer got a picture of a woman helping the girl to her feet. Publication of the photo in the newspaper was not actionable; it was a news picture used to convey a news event. Twenty months later, the *Saturday Evening Post* used the picture to illustrate an article titled "They Ask to Be Killed." The photo caption included "unpredictable darting through traffic still takes its sobering toll" and a box by the headline said, "Do you invite massacre by your own carelessness? Here's how to keep them alive." A Federal Court of Appeals wrote: "the legitimate subject for publicity for one particular accident, now becomes a pictorial, frightful example of pedestrian carelessness. This, we think, exceeds the bounds of privilege."[13]

Nelson and Teeter write:

The lesson, for photo editors, should be plain: if a picture is not taken in a public place or if that picture—or its caption—places someone in a false light, don't use it. The exception, of course, would be when you have received permission, in the form of a signed release, from the persons pictured.[14]

When a picture or account of an event ceases to be news and becomes a symbolic but false illustration, or entertainment, or commercial in nature, it may become the subject of successful litigation by the person pictured or described.

Magazines should insist upon written consent for the use of pictures that may not be deemed newsworthy. Public relations magazines vary in their practice about getting releases from employees. Some insist upon signed releases from everyone pictured, others assume that the employee implied consent when he or she had the picture taken, knowing the use to which it would be put.

Permission to use a photograph does not automatically include permission to use a person's name. That must be specified in the same or a different release, or the magazine will be open to suit for invading a person's privacy for using his or her name without consent.

A model release gives written consent of the persons pictured to use the photograph for specified purposes. From the editor's viewpoint, a blanket release permitting all uses is desirable. From the model's viewpoint, a more restricted use may be better. A sample release is:

The undersigned hereby irrevocably consents to the unrestricted use by ***
[photographer's name], advertisers, customers, successors and assigns of my name,
portrait, or picture for advertising purposes or purposes of trade, and I waive the right to
inspect or approve such completed portraits, pictures, or advertising matter used in
connection therewith***.[15]

Some caution should be taken in using pictures even with unrestricted releases. In one case the model sued because the photo had been retouched to suggest a completely different situation than had originally been photographed. She won.[16] In Louisiana a man agreed to "before" and "after" photos for a health studio's bodybuilding course. However, when the photos were used in an ad 10 years later, the court held that his privacy had been invaded.[17]

If you are buying a photo from an agency or photographer, you are buying the right to publish it in your magazine one time. It is possible to buy exclusive rights. Magazines in competitive markets generally want exclusive rights. Smaller or more specialized magazines may not.

Photos taken by a magazine's staff are no problem beyond the routine of getting written releases because the magazine has exclusive rights and can sell or assign any or all of them.

The right of privacy is not restricted to photographs, although more cases have involved them than articles. Two significant cases illustrate how articles can be involved, and how courts have tended to support the media when the material they publish has strong public interest.

William J. Sidis was an 11-year-old mathematical prodigy in 1910. He was graduated from Harvard at age 16 and received much publicity. An article about him in the August 14, 1937, issue of *The New Yorker* was accompanied by a cartoon with the captions, "Where Are They Now?" and "April Fool." The article told how Sidis lived in a "hall bedroom of Boston's shabby south end," and worked at a routine clerical job. He sued for invasion of privacy, but the court held that although *The New Yorker* had published "a ruthless exposure of a once public character, who has since sought and has now been deprived of the seclusion of private life," it found

"The article in the *New Yorker* sketched the life of an unusual personality and it possessed considerable popular news interest." The court would not comment on whether newsworthiness would always constitute a complete defense. It further observed:

. . . Revelations may be so intimate and so unwarranted in view of the victim's position as to outrage the community's notions of decency. But when focused upon public characters, truthful comments upon dress, speech, habits, and the ordinary aspects of personality will usually not transgress this line. Regrettably or not, the misfortunes and frailities of neighbors and "public figures" are subjects of considerable interest and discussion to the rest of the population. And when such are the mores of the community, it would be unwise for a court to bar their expression in the newspapers, books, and magazines of the day.[18]

"Fictionalizing" was a factor in the first privacy case to reach the United States Supreme Court. The February 28, 1955 issue of *Life* carried an article titled "True Crime Inspires Tense Play," relating how the James Hill family of Whitemarsh, Pennsylvania, near Philadelphia, had been held captive in its own home in 1952, and that this had been used as the basis for a novel by Joseph Hayes titled *The Desperate Hours.* The article said, "Now they [Americans] can see the story re-enacted in Hayes's Broadway play based on the book, and next year will see it in his movie." In the next paragraph it said, "LIFE photographed the play during its Philadelphia tryout, transported some of the actors to the actual house where the Hills were besieged. On the next page scenes from the play are re-enacted on the site of the crime."[19]

The play and novel, though, did not match the "true crime." The Hills, called Hilliards in the fiction, had not been harmed by the convicts in any way, but in the novel and play father and son were beaten and the daughter subjected to "a verbal sexual assault." Hill, who had moved to Connecticut to avoid public scrutiny, sued for invasion of privacy under the New York statute on the grounds that the *Life* article "was intended to, and did, give the impression that the play mirrored the Hill family's experience, which, to the knowledge of the defendant . . . was false and untrue."

Time Inc. in its defense contended that the subject of the article was "a subject of legitimate news interest," "a subject of general interest and of value and concern to the public" at the time of publication, and that it was published "in good faith without any malice. . . ."

The trial court jury awarded $50,000 compensatory and $25,000 punitive damages to the Hills. On appeal, a new trial on the question of damages was ordered but the finding that *Life* had invaded the Hills' privacy was upheld. A jury was waived and the court awarded $30,000 compensatory and no punitive damages.

Writing the opinion on the appeal to the United States Supreme Court, Justice Brennan noted that truth was a complete defense under the statute but that Hill was entitled to sue to the extent that *Life* "fictionalized" and "exploited for the defendant's commercial benefit." He also noted that Hill was a newsworthy person substantially without a right to privacy as far as his hostage experience was involved. He then brought in the *New York Times v. Sullivan* libel case:

Material and substantial falsification is the test. However, it is not clear whether proof of knowledge of the falsity or that the article was prepared with reckless disregard for the truth is also required. In *New York Times Co.* v. *Sullivan,* 376 U.S. 254, we held that the Constitution delimits a State's power to award damages for libel in actions brought by public officials against critics of their official conduct. Factual error, content defamatory of official reputation, or both, are insufficient to an award of damages for the false statements unless actual malice—knowledge that the statements are false or in reckless disregard of the truth—is alleged and proved. . . .

We hold that the Constitutional protections for speech and press preclude the application of the New York statute to redress false reports of matters of public interest in the absence of proof that the defendant published the report with knowledge of its falsity or in reckless disregard of the truth.[20]

Although five justices voted for *Life,* they were split in their reasons, three agreeing on use of the *New York Times* rule, and two concurring in the decision on other grounds. The Chief Justice joined two other justices in a dissenting opinion. The Brennan opinion did not establish truth as a dependable defense in invasion of privacy suits. His majority opinion placed the benefits of freedom of the press to society ahead of an individual's right to privacy and allowed for incidental, non-malicious error to creep into an article as part of the risk of freedom:

> We create grave risk of serious impairment of the indispensable services of a free press in a free society if we saddle the press with the impossible burden of verifying to a certainty the acts associated in news articles with a person's name, picture or portrait, particularly as related to nondefamatory matter. Even negligence would be a most elusive standard. . . . A negligence test would place on the press the intolerable burden of guessing how a jury might assess the reasonableness of steps taken by it to verify the accuracy of every reference to a name, portrait or picture.[21]

Although the lower courts had found that the *Life* article was not legitimate news but fictionalized entertainment for purposes of trade, Justice Brennan wrote, "We have no doubt that the subject of the *Life* article, the opening of a new play linked to an actual incident, is a matter of public interest. 'The line between the informing and the entertaining is too elusive. . . .' "[22]

Author Hayes had said the Hill incident triggered his writing of the book and the play, but that he had not attempted to portray the Hill family's experience, and that he had used incidents from California, New York, Detroit, and other places in shaping his story. Brennan rejected the question of commercial exploitation by quoting a 1952 Supreme Court decision:

> That books, newspapers, and magazines are published and sold for profit does not prevent them from being a form of expression whose liberty is safeguarded by the First Amendment.[23]

Future courts may find differently, and the split in the court in this decision muddles the question, but this decision did bring to bear on an invasion of privacy suit many aspects of press freedom and protection that had been established, including nonmalicious error, difficulty of attributing commercial exploitation, and the element of newsworthiness.[24]

Four different rights of privacy have evolved from decided cases: (1) intrusion, (2) appropriation of one's name or likeness, (3) publicity that places the person in a false light before the public, and (4) publicity that discloses private and embarrassing facts.

Intrusion is the acquisition of information from or about a person by physical trespass or other means from which an ordinary person could expect a reporter to be excluded. In one case reporters posed as patients to gain admittance to the home-office of an alleged medical quack and, once there, surreptitiously took photographs and made sound recordings. This was found to be an invasion of privacy, and the fact that the ruse was undertaken to gather news was not accepted as a defense. Privacy was invaded when the intrusion took place, and existed whether or not the information was published. Electronic eavesdropping, wire-tapping, harassment, and conversion of another's personal documents have been alleged to be intrusive invasions of privacy.[25]

Appropriation involves using a person's photograph or name for advertising purposes or in trade without written consent. Use of a living person's name or likeness in an intentionally fictionalized version of a topic of news or general interest may be a case of appropriation. In one case in 1966, Warren Spahn, a well-known baseball pitcher, won a privacy suit over publication of an unauthorized biography because there were significant amounts of intentionally fictionalized material in the book.[26]

Much promotional material is published as editorial content, but the determination of whether it is informational or commercial will be carefully made by a court. One teenage woman who was featured in *Seventeen* magazine's "make-over" section inadvertently did not sign the routine permission forms and release. Teenagers featured in this section are paid and are given clothing, cosmetics, and advice on how to improve their appearance. The article includes before-and-after pictures and mentions brand names of products in discussing the make-over. The teenager sued, contending that her name and likeness had been appropriated for trade purposes. She lost when the court ruled that the article about grooming, makeup, and clothing was newsworthy to the teenage audience at which it was aimed (*Lopez v. Triangle Communications,* 1979).

Family Circle bought the rights to publish portions of the revised book, *Your Baby's Sex: Now You Can Choose It.* It contained an unsolicited letter from a woman who had successfully used the techniques recommended in the first edition. The woman sued *Family Circle,* contending publication of her letter was an advertisement for the book and that the entire article was an advertisement for the book, using her name for trade purposes. The Appellate Division of the New York Supreme Court noted that the book's publisher, Dodd, Mead & Company, had not paid for the publication but that *Family Circle* had purchased the rights to the material (*Heller v. Family Circle*).

A magazine may, however, use editorial material from previous issues in its own advertising. In *Booth v. Curtis Publishing Company* (1962), the court held that a *Holiday* magazine ad reproducing a photograph of actress Shirley Booth from an article that had appeared earlier in editorial pages was not an invasion of privacy.[27] In *Namath v. Time, Inc.* (1976), New York State's highest court upheld lower court decisions that use of a picture of Namath in the 1969 Super Bowl game and his name in an ad promoting *Sports Illustrated* did not invade his privacy. However, had the ad contained words that implied that Namath endorsed the magazine, "a completely different issue would have been presented," wrote an appeals judge whose decision was upheld. Namath had sued for $2.5 million.[28]

Under both these New York State court decisions, as long as the names and likenesses have been previously published editorially and are used in advertising to illustrate the quality and content of the publication, written consent is not required and appropriation has not taken place.

Forum magazine used a picture of Cher, the entertainer, to promote an edition of the magazine, stating that Cher endorsed the magazine, which was not true. A United States district court in California ruled that use of Cher's name and picture went much further than establishing the news content and quality of the magazine. The advertising was not merely incidental to the original publication of an interview with Cher (*Cher v. Forum International,* 1982).

False light deals with publication of untrue information that is not defamatory but which places the individual in a false light before the public and therefore invades the person's privacy. In the *Time, Inc. v. Hill* case, the U.S. Supreme Court ruled that damages for a false light invasion of privacy could not be awarded unless the untrue material was published "with knowledge of falsity or reckless disregard for the truth."

In *Cantrell v. Forest City Publishing Co.* (1974) the court found that the plaintiff had been portrayed in a false light through knowing or reckless untruth ("calculated falsehoods") in an article that falsely implied that she had been present during the reporter's visit to the family home, that he had observed her facial expression, and that she was reluctant to talk about the tragedy of a widely publicized bridge collapse in which her husband had been killed.[29] There are two qualifications for false light: (1) The published false information must be highly offensive to a reasonable person, and (2) It must be shown that the publisher knew the information was false when it was published, or acted with reckless disregard of the truth or falsity of the information.[30]

In another case, the *National Enquirer* published a story about a woman who killed her three children and then herself and indicated she was happy and had no reason to commit suicide. Her husband sued the *Enquirer* for false light. He proved that the writer had access to records that indicated his wife was depressed and despondent before the incident and that the reporter had a copy of her entire suicide note, of which the *Enquirer* printed only a portion, leaving out the part that clearly explained the reasons for the murder-suicide. The federal court of appeals ruled that this was reckless disregard for the truth.[31]

Public disclosure of private and embarrassing facts is much less of a problem; publishers have won most of the cases filed against them so far. The case of William J. Sidis is an early example. In two California cases, the appellate courts indicated that crimes committed in the past are matters of public interest, but that names of the individuals involved may not be when many years have passed and the individuals have reformed. Such persons have regained some right of privacy that had earlier been forfeited.[32]

"Who Let This Doctor in the O.R.? The Story of a Fatal Breakdown in Medical Policing" in *Medical Economics* described an anesthesiologist's patients who suffered disabling or fatal injuries in the operating room, focusing on the lack of self-policing by physicians. In documenting his allegations, the writer discussed the anesthesiologist's psychiatric and related personal problems. Her name and picture were included in the article. She conceded the story was newsworthy, but argued that publication of her photograph, name, and private facts revealing her psychiatric and marital histories added nothing to the story and was an invasion of her privacy. The court ruled otherwise, stating that the inclusion of the name and photograph strengthened the impact and credibility of the article. "They obviate any impression that the problems raised in the article are remote or hypothetical, thus providing an aura of immediacy and even urgency that might not exist had plaintiff's name and photograph been suppressed." Her psychiatric and marital problems were connected to the newsworthy topic by the rational inference that her personal problems were the underlying causes of the acts of alleged malpractice (*Gilbert v. Medical Economics,* 1981).

A *Sports Illustrated* article about a bodysurfer included alleged private and embarrassing facts, such as that the surfer extinguished cigarettes in his mouth to impress women, intentionally injured himself so he could collect unemployment and have time for surfing, and ate insects. He had told the reporter these but claimed that prior to publication of the article he forbade publication of them. The federal district court said that to lose First Amendment protection the offensive facts must first be highly offensive as a matter of community mores and, second, the revelation must be for its own sake. These facts, however, were not sufficiently offensive and "were included as a legitimate journalistic attempt to explain Virgil's extremely daring and dangerous style of bodysurfing" (*Virgil v. Time, Inc.*).[33]

People close to public figures sometimes lose some of their privacy. *Saturday Evening Post* published names of the children of "Tiger Lil" Corabi in an article that said she was accused of planning a complex burglary. The Pennsylvania high court ruled that she was a public figure, and anyone could publish her biography without her consent and could include names of family members (*Corabi v. Curtis Publishing Co.,* 1971).

Reader's Digest published a story about the tremendous number of truck hijackings nationally and mentioned, only as a detail, an incident in which Marvin Briscoe hijacked a truck. It did not mention that this had taken place eleven years earlier. Briscoe asserted that he had served his time in jail and had led an exemplary life since he was freed. The story revealed to friends, neighbors, and family part of his life he had hidden. The California Supreme Court questioned the value of re-telling this story, which negated the state's rehabilitation of him. The suit was sent back to the state court for trail, but *Reader's Digest* had it removed to a federal district court and a federal judge granted a motion for summary judgment for the magazine (*Briscoe v. Reader's Digest Association,* 1971).

Copyright

Editors should be certain the material they are buying is original with the author. Brilliant articles often are accepted, later to be found as having been cribbed from other publications.

Copyright in the United States protects a work for the life of the author plus 50 years or, in the case of a work made for hire or an anonymous or pseudonymous work, the lesser of 75 years after publication or 100 years after creation. Federal copyright protection begins as soon as a work is created, even though a notice of copyright is not required until the work is published. Publication is defined as "the distribution of copies or phono-records of a works to the public by sale or other transfer of ownership, or by rental, lease, or lending."[34]

When a person creates a work while employed by a corporate publisher, unless there is a written agreement to the contrary, the employer is considered to be the author and the actual author (employee) is considered to have produced the "work for hire."

If a publisher expects to use material produced by contributors who are not employees as works for hire, he or she must have a written agreement to that effect with the contributors.

Any transfer of copyright greater than a nonexclusive license is valid only if in writing and signed by the owner of the rights conveyed. In other words, a publication wanting to buy exclusive rights to an article, photographs, or illustrations must have a written agreement specifying exclusive rights with the copyright owner of the article, photographs, or illustrations. A magazine intending to use material in a book or as a reprint or to protect itself from having the piece turn up elsewhere must enter a signed agreement with the contributor.[35]

Copyright registration of an issue of a magazine protects all editorial content and those advertisements on behalf of the magazine's owner. No separate notice is required to protect an individual contributor's work. All other advertisements have to bear their own copyright notice to be protected.

Before the current copyright law took effect January 1, 1978, copyright in the United States was for a term of 28 years, with one renewal permitted to extend the total period to 56 years. After that, material was in the public domain and could be reprinted with impunity. But in this transition period from the former law to the current law, further checking is required to determine whether a copyright has expired.

The current law extended the copyright of works in their second term of copyright in 1978 to 75 years from their first publication and provided that works in their first term can receive a second term of 47 years. So works copyrighted before 1921 may still enjoy copyright protection.

Copyright protects the actual expression of the piece, not the ideas or facts contained in it. Further, if copyright is infringed, it is necessary for the copyright owner to file suit to recover damages. The Copyright Office in the Library of Congress merely registers copyright claims, it does not grant copyrights. Most consumer and business magazines are copyrighted to protect material that could be used advantageously by competing magazines. Magazines of associations and those with public relations objectives often are not copyrighted and often contain instead of a copyright notice a statement like this one from *Dodge Adventurer:* "Other media are invited to use all content, partially or full, of this publication, with or without credit." An association or public relations magazine sees this as a possibility for extra publicity for its sponsor.

Whether to copyright a magazine is a policy decision that must be made in the light of a magazine's competition, purposes, proprietary interest in its articles and photographs, and similar factors. It might suffice to ask whether the magazine would go to court to collect damages if its material were reprinted without permission, and if the magazine expects to sell reprint rights. If the answer is yes in either case, the magazine should be copyrighted.

To obtain post-publication copyright, one must (1) produce copies with a copyright notice, (2) publish the work, and (3) register the claim with the Copyright Office. The first step is accomplished by placing copyright notice, the year of publication, and the name of the copyright owner on the title page or the first page of text. The second is completed when copies are placed on sale, sold, or publicly distributed by the copyright owner. The third is done by sending two copies of the work and a completed application form to the Register of Copyrights, Library of Congress, with payment for the copyright fee. Full information and necessary forms are available from the Register of Copyrights, Library of Congress, Washington, D.C. 20559.

Omission of the copyright notice or an error in it can be remedied by registering within five years with the Register of Copyrights and making a reasonable attempt to add notice to all copies that are distributed to the public after the omission or error has been discovered. In the meantime, an innocent infringer would not be liable.

Nation was found to have infringed copyright in publishing a 2,000-word excerpt from the copyrighted memoirs of former President Gerald Ford. The memoirs were soon to be published in book form by Harper and Row and the Reader's Digest Association. *Time* magazine had purchased the right to publish excerpts before publication of the book. *Nation* published a section of the memoirs without permission and argued in defense against Harper and Row's suit that the material it published was newsworthy and should be protected by the fair use doctrine. *Time* abandoned its agreement to publish excerpts, costing Harper and Row the fee *Time* had agreed to pay for pre-publication rights. (*Harper and Row v. Nation,* 1983). *Nation* has filed an appeal.

In an ad promoting its new TV magazine, the *Miami Herald* showed copyrighted covers of *TV Guide.* The Fifth United States Court of Appeals ruled that it was fair use of copyrighted material, that the use of the covers in the ad had no effect on the potential market or value of the *TV Guide* covers. The ad might hurt sales of *TV Guide,* but that would be the effect of the advertisement, not the copyrighted covers. The court also said that the effect of the use on the market for the copyrighted work "is widely accepted to be the most important factor" (*Triangle Publications v. Knight-Ridder Newspapers, Inc.,* 1980).

Postal Regulations and Obscenity

Most magazines distribute a substantial amount of their circulation by mail and must be aware of postal regulations, which provide that obscene, filthy, lewd, or lascivious publications may be barred from the United States mails. Knowing violation of this provision can result in a fine or imprisonment or both. The fine or imprisonment would not necessarily be imposed unless copies containing the nonmailable matter were deposited in the mails after determination by the Postal Service that the copies were nonmailable under the statute.

Also nonmailable are material about lotteries, except state-operated ones, fraudulent matter relating to obtaining money under false pretenses, matter deemed disloyal to the United States or advocating or urging treason, including insurrection or forcible resistance to any law of the United States.

Obscenity has been an issue in magazine problems with the U.S. Postal Service. Ralph Ginsburg ran afoul of the liberal interpretations of obscenity of the mid-1960s by promoting his publications, which did not appear to be obscene under the law, as if they actually were.

Ginsburg's three products were *Eros,* a hardcover magazine devoted to sophisticated sexual themes; *Liaison,* a biweekly newsletter; and *The Housewife's Handbook on Selective Promiscuity,* a short book. According to Justice William Brennan's opinion for the Supreme Court, evidence showed

that each of the accused publications was originated or sold as stock in trade of the sordid business of pandering—"the business of purveying textual or graphic matter openly advertised to appeal to the erotic interest of their customers." EROS early sought mailing privileges from the postmasters of Intercourse and Blue Ball, Pennsylvania. The trial court found the obvious, that that hamlets were chosen only for the value their names would have in furthering petitioners' efforts to sell their publications on the basis of salacious appeal; the facilities of the post offices were inadequate to handle the anticipated volume of mail, and the privileges were denied. Mailing privileges were then obtained from the postmaster of Middlesex, New Jersey. EROS and Liaison thereafter mailed several million circulars soliciting subscriptions from the post office; over 5,500 copies of the *Handbook* were mailed.

The "leer of the sensualist" also permeates the advertising for the three publications. . . .[36]

Four of the nine justices dissented. Ginsburg appeared to be taking advantage of the landmark 1957 Roth decision, in which Justice William J. Brennan wrote that the test of obscenity is

. . . whether to the average person, applying contemporary community standards, the dominant theme of the material taken as a whole appeals to prurient interest.[37]

Thus the work as a whole and its effect on the "average" person were to be the considerations, not the effect of selected passages on a susceptible person. The Roth decision also reaffirmed that obscenity is not protected by the First Amendment:

All ideas having even the slightest redeeming social importance—unorthodox ideas, controversial ideas, even ideas hateful to the prevailing climate of opinion—have the full protection of the guaranties, unless excludable because they encroach upon the limited area of more important interests. But implicit in the history of the First Amendment is the rejection of obscenity as utterly without redeeming social importance.[38]

Chief Justice Earl Warren's concurring opinion helped to change the focus of future obscenity actions. He suggested that the conduct of the defendant should be the central issue. Nine years later the Ginsburg decision revolved on this point, that Ginsburg had commercially exploited the prurient interest even though his publications in themselves apparently were not obscene. The Supreme Court decision upheld a $28,000 fine and five-year prison sentence. Ginsburg finally went to prison in 1972 and was paroled after eight months.

In 1973 another 5-4 decision involving an unsolicited, sexually explicit advertising mailer changed the obscenity situation a bit, but not as much as some people thought.

In *Miller v. California* the court ruled that states could regulate obscene materials, but only those that depict or describe sexual conduct that is clearly defined in the applicable state statute. Chief Justice Warren Burger wrote the decision, which said in part:

. . . State statutes designed to regulate obscene materials must be carefully limited. As a result, we now confine the permissible scope of such regulations to works which depict or describe sexual conduct.

That conduct must be specifically defined by the applicable state law, as written or authoritatively construed. A state offense must also be limited to works, which, taken as a whole, appeal to the prurient interest in sex, which portray sexual conduct in a patently offensive way, and which, taken as a whole, do not have serious literary, artistic, political or scientific value.

The basic guidelines for the trier of fact must be (a) whether "the average person applying contemporary community standards" would find that the work, taken as a whole, appeals to the prurient interest, (b) whether the work depicts or describes, in a patently offensive way, sexual conduct specifically defined by law, and (c) whether the work, taken as a whole, lacks serious literary, artistic, political, or scientific value.[39]

Although local police and other officials in several communities cleared *Playboy, Penthouse, Oui,* and similar magazines from newsstands,[40] such action was not covered by the ruling and the magazines soon reappeared.

In fact, the Supreme Court decision had stated:

Under the holdings announced today, no one will be subjected to prosecution for the sale or exposure of obscene material unless these materials depict or describe patently offensive "hard core" sexual conduct specifically defined by the regulatory state law, as written or construed. We are satisfied that these specific prerequisites will provide fair notice to a dealer in such materials that his public and commercial activities may bring prosecution.[41]

Hamling v. U.S. (1974) clarified that jurors may rely on their own knowledge of standards in their community; however, they are not to use their own standards but rather to draw on their knowledge of the standards of the average person in that community so that the "material is judged neither on the basis of each juror's personal opinion nor by its effect on a particular sensitive or insensitive person or group."[42]

The U.S. Supreme Court has been generous in what it accepts as definitions of "patently offensive 'hard-core' sexual conduct," but overall there has been little change in arrests, prosecutions, and convictions since Miller and Hamling.[43]

Ideas, then, remain absolutely protected by the First Amendment. Obscenity continues not to be protected, and state laws can regulate only that obscenity which describes or depicts sexual acts specifically defined in those laws.

Although it does not affect the vast majority of magazines or even books, the Pandering Advertisement Act of 1968 permits the individual to define obscenity for himself or herself. He or she can have the Postal Service order the sender of unsolicited mail to strike his or her name from their mailing lists by swearing that he or she has been sexually aroused by their mail. Complaints under this act have been filed, among others, against advertisements for the *Christian Herald,* an electronics magazine, and auto seat covers.

Another act permits an individual to protect himself or herself and his or her children under age 19 for a five-year period from receiving sexually oriented advertisements in the mail by filing form 2201 at the post office.

Other Legal Matters

Reproducing Currency

Federal law forbids publication of illustrations of U.S. currency or uncancelled stamps unless the illustrations are for historical, educational, or numismatic purposes. Then the illustrations must be in black-and-white and either less than three-quarters (75 percent) or more than one and one-half times (150 percent) the size of the original currency or uncancelled stamp.[44]

Lottery

Lotteries, except state lotteries, cannot be promoted by editorial or advertising matter sent through the mail. A lottery exists when there are three elements—prize, chance, consideration. Generally a prize is an award of greater value than any or all of the other participants receive. Most contests have this element of lottery. Chance means that the outcome is beyond the control of the participants, is not based on skill, talent, or persistence. Most contests also have this element. Consideration is not so easily defined, but it involves payment to enter, buying a specific product, or being present when prize winners are announced. The most common technique for eliminating consideration is to permit a brand name to be written in block letters on a 3″ × 5″ piece of paper in place of submitting a wrapper or proof of purchase from the sponsor's product.

Because *all three* elements must be present to constitute a lottery, elimination of any one makes the material publishable in editorial or advertising content. But apparently innocent items often are lotteries: a door prize when one pays to enter the event, or an auto raffle or turkey raffle, or a bingo party when one pays to play. The absolute prohibition against material about lotteries was softened in 1947 when the Post Office Department ruled that lotteries may be mentioned if "the element of lottery is only incidental to a newsworthy event." Few publications are harassed by postal authorities for mentioning lotteries, but they can be.

Trademarks

Magazine editors quickly find that trademarks are valuable company property and must be protected. If you misuse a trademark, by not capitalizing it, for example, you are likely to get a letter from a company attorney warning that it must be capitalized and should be followed by the generic term of the product: Scotch Brand cellophane tape, L'eggs pantyhose, Zenith color television receiver.

The danger to a company is that if a trademark is accepted into everyday use in place of the generic term and the company has not protested such use, it is likely to lose its legal claim to the trademark. Aspirin, cellophane, escalator, shredded wheat, milk of magnesia, linoleum, and lanolin once were trademarks, but all lost their protection when they came to designate the item rather than a brand name of the item. An irony is that a company may spend millions of dollars to get the public to think of its brand synonymously with the product but that it must protect the distinctiveness or identity of its trademark independent of the item.

When you use a trademark in place of a generic name, you may receive a letter from a trademark lawyer politely and firmly reprimanding you. The important thing to the lawyer is to have on record a copy of the complaint so that if there is litigation involving the trademark, it can be introduced as evidence that the company did attempt to protect the trademark from falling into generic use. Most stylebooks suggest using generic terms in place of trademarks, but the New Journalism finds it fashionable to tell what brand of cigarettes someone smokes, what brand of suit he or she wears, or what brand of auto he or she drives.

Lack of evidence in protesting misuse of trademarks can cause courts to find that the trademark has lost its distinctiveness and the company has lost its exclusive right to use it. An unusual case of this type was legal action the King-Seeley Thermos Company took against Aladdin Industries for calling its vacuum bottles "thermos." The court found that the company not only had not protested the use of "thermos" in place of "vacuum bottle" but had mildly encouraged that use. It ruled that Aladdin could call its vacuum bottles "thermos" but that King-Seeley Thermos retained the right to the "Thermos" trademark.[45]

Editors of company-sponsored publications become keenly aware of ways to protect trademarks, and many company magazines use the encircled R ® after every company-owned trademark in editorial copy as well as in advertising. Others list all company trademarks in the magazine. An example is the *Sohioan* of Standard Oil Company (Ohio). On the last page before the inside back cover it lists the photo credits then:

TRADEMARKS

The following trademarks and service marks are the property of The Standard Oil Company (Ohio) and its subsidiaries: Barex, Boron, Canfield, Cetron, Farmex, Filon, Filon-Stripes, Frostex, Gas & Go, Golden Duron, Ice-gard, Lubri-Chart, Lubri-Check, MOCAR, Nitrex, Octron, Oxco, Parowax, Piston Seal, Premex, Pro, Profile, Prolon, Pro-phy-lact-tic, QVO, Ree-Juve, Silmar, So-clear, Sohigro, Sohio, Solar, Trolkote, Trolumen, Valve Ease, Vistron, and Wm. Penn. BP and BP in shield are used by license.

Names of magazines cannot be copyrighted but they can be registered as trademarks. A trademark must be used in commerce *before* it is registered. Intent to register a trademark is indicated by the small letters "TM" after the trademark. A trademark applies only to the class of goods on which it is used and only as long as it continues to be used. In other words, a magazine cannot prevent a manufacturer from using its name on pet foot or clothing or furniture. In some cases, however, courts have broadly interpreted the law and have ruled that a business, such as a restaurant, was using the good reputation of a publication's name to promote its business and must cease using the name.

When a magazine discontinues publication, its owners lose the right to its name because it is no longer being used in commerce. Some publishers protect names by incorporating them into other magazines they issue, such as *Redbook, incorporating American Home.* At some later date the publisher may revive the defunct magazine or sell its name to another publisher.

Even though magazines lose their names when they cease publication, publishers planning to use the name of a defunct magazine generally buy the name from the previous publisher to ensure that no lawsuit will be filed. For large publishers, this often is an economical form of protection.

Labor Law and Employee Magazines

Editors of company-sponsored magazines for employees must be aware of actions of the National Labor Relations Board under the Taft-Hartley Act. Employers often convey information about employee benefits and contract negotiations and offers in their employee publications. They are free to do this as long as the material does not threaten the employee or promise benefits for adopting the employer's position. Section 8(c) of the Taft-Hartley Act specifies the conditions:

The expressing of any views, argument, or opinion, or the dissemination thereof, whether in written, printed, or graphic, or visual form, shall not constitute or be evidence of an unfair labor practice under any provisions of this Act, if such expression contains no threat of reprisal or force or promise of benefit.

Material that affects labor relations usually will come from the company personnel department and will be checked routinely with its legal counsel, so the main point here is that the editor be aware of the potentially damaging situation. An employer, for example, may campaign against a union seeking to represent employees, indicate a preference for one union over another, urge employees to change unions or start a new one or have none at all, or tell employees it does not like to deal with unions. An employer may not threaten employees with economic reprisal for participating in union activities, promise benefits to employees if they reject the union or choose a union the employer prefers, or give financial support or other assistance to a union or to employees who are opposing or supporting a union.

A helpful reference for public relations magazine editors is Morton J. Simon, *Public Relations Law* (New York: Appleton-Century-Crofts).

Advertising

Although primarily concerned with editorial content, the editor is interested in advertisements and what they look like and say in the publication. A McGraw-Hill attorney recommends that every advertising rate card have a provision giving the publisher the right to reject any advertising believed to be inappropriate and a protective clause that makes the advertiser and advertising agency totally responsible to the publisher for the content of any advertisement published in the magazine. At McGraw-Hill, each magazine sets its own criteria for accepting or rejecting ads.[46]

Avoiding Legal Problems

The preceding discussions of potential legal problems suggest some ways to avoid those problems. An editor can reduce the possibility of being subjected to legal action if he or she:

1. Attains a reasonable knowledge of federal and state law affecting publications and especially court decisions involving publications. Knowledge of potential dangers can help one consider ways to avoid or overcome them.

2. Consults routinely with counsel before entering danger areas. A courageous editor must be willing to risk litigation in serving readers or society at large. But he or she should not take unnecessary risks that leave the magazine open to unnecessary suits. McGraw-Hill's general counsel told a company legal seminar:

   Our job as lawyers is to counsel you on how to avoid litigation or defend yourself against it. Your obligation is to identify a potential legal problem and let us know, as soon as possible, when you have one. We are not censors; we don't want to kill articles. We want to get your stories published by working with you on reducing the possibilities of legal risks.[47]

3. Insists upon careful editing that makes every effort to avoid error. A substantial number of lawsuits against magazines originate from error rather than intent.

Notes

1. Harold L. Nelson and Dwight L. Teeter, Jr., *Law of Mass Communications,* 3d ed. (Mineola, N.Y.: The Foundation Press, 1978), p. 59.
2. Curtis Publishing Co. v. Butts and Associated Press v. Walker, 388 U.S. 130 157–58 (1967).
3. Don R. Pember, *Mass Media Law,* 3d ed. (Dubuque, Iowa: Wm. C. Brown Company Publishers), 1984, pp. 123–125 and 146.
4. Ibid., p. 131.
5. 418 U.S. 351 (1974).
6. Harry Johnston III, "Libel and the magazine publisher," *Folio,* December 1976, p. 34.
7. *The News Media & The Law,* June/July 1981, pp. 26–27.
8. *The News Media & The Law,* February/March 1981, p. 21.
9. *The News Media & The Law,* February/March, 1981, p. 24.
10. Pember, pp. 154–155.
11. Lahiri v. Daily Mirror, Inc., 162 Misc. 776, 295 N.Y. Supp. 382 (1937).
12. Molony v. Boy Comics Publishers, Inc., 277 App. Div. 166, 98 N.Y.S. 2d 119 (1950).
13. Leverton v. Curtis Publishing Co., 192 F.2d 974 (1951).
14. Nelson and Teeter, p. 188.
15. Ibid., p. 216.
16. Russell v. Marboro Books, Inc., 13 Misc. 2d 166, 183 N.Y.S. 2d 888 (1955).
17. McAndrews v. Roy, 131 So. 2d 256 (1961).
18. Sidis v. F-R Publishing Corp., 113 F. 2d 806 (C.C.A.N.Y. 1940).
19. 385 U.S. 374, 377, (1967).
20. 385 U.S. 374, 386–88 (1967).
21. 385 U.S. 374, 389, (1967).

22. 385 U.S. 374, 388, (1967), quoting Winters v. New York, 333 U.S. 507, 510 (1948).
23. Quoting Joseph Burstyn, Inc. v. Wilson, 343 U.S. 495, 501–2, (1952).
24. In an earlier stage of the Hill case Presiding Judge Bernard Botein had held that "showing that a noteworthy item has been published solely to increase circulation injects an unrealistic ingredient into the complex of the right to privacy and would abridge dangerously the people's right to know. In the final analysis, the reading public, not the publisher, determines what is newsworthy, and what is newsworthy will perforce tend to increase circulation."
    [Hill v. Hayes, 18 A.D. 2d 485, 240 N.Y.S. 2d 286, 293 (1963)]
25. Harry M. Johnston III, "Invasion of privacy," *Folio,* February 1977, p. 66.
26. Ibid., pp. 66–67.
27. Ibid., p. 67.
28. *Advertising Age,* June 14, 1976, p. 88.
29. Johnston, "Invasion of privacy," p. 68.
30. Pember, p. 227.
31. Pember, pp. 230 and 234.
32. Ibid., pp. 225–226.
33. Ibid., pp. 220–221.
34. Public Law 94–553 (October 19, 1976), Sections 302, 401, and 101.
35. Harry M. Johnston III, "What the new copyright law means to you," *Folio,* June 1977, p. 30.
36. 383 U.S. 463, 467–68, (1966).
37. 354 U.S. 476, 489, (1957).
38. 354 U.S. 484 (1957).
39. 413 U.S. 23–24 (1973).
40. *The Quill,* October 1973, p. 9.
41. 413 U.S. 27 (1973).
42. Pember, p. 387.
43. Ibid., pp. 391–395.
44. *McGraw-Hill News,* July 12, 1979, p. 2, reporting a company seminar on "Magazines and the Law."
45. Judge Robert P. Anderson ruled in June 1962 that "thermos" is generic and in the public domain as a synonym for "vacuum insulated" and as an "adjectival noun meaning a vacuum insulated container." Aladdin was permitted to use "thermos" only when the word "Aladdin" preceded it and only in all lower case letters. [*Advertising Age,* July 2, 1962, p. 2, and January 13, 1964, p. 16.]
46. *McGraw-Hill News,* July 12, 1979, p. 2.
47. *McGraw-Hill News,* July 12, 1979, p. 1.

Glossary of Terms

AAAA American Association of Advertising Agencies, an organization that sets standards for colors, sizes, and other aspects of advertising production, for advertising research, and for ethical conduct. Also called *4As*.

ABC Audit Bureau of Circulations, an organization of advertisers, advertising agencies, and publishers that defines circulation classifications and audits member publications to verify their claims.

ABP Association of Business Publishers, an organization of specialized business publications.

Agency commission Rate allowed to advertising agencies for normal services, usually 15 percent of the billing.

Area composition Sophisticated type-setting with the output placed in several columns to fill a desired rectangular area rather than in one long column.

Ascender In a type face, a stroke that rises above the center body of a letter.

Audience The readers, viewers, or listeners of an item of communication; larger than the number of subscribers because it includes *all* who read, see, or hear the message.

Author's alterations Changes made by an author after his or her work has been set in type.

Backleading A capability of modern type-setting machines to back up after setting type, thus permitting reduction of space between lines, overlapping, or the setting of type in several columns under one headline.

Backbone The binding edge of a magazine.

Backward reader One who views a magazine by flipping pages from the back to the front.

Bar graph An explanatory illustration relying on differences in the length of bars to show statistical differences.

Baseline In typography, the line formed by the bottom of the center body letters and all capitals; descending strokes extend beneath the baseline.

Basic paper weight The weight in pounds of a ream of paper in the standard size for a given grade; book is 25″ × 38″ and cover is 20″ × 26″.

Benday A process for artificially adding shading to a line illustration.

Bind-in card A promotional card attached to the binding of the magazine.

Bingo card Reader service card on which a reader can circle or check items to request further information about products or services advertised in the magazine.

Bit A binary digit; the smallest piece of computer information represented by a zero or 1; a switch on or off.

Bleed The extension of an illustration beyond the edge of a page.

Blow-in card Promotional card loose in the magazine, not bound.

Blueline Paper proofs in offset lithography, so-called because the printing areas show in blue. Also called *blue-print*.

Blue pencil Journalese for making corrections.

Blueprint See *blueline*.

Blurb Further information about an article than that given in the title or headline, often information about the author; also cover lines or article titles used on the cover to lure readers inside.

Body The part of a piece of type that serves to hold the face at the right height for printing; the main text of a message.

Body type Type of the smaller sizes (13-point and smaller) used to present the main text (body) of a message.

Boldface The darker version of a type design.

Bond A basic class of paper used for printed office forms.

Book Trade slang for magazine.

Book paper A basic class of paper used for books and magazines.

Box A frame for a type area, formed by plain or decorative lines.

Break-of-the-book Allocation of space within a magazine.

Brightype A method of converting metal type to a photographic image that can be efficiently used in offset printing.

Brownline Paper page proof in offset lithography on which the printing image shows in brown. Also called *brownprint*.

Brownprint See *brownline*.

Bulk The thickness characteristic of paper as compared to weight or feel.

Bulk discount A discount offered to an advertiser based on the number of pages or total linage placed in one magazine.

Burn In offset printing, exposing light through a negative onto the photosensitive surface (plate) below.

Business magazines Those published to serve readers engaged in a business, profession, or other vocation.

Byte A set of binary digits (bits) sufficient to represent a verbal piece of information, such as a character or a number; usually eight or six bits represent one byte.

Calendering The paper finishing process involving running paper between rollers to increase its smoothness.

Camera ready Type and/or illustrations ready to be photographed to print by offset lithography.

Caps and lower case In typesetting, refers to material to be set in capitals and small letters.

Caption The words printed with an illustration to describe the illustration.

Cathode ray tube A high speed typesetter that uses a video screen for putting images on photo paper; a computer terminal with a video screen.

Center body In typography, those letters having no ascenders or descenders, such as *a, c, e*.

Closing date Last day on which a magazine will accept advertising material for a given issue.

Coated paper A basic class of paper that has been given a coat of enamel; a glossy coat is necessary for fine reproduction of photos in letterpress printing.

Cold type Any type not set with hot metal.

Color separation Refers to separating the three primary colors and black from a full-color image through the use of filters.

Combination An illustration or engraving combining line and continuous tone.

Command In computerized printing production, a string of bytes of information that force an action by the computer.

Company publication A periodical produced by a company to promote its own interests.

Composition Typesetting.

Comprehensive A precise layout intended to show exactly how a finished page will look.

Consumer magazine Magazines intended to circulate among the general buying public and usually advertising consumer goods; any magazine that can be bought at a retail outlet.

Contents page The page or pages containing a listing of the contents.

Controlled circulation Circulation to qualified readers only, usually free or at a token price.

Copy Material (words and illustrations) intended for printing reproduction.

Copy editing The process of reading and correcting copy.

Copyfitting Computation of space requirements for copy.

Copy schedule A record of the copy that has been processed for an issue.

Cover The front page of a magazine plus the other three pages making up the outside wrap: inside front, inside back, and back cover.

Cover lines Article titles, blurbs, or other lines on the cover that tell the reader about the contents inside. Also called *sell lines*.

CPM Cost per thousand, the cost of a full-page ad per 1,000 circulation of the magazine; also recently per 1,000 readers extrapolated from readership research findings.

Crop The figurative removal of a portion of either dimension of a photo.

Cursor The blinking light on a video terminal screen that is used to locate any text changes as they are made on the screen.

Cut A photoengraving; to eliminate some of the wordage in copy.

Cutlines The descriptive lines accompanying an illustration.

Cylinder press See *flat-bed*.

Demographics Social and economic characteristics of individuals and households (age, income, education, sex, occupation, home ownership, etc.).

Descender The vertical stroke extending below the center body of a letter.

Dingbat A decorative typographical device such as stars, circles, check marks.

Direct entry A typesetter that is operated via a keyboard that is part of the typesetter.

Display type The larger sizes of type, from 14-point up.

Doctor blade In gravure printing, the blade that cleans the surface of a plate, leaving ink only in the depressed image areas.

Double-burn In offset, the exposure of light through each of two flats onto one plate in order to get close positioning of elements.

Double print See *surprint*.

Double truck A layout across two facing pages, traditionally those pages at the binding center.

Drop-out A special halftone treatment involving elimination of dots to create areas of pure white.

Dummy A pattern of a page or pages provided to printers to show location of all elements; it may be simply a drawing or proofs pasted in position to form the pattern.

Duotone Reproduction of a halftone in two colors from two plates.

Electroplating A process for duplicating letterpress plates or printing forms.

Em A measure of quantity in type; a square in the type size being used; common amount of indentation for a paragraph.

Engraving A plate used to reproduce illustrations in letterpress printing; also the process of making such plates.

External A public relations magazine prepared for and circulated to a group of readers outside the organizational structure, such as customers.

Face The printing image of type.

Facsimile Transmission of pages by way of FM radio waves.

Family In typography, a collection of types so similar as to be from the same family and carry the same family name, such as Melior.

Family variations In typography, the variations in weight, width, posture, and size with a family classification, such as Melior Light, Melior Bold, Melior Italic, Melior Extended, Melior Condensed.

Flat An opaque sheet of paper containing the negatives taped in position for the making of an offset printing plate. Also called a *mask*.

Flat-bed press A printing press using a flat form rather than a curved plate to carry ink to paper. Also called *cylinder press*.

Floppy disk A data storage device that resembles a 45 rpm record in appearance.

Folio Page number; also refers to other marginal information that may be included with the page number, such as date and name of a periodical.

Font One size of one branch of one family of type in sufficient quantity to do normal typesetting.

Form Type and plates enclosed in a metal frame (chase) for printing; an offset plate containing all the pages for one press run.

Format Size, shape, and other characteristics giving identity to a periodical. In typesetting, the instructions as to type size, etc., that are fed into an automated typesetter.

Formatting In computerized typesetting, the capability of calling for a set of markup instructions for a piece of typesetting with one keystroke.

Four-color Reproduction in four colors; four-color process involves the use of a full-color original from which the primary colors (red, yellow, and blue) plus black are filtered onto separate negatives and then onto printing plates for reproduction; spot color reproductions in four colors require the preparation by the artist of a separate mechanical for each color from which negatives and plates are made without filtration.

Free-lance A nonstaff contributor; also the material he contributes.

Frequency discount A discount offered to an advertiser based on the number of insertions within a contract period; contrasts with bulk discounts for total quantity.

Fulfillment In circulation, the activities necessary to deliver the magazine to the subscriber, including start-up date, billing, maintaining the address file, and cut-off upon expiration.

Galley proof A type proof taken of type before it has been put into page forms.

Gatefold A cover or insert folded to open out to dimensions larger than the conventional spread to create unusual horizontal display.

Goldenrod An offset flat of that color.

Gothic A basic group of type faces that are skeletal and monotonal in nature.

Gravure A system of printing that relies on depressed areas to carry ink to the paper; also called *roto*.

Gridding A design technique in which space is divided into rectangles and elements are confined in those rectangles, thus creating a Mondrian-like geometric design.

Group In typography, one of five basic classes of type: Text, Roman, Gothic, Script and Cursive, or Novelty.

Gutter The binding edge of a page; the margin that is at the binding edge.

Halftone An illustration that reproduces continuous tones; also the plate needed to reproduce such illustrations.

Hard copy A printout copy of material in a computerized system as compared with *soft* copies that appear only on a video screen.

Highlight A halftone reproduction containing areas from which all dots have been removed in order to get a pure white.

Hot type Type cast with molten metal.

House organ A public relations periodical.

Iconography Communicating with pictures or other images.

Imposition The arrangement of pages in a printing form so that, when the sheet they are printed on is folded, the pages will be in proper sequence.

Impression Each contact of a printing form to paper.

Indicia Mailing information that post office requires permit holders to include in a magazine.

Initial In magazine layout, a letter that has been given special size and form to start a copy area.

In-house From within the publishing firm as distinguished from an outside supplier.

Insert A separate sheet of printing containing fewer pages than the normal signature and added to a magazine during binding.

Intelligent terminal A computer terminal with enough storage capacity within itself to permit execution of some functions without using the central computer's capability.

Internal A public relations magazine prepared for and circulated to a group of readers within the organizational structure of the sponsor, such as employees.

Italic The slanted posture version of a type family.

Jump To continue a portion of an article to the back of a magazine; also refers to the continued portion.

Justify To make type lines flush to the right as well as to the left.

Key The drawing, layout, or plate that is used as the basis for the positioning of others to be printed in color.

Kill fee Fee paid to a free-lance writer when an assigned article or previously accepted article is not used.

Layout A drawn or pasted-up pattern for a printer to follow in making up a page. Also see *dummy*.

Leading Pronounced "ledding." The addition of white space between type lines, usually by adding nonprinting strips of lead between lines of hot type.

Lede Journalese for the beginning of an article or most important element of a layout.

Legibility The factor of graphic presentation that relates to ease of reading.

Letterpress   System of printing that uses a raised surface to carry ink to paper.

Little magazine   A magazine that publishes artistic works not sufficiently popular for large-circulation magazine use.

Line conversion   Special illustration technique that converts continuous tone originals to line reproductions.

Line illustration   Any illustration without continuous tones, including type lines, if they are to be produced as an illustration.

Linotype   A basic linecasting machine for letterpress printing manufactured by the Mergenthaler Linotype Corp.

Line gauge   A printer's ruler, marked off in picas, inches, and perhaps units of 5½, 8, and 10 points.

Lithography   A planographic printing process that relies on the mutual resistance of water and ink to achieve printing; in modern usage, a synonym for photo-offset, the indirect, planographic system of printing using photography for etching images on metal plates.

Logo   Nameplate.

Lower case   The small letters as contrasted with capitals.

Make-ready   Getting a letterpress printing form ready for the press by removing height inequalities that prohibit equal impression for the elements in the form.

Markerupper   The person who assigns the codes to copy to be printed so automated typesetters will produce type with the desired characteristics.

Mask   The vehicle, usually a sheet of opaque paper, that holds negatives in position so offset plates can be exposed. Also called a *flat*.

Masthead   The small area in which a publication presents its staff names and related information.

Measure   The length of a line of type.

Mechanical   A layout or dummy with all type and line illustrations pasted in position, ready to be photographed and transferred to a printing plate.

Metropolitan magazines   Those serving the residents of a particular metropolitan area.

Miniature   A scaled, small version of a layout or dummy.

Moiré   An undesired screen pattern created by the clashing of two or more screens used in preparing continuous tone illustrations.

Monotype   A typecasting machine that differs from most others in that it casts individual letters rather than lines of type.

Montage   An illustration composed of several images pasted together to form one illustration; when it is made by the photographer with his enlarger, it is called a photomontage.

Mortise   An illustration with a portion of it removed from within its outer borders.

MPA   Magazine Publishers Association.

Nameplate   The magazine's name as presented in type or illustration on the front cover.

Notch   An illustration with a portion of it cut away from one or more of its outer dimensions.

Nyloprint   A trade name for one of the types of thin plates used for rotary letterpress printing.

Offset   A system of printing that is chemical, planographic, and indirect. An inked image on a flat plate is transferred to a rubber surface before being pressed to paper; the plate surface is treated to accept greasy ink in image areas that resist water and to accept water in nonimage areas while resisting the ink in those areas.

One-shot   A magazine published only once rather than periodically; also called a *special*.

On line   In computerized systems, being hooked together by wire.

Opaque   Elimination of flaws in a negative by painting clear spots with an opaque substance.

Opinion magazines   Those whose content deals with public affairs, usually from a definite point of view.

Optical Character Recognition   (OCR) A system or device that scans typewriter copy and converts the alphanumeric symbols to the code that produces tape or communicates directly with a typesetter thus automatically producing type.

Outline   In magazine production, an illustration that is silhouetted against a plain white background.

Overlay   A transparent sheet placed over the face of an illustration or layout to position material to be printed in color or to provide instructions for preparation.

Overset   Type that is set but not used.

Page proof   Proof provided to check position of elements on a page.

Paste-ups   Pages formed by pasting up proofs of body and display type.

Perfect binding   A binding system using flexible glue to serve as the backbone of a publication.

Perfecting press   One that prints on both sides of a sheet or web at one impression.

Photocomposition   Type that is set by light exposure to film or paper, as contrasted to the key striking of typewriters or the casting of metal type.

Photoengravings   Metal plates with raised image areas created through photography and acid etching.

Pica   A basic unit of printer's measurement that is one-sixth of an inch or 12 points.

Piece   A story or article.

Pie chart   An explanatory illustration using a circle split into segments to show relationship of quantities.

Plate burner   The device used to beam light through the negatives in a mask to a photosensitive plate used for offset printing.

PMT   A machine used to transfer the dotted image of a halftone negative to photo paper thus creating veloxes.

Point   Unit of printer's measurement equal to 1/72nd of an inch, 1/12th of a pica.

Press proof   A proof taken of a press form while it is on the press.

Press run One run of the press to produce the required number of copies of a signature or other unit; a magazine with 10,000 circulation printed in two colors would have two press runs of 10,000 each.

Process color Lifelike color that is achieved by printing from four plates created by separating the primary colors plus black.

Progressive margins A system of margins in which the bottom is largest, and the others become progressively smaller in this order: outside, top, and gutter.

Progressive proofs In process color, proofs that show the reproduction of each color plate separately and in combination.

Proportioning The process of computing the proportions of enlargements or reductions of illustrations.

Public relations magazine Any magazine published to promote the activities of the sponsor.

Pulps Slang for a class of magazines originally printed on a pulpy paper and appealing to an unsophisticated audience.

Ragged right Type set so that lines do not end flush to right as in a uniform or justified column, but in an irregular pattern on the right; unjustified right.

Readability The clarity of a message; ability of a receiver to read a message.

Ream A quantity of paper, 500 sheets.

Register Positioning of elements in printing so their image will be located exactly as desired on the printed sheet or web; especially with reference to applying additional colors on the sheet.

Reproduction proof A proof taken after make-ready in order to get the quality necessary for the proof to be camera-ready.

Reverse In illustrations, reproducing blacks as whites and whites as blacks.

Reverse leading (See backleading)

Rollout Large direct mail campaign; usually follows a test mailing.

Roman A basic type group characterized by serifs and variation in thicknesses among basic strokes; also upright posture as opposed to italic.

Rotary press A press that prints from plates on rotating cylinders.

Rotogravure Printing from depressed (engraved) areas on a rotating cylinder.

Rough A full size layout that has been roughly sketched.

Run The number of impressions for a sheet or web going through a printing press.

Saddle-stitch A type of binding in which sections of a magazine are inserted rather than stacked and staples are driven through the fold from the outside. Also called *saddlewire*.

Sans serif Type without serifs, the small strokes that run counter to main strokes in some type designs.

Scaling Computation of the dimensions of illustrations after enlargement or reduction.

Scanner See *Optical Character Recognition*.

Screen A sheet of film containing intersecting opaque lines that is placed over the film in an engraver's camera to break a continuous tone image into dots as it exposes the film. The dots are the vehicle for reproducing the various tones present in photographs.

Script A basic group of type styles resembling handwriting.

Self-cover A magazine whose cover is part of a large sheet that folds into a section of the magazine.

Serif The small stroke that runs counter to a main stroke of a letter in some styles of type, especially Roman.

Sheet fed Presses that print on sheets of paper rather than rolls.

Sheetwise A system of imposing half the pages of a magazine section in a printing form so that when the sheet is printed with the remaining pages on the other side and folded into a magazine section, the pages will be in proper sequence.

Shelter books Magazines whose subject matter is homes.

Shoulder The nonprinting area above and below the face of a piece of type.

Side-stitch A binding system in which staples are driven through stacked magazine sections about one-eighth inch from the backbone. Also called *sidewire*.

Signature A section of a magazine, usually 8, 16, or 32 pages, formed when a press sheet is folded to format size.

Silhouette An illustration treatment that eliminates all background to permit the subject to stand in outline against the paper.

Slave A television terminal that relies entirely on its host computer for the capability to perform desired functions.

Slicks Slang for quality magazines printed on smooth paper.

Slug A word or two used to identify a piece of copy.

Solid Unscreened, as in a 100 percent tint block; also, in typesetting, no added leading between lines.

Special position Requested specific position for an advertisement; usually charged at higher rates.

Split-roller A printing technique in which ink rollers and fountains are split so a different color can be rolled over a form from each segment.

Spot color Any color other than process color.

Square serif Type style that is monotonal in nature but contains rectangular serifs.

SRDS Standard Rate and Data Service, a company that provides directory listings of publications and their advertising rates and production requirements.

Stand-alone A television terminal not connected to a computer; it has capability to perform useful functions on its own, such as produce a perforated tape to run a typesetter.

Stereotyping   A process for duplicating letterpress plates or forms by injecting molten lead against a mold pressed into a sheet of fibrous material.

Stock   Paper for printing.

Strike-on   Type composition by way of a typewriter-like device through which the alphanumeric characters are placed on paper with the striking of a key.

Stripping   Fastening negatives into a flat or mask.

Supercalendered   A paper with a smooth surface created by extensive rolling of pulp between smooth cylinders.

Surprint   An illustration that combines continuous tone and line images in one area; created by exposing continuous tone and line negatives in sequence to the same plate area. Also called *double print*.

Syndicate   An organization selling photos or other copy to publications.

Teaser   An article used on the cover to try to lure the reader inside.

Technical service magazine   A public relations magazine designed to provide technical assistance to users of the sponsor's products.

Text   The body of an article; also an ornate type group appropriate for religious and ceremonial subjects.

Thumbnail   A miniature, either picture or layout.

Tint block   A flat tonal area or the plate used to create it.

Tip-in   A one-sheet insertion glued into the binding of a magazine or book.

Trade out   Two magazines exchange advertising space to promote their magazines in the other one with no cash involved; often the exchange is based on the ratio of the magazines' circulations.

Type page   The image of a page; the page exclusive of margins.

Typo   Short for typographical error.

Upper case   Printer's term for capital letters.

Velox   A screened photoprint that can serve as a line illustration.

Video display terminal   A keyboard and television screen that displays text on the screen and permits manipulation of the text via the keyboard. May be part of a computer system or a standalone unit.

Vignette   A special finish for reproduction of photographs in which the edges fade into the background.

Waste circulation   Part of a magazine's circulation who are not prospects for an advertised product or service, such as in an area where the advertiser has no distribution.

Web-fed   A printing press fed from a roll of paper rather than sheets.

Word wrap   In computerized systems, the ending of lines after complete words only with no hyphenation on video terminal screens.

Work-and-back   See *sheetwise*.

Work-and-tumble   A system of imposing the pages in a printing form whereby: 1) all the pages of a signature are printed on both sides of the sheet and the sheet is cut into two signatures; and 2) after being printed on one side, the sheet is tumbled so that the back edge becomes the front (gripper) edge.

Work-and-turn   Same as work-and-tumble except that after one side is printed the sheet is turned over sideways so the same front edge is retained.

Wrap   A four-page insert that is wrapped around a signature for binding.

Wrap-around plates   Shallow-etched plates used on letterpress rotary presses, permitting the use in letterpress of the composition, paste-up, and photographic techniques usually associated with offset lithography.

Wrong font   A proofreading designation indicating a type character that is the wrong size or style.

x-height   In typography, the height of the lower case *x* and other center body letters.

Zinc   Slang for a photoengraving made from zinc.

Bibliography

Baird, Russell N., and Turnbull, A. T. *Industrial and Business Journalism.* Philadelphia: Chilton Company, 1961.

Backstrom, Charles H., and Hursh, Gerald D. *Survey Research.* 2d ed. Evanston: Northwestern University Press, 1981.

Compaine, Benjamin M. *The Business of Consumer Magazines.* White Plains, N.Y.: Knowledge Industry Pub., 1982.

Cousins, Norman. *Present Tense.* New York: McGraw-Hill Book Company, 1967.

Dembner, S. Arthur, and Massee, William E., eds. *Modern Circulation Methods.* New York: McGraw-Hill Book Company, 1968.

Elfenbein, Julien. *Business Journalism.* 2d ed. New York: Harper & Bros., 1960.

————, ed. *Businesspaper Publishing Practice.* New York: Harper & Bros., 1952.

Ferguson, Rowena. *Editing the Small Magazine.* 2d ed. New York: Columbia University Press, 1976.

Flesch, Rudolf. *The Art of Readable Writing.* Rev. ed., New York: Harper & Bros., 1974.

Ford, James L. C. *Magazines for Millions: The Story of Specialized Publications.* Carbondale, Ill.: Southern Illinois University Press, 1969.

Franklin, Marc A. *The First Amendment and the Fourth Estate.* 3d. ed. Mineola, N.Y.: Foundation Press, 1985.

Gillmor, Donald M., and Barron, Jerome A. *Mass Communication Law.* 4th ed. St. Paul, Minn.: West Publishing Co., 1984.

Gunning, Robert. *The Technique of Clear Writing.* Rev. ed. New York: McGraw-Hill Book Company, 1968.

Hamblin, Dora Jane. *That was the LIFE.* New York: W. W. Norton, 1977.

Huff, Darrell. *How to Lie with Statistics.* New York: W. W. Norton & Co., 1954.

Hurlburt, Allen. *Publication Design.* 2d ed. New York: Van Nostrand Reinhold, 1976.

Hurley, Gerald D. and MacDougall, Angus. *Visual Impact in Print.* Chicago: American Publishers Press, 1971.

Kerlinger, Fred N. *Foundations of Behavioral Research.* 2d ed. New York: Holt, Rinehart and Winston, Inc., 1973.

Klare, George R. *The Measurement of Readability.* Ames: Iowa State University Press, 1963.

Kobler, John. *Luce: His Time, Life and Fortune.* New York: Doubleday, 1968.

Lyon, Peter. *Success Story: The Life and Times of S. S. McClure.* New York: Charles Scribners Sons, 1963.

Magazine Publishing Management. New Canaan, Conn.: Folio Magazine Publishing Corp., 1977.

McCloskey, James. *Industrial Journalism Today.* New York: Harper & Bros., 1959.

McLean, Ruari. *Magazine Design.* London: Oxford University Press, 1969.

Mayes, Herbert R. *The Magazine Maze.* Garden City, N.Y.: Doubleday, 1980.

Meyer, Philip. *Precision Journalism.* 2d ed. Bloomington: Indiana University Press, 1979.

Mogel, Leonard. *The Magazine.* Englewood Cliffs, N.J.: Prentice-Hall, 1979.

Nelson, Harold L., and Teeter, Dwight L. Jr. *Law of Mass Communications.* 5th ed. Mineola, N.Y.: The Foundation Press, 1985.

Nelson, Roy Paul. *Articles and Features*. Boston: Houghton Mifflin, 1978.

————. *Publication Design*. 3d ed. Dubuque, Iowa: Wm. C. Brown Company Publishers, 1983.

Palmer, Lane M. *Publishing Magazines to Meet Reader Needs and Interests*. Madison, Wis.: Department of Agricultural Journalism, University of Wisconsin, 1971.

Pember, Don R. *Mass Media Law*. 3d ed. Dubuque, Iowa: Wm. C. Brown Company Publishers, 1984.

Peterson, Theodore. *Magazines in the Twentieth Century*. 2d ed. Urbana: University of Illinois Press, 1964.

Rivers, William L., and Work, Alison R. *Free Lancer and Staff Writer*. 4th ed. Belmont, Cal.: Wadsworth Publishing Company, Inc., 1986.

Rivers, William L., Schramm, Wilbur and Christians, Clifford G. *Responsibility in Mass Communication*. 3d ed. New York: Harper & Row, 1980.

Rothstein, Arthur. *Photojournalism: Pictures for Magazines and Newspapers*. 3d ed. Philadelphia: Chilton, 1973.

Schoenfeld, A. Clay, and Diegmueller, Karen S. *Effective Feature Writing*. New York: Holt, Rinehart and Winston, 1982.

Schuneman, R. Smith, ed. *Photographic Communication*. New York: Hastings House, 1972.

Simon, Morton J. *Public Relations Law*. New York: Appleton-Century-Crofts, 1969.

Stempel, Guido H. III, and Westley, Bruce H., eds. *Research Methods in Mass Communication*. Englewood Cliffs, N.J.: Prentice-Hall, 1981.

Strunk, William Jr., and White, E. B. *The Elements of Style*. 3d edition. New York: Macmillan, 1979.

Thurber, James. *The Years with Ross*. New York: Grosset & Dunlap, 1959.

Turnbull, A. T. and Baird, Russell N. *Graphics of Communication*. 4th ed. New York: Holt, Rinehart & Winston, Inc., 1980.

White, Jan V. *Editing by Design*. 2d ed. New York: R. R. Bowker, 1982.

Wolseley, Roland E. *The Changing Magazine: Trends in Readership and Management*. New York: Hastings House, 1973.

————. *The Magazine World*. New York: Prentice-Hall, 1951.

————. *Understanding Magazines*. 2d ed. Ames: Iowa State University Press, 1969.

Index

*An italicized page number indicates an illustration